FRANZ KAFKA
Parable and Paradox

FRANZ KAFKA

Parable and Paradox

Heinrich

By (Heinz) Politzer

Cornell Paperbacks

CORNELL UNIVERSITY PRESS

ITHACA, NEW YORK

To Jane

Note on This Edition

SINCE this book was first published in 1962, the stream of Kafka criticism has continued unabated. For this edition I have tried to take into account the most important recent work on Kafka by modifying my text, within the limits of technical expediency, wherever a new critical contribution seemed to demand a change.

A rather momentous event occurred in the spring of 1963, when a conference on Kafka was convened in the castle of Liblice, near the writer's native Prague. This meeting was to provide an impetus to Kafka studies behind the Iron Curtain. In adding a new chapter—Chapter X—on Kafka and communist literary theory, I hope to have broadened the scope of my book. I wish to thank Professor Emil Kovtun of the Department of Slavic Languages and Literatures at Berkeley, as well as my friend and student Ehrhard Bahr, for invaluable help in collecting and translating the material discussed in this chapter. I am also beholden to Professor J. Peter Stern of St. John's College, Cambridge, England, for his most careful and productive scrutiny of the new chapter.

In the fall semester 1963–1964 I repeated my graduate seminar "Kafka and Expressionism," exposing the first edition of this book to the criticism of students whose alertness was matched only by their mercilessness. My sincere thanks go to them and to those professional critics who suggested improvements. Thanks are also due to Mrs. Louise McClendon, who read the proof and revised the index for this edition.

Finally I wish to thank the staff of Cornell University Press for their understanding and good will, their patience and expert counsel, as well as for the encouragement they gave me while I prepared this edition.

                                                                    H. P.

Berkeley, California
December 1, 1965

Preface

ON March 31, 1961, *Time* magazine published a cover story reporting on certain aspects of the contemporary American scene. The piece was called "The Anatomy of *Angst*." Its first two paragraphs, a quotation printed in italics, read as follows:

The automatic elevator stops with a jolt. The doors slide open, but instead of the accustomed exit, the passenger faces only a blank wall. His fingers stab at buttons: nothing happens. Finally, he presses the alarm signal, and a starter's gruff voice inquires from below: "What's the matter?" The passenger explains that he wants to get off on the 25th floor. "There is no 25th floor in this building," comes the voice over the loudspeaker. The passenger explains that, nonsense, he has worked here for years. He gives his name. "Never heard of you," says the loudspeaker. "Easy," the passenger tells himself. "They are just trying to frighten me."

But time passes and nothing changes. In that endless moment, the variously pleading and angry exchanges over the loudspeaker are the passenger's only communication with the outside world. Finally, even that ceases; the man below says that he cannot waste any more time. "Wait! Please!" cries the passenger in panic—"Keep on talking to me!" But the loudspeaker clicks in silence. Hours, days or ages go by. The passenger cowers in a corner of his steel box, staring at the shining metal grille through which the voice once spoke. The grille must be worshiped; perhaps the voice will be heard again.

At this point the *Time* writer himself interrupted to assure his readers that this was not a story by Franz Kafka. Of course it was not, if only for the reason that Kafka's houses did not rise twenty-five stories high and could not boast of automatic elevators equipped with loudspeakers and metal grilles. However, the hasty assurance implied that *Time* expected many readers to associate with this anecdote the name of an author who had died, thirty-seven years earlier, in the center of Europe, at the very threshold of our time.

Franz Kafka's fame is not the least among his paradoxes. When this book was first conceived in the early nineteen-thirties his name was familiar only to a small group of initiates, many of whom had known him in the flesh. To a greater or lesser degree they shared his background and the experiences which had inspired him to tell his tales. They formed a sect, an intellectual conspiracy, and an elite.

Today Franz Kafka has become a household word. To be sure, the household to which it refers is presided over by fear—or, to accept the dubious compliment *Time* paid the German language, by *Angst*—and is quite generally not in the best order. But the fact remains that this household, our Western civilization, has chosen as a catchword for its frustrations and darkest moods the name of a writer who was endowed with the unique gift of preserving his painful visions in images of great lucidity and of presenting his symbols with a logic all his own.

It turns out that *Time*'s Kafka story is a "dream remembered in precise detail by a successful New Yorker (one wife, three children, no analyst)"; the absence of the analyst seems to be mentioned to stress the normalcy of the dreamer and the validity of his *cauchemar* even for the general reader. Let us not be misled by *Time*'s comment; Franz Kafka's stories can hardly be called dreams. If they were hallucinations anticipating, at times with astonishing clairvoyance, the reality of things to come, they were also meticulously controlled artistic exercises undertaken by one of the most skilled prose writers to appear so far in the twentieth century. What distinguishes an actual Kafka story from a Kafkalike dream is the style of the story.

This book aims at assessing the elements which compose Kafka's style. Rather than stress the timeliness of his vision, it attempts to explore the timelessness of his imagery. Its main subject is not Kafka, the man who indulged in nightmares, even if these nightmares are pertinent today, but Kafka, the narrator who told remarkably illuminating stories while searching for a way through the shadows which extended from his age to ours. If his work is a revelation of darkness, it is also the manifestation of a profoundly creative literary mind.

In spite of the horror spread by many of Kafka's stories (characteristically, they are among his most popular), there is comfort in the inevitability of his symbolic language and in the mastery with which he executed even their most frightful detail. While probing the nature of Kafka's art, this book does not undertake to answer the questions Kafka himself left open as part of his grand design. His greatness lies in his endeavor to formulate these questions ever anew even though he did not hope to receive an answer.

Some of his aphorisms reflect a glimmer of the light that Kafka knew existed, but not for him. Accordingly, this glimmer is hidden in tortuous conditional phrases and enhances the darkness surrounding it. Kafka's life would have been easy to live, and his task as a writer simple to accomplish, if he had been an agnostic. He had an eminently analytical mind and saw no reason to believe in anything; yet he continued to suspend even his disbelief and to inquire why it had become impossible for him to see the light.

Since I do not propose to offer an unambiguous solution to the Kafka problem, I find it impossible to round out my book with a neat set of conclusions. Instead, I have attempted, in the last chapter, to compare Kafka and Camus, choosing the younger French writer to show that the questions raised by the older German one continue to reverberate in the conscience of the present.

I have discussed the methodology of my approach in the first chapter. Having first chosen a representative piece from Kafka's most mature time for the sake of demonstration, I felt free thereafter to restrict myself in the selection of texts. I have given preference to the stories Kafka prepared for print during his lifetime because they have come down to us in a form authenticated by him. Next to these pieces I have concentrated on the great novel fragments which make up the bulk of his literary estate. Since I am concerned with his accomplishments as a narrator, I have drawn on his aphorisms and personal utterances primarily for supporting evidence. I have omitted what seemed not to need explanation, what could be explained by combining interpretations already given, and what remained inexplicable to me after long study.

The time during which this book was taking shape also witnessed the production of an impressive wealth of Kafka criticism. As far as I am conscious of my indebtedness to others, I have documented it in the notes. Being part of a critical study, however, the acknowledgment of my debt occasionally takes the form of criticism. This does not detract from my gratitude, which is genuine, especially when it comes to thanking Martin Buber, who during the crucial years 1940–1947 encouraged me, guided me, and enlightened me in the pursuit of my studies; Erich Heller, who in his book *The Disinherited Mind* opened new vistas to Kafka scholarship and who furthered my work by allowing me to keep in touch with his; and Wilhelm Emrich, the author of the most comprehensive Kafka study to date, a most erudite and gracious opponent in the never-ending debate on our common subject.

My book is meant to contribute to this debate first and foremost by concentrating on the text as such. Written in English by an author whose native tongue is German, it tries to convey to the English reader some of the feats Kafka performed in the medium of his language, his wordplays, his ironies, and the other transparencies of his style.

My task was made possible by Kafka's generally sensitive and conscientious translators. But not all his writings have been rendered into English by the same hand, and even the Muirs, who have done the greatest part, preferred, understandably enough, fluency and coherence to literalness. Therefore I have taken the liberty of modifying the existing translations here and there in order to harmonize them with one another or to obtain a more literal rendering closer to the German original. Significant departures from the standard translations have been explained in the text or the notes. The rest—adaptions of inflection, sentence structure, or individual words—are not intended to be read as a criticism of the texts as they exist in English today, nor do these adjustments suggest a new version or retranslation. They are simply meant to illustrate, for the purpose of a critical study, the cadence of Kafka's diction and the *double-entendre* inherent in his language.

References to Kafka's writings are incorporated in the text. Digressions are added at the bottom of some pages. Secondary sources are quoted in the notes at the back of the book. By keeping this system somewhat flexible I hope to have achieved as full a measure of documentation as possible without putting too many obstacles in the path of the reader.

Acknowledgments

THE final version of this book was drafted during the academic year 1958/1959, while I held a fellowship from the John Simon Guggenheim Memorial Foundation. Earlier research was made possible by grants I received from the American Philosophical Society in 1953 and 1954. The University of California at Berkeley, through its Committee on Research, has greatly aided me during the final stages of preparing the manuscript. To these institutions go my sincere thanks.

I am also grateful to President Deane W. Malott of Cornell University and the Cornell Committee on University Lectures for their invitation to deliver the Messenger Lectures in the fall of 1962, lectures which were based on the material presented in this book. Further thanks are due to Mr. Jonathan Brazin and the Telluride Association of Ithaca, New York, whose hospitality I enjoyed during my stay at Cornell University.

To Mr. Victor Reynolds, University Publisher, and Miss Catherine Sturtevant, Executive Editor of the Cornell University Press, and their staff I am indebted for the care they took of my manuscript and for the cooperation they have given me during the difficult period of readying it for print.

To the editors of *Chicago Review, The Germanic Review, Modern Fiction Studies, Modern Language Quarterly, Monatshefte für deutschen Unterricht,* and *PMLA* I am indebted for their permission to use in this book material previously published in the pages of their journals.

The following publishers have kindly consented to my quoting from the works of Max Brod, Albert Camus, and Franz Kafka: S. Fischer Verlag, Frankfort-on-Main; Alfred A. Knopf, Inc., New York; New Directions, Norfolk, Conn.; and Schocken Books, Inc., New York. Full bibliographical credit is given to them on pages xv–xvii of this book. I am also indebted to the publishers who gave their permission to quote from the following supplementary works: Erich Auerbach, *Mimesis, The Representation of Reality in Western Literature,* translated by Willard R. Trask, copyright 1953 by Princeton University Press, Princeton, N.J.; Martin Buber, *Tales of the Hasidim, The Early Masters,* translated by Olga Marx, copyright 1947 by Schocken Books, Inc., New York; Martin Buber, *Two Types of Faith,* translated by Norman P. Goldhawk, copyright 1951 by Routledge & Kegan Paul, Ltd., London, England; Albert Camus, *The Myth of Sisyphus and Other Essays,* translated by Justin O'Brien, copyright 1957 by Alfred A. Knopf, Inc., New York; Wilhelm Emrich, *Franz Kafka,* copyright 1958 by Athenäum-Verlag, Bonn; Erich Heller, *The Disinherited Mind,* copyright 1952 by Bowes & Bowes, Cambridge, England; Thomas Mann, *Death in Venice and Seven Other Stories,* translated by H. T. Lowe-Porter, copyright 1954 by Vintage Books, Inc., New York; Thomas Mann, *The Magic Mountain,* translated by H. T. Lowe-Porter, copyright 1951 by Alfred A. Knopf, Inc., New York; Rainer Maria Rilke, *Requiem,* translated by J. B. Leishman, copyright 1957 by the Hogarth Press, Ltd., London, England; Gershom S. Scholem, *Major Trends in Jewish Mysticism,* copyright 1941 by Schocken Publishing House, Jerusalem, copyright 1946 by Schocken Books, New York, copyright 1954 by Schocken Books, Inc., New York; and Franz Werfel, *Schlaf und Erwachen,* copyright by S. Fischer Verlag, Frankfort-on-Main. Bibliographical references to these quotations are to be found in the notes on pp. 359–365 of this book. *Time* magazine permitted an extensive quotation from its issue of March 31, 1961. The facsimile facing page 1 is reproduced by courtesy of Schocken Books, Inc., New York.

Professor Eric A. Blackall of Cornell University has given my manuscript much of his time and scholarly love. His encouragement, criticism, and insight into the Kafka problem have immensely contributed to the final shape of my book. It was on his advice that I added the analysis of "The Burrow" to the manuscript. As a sign of my gratitude I dedicate this chapter to him.

My friend and colleague Professor Blake Lee Spahr, a Kafka expert of no mean merit, has given me invaluable advice on many a point of detail. I also enjoyed the support and counsel of my Berkeley friends Mrs. Ruth Angress, Professor Marianne Bonwit, Mrs. Jean Jászi, Professor Andrew O. Jászi, Mrs. Susanne Lehmann, Professor Erich L. Lehmann, and Professor Philip Motley Palmer. To all of them I wish to express my thanks.

Miss Martha Mayo has helped me in the final stages of research. She and Mr. Peter G. Hinman assisted me conscientiously with many questions of stylistic detail, stimulating new ideas and checking others. They also helped me assiduously to read proof and prepared the index of the book.

My all but illegible manuscript was typed by Mrs. Helga W. Kraft. Her charm and devotion to the work at hand considerably brightened the grim aspects of the world which I tried to recreate.

Finally I want to thank all the members of a graduate seminar on "Kafka and Expressionism" which I gave in the fall semester of 1961/ 1962 at Berkeley. Their own studies and the criticism to which they subjected my interpretation have left an imprint on these pages which I am all the more eager to acknowledge since it is visible only to their eyes and mine.

H. P.

Berkeley, California
August 15, 1962

Editions and Key
to Abbreviations

THE following English editions of Kafka's works were used:

Amerika, trans. Edwin Muir, copyright © 1946 by New Directions, New York. Reprinted by permission of New Directions, Publishers. = *A.*

The Penal Colony, trans. Willa and Edwin Muir, copyright 1948 by Schocken Books, Inc., New York = *PC.*

The Great Wall of China, trans. Willa and Edwin Muir, copyright 1948 by Schocken Books, Inc., New York = *GW.*

The Diaries of Franz Kafka, 1910–1913, ed. Max Brod, trans. Joseph Kresh, copyright 1948 by Schocken Books, Inc., New York = *DI.*

The Diaries of Franz Kafka, 1914–1923, ed. Max Brod, trans. Martin Greenberg and Hannah Arendt, copyright 1949 by Schocken Books, Inc., New York = *DII.*

Letters to Milena, trans. Tania and James Stern, copyright 1953 by Schocken Books, Inc., New York = *LM.*

Gustav Janouch, *Conversations with Kafka,* trans. Goronwy Rees, published 1953 by Frederick A. Praeger, Inc., New York = *J.*

Dearest Father, trans. Ernst Kaiser and Eithne Wilkins, copyright 1954 by Schocken Books, Inc., New York = *DF.*

The Castle, trans. Willa and Edwin Muir, Eithne Wilkins, and Ernst Kaiser (Definitive ed.), copyright 1954 by Alfred A. Knopf, Inc., New York = *C.*

The Trial, trans. Willa and Edwin Muir and E. M. Butler (Definitive ed.), copyright 1957 by Alfred A. Knopf, Inc., New York = *T.*

Description of a Struggle, trans. Tania and James Stern, copyright 1958 by Schocken Books, Inc., New York = *DS.*

Max Brod, *Franz Kafka,* trans. G. Humphreys Roberts and Richard Winston, 2d ed., copyright 1960 by Schocken Books, Inc., New York = *FK.*

No English edition of Kafka's letters (except those to Milena) was available at the time I was writing this book. Quotations from the letters are from the German edition (*Briefe 1902–1924* [Frankfort: Fischer, 1958], copyright 1958 by Schocken Books, Inc., New York) and appear, identified by the letter *B,* in my translation.

For the ninth chapter the following works by Albert Camus were used:

The Stranger, trans. Stuart Gilbert, copyright 1954 by Vintage Books, Inc., New York = *S.*

The Plague, trans. Stuart Gilbert, copyright 1957 by Alfred A. Knopf, Inc., New York = *P.*

The Fall, trans. Justin O'Brien, copyright 1957 by Alfred A. Knopf, Inc., New York = *F.*

The following German editions of books by or about Kafka were consulted:

Franz Kafka, *Gesammelte Schriften,* ed. Max Brod, the first 4 vols. in cooperation with Heinz Politzer; 6 vols. (Berlin: Schocken; Prague: Mercy, 1935–1937).

Franz Kafka, *Gesammelte Werke,* ed. Max Brod; *Briefe an Milena,* ed. Willy Haas; 9 vols. (Frankfort: Fischer, 1946–1958).

Gustav Janouch, *Gespräche mit Kafka* (Frankfort: Fischer, 1951). Republished as volume 417 of the *Fischer-Bücherei,* augmented by a set of notes and biobibliographical references by Alma Urs.

Max Brod, *Franz Kafka: Eine Biographie* (Frankfort: Fischer, 1954).

A new edition of Kafka's stories (*Die Erzählungen* [Frankfort: Fischer, 1961]) contains for the first time a detailed chronology of the individual pieces. Unfortunately the editor, Klaus Wagenbach, was prevented by lack of space from substantiating the dates.

Whenever reference is made in this book to the German originals, the quoted passages are not to be found in the American editions. They are quoted from the second German edition.

A Brief Chronology of
Franz Kafka's Life and Works

1883   Born July 3 in Prague.

1889–1893   Attends elementary school.

1893–1901   Attends German Gymnasium.

1901   Begins to study law at the German Karl-Ferdinand University in Prague.
Considers studying German literature in Munich.

1902   Meets Max Brod.

1906   Starting in April, works as secretary (*"Konzipient"*) in the law offices of Dr. Richard Löwy.
June: Receives doctorate in jurisprudence from the Karl-Ferdinand University.
October 1, 1906—October 1, 1907, practices law first at the criminal court, then at the civil tribunal in Prague.

Before 1907   Writes "Description of a Struggle" and "Wedding Preparations in the Country."

1908   October: Temporarily employed in the Assicurazioni Generali, an Italian insurance company.

1908   Appointed to post with government-sponsored Workers' Accident Insurance Institute.
First publication: eight sketches printed in Franz Blei's literary periodical *Hyperion*.

1909   September: Takes trip to Riva and Brescia with Max Brod and
       Brod's brother, Otto.
       Two dialogues from "Description of a Struggle" published in
       Hyperion. "The Aeroplanes at Brescia" published in the
       Prague daily newspaper *Bohemia.*

1910   Begins his diary in the quarto notebooks.
       The Yiddish theater troupe performs in Prague (also in 1911).
       October: Takes trip to Paris with Max and Otto Brod.
       December: Takes trip to Berlin.

1911   January–February: Sent on official trip to Friedland and Rei-
       chenberg in northern Bohemia.
       Summer: Visits Zürich, Lugano, Milano, and Paris with Max
       Brod.
       Then goes to sanitarium Erlenbach near Zürich (alone).
       Writes travelogues.

1912   (or before?) Begins *Der Verschollene* (*Amerika*).
       Summer: Takes trip to Weimar with Max Brod.
       Then goes to sanitarium Jungborn in the Harz Mountains (Ger-
       many).
       August 13: Meets Felice Bauer.
       August 14: Sends the manuscript of *Meditation* to the publish-
       ing house of Rowohlt.
       Meditation published.
       Writes "The Judgment" and "The Metamorphosis."

1913   "The Judgment" published in Max Brod's literary yearbook
       Arkadia.
       "The Stoker," first chapter of *Der Verschollene,* published in
       Kurt Wolff's series *Der jüngste Tag.*
       Takes trip to Vienna, Venice, and Riva (alone).

1914   End of May: Becomes formally engaged to Felice Bauer.
       July: Breaks engagement.
       Summer: Visits Hellerau, Lübeck, Marienlyst (Germany).
       Writes first draft of "In the Penal Colony."
       Begins *The Trial.*

1915   Reunion with Felice Bauer takes place.
       Moves from house of parents into a rented room.
       Continues work on *The Trial.*

Takes trip to Hungary with his sister Elli.

Receives the Fontane Prize for "The Stoker."

1916 July: Visits Marienbad (Bohemian spa) with Felice Bauer.

"The Judgment" and "The Metamorphosis" published in *Der jüngste Tag*.

Winter: Writes "A Country Doctor" and several other stories to be included in the volume *A Country Doctor*.

November: Reads "In the Penal Colony" before a Munich audience.

1917 Moves into a room in Prague's Alchemists' Lane, then into the Schönborn Palace.

Continues work on *A Country Doctor*.

July: Engaged for a second time to Felice Bauer.

September 4: Tuberculosis diagnosed.

Takes sick leave from the Workers' Accident Insurance Institute.

Lives in Zürau with his sister Ottla.

[?] Writes aphorisms (octavo notebooks).

December: Engagement with Felice Bauer again broken.

1918 Stays in Zürau.

Studies Kierkegaard intensively.

Summer: Returns to Prague.

September: Lives in Turnau.

November: Lives in Schelesen (Želisy).

Meets Julie Wohryzek.

1919 *A Country Doctor* and *In the Penal Colony* published by Kurt Wolff.

Summer: Stays in Prague.

Engaged briefly to Julie Wohryzek.

Winter: Returns to Schelesen with Max Brod.

Writes "Letter to His Father."

1920 Takes sick leave in Merano (southern Tyrol).

Correspondence with Milena Jesenská begins.

Summer and autumn: resumes work in his Prague office.

December: Stays in sanitarium at Matliary in the Tatra Mountains.

Meets Robert Klopstock.

1921   Until September: Remains in Matliary, then returns to Prague.
       "The Bucket Rider" published in the Prague daily *Prager Presse*.

1922   January–February: Lives in Spindelmühl (northern Czechoslovakia), then returns to Prague.
       March 15: Reads the beginning of *The Castle* to Max Brod.
       May: Last conversation with Milena.
       End of June to September: Lives with his sister Ottla in Planá.
       Continues work on *The Castle*.
       The story "A Hunger Artist" published in *Neue Rundschau*.

1923   July: Stays in Müritz on the Baltic Sea.
       Meets Dora Diamant (Dymant).
       From end of September: Lives with Dora in Berlin–Steglitz.
       Writes "The Burrow."
       Dispatches the volume *A Hunger Artist*.

1924   March: Returns to Prague.
       April 10: Stays at Sanitarium Wiener Wald near Vienna.
       Then Vienna: Becomes patient in clinic of Professor Hajek.
       Finally: Stays at Sanitarium Kierling near Vienna, with Dora Diamant and Robert Klopstock.
       Finishes "Josephine the Singer."
       Dies June 3.
       Buried June 11 in the Jewish cemetery in Prague–Strážnice.
       The collection of stories *A Hunger Artist* published by *Die Schmiede*. (Based on *B*, 522–524, and *D II*, 333–335).

Contents

Contents   xxvii

FRANZ KAFKA
Parable and Paradox

"Gibs auf!"

FACSIMILE OF KAFKA'S MANUSCRIPT

Ein Kommentar

Es war sehr früh am Morgen, die Strassen rein und leer, ich ging zum Bahnhof. Als ich eine Turmuhr mit meiner Uhr verglich, sah ich dass schon viel später war als ich geglaubt hatte, ich musste mich sehr beeilen, der Schrecken über diese Entdeckung liess mich im Weg unsicher werden, ich kannte mich in dieser Stadt noch nicht sehr gut aus, glücklicherweise war ein Schutzmann in der Nähe, ich lief zu ihm und fragte ihn atemlos nach dem Weg. Er lächelte und sagte: "Von mir willst Du den Weg erfahren?" "Ja" sagte ich "da ich ihn selbst nicht finden kann." "Gibs auf, gibs auf" sagte er und wandte sich mit einem grossen Schwunge ab, so wie Leute, die mit ihrem Lachen allein sein wollen. (An English translation is on the opposite page.)

CHAPTER I

"Give It Up!"
A Discourse on Method

"IT was very early in the morning, the streets clean and deserted, I was on my way to the railroad station. As I compared the tower clock with my watch I realized it was already much later than I had thought, I had to hurry, the shock of this discovery made me feel uncertain of the way, I was not very well acquainted with the town as yet, fortunately there was a policeman nearby, I ran to him and breathlessly asked him the way. He smiled and said: 'From me you want to learn the way?' 'Yes,' I said, 'since I cannot find it myself.' 'Give it up, give it up,' said he, and turned away with a great sweep, like someone who wants to be alone with his laughter" (*DS*, 201).

This paragraph was discovered among the papers which Franz Kafka left at his death. On its upper left corner the manuscript page shows in faded ink, but unmistakably in Kafka's handwriting, the title "A Commentary." Max Brod published the piece in 1936 calling it: "Give It Up!" Presumably it was written during Kafka's last years.*

At first sight it is simple enough. It does not make any extravagant demands on the reader's sensitivity or imagination, nor does it lead to

---

* Klaus Wagenbach (*Franz Kafka, Die Erzählungen* [Frankfort: Fischer, 1961], pp. 417–419) dates the piece between November and December 1922. References to this chronology are hereafter cited as "Wagenbach."

any staggering conclusions. It seems to be self-contained and to say neither more nor less than what it actually says. For this reason it may serve us as an example of Kafka's narrative style. We shall try to determine its form and meaning, then apply some current methods of interpretation to test their validity for this particular text, and finally draw a few conclusions of our own. In the chapters to come there will be ample opportunity to check these conclusions against the evidence offered by Kafka's work at large.

At the outset one must admit that the form of our literary document is somewhat puzzling. It is both a narrative and a statement of truth, although a negative one. Its few lines contain lyrical impressions as well as a dramatic dialogue which is resolved at the end into one decisive silent gesture. For the moment one might call the piece an aphorism extended into an anecdote.

The hybrid form of the story is appropriately reflected by the variety of stylistic devices Kafka has brought into play. The first sentence is composed of three short and almost disconnected phrases; its character is determined by monosyllabic words, which occur much less frequently in German than they do in English. The statement it makes is realistic. The early hour of the day explains the clean and empty streets. Undoubtedly the city will be full of noise and dirt once dawn has turned into day, and people have appeared to fill the streets. Nor is there anything conspicuous about the man who is introduced in the first person as "I." One is tempted to feel that he represents the narrator. At the same time he seems to be shy, for it strikes us as a personal trait that he mentions himself only after having described the time and place of the sketch. The early hour provides a good setting for him; we imagine him to be as fresh and lonely as the streets through which he makes his way to the railroad station.

There is no one to accompany him, nor does he mention anyone whom he may leave behind. He does not say why he turns his back on the place, nor does he indicate where he wants to go. We see him before us, but his figure is determined by what we are not told about him rather than by a description dwelling upon his distinctive features. We are able to make a few assumptions about his person; yet they are not based on what he actually is or does but on what he fails to disclose about himself.

The basic structure of the second sentence resembles that of the first except that the number of individual phrases is now greater, which makes the tempo of the whole sequence seem faster. Here the many commas no longer separate the short statements: instead they have the effect of clamping the parts together. The musical cadence of this sentence has a staccato quality. The word "breathlessly" which falls toward its end expresses the character of the whole. Thus the story moves to its climax; we are astonished, however, to notice that even though this sentence marks a turning point in the narrative, it does not abandon reality anywhere. It reports nothing a realist could not have expressed in exactly the same terms. On the other hand, if we probe the sentence for its actual content, we shall see that the words have been chosen in such a way that the reader is forced to focus his attention on what remains hidden behind and below the realistic narrative.

Let us examine this second sentence more carefully. The man compares his watch with a clock in a tower and discovers that he is late. This is an everyday occurrence; yet we feel strangely compelled to ask for the motivation of the wanderer's trivial action. His watch was slow; he must have sensed that he was behind time, or he would have had no reason to check up on it. Here two time systems seem to diverge: the man's personal time which had determined his way, the time which he carries as a watch on his own body and which has become almost as much a part of himself as his own heart, dissociates itself from the impersonal time, which runs its way up on the tower, completely unconcerned with the wanderer and the watch that had been setting his pace. He "had" believed in it. Kafka deliberately chooses the pluperfect tense to indicate a past now left behind by the man. He starts to run. Now he no longer believes in his personal time; without even the slightest hesitation he accepts the impersonal time as correct. And yet—is it not possible that his personal time was right and that the clock in the tower was too fast?

The fact that the wanderer's watch disagrees with the clock in the tower has led him to what he calls a "discovery": he realizes that it is later than he thought. Because of the urgency of this insight he fails to consult a third watch or to check the time on the clock before he completely surrenders to panicky haste. The reader will sympathize with the man in the anecdote, for he may remember having done the same thing himself. Thus an identification with the man is established which will prevail until the end of the story. It may have been that the wanderer was overcome by the height, the nearness to heaven, of the clock in the tower. More likely than not, however, he was swayed by the mere fact that this clock showed a time outside and beyond

himself. Not only is he willing to give precedence to whatever is outside of himself—as the first sentence of the anecdote has already
demonstrated—he feels compelled to trust the extrapersonal power of
the clock without any further ado. Hence the word "shock," which
breaks through the hitherto smooth surface of the narration with
primitive force. The panic causes a second awakening, but this time
the man is intellectually awakened. He realizes that his walk is no
longer in step with a higher order of things. This realization tempts
him to run; yet by running, he loses his way. Or to say it in other
words, the attempt to regain the right time by running deprives him
of the right direction in space.

At this point of the story we meet the phrase, "I was not very well
acquainted with the town." First and foremost it seems to suggest
that the narrator is neither a native nor a casual visitor, for in neither
case would the problem of familiarity with the town have arisen. The
fact that the man was not quite familiar with the city could explain
his insecurity. Then his fear of being late would be associated with
his fear of being a stranger, and both fears could have been allayed
if he had only stayed in the neighborhood long enough to become
acquainted with it. "Why don't you know your way?" he seems to be
asking himself. "You could have known it better if only you had stayed
a little longer."

Again, and this time more urgently, we are asking for the reasons
behind the man's departure. The haste to which he has succumbed
suggests a possible solution to the puzzle: it was impatience which
caused him to leave the city before he had become sufficiently familiar
with it. Because of impatience the wanderer was likewise incapable of
stopping to check the time again or to contemplate his condition.
Instead he surrendered to a panic incommensurate with the simple
discovery that his watch was slow. Here is another, deeper motivation
for the man's following the clock in the tower instead of his own watch:
the fact that the impersonal time of the clock was later than his own
time met his innate impatience halfway.

Impatience brings a sigh of relief from the wanderer when he
catches sight of the policeman. German uses the words *Polizist* and
Schutzmann interchangeably; yet here Kafka introduces the policeman
deliberately as *Schutzmann*. It is *Schutz* which the man now craves
most—protection from the strange city, from the elapsed time, from
his own insecurity. Moreover, the policeman has not appeared suddenly, nor did he catch the eye of the running man by mere chance.

He was nearby, standing there as if he had been on that very spot since time immemorial and intended to remain there forever. Towering there, the policeman seems to be associated with the tower that holds the clock; like the clock tower he represents a system of order ruling the world outside. And just as the man previously had accepted the "outer" time of the tower, so now he surrenders to the extrapersonal authority of the policeman. He does not stop to think or ask himself what business the officer had in this place at so early an hour. Because the street itself is deserted and free from traffic, a policeman is not needed. Destiny itself has clearly ordered the *Schutzmann* to take up his position at this spot and to protect the man for whom he seems to have been waiting.

The word "fortunately" is intended to express the fact that the man believes he has found again a complete agreement between the reality outside and the sense of direction inside himself; he again sees the relationship between the time shown by the clock in the tower and the way he was afraid he had lost, between a well-ordered world and his position in it. His haste now proves to have been utterly unnecessary. The policeman is to show him the way to the railroad station, the lost time will be regained, and all will end well. Our wanderer now relaxes to the extent that, for the first and only time in the story, he is able to describe himself directly. By calling himself "breathless," he reflects the impression which he is bound to give the policeman. For one split second he sees himself as he must appear to the outside world. Yet in this moment of extraversion he accepts, ironically, the policeman's point of view; from now on he will doubt the information given him by the official as little as the time revealed to him by the clock.

During this second, fate appears to be favorably inclined toward the hapless wanderer. The policeman smiles. However, the smile immediately assumes a second, ominous meaning by the words which the policeman adds to it. Kafka has formulated the sentence in which this change occurs in a peculiarly skillful way. Its meaning is at first hidden under the policeman's smile, which only later turns out to have been false or at least ambiguous. The discomfort that the change intends to convey arises in the reader only gradually. Some time is needed to realize the strangeness of this information giver who answers a question with a counterquestion: "From me you want to learn the way?" Signposts are meant to point the way, not to raise questions about themselves. Nor can we miss the undertone of arrogance and indignation in the words of the policeman, who puts himself first in his question (in contrast to the man who had hidden himself at the end of the introductory sentence). The "I" of the official towers so forcefully above the "Thou" of the man that we do not realize right away the presumption underlying his words. He actually addresses the man with a "Thou" (*du*), instead of the formal "you" (*Sie*). In German one says *du* to inferiors, to children, or to animals, not to a solid citizen, with whom one conducts an official exchange of words. Putting his Ego before the humiliating "Thou," the policeman downgrades the information seeker.

And yet, are we not falling prey to a deception when we accept the impression the policeman is giving the man? His counterquestion, which is bound to sound like the epitome of unreasonble pride to the ears of the disappointed questioner, may just as well have been prompted by diffidence or uncertainty. The policeman may have resorted to parrying question with question because the answer was not known to him either. He may not have been familiar with this part of the city, may himself have been ignorant of the right way. The ambiguity of his return question may have been a sign of his incompetence, the *du* of his address an attempt to ingratiate himself with the man, for the German *du* also implies human proximity and brotherliness. Again the wanderer is offered an opportunity to deliberate and evaluate the situation confronting him. Again he misses it. Meekly, like a horrified child, he admits his helplessness.

The exchange between man and policeman is restricted to the barest minimum of words. While it is taking place, however, a general change occurs, unnoticeably but undeniably. In the beginning an ordinary man was asking for an ordinary way, but by now it has become clear to us that it could not have been the everyday way to an everyday railroad station which was on the policeman's mind. Although his counterquestion is phrased in the simplest of words, it points to another, more complex meaning of the word "way." It hints at an infinite variety of ways, without pointing them out or making a binding statement about them. After all, what answer could be more noncommittal than a question? Although man and policeman are conversing in the same language, they do not agree on the exact meaning of this one syllable "way." They talk past one another. Nevertheless, it is not impossible that the man, out of submissiveness and self-denial, eventually will make the policeman's deeper and darker idea of the way his own—whatever this idea may be.

Simultaneously the background of the story has changed without, to be sure, resulting in a change of the external scene. Since the way with which the policeman is concerned, cannot possibly be identical with the one sought by the man in reality, the very reality of the street on which the encounter is taking place has begun to dissolve. The setting which we assumed at first to have the three-dimensional quality of a real town has become unreal and intangible. Even the clock tower has disappeared from the story. Thus the man is deprived of his last pointer, and nothing is left to give him direction.

We are now prepared for the words, "Give it up!" with which the information giver finally dismisses the man. The finality of these words is stressed by their being repeated. On the other hand, it could also be that this repetition is due to the policeman's realization of the man's limited understanding: he talks to him as one talks to an infant or a person who is hard of hearing. We remain in the dark about the precise meaning of these syllables, which descend upon the man like a sixfold thunderbolt. What is he being asked to give up? As little as Kafka allows himself to be pinned down with regard to the meaning of the word "way," so little does he enlighten the reader about the intention of the truly impersonal pronoun "it" in "Give it up!" * This "it" is so elastic that it can easily be extended to mean the man's unreasonable haste. If this were the case, the policeman would seem to intimate that the man should abandon his breathlessness and impatience, that is, that he should quiet down. Similarly, the "it" may be understood as a reference to the man's travels and wanderings, or his departure in particular. Then the grim warning would have changed its tone completely and have become a friendly invitation encouraging the man to stay in the city, to look around and linger a while until he would know his way better than before. And yet we are already so intensely identified with the man and his way of thinking that we, too, hasten to substitute an "everything" for this "it." "Give everything up!" the policeman seems to be saying, "let all hope go, abandon the way and the desire ever to find it, give up your quest, your drive and your yearning, your very existence—yourself!" He has pronounced this verdict without giving his reasons, without specifying how it should be carried out, without even pronouncing it. He has simply repeated a few syllables, which can mean anything from benevolent advice to the most sinister urge to self-destruction.

* In the German original this "it" is even more obscure: there the pronoun "*es*" has been reduced to the letter *s*, which is fused with the imperative *gib* to "*Gibs auf!*" where "it" becomes almost inaudible.

The man listens to the verdict in complete silence. He neither questions nor contradicts it and seems to accept it fully. He still notices the "great sweep," with which the official turns away: yet this baroque gesture of the policeman seems even to precipitate the man's disappearance from the scene. The information giver remains silent with a flourish, as it were; thus he avoids giving an answer and shuns, ultimately, his duty. He "turned away . . . , as people do who want to be left alone with their laughter." Kafka uses the present tense here: the policeman's preoccupation with himself is meant to continue as a *praesens infinitum* while the narrator narrates and the reader reads this story.

The policeman returns to his duty, which, whatever it may be, has nothing to do with the claims the man has made upon him. The man has disappeared like the town around him. This statement is, however, only a surmise, unsupported by any textual evidence. By interrupting his narrative at this point, Kafka saves himself the trouble of informing us about the eventual outcome of his story. We are never told whether the man really found his way in the end.

Nor do we find any indication of the outcome in the tone of the story. We cannot decide whether we have been reading a tragic or a grotesquely comic tale. Its scene is plunged in a twilight in which the horrible freely blends with the absurd, and if we are in the right mood, even with the funny. The policeman smiles when his eyes catch the man; the man sees in the information giver a figure of monumental seriousness. The wanderer appears ludicrous to the reader, the official petty, pompous, and awe-inspiring. Yet Kafka does not decide for any one of these conflicting points of view. Instead he forces the reader to change continuously from one to another. Moreover, these shifts of perspective occur so quickly that the contrasts are blurred, the opposites merge, and the contradictions are shrouded by an all-encompassing ambiguity.

Whoever intends to extract an unequivocal meaning from this story will, like the man who is its central figure, hear a question instead of an answer. The policeman's "Give it up!" is also spoken to all those interpreters of Kafka who seem to assume that he believed in the existence of only one way leading in one direction to one aim.

Kafka's ultimate evasiveness can be demonstrated by subjecting our anecdote to some of the interpretations which the different approaches of literary criticism would suggest.

Historically the man who wants to leave the city at any cost suffers from acute claustrophobia. "Out of here—this is my aim," Kafka exclaims in a story which is the companion piece of our anecdote (*DS*, 200). As a German Jew in Czech Prague, Kafka lived in a triple ghetto: the Jewish community was encircled by hostile Slavs, who in turn were hemmed in and held down by the Austrian bureaucracy that ruled the city in the name of the Habsburg empire until the revolution of 1918. Also Kafka "was not very well acquainted with the town," even though he was born there. The German language, in which his books are written, separated him from the Czechs. Yet the servants and employees of his father were self-conscious and aggressive Slavs. On the other hand, his Jewish origins kept him estranged from the Austrian upper class, which more often than not indulged in a covert and inconsistent anti-Semitism and administered the city according to the prejudices of the moribund monarchy.

Kafka was not unaware of his relation to history. On January 13, 1921, he wrote Max Brod about his "present inner condition":

It is somewhat reminiscent of Old Austria. To be sure, it went quite well at times, in the evening one would lie on the couch in the nicely heated room . . . and enjoy some measure of peace, but it was only a peace of sorts, and not one's own. Just a trifle, the question of the Trautenau district court, perhaps, was needed to start the throne in Vienna rocking. A dentist's assistant . . . studies in a whisper on the balcony above, and the whole empire—really, the empire in its entirety—suddenly goes up in flames (*B*, 288–289).

With this statement in mind, one could interpret the policeman in our story as the representative of an administration that is feared as well as despised. The old order still survives, and although its offices are still functioning, its subjects are unable to obtain any pertinent information, let alone effective protection. The policeman's withdrawal from the man's question could then be understood as Old Austria's admission that she was helpless and incapable of assisting her citizens politically. His retort, "Give it up!" would be the expression of historical apathy, symbolizing the death wish of the Habsburg empire, whose subjects felt that it was doomed to decline. Yet Kafka leaves the relationship between man and policeman, central figure and official, individual and society, wide open. Is our narrator merely a passive victim of the law's delay, the insolence of office? Does not, rather, a hidden rebellion smoulder in his insistence on finding the right way in a time out of joint? The fragmentary nature of the anecdote excludes any clear-cut answer. Yet the historical approach enabled one historically minded interpreter (E. B. Burgum) to ascribe pre-Fascist tendencies to Kafka's heroes,[1] while another, likewise guided by political considerations (Paul Reimann), claimed them as proto-Communists.[2] Posing more questions than it is able to answer, the historical approach has a tendency to lead interpreters to mutually exclusive extremes. The central problem remains untouched by it.

A psychological approach might indicate that our anecdote is first and foremost a case study in neurasthenia. Three times the narrator's nerves fail him: when he discovers that he is late, when he is mystified by the policeman's return question, and when in the end he succumbs to total silence. Age-old anxieties expose him to situations which he does not even try to master—the fear of arriving too late, which, to be sure, is only a thinly veiled fear of death, of losing one's life before one has come to its end and reached his goal. This phobia is accentuated by the horror inflicted upon the man by the policeman's blocking the very way he was supposed to have shown him.

It is possible to see in this fright an allegory of Kafka's childhood experiences, particularly of the role his father played in his upbringing. The long letter he wrote to his father in 1919 offers an abundance of material supporting a psychological interpretation of the story before us. For example, in the letter Kafka wrote, "For me you took on the enigmatic quality that all tyrants have whose rights are based on their person and not on reason"; in the story the policeman rises to a grandeur which stifles all the independent thoughts necessary to solve the enigma. Similarly Kafka wrote to his father, "It sometimes happened that you had no opinion whatsoever about a matter and as a result all opinions that were at all possible with respect to the matter were necessarily wrong, without exception"; the policeman first answers the man with a counterquestion and crushes him finally with the weight of his verdict—which is based on no opinion whatsoever. And finally he wrote, "When I began to do something you did not like and you threatened me with the prospect of failure, my respect of your opinion was so great that the failure then became inevitable" (*DF*, 145, 152); in the story the man yields silently to the inevitable, which Kafka had taken great pains to describe as quite avoidable.

Furthermore, as a dream symbol the policeman would turn into a phallic image, as does the clock tower to which the policeman's symbolic relationship is thus again revealed. Following these associations, the reader might perceive behind the figure of the policeman the immensely inflated dream image of Kafka's father. It would bar the son's way into a life of normalcy, which appears to Kafka more and more as the only possible, the true, way. In letting the father figure pronounce the verdict, "Give it up!" over the son, Kafka might have been expressing doubts regarding his own virility. To be sure, he could write to his father: "Marriage is certainly the guarantee of the most acute form of self-liberation and independence, I should have a family, the supreme thing that one can achieve and so too the supreme thing you have achieved, I should be your equal, all old and everlasting new shame and tyranny would then be a mere history of the past." But then he recoils before the father—just as the man shrinks back from the policeman—when he cries out to him, "But we being what we are, marrying is barred to me through the fact that it is precisely and particularly your most intimate domain" (*DF*, 190, 191).

The obvious flaw in this psychological interpretation is the all-too-frequent use it makes of the extraliterary raw material of personal confessions. If the policeman in our anecdote really functions as a dream symbol, a father image expanded to the proportions of a veritable nightmare, why does he still strike the reader with an impersonal, almost universal terror? The psychological interpretation goes a long way in elucidating the origins from which Kafka's visions sprang, but fails to explain their horrible individuality and their equally terrible general appeal. Moreover, it does not clarify the relationship between day and dream, reality and unreality in Kafka's books—it simply reduces the latter to the former. But did our narrator not wake up shortly before setting out on his way through the city? Was this awakening part of his dream? Did it merely open a trap door through which he tumbled from one level of unreality to another, deeper one? On the other hand, does not reality betray its transient and transparent character, that is, its innate unreality, by being exposed to the inexorable dream logic of Kafka's nightmares? Does the abrupt ending of this anecdote, its *fragmentary* character, result from a shocklike transition from the unreality of a dream experience to the rational sphere of reality? Or does Kafka interrupt his narrative because he (and the reader with him) awakened from a bad dream? The text of our anecdote holds no answer to these questions.

If we choose to interpret our story in the light of religion, then the policeman would no longer be a substitute for Kafka's physical father, but a messenger from a spiritual realm. As such, however, he has nothing to communicate to the human sphere but the command to "give it up," whereupon he turns majestically away and minds his own business. His own concerns are so remote from human understanding that they can only be expressed by the silence following the end of the story. Man's unfamiliarity with his familiar surroundings, his alienation on earth, now acquire a metaphysical meaning. Nameless and yet as clearly allegorical as the Everyman in the mediaeval morality play, the man in our anecdote faces eternity, comparing his watch, the symbol of temporal time, with the clock in the tower, the image of infinity. Kafka knew that the balance between the "inner" time of man and the "outer" time of the universe was seriously disturbed. "The clocks are not in unison," he jotted down in his diary on January 16, 1922; "the inner one runs crazily on at a devilish or demoniac or in any case inhuman pace, the outer one limps along at its usual speed. What else can happen but that the two worlds split apart, and they do split apart, or at least clash in a fearful manner" (*DII*, 202). The time symbolism in this diary entry contradicts the imagery of our anecdote in that there the narrator's "inner" time is slower than the "outer" time of the clock in the tower. And yet the diary version seems truer, at least as far as Kafka and his figures are concerned. For the unbalanced speed of human time stems from a restlessness which drives these figures mercilessly in a metaphysical direction.

We have seen that this restlessness prompted the narrator to depart from the city, caused him to lose his way and to entrust himself to the policeman. Impatience assumes in Kafka's mind an importance almost equal to the weight attributed to original sin in a Christian conscience. "All human errors are impatience," he says in one of his aphorisms, "a premature breaking off of what is methodical, an apparent fencing in of an apparent thing." And still more outspoken: "There are two main human sins from which all the others derive: impatience and indolence. It was because of impatience that man was expelled from Paradise; it is because of indolence that he does not return. Yet perhaps there is only one major sin: impatience. Because of impatience man was expelled, because of impatience he does not return" (*DF*, 34). This impatience is of a mystical nature; it was the reason why man once forfeited the divine realm, the very sphere he is now assailing in order to force his reentry. Yet because of this impatience the realm beyond remains forever inaccessible to the human grasp, for the domain of God cannot be taken by storm. From his impatience grows the man's uneasiness in the city as well as his fear of being too late, or rather, that it is too late for him. Impatience causes his anxiety that he will never be on time, that the clock in the tower will never agree with his watch, that no policeman will ever be there to point out the way he is seeking. Thus the misunderstanding between man and policeman is no longer due to semantic differences; it is a last, painfully lingering reminiscence of Paradise Lost. The verdict "Give it up" reverberates with the echoes of a divine judgment.

In view of such a total alienation of the physical from the metaphysical world, the word "fortunately," with which the narrator hails the appearance of the policeman, acquires an air of religious irony. For the man, unsheltered and homeless as he finds himself on earth, must consider it an unprecedented stroke of luck to catch even a glimpse of the policeman. The *Schutzmann* is, after all, a security officer and establishes some kind of order in an otherwise disorderly universe. In the end, the policeman deprives him of the security which it should have been his official duty to provide. Bitter sarcasm lies in the fact that the man will never benefit from the fortune his "fortunately" had so boldly and blindly anticipated. But it is a metaphysical sarcasm, and the whole anecdote represents a statement about a situation in human history in which there is no certainty left to the individual. It depends on the individual's religious orientation whether or not he interprets this uncertainty metaphysically and sees in it a sign of the world's apostasy from its creator. "Is there any connection left at all between a sense and order in the universe and this nonsense, the disorder of the human world?" Martin Buber has asked, with Kafka's stories in mind.[3] Our story does not answer this question.

It is possible to claim the man in our anecdote as an existential hero. Then the policeman would appear as the spokesman of a universe totally unconcerned with the information seeker's personal destiny and radically hostile to him. This universe answers man's claim for direction with an icy silence.

Yet this silence releases the man from any and all obligation. Committed to nobody and nothing, he can easily leave the town. He can turn wherever he pleases; he does not even indicate to which destination the railroad is going to carry him. This is his existential advantage. How does he use it? Shocked by the discrepancy between his existence and the world outside—the comparison of his watch with the clock in the tower—he plays into the hands of the absurd policeman. It is perhaps the gravest symptom of the disorder disrupting Kafka's

world that he can no longer distinguish between the social and the
metaphysical authorities who govern it. And how could he distinguish
between them since they seem united in opposing him?

This central problem has been formulated by Wilhelm Emrich, who
asks, "How is it possible to assert the free 'self' amidst all the moving
forces of life which converge upon us, in the final analysis, collec-
tively?" [4] Emrich's study is the most thorough analysis of Kafka's
imagery that we possess to date. Yet he uses the writer's images as
building stones in an elaborate philosophical structure which presupposes that Kafka's "self" is basically free. He sees Kafka's heroes
involved in a struggle with life's antinomies which can eventually be
overcome, if only by the hero's tragic end. "Only then," Emrich says,
"when *everything* is negated, both life with its contradictions and
limitations, and the claim for the absolute, . . . only then can responsibility be conferred upon the man. . . . Beforehand . . . he submitted to the conditions of life or to an unconditional command. Now
he stands above both. Only this is his genuine position." [5] To be sure,
Emrich did not have our anecdote in mind when he arrived at this
conclusion. But his study so thoroughly integrates all of Kafka's images
and ideas into one philosophical pattern that we feel justified in applying it also to the text at hand. Our anecdote, however, knows of the
existential freedom stipulated by Emrich only as an opportunity patently missed by the narrator. Perhaps he wanted to grasp it when he
started out on his journey, yet he allows himself to be bound—spellbound—by any and all restrictions he encounters on his way. The
responsibility which the policeman's catastrophic "Give it up!" confers
upon him either throws him back and forces him to stay in the place
he had wanted to leave, or it advises him to end his way voluntarily
rather than be destroyed by fate. The existential freedom to which he
is released in the end may very well be tantamount to a freedom *from*
all existence, the freedom one finds in death. In no case can we discern
the trace of a victory—however hypothetical this victory may be—in
the text of our story.

The interpretations so far presented are not mutually exclusive. On
the contrary, if they are added together they still do not suffice to
exhaust the meaning hidden in the anecdote. For Franz Kafka was
incomparably more than a neurotic God-seeker whose whims and
quirks were historically conditioned by the intellectual climate of his
native country and his era. He was a writer in his own right, a *lit-*

térateur if ever there was one, the creator of word images, interested in their relationships to one another (which, however, he never clearly defined) and to their background (which he was altogether incapable of exploring).

Since he was a border case in the literal meaning of the word, given to analytical thinking as well as to vision, a psychologist as well as a mystic, ambiguity became the very essence of his language. With the help of his imagery he was able to straddle the two realms of his experience: the pseudomythical underworld of his childhood, where the father held sway, and the cryptoreligious universe of his poetic vision, where God reigned in perfect inaccessibility. As the result of an ingrained *double-entendre* Kafka's imagery stands widely exposed to a background spanning both the abysm below and the abysm above, which he sometimes, erroneously, called "heaven."

That his images are endowed with an uncanny persuasiveness and that his epical structures have proved durable beyond his and anybody else's expectation are due to their utter simplicity; like most great documents of literature they reflect the tension between the individual and the universe. To be sure, Kafka refrains from discharging this tension tragically; nor does he dissolve it in the happy ending of a comedy. Yet farcical elements, like the change from smile to sternness on the policeman's face, merge with the stark brutality of a tragic ritual, like the policeman's almost hieratic "great sweep." Nor is this basic tension channeled into the chronological sequences of a conventional tale. Caught in an impressive image, it suddenly bursts on the reader, who, with the shock of recognition, may perceive in it the very condition of man. Thus this tension betrays the inexpressible without expressing it. Ludwig Wittgenstein may have had similar experiences in mind when he remarked in his *Tractatus Logico-Philosophicus:* "There is indeed the inexpressible. This *shows* itself, it is the mystical." [6] Wittgenstein italicized the word "shows" in order to impress upon the reader his conviction that the mystery of existence may appear but cannot be translated into the logic and grammar of coherent language.

The suddenness with which Kafka's images show themselves frees them from the restrictions and limitations of epical time. They may deal with time, or play with it, but they are not to be measured or judged by the usual processes of time. Our anecdote, too, is set outside the flux of time; being a fragment, it has neither a beginning nor an end. The background into which the fragment opens swallows the time on the man's watch, the time of the clock in the tower, and any time which may have passed between the hour of the wanderer's awakening and his encounter with the policeman.

While the content and the purpose of Kafka's narratives are both ultimately and uniquely ambiguous, their style and structure nonetheless permit some closer exploration. The word "background" has repeatedly emerged in our argument. It is meant to be understood in the sense given it by Erich Auerbach in his book entitled *Mimesis: The Representation of Reality in Western Literature*. In the first chapter Auerbach compares the extensive style employed by Homer in the nineteenth book of the *Odyssey* with the intensive style which distinguishes the account of Isaac's sacrifice, given by the so-called Elohist in the twenty-second chapter of Genesis. He makes the following observation:

It would be difficult, then, to imagine styles more contrasted than those of these equally ancient and equally epic texts. On the one hand, externalized, uniformly illuminated phenomena, at a definite time and in a definite place, connected together without lacunae in a perpetual foreground; thoughts and feelings completely expressed; events taking place in leisurely fashion and with very little of suspense. On the other hand, the externalization of only so much of the phenomena as is necessary for the purpose of the narrative, all else left in obscurity; the decisive points of the narrative alone are emphasized, what lies between is nonexistent; time and place are undefined and call for interpretation; thoughts and feeling remain unexpressed, are only suggested by the silence and the fragmentary speeches; the whole, permeated with the most unrelieved suspense and directed toward a single goal (and to that extent far more of a unity), remains mysterious and "fraught with background." [7]

To enlarge upon this comparison between the Elohist and Homer, it would be attractive to extend it to a comparison between Franz Kafka and James Joyce, whose *Ulysses* belongs by orientation—and title—in the Homeric tradition. Kafka's monolithic laconism would thus appear as the perfect counterpart of Joyce's mania for rendering the total picture, even the unconscious of the persons depicted. As Joyce's ideal form we could imagine a catalogue so complete as to become unreadable and, by including even the inexpressible, dissolving reality into absurdity; as Kafka's ideal form, a paragraph bursting with the absurdity of existence.* Yet even if we concentrate on the interpre-

* A further example may be helpful to clarify the difference between "foreground" and "background" in modern fiction. When Thomas Mann, in 1939, delivered an introductory speech to his *The Magic Mountain* before the students

tation of our anecdote, we cannot fail to observe that Auerbach's characterization of the Elohist contributes considerably to our understanding of Kafka's style. From its beginning the anecdote has been calling for interpretation. The man's awakening, his walk through the early morning, the comparison of his watch with the clock in the tower, are told in such a fashion that they seem to be the last visible signs of invisible chain reactions which originate in the unknown, the not-knowable.

There is not one self-explanatory word in a typical Kafka narrative. His mature prose shows nothing but a surface spread over happenings that remain profoundly impenetrable. Paradoxically this enables Kafka, the visionary, to furnish his stories amply with realistic detail. Since even the inanimate objects he describes point to an undefined and mysterious background, they no longer relate to one another according to the customs and conventions of reality. Clefts, cracks, and crevices open, revealing the depth behind the realistic detail. The same is true of the figures acting on a stage thus prepared. Ostensibly most of them are well grounded in reality, even in the reality of Kafka's own life. Sometimes he provided them with assonances of his own name and other hints of his own biography, even if he didn't wish to introduce them simply as "I," as he does in the anecdote before us. Consequently, we are tempted to interpret the wanderer as Kafka. Yet the opposite may be true. The man in our story may be an image rather than the more or less true likeness of the author. For throughout these stories we are not dealing with portrayals of actual beings but rather with code ciphers conveying indecipherable messages, pawns in a game of chess played by invisible hands and obeying a master mind totally incomprehensible to them as well as to us. By calling this man "I," Kafka committed consciously, purposefully, and, we dare say, mischievously an "intentional fallacy." [8]

It is more than probable that he even shaped the "I" which expresses itself in his letters and diaries after the model of the heroes in his

---

of Princeton University, he felt compelled to defend his book against the idea that it was a social novel. "The critique of the sanitarium and its therapeutical methods is foreground, one of the foregrounds in a book the very essence of which is fraught with background" (*Der Zauberberg* [Frankfort: Fischer, 1958], p. xii). Thereupon he proceeded to acclaim some critics who had interpreted his novel as an "initiation story" and a "quester legend." Mann's self-interpretation cannot be discussed here any further. Suffice it to say that he too chose the term "background" when he wished to indicate that his work was constructed on a level higher than reality.

books—one more reason to be careful in the use of this biographical
material for the interpretation of his literary writings. Instead of lifting
the material of his books out of the shapeless mass of his life experiences, he may very well have lived his life as if it were one of his
writings. Stylizations of this kind are not infrequent in modern literature, which to such a large extent describes the decomposition of
human identity and substitutes literary symbols for it. We need only
remember Dostoyevsky's diaries and Rilke's letters to realize that this
literary treatment of biographical data has become a major preoccupation of modern writers in general. By the same token we shall have
to admit the general unreliability of these personal documents as far
as the discovery of the man behind the mask, the writer behind the
writing, is concerned. Although it is impossible to disregard them,
Kafka's diaries, conversations, letters, and aphorisms have to be treated
with extreme circumspection and tact. The information they contain
is tenuous and, more often than not, misleading. We cannot identify a
reflected image by reflecting it in a second mirror.

We shall not be able to say much more about Kafka's figures than
that they too are congenitally and intimately connected with their
background. The background penetrates their words, determines their
attitudes, and fills up their silences. This again makes them late
descendants of the figures in the text of the Elohist. Even they, Auerbach notes, "can be represented as possessing 'background,'" more
background, in any case, than Homer's heroes, for they

have greater depths of time, fate, and consciousness . . . ; although they
are nearly always caught up in an event engaging all their faculties, they
are not so entirely immersed in its present that they do not remain continually conscious of what has happened to them earlier and elsewhere;
their thoughts and feelings have more layers, are more entangled. Abraham's actions are explained not only by what is happening to him at the
moment, nor yet only by his character . . . , but by his previous history;
he remembers, he is constantly conscious of, what God has promised him
and what God has already accomplished for him—his soul is torn between
desperate rebellion and hopeful expectation, his silent obedience is multilayered, has background.[9]

The man in our story resembles the Abraham of the Elohist in that
his person is likewise both impersonal and more than personal: he is
nameless as well as representative. His face is a complete blank, and
yet it reminded us of Everyman. Similarly his actions cannot be explained by the events that actually occur, but by reasons hidden both

below the threshold of his consciousness and beyond the frame of reference of what is actually told in his story. He too is suspended between hope and despair, indignation and expectation; and the silence in the end is so multilayered that we are unable to state with any degree of assurance whether it indicates his end and not, perhaps, a new beginning. Completely absorbed in his meeting with the policeman, the man experiences at the same time a meeting with powers which seem to draw him back to his childhood and, further still, to the unfathomable recesses of the memories of his race. Since, however, time seems to be suspended with regard to everything Kafka wrote, his narratives also point forward, to the future.

Kafka died in 1924. The generations that followed have frequently recognized their own destiny in the seemingly unreal fate of his heroes. In his fantastic visions he anticipated the Waste Land as the landscape of modern man. There he lives unsheltered and totally exposed to a regimen fraught with horror and imbued with nonsense. The *Schutzmann* who substitutes condemnation for protection is as contemporary an image as the man who wanders without knowing his way.

But here the parallels with the Elohist end. Biblical Abraham is open to a background replete with the presence of his God. He remembers Him when he accepts the unintelligible command to slaughter his firstborn son. His promise fills Abraham's consciousness even when he prepares for the sacrifice. The certainty of this belief not only connects Abraham with his background, it is identical with it. The background of Kafka's man, on the other hand, consists of a darkness symbolizing the complete absence of any such certainty. It is an eclipse of God, a *Gottesfinsternis,* like the one conjured up in a poem (1935) by Kafka's sometimes admired, sometimes scorned, friend and fellow countryman, Franz Werfel:

> Even from the heaven of your day
> Hangs suddenly God's eclipse . . .
>
> From the horizon, icy-grained
> The charging storm engulfs your house.
> All trees have eery shadows
> The like were never seen before.
> The leaves hang flabby and swollen
> Like soggy fruit that grew too big.
> The waters in the reed beyond
> Gurgle out a gruesome dialect . . .

But insectlike
You quite forgot the former light
And give not one astonished moment
To the distorted picture of the world
And to its frozen heartless waste.

At least be shocked and startled
When the bats aroused at day
Dash against your window in despair!

(Auch an dem Glaubenshimmel deines Tages
Hängt plötzlich Gottesfinsternis . . .

Von Horizonten hagelt Sturmangrit
Eishältig dir ums Haus.
Die Bäume alle werfen
So fremde Schatten, wie man nie gesehn.
Die Blätter hängen schlaff
Und aufgeschwemmt gleich überwachsnen Früchten.
Das Wasser selbst im Rohr
Vergurgelt schauerlichen Dialekt . . .

Du aber hast
Insektenhaft das einstige Licht vergessen
Und schenkst dem ganz zerzognen Bild der Welt
Und ihrer Herzerfrorenheit
Nicht einen Augenblick Verwunderung.

Erschrick doch wenigstens,
Dass die am Tag erwachten Fledermäuse
Verzweifelt sich an deine Fenster werfen! [10])

A lyrical paraphrase may be called for where textual analysis has proved unsatisfactory. Werfel's "completely distorted image of the world" holds all the realism Kafka ever attained in the description of his world. In the poem this distorted image is linked to the frozen heart of creation. But neither Werfel nor Kafka establish the principle of cause and effect between the emptiness of the heart and the disfiguration of the world outside. They simply mention one symptom after the other *as if* they belonged together. There is no light in this world, and yet the shadows deepen. The sun, the central source of life, has disappeared; certain forms stand out in a twilight produced by other, unnamed sources. Inanimate objects change their shape and function: leaves turn into fruit as, conversely, fruit may turn into leaves, thus rendering nature fruitless. Water speaks a dialect, like man, but it is an idiom which spreads horror before the trickle dries up and ends in silence. Man is like an insect; yet he is not, like a moth, attracted by the light but forgetful of it. Nocturnal bats join forces with the elements of nature to attack the last stronghold of man, his house, which is as empty and as frail as his heart.

Again, the border line between the inner and the outer world is extinguished, as is the difference between day and night. The background advances to envelop and engulf it all. Werfel differs from Kafka merely in calling this background by its name, *Gottesfinsternis*. Kafka, however, kept silent. All that Kafka ever wrested from the silence surrounding him was the insight "that the incomprehensible is incomprehensible, and this we knew already." The phrase is taken from a longer aphorism with the revealing title, "On Parables" (*GW*, 258).

The anecdote about the man and the policeman is such a parable about the incomprehensibility of the incomprehensible. It culminates in the policeman's "Give it up!" in which the incomprehensible asserts its intention to remain obscure. The tradition of his family's religion, the Jewish belief, exerted on Kafka an aftereffect still strong enough to suggest to him hidden depths of existence and powers holding sway beyond man's life. The policeman is nearby. Yet these extrahuman powers cannot be asked for information, let alone assistance. They vanish before man's grasp. The policeman turns away, as people do who want to be left alone. The parable merely leads in the direction of these powers like a bridge dissolving in mist before it has reached the bank on the other side.

The command "Give it up!" reveals to the man the dilemma of his existence. Yet Kafka did not try to solve this dilemma, nor to translate it into any doctrinal message. He simply stated it with all the strength he could muster from the weakness of a man born late in the development of his civilization. His parables are as multilayered as their Biblical models. But, unlike them, they are also multifaceted, ambiguous, and capable of so many interpretations that, in the final analysis, they defy any and all. Like literary Rorschach tests they reveal the characters of the interpreters rather than their own.

Yet, taken by itself, the "Give it up!" of the policeman is a paradox, since it represents the only information given by an official whose task consists in giving information. Such a paradox will be generated wherever the natural and the supernatural meet, that is, when a message

which is inaccessible to ordinary verbalization is to be translated into
the vernacular of reasonable and generally intelligible communication.
Kierkegaard already had recognized this function of the paradox when
in *Fear and Trembling* he expressed the remoteness of his God by
retelling the sacrifice of Isaac in a set of highly paradoxical parables.
But he was still commenting upon a text to which he was committed
by his belief, whereas Kafka turned the paradoxical parable into an
independent literary genre.

Generally speaking, Kafka's parables center on their paradox, just
as our anecdote revolves around the policeman's verdict. Circling
around this nucleus, they maintain a suspense originating in the never-
defined relation their actual plots maintain with their backgrounds.
Only when the narrative stops to reveal its essentially fragmentary
character will this background be thrown into bold relief. Otherwise
it is reflected and refracted by an abundance of ambiguous word
images. Thus imagery as well as background appear as expressions
of the narrator's incapability of saying what these parables have been
meant to say in the beginning. Franz Kafka's importance derives from
the fact that he was probably the first and certainly the most radical
writer to pronounce the insoluble paradox of human existence by
using this paradox as the message of his parables. Therefore, any
interpretation of his work will have to return to the text itself:

"It was very early in the morning, the streets clean and deserted, I
was on my way to the railroad station. As I compared the tower clock
with my watch I realized that it was already much later than I had
thought, I had to hurry, the shock of this discovery made me feel uncertain of the way, I was not very well acquainted with the town as
yet, fortunately there was a policeman nearby, I ran to him and breathlessly asked him the way. He smiled and said: 'From me you want to
learn the way?' 'Yes,' I said, 'since I cannot find it myself.' 'Give it up,
give it up,' said he, and turned away with a great sweep, like someone
who wants to be alone with his laughter."

CHAPTER II

Juvenilia

The Artist as a Bachelor

FRANZ KAFKA'S literary beginnings were not very impressive. While he was still a law student at Prague University, he wrote a long narrative, "Description of a Struggle" (*DS*, 11–96). In 1909 he published two fragments taken from this story in Franz Blei's magazine, *Hyperion*.[1] Shortly after he received his academic degree in 1906, the twenty-three-year-old writer started work on another long story, "Wedding Preparations in the Country" (*DF*, 2–31), which he continued to work on well into the following year, 1907.

Both narratives reveal that the young writer was searching frantically for a form capable of controlling a continuous flow of amorphous images. The works remind us of the Impressionists in that their innate lack of contour and coherence reflects a reality which is itself in the process of dissolution. In this respect they are "modern"; they alter the style of the decadent neoromantic Young Vienna School to the idiom and scenery of Prague. Like his Viennese contemporaries, Kafka seems to have been influenced by Far Eastern art.[2] This influence is revealed especially in the subtle techniques of omission and intimation. The interpenetration of life and dream, which the Viennese had taken over as part of their baroque heritage, led the young Kafka to a somewhat tired mingling and merging of reality and unreality. Unabashed lyricism alternates with conversation, subjective wanderings with the more detached and distant dialogue form. The two *Hyperion* pieces are dialogues in this vein; a third conversation will be considered a little later.

These fledgling exercises in the art of the drama anticipate the only dramatic fragment we have from Kafka's hand. Although "The Warden of the Tomb" (*DS*, 147–178) appears in the Octavo Notebooks of Kafka's middle period,* it still moves on the neoromantic border line which divides, and unites, life and death. The living are ghosts, and the shadows of the departed prove more powerful than the figures actually present on the stage. One cannot help being reminded by "The Warden of the Tomb" of Hugo von Hofmannsthal's dramatic sketch *Death and the Fool* (1893). However, Hofmannsthal's verse succeeds in merging a few short scenes into a powerful theatrical statement, whereas Kafka's prose reveals how poorly the dramatic form suited the tragic ironies which inform his vision. As little as in the earlier attempts was he able in the later fragment to derive from the meetings of his characters the clear-cut clashes and fully realized reconciliations required of genuine dialogue. In its execution, though perhaps not in its intent, "The Warden of the Tomb" still betrays a beginner's hand.

His lyrical mood, on the other hand, is well expressed in the movingly fragile poem he chose as a motto for "Description":

> And people in their clothes
> Stroll about, swaying over the gravel
> Under this enormous sky
> Which, from hills in the distance,
> Stretches to distant hills (*DS*, 11).

> Und die Menschen gehn in Kleidern
> Schwankend auf dem Kies spazieren
> Unter diesem grossen Himmel,
> Der von Hügeln in der Ferne
> Sich zu fernen Hügeln breitet.

This is indeed a poor man's Hofmannsthal. The poem draws from the mood of the Young Vienna School in its resignation to the transitoriness of life and its infatuation with fleeting images. Yet the austere treatment of the language and the timidity revealed by the few unassuming

---

* Max Brod's postscript to the German edition of *Beschreibung eines Kampfes,* pp. 352–354.

objects in the poem point to the provincialism of its origins. To be sure, Hofmannsthal's love of costume and beautiful gesture is absent; instead, we are touched by the innocence of Kafka's poetic view. Stressing the clothes in which the people go for their everyday walks and the greatness of the sky against which they are silhouetted, he betrays a child's astonishment at a world still full of wonders. But the wonders are lost in the great distances which the poem tries to evoke by repeating, in the manner of an amateur, the very word "distant" which denotes them. Is it this feeling of alienation which makes the people sway? Is their dress mentioned so prominently because it too hints at artificial estrangement from a more natural, more paradisiacal state of humankind, where heaven is near? Whatever the answer may be, the feeling of distance permeates the five unrhymed lines and dissolves a vision into an impression. Economy of vocabulary borders on monotony. The whole vignette reflects the nervous aimlessness, the surrender to mood for the sake of surrender, the oscillating vagueness of the *fin de siècle,* without the richness of nuance and transition which distinguishes this period. Kafka's early prose shares with this poem both integrity (even then he did not say a word for which he could not answer) and lack of artistic control. There, too, the images seem to be lost in the greatness of the distances which separate object from object and man from man. More often than not, the sparsity of the language seems to give place to an overabundance of ideas and images. Yet behind the hectic and unharnessed movement of Kafka's early prose we notice again the self-consciousness of provincialism.

It does not suffice to attribute this sparsity of Kafka's early style to the language he spoke in his youth.[3] To be sure, *Prager Deutsch* was the idiom of a small and inbred community which repressed and repulsed the best of its sons and planted the germs of self-hatred in them. It is likewise true that this German, cut off from a constant exchange with the outside world, was interspersed with scraps from the vocabulary of the neighboring Czechs and that its pronunciation, idiom, and syntax suffered from being exposed to the Slavic influence.[4] Finally, the linguistic corruption was completed by the Yiddish expressions and inflections that had survived in the Kafka household, as the "Letter to His Father" shows, "Your opinion was correct, everyone else was . . . *meshugge,* not normal" (*DF*, 145). But similar conditions did not prevent Franz Werfel from embarking on his literary career, at the age of twenty-one, with the brilliantly rich verbal display of his *Weltfreund* poems.

Nor can the ever-precarious position of the Jewish writer in German literature alone account for the shapelessness and lack of focus disfiguring Kafka's early style. In retrospect Kafka found a dubious consolation in explaining the shortcomings of *all* German-Jewish writers by this rationalization. In a letter to Max Brod, probably written in June 1921, he observed that these writers must choose from among three impossibilities:

the impossibility of not writing, the impossibility of writing in German, the impossibility of writing differently. One could almost add a fourth impossibility: the impossibility of writing. . . . Thus it was in many ways an impossible literature, a gypsy literature, which had stolen the German child out of his cradle and with great haste tricked him up in some fashion because somebody had to dance on the rope, after all (*B*, 337–338).

The later development of Kafka's own art belies this generalization. Only a very ungypsylike responsibility for one's own work could produce a prose which, in spite of its ambiguities, was as unadorned and translucent as his.

There are many more partial explanations for Kafka's painfully slow, painfully disorganized beginnings; yet even when taken all together, they do not form a conclusive pattern. We touched on what is perhaps the most basic of them when we mentioned his estrangement from reality. This, of course, he shared with many a "modernist" among his contemporaries around the turn of the century. However, he was still unable to use this estrangement creatively, to conquer a decaying world by giving its decay a meaning and, through meaning, form. This alienation from reality did not make sense even to him; its meaning still remained obscure. Thus it produced in him a kind of frigidity, which made him sometimes stammer and sometimes precipitate a rush of words. It almost reduced him to silence.* In the "Conversation with the Supplicant" from the story "Description of a Struggle" he has

---

* A similar experience is related in Hofmannsthal's "Letter of Lord Chandos" (1902). Here a fictitious young English writer and scholar explains his decision never to write again because he had grown "by degrees incapable of discussing a loftier or more general subject in terms of which everyone, fluently and without hesitation, is wont to avail himself." Words no longer fit the reality they are supposed to express. The only language Lord Chandos declares himself willing to use is one "in which inanimate things speak to me and wherein I may one day have to justify myself before an unknown judge" (Hugo von Hofmannsthal, *Selected Prose*, trans. Mary Hottinger and Tania and James Stern [Bollingen Series, XXXIII; New York: Pantheon, 1952], 133, 141).

the narrator's "I" cry out to a "praying man," who is but another projection of the narrator's Ego:

Of course I guessed the first time I saw you, what kind of state you were in. I have had some experience, and I don't mean it as a joke when I tell you it is like being seasick on dry land. It is a condition in which you can't remember the real names of things and so in a great hurry you fling temporary names at them. You do it as fast as you can. But you have hardly turned your back on them before you have forgotten what you called them. A poplar in the fields which you called "the tower of Babel," since you either did not or would not know that it was a poplar, stands wavering without a name again, and so you have to call it "Noah in his drunken state."

The images in this passage are so absurdly farfetched, the connection between the poplar and the Tower of Babel, let alone the drunken Noah, so arbitrary and tenuous, that the reader will heartily agree with the supplicant's reply: "I am thankful to say that I don't understand what you have been talking about" (*DS*, 60). Of course it is possible to use a rising tower as a simile for a tree which stands silently in the field and a staggering drunkard for a tree which sways back and forth in the wind.* But by using Old Testament names to connote both the tower and the tottering man, Kafka blurred whatever possibility of comparison was inherent in his similes. It is noteworthy that even in this early stage it was Old Testament names which Kafka chose to qualify his images and provide them with "background."

Generally speaking, there are many correspondences between these early exercises and the more mature work. As a striking example consider the daydream of Raban, the hero of "Wedding Preparations." He imagines lying in bed one morning, dreamily assuming "the shape of a big beetle, a stag beetle or a cockroach" (*DF*, 6), thus anticipating the change of a traveling salesman into a monstrous insect in "The Metamorphosis" (*PC*, 67). "I would pretend," Raban thinks, "it was a matter of hibernating, and I would press my little legs to my bulging belly. And I would whisper a few words, instructions to my sad body, which stands close beside me, bent. Soon I shall have done—it bows, it goes swiftly, and it will manage everything efficiently while I rest" (*DF*, 7). What Raban's body is meant to accomplish is a dreaded visit with his fiancée in the country, while his imagining mind rests in his bed, snug as a bug. The obvious difference between the earlier and the

* According to Genesis 9:21, drunken Noah was, however, *lying* in his tent.

later story lies in Raban's merely imagining his transformation, whereas Gregor Samsa must actually undergo it. Raban is "like" a bug; Samsa awakens and "is" one. Or as Walter Jens has put it: "For Kafka, Gregor Samsa does not live symbolically like an insect, he has actually changed into a bug." [5]

The diaries and letters show that for the rest of his life Kafka drew on the experiences he had collected before and during his early manhood. Yet in his beginnings as a writer his approach to them was primarily passive. He attempted to project what he saw with his inner eye onto the reality outside him and to establish psychological motivations and other causal relations. He talked *about* the ideas that crossed his mind instead of changing them into images which needed no further explanation other than their very existence. His mind was filled with impressions. These, however, he reproduced impressionistically, and impressionism in literature as well as in painting is nothing but the last consequence of a materialistic point of view. He saw the unreality of reality but did not yet trust his eyes. Therefore he did what after him his interpreters were time and again tempted to do: he translated unreality into reality.

His early images reveal their importance only through hindsight. Since we know the shape they eventually took, we are able today to appreciate the role they were playing during Kafka's formative years. But we must not use them in the same way that we use Kafka's accomplished imagery to construct a coherent system of Kafka symbolism. These early images are quicksand, unable to carry any structure, however hypothetical such a structure may be in itself. To Kafka's contemporaries, ignorant as they were of his future development, his early endeavors may have seemed to set a new tone and to attain a high literary level. As early as 1914 Robert Musil, the future author of *The Man without Properties,* observed in Kafka's style "something of the conscientious melancholy in which an ice skater indulges when he executes his long slides and serpentines." Musil's critical style shows a predilection for late impressionist mannerisms, which made him susceptible to Kafka's delicate creations. He goes on to note Kafka's "artistic self-control" and, very sharp-sightedly, "a transition into emptiness of the small infinities," the infinities referring, of course, to the fragmentary character of these sketches. Finally he speaks of Kafka's "very soft and somber overtones, which are very attractive, only too vague and soft." [6] The loose texture of these early exercises justifies Franz Werfel's embarrassed reaction when Max Brod read to him for the first time pieces of Kafka's prose. "This will never go farther than Bodenbach," Werfel said.[7] Bodenbach was at that time the border station between Bohemia and Germany.

Kafka used his early work as a kind of quarry from which he extracted many of the sketches published in 1913 in his first volume, *Betrachtung*, which is in English the chapter "Meditation" contained in *The Penal Colony*. According to Brod, the first of the eighteen pieces, "Children on a Country Road" (*PC*, 21–25), was originally meant to take the place of the third main section of *Description of a Struggle*.[8] The fifth piece, "Excursion into the Mountains," corresponds to a passage close to the end of the first piece in the second main section of *Description* (*PC*, 29–30; *DS*, 36–37), the twelfth, "Clothes," is, but for a few small changes, identical with a part of a paragraph in the third main section of the same fragment (*PC*, 36; *DS*, 89–90), and the seventeenth, "The Trees," consists, in the German original, of one short paragraph lifted in its entirety from "The Continued Conversation between the Fat Man and the Praying Man,"[*] a part of the second main section (*PC*, 39–40; *DS*, 84). The eleventh, "The Passenger on the Tram," is a free variation of a theme touched upon even more fleetingly and playfully in the "Wedding Preparations" (*DF*, 9–10). There is no recognizable principle of selection or organization governing this short book; its parts are united by a mood of sophisticated wistfulness rather than by any theme or aim. They share their fragmentary air with the other pieces in the collection, which likewise begin at random and indicate their end, if at all, only by a slight rise in emphasis. They are five-finger exercises, models of the *kleine Form*, developed at that time by the Prague writer Gustav Meyrink, the Viennese Peter Altenberg, and the Swiss Robert Walser. Although "Meditation" abounds in colors (pastel) and figures (vague) and gives an early example of Kafka's skill in packing a multitude of sensations into one evenly sustained sentence, it is far from "divine," the term with which Brod hailed the book (*FK*, p. 127). Rather it is a hodgepodge of reminiscences and promises, an odd assortment of paragraphs, gleaned from a poet's imaginary diary.

Kafka began to keep a diary as early as 1910. Since a diary is by its very nature and purpose devoted to the exploration of the writer's mind and soul and can neglect the reality around him, Kafka soon found here his own mode of expression—found it much earlier at least than when he tried to produce literature for literature's sake.

---

[*] The work of different translators, these pieces snow textual differences in the respective American editions.

Nevertheless, his literary visions kept interfering with his work as a diarist, and the beginning of many a Kafka story can be found on the same page with his most intimate private observations. Conversely, "Bachelor's Misery," one of the most telling subsections in "Meditation," is an adaption of a diary entry for November 14, 1911, which follows. (Italics indicate phrases which were used directly in the "Meditation" piece.)

Before falling asleep.

It seems so dreadful to be *a bachelor, to struggle as an old man desperately to keep one's dignity while begging to be accepted whenever one wants to spend an evening in company, to carry one's* meal *home in one hand,* unable to expect anyone with a lazy sense of calm confidence, able only with difficulty and vexation to give a gift to someone, *to say good bye at the front door* [Haustor], *never to* be able *to run up the stairway pressed close to one's wife, to lie ill* and have only the solace of the view from one's window when one can sit up, *to have in one's room only side doors leading into strange people's apartments,* to feel the strangeness of one's relatives, with whom one can keep on close terms only by means of marriage, first by the marriage of one's parents, then when the effect of this has worn off, by one's own, *to have to admire other people's children and not be allowed to go on saying: "I have none,"* to feel one's old age continuously since there is no family growing up around one, *to model oneself in appearance and behavior on one or two bachelors remembered from* our *childhood.* All this is true, *except that* it is easy to make the error of unfolding so many future sufferings in front of oneself that one's eye is forced to pass far beyond them never to return, while *in reality today and later one will be standing there with a* palpable *body and a real head,* a real *forehead, that is, for smiting on with one's hand* (DI, 150–151).

In "Meditation" the passage reads as follows. (Here italics indicate deviations from the wording of the diary entry.)

It seems so dreadful to *stay* a bachelor, to struggle desperately as an old man to keep one's dignity while begging to be accepted whenever one wants to spend an evening in company, to lie ill *gazing for weeks from the corner where one's bed* is, *always* to say good bye at the front door, never to run up the stairway pressed close to one's wife, to have in one's room only side doors leading into strange people's apartments, to carry one's *supper* home in one hand, to have to admire other people's children and not be allowed to go on saying: "I have none myself," to model oneself in appearance and behavior on one or two bachelors remembered from *one's* childhood.

That's how it will be, except that in reality today and later one will be standing there with a palpable body and a real head, a real forehead, that is, for smiting on with one's hand (*PC*, 30.)

At the time of the diary entry Kafka was twenty-eight years old, at that of the publication of "Meditation," thirty. The dates are revealing since Kafka experienced these two years of his life as a period of extreme crisis. It was at this same age that his father, who was setting the standards of his life, had begotten him as his firstborn son.* Whereas the father had established himself and founded a family by his thirtieth year, the son at the same age was stricken by the misery of a bachelor's life. Sometime between 1911 and 1913 he must have accepted his fate as inevitable, for the diary version laments the misery of *being* a bachelor, the version in "Meditation," of having to *stay* one. The diary merely reflects the present by stating: "All this is true." The passage in "Meditation," on the other hand, has already resigned itself to the future and submits to its sufferings with a tired: "That's how it will be."

Both versions speak of the bachelor as if he were an old man. Yet time is suspended in both texts by the simple trick of putting most verbs into the infinitive instead of using them in the indicative. Present and past time are indistinguishable; only in the end the future will win out, even grammatically. There is, however, a difference in the two texts. The infinitives in the diary seem to be chosen by a young man tormented by the prospect of aging and frustrated by the immensity of sorrows he anticipates as "future sufferings." The published version uses the timelessness of the infinitive to emphasize the generic elements of bachelorhood. Most personal touches are omitted here. Whereas the bachelor of the diary modeled himself on the bachelors remembered from "our," that is, his, childhood, the possessive pronoun "our" proved too intimate for the bachelor of "Meditation" and it was replaced with an impersonal "one" ("one's childhood"). With a conscious effort Kafka leaves autobiography behind and moves, still cautiously and gropingly, toward the creation of a literary figure common to all three of his novel fragments and most of his shorter stories. The typical Kafka hero is, and remains, a bachelor.

Bachelorhood itself is decried as a dreadful state: cumbersome, vex-

---

* According to his tombstone, Herrman Kafka lived from 1854 to 1931 (*Franz Kafka a Praha* [Prague: Žikeš, 1957], pl. 31). The marriage register has 1852 as his birth date (Wagenbach, 16, 192 n. 28). Either date will do; at the critical time Herrman Kafka was as old as Franz, the diarist, or as Franz, the author. It is no accident that *The Trial* takes place during Joseph K.'s thirtieth year.

atious, and evil. Any attempt to balance the bachelor's misery by an ever so slight reference to the less sunny side of matrimony is patently absent. So is any observation of the marital bliss of others. This bachelor coolly and abstractly views marriage as a social institution. In the diary he justifies the married state as a means to keep the family structure intact, "first by the marriage of one's parents, then . . . by one's own." In "Meditation" he drops this argument. Yet even there he presents the isolation of the bachelor primarily in its social aspects: the lonely man loses his dignity when he has to beg for dinner invitations. He exposes himself to ridicule when he shops for his solitary meals. So minimal are his needs and so overwhelming his self-consciousness that he carries his food "in one hand," covering it, we may assume, with the other. The final version specifies this meal as supper, *Nachtmahl,* tingeing the scene with the shades of night. The single man is unloved, of course. He feels his predicament most acutely when, before everyone and exposed to the contempt of all, he must say good-bye at the main door of his apartment house, while the married man enjoys the privilege of "pressing close to his wife" when he runs up the stairway, thus satisfying the curiosity of the neighbors and impressing, by a public caress, the bachelors among them. Characteristically Kafka fails to mention the intimacy of living room and bedroom, for these are closed to the public and hence socially nonexistent.

The epitome of the bachelor's solitude is an illness which confines him to a room without a separate entrance. (Gregor Samsa in "The Metamorphosis" sleeps in such a room, which is reminiscent of the bed chambers assigned to servants. We may assume that the bachelor's room, like Samsa's, is part of the family apartment.) In this position not only is he at the mercy of every intruder because his room has no key, but he finds no assistance from outside; these side doors lead to the rooms of strangers, the strangers being no one else than his family. The only main door available to him is the front door of the house. It disgorges him into the hubbub of the streets yet excludes him from sharing the privacy of the interior with anyone who may have accompanied him to the house. Prague front doors were at that time jealously guarded by a Cerberuslike race of doorkeepers.

The single items in this catalogue of solitude are enumerated differently in 1911 and 1913. The diary is still close to logic and reality: if the bachelor thinks it below his dignity to ask for a supper invitation, then it follows that he is forced to buy his own food and carry it home. (Sharing the meal with the family seems to be out of the question.)

This relation of causality is suggested merely by the proximity of the two phrases, but the contrast with the corresponding passage in "Meditation" is clear. Here the bachelor's illness has been substituted for his lonely shopping trip; solitude has been transformed into sickness. The inherent truth of this substitution compensates for what it may lack in logical correctness. Without explicit mention we are given to understand that the origins of the bachelor's illness are of a psychosomatic nature, that his solitude is just as much the reason for his illness as, in the diary, his seclusion is the reason for his lonely errands to the grocer. By the rearrangement of realistic detail in the later version, Kafka has succeeded in penetrating reality, in practicing some sort of depth psychology, and in illuminating the bachelor's mind, without changing a word in the verbal content of the two phrases. Transpositions of this kind will be typical of Kafka's later, suprarealistic style.

The sick bachelor of the diary can still seek consolation in the view from his window, provided he can muster enough strength to sit up in bed. The bachelor in "Meditation" is deprived of any such comfort. His bed now stands in the corner, an image which indicates his complete removal from the outside world. He is left to his own devices, a helpless bundle of miserable matter. The room is empty, the imprisonment complete. Since, however, his disease is only a symptom, the symptom of his loneliness, and since this solitude is self-imposed and self-inflicted, Kafka by this intensification indicates that the real prison of the bachelor is not the empty room in which he languishes but the equally hopeless barrenness of his soul. Again, he did not have to add a single word to effect this turn in our interpretation.

Doors—closed doors, locked doors—and doorkeepers all play an important part in the lives of Kafka's bachelors. Even the sketch in "Meditation" is filled with *Torschlusspanik*, the panic fear of having the door of life slammed in one's face, a remarkable symptom in a man not much older than thirty. Life—a good life—was at least at times synonymous with married life for this bachelor. To be barred from marriage, once and forever, filled him with a despair which was to grow to metaphysical proportions in his mature works.

On the biographical level of "Meditation," one cannot help noticing certain contradictions which foreshadow the paradoxical nature that the image of the door will acquire later on. Among the places where an unmarried man might miss a wife one would normally not expect a staircase, but this bachelor does not seem to be interested in matrimony as the marriage of true minds, nor, for that matter, of warm bodies. To him wedlock is primarily a means of reassurance, before the world, before his family, and before himself. Most of the iniquities which constitute his misery can be avoided only by the service of another person. Kafka's bachelor seems not to lack companionship and love so much as he misses a relief from tedious everyday duties, the enacting of the wife's role before the outside world, the bearing of his progeny. For these things no specific personality is required; any woman will do and she is easily replaceable. Here the bachelor of "Meditation" anticipates the infidelity in which the two K.'s in *The Trial* and *The Castle* indulge. They are polygamous; yet they are not driven by passion but by a downright universal need for help, which cannot find hands enough for its satisfaction. "Women," says Joseph K. in *The Trial*, "have great influence. If I could move some women I know to join forces in working for me, I could not help winning through" (*T*, 265). Kafka's bachelor is a Don Juan of helplessness.

It is as hard to imagine this bachelor as a father as it is to see him as a husband. The diary describes him as a man "able only with difficulty and vexation to give a gift," and mentions that in contrast to the happy family man the bachelor has no opportunity "to expect anyone with a lazy sense of calm confidence." These, to be sure, are petty particulars of self-incrimination, and Kafka was well advised when he left them unmentioned in the final version. But their very pettiness betrays the bachelor's inability to bear the responsibilities, necessarily often trivial, of fatherhood. This inner reluctance reveals itself in a slip of the tongue. "Having to admire other people's children . . ." he says in both texts, understandably preferring that other people might admire his. Then he continues: ". . . and not being allowed to go on saying: 'I have none myself.'" "To be allowed" suggests that the very fate the bachelor laments is actually a favor bestowed upon him. The expression contradicts the tortures afflicted upon him by his solitude. To put it more pointedly, the first half of the sentence condemns the frustrations of childlessness, the second accepts it with an air of secret gratitude. The slip recurs in the text of "Meditation," which Kafka himself had prepared for print; if he remained ignorant of it, then his subconscious proved here its superiority over the painstaking control to which he subjected every line he ever published. It is, however, much more probable that he noticed the slip and preserved it as an early example of what was to become the ambiguity of his style.

It has been suggested that the world of children was the only world that held out a hope of salvation to Kafka and his heroes.[9] Although he may have been willing as a young writer to accept consciously such a cliché, his subconscious self was sincere enough, even then, not to deceive him. His very language gives him away, and even more so the images he derives from it. "Meditation" contains as its first piece the fleeting vision of "Children on a Country Road," and in it is the statement, rare indeed in any of Kafka's writings, that "nothing was lost" (*PC*, 22). Yet these children are lifted out of any social context; they roam on roads and sleep in ditches. Their world is lost in relativity; it moves, it soars, it floats; the law of gravity has been suspended. The narrating child loses his equilibrium when he follows a swarm of birds with his eyes and observes "not that they were rising but that I was falling" (*PC*, 21). The swing on which he sits offers but a poor, rational excuse for a feeling of "being seasick on dry land" (*DS*, 60), which pervades the story. Rather it is a sensation imparted to him by a world in which names have lost their meaning and things their defining contour: "We pierced the evening with our heads" (*PC*, 22). Even the boy who indulges in these memories is ready to admit, "When one joins in song with others it is like being drawn on by a fishhook" (*PC*, 24). He too is surrounded by solitude, and is conscious of it. A prospective bachelor, he is running away on this country road, escaping from his child's paradise, unable to retrace his hasty steps. That "Meditation" also closes with a story about a child suggests that the theme was very much on Kafka's mind when he made this selection. This time the motifs of child and bachelor are intertwined: the child pays a visit to a lonely man. Again, we are surprised to hear a soothing, positive remark: " 'Hush, hush,' said the child over his shoulder, 'It is all right' " (*PC*, 41). But the comforting words are uttered by an apparition which is repeatedly identified as a ghost, a will-o'-the-wisp of solitude, whose flighty utterances are bound to lead the poor man still further astray. The title of the sketch is "Unhappiness." The bachelor enters his room with a scream and is perplexed by this unmotivated outcry "which met no answer nor anything that could draw its force away" (*PC*, 40). At the end of the story he falls asleep, terminating Kafka's first volume on a note of despondency and exhaustion.

Far from promising the bachelor any salvation, the children offer him here yet another instrument with which to carry on his self-torture. He sees them primarily as links in the chain of generations; he desires them for the sake of continuity and as a living testimony that he could hold his own before the man who had engendered him, his father.

Confronted with them in reality, he is said to have shown them many
a sign of kindness and understanding; but when it came to including
them as figures in his books, he gave them their full share in the solitude and sorrow which inform the world of their elders.

The bachelor was the first mask Kafka put on to stylize his mode of
expression and raise his monologues beyond the level of a private confession. At the time of "Meditation" he was not yet able to construct
a stage sufficiently elaborate to allow the utility of this mask to be
displayed. Hence the brevity of "Bachelor's Misery," and its lyrical,
elegiac quality. No antagonist has yet appeared to challenge the bachelor and involve him in any kind of action.

So far back does this image reach in Kafka's fantasies that the diary
of 1910 presents us with a conversation in which an imaginary "I" faces
an equally imaginary "You," who turns out to be a bachelor.
In him there appears the whole paradox of Kafka's later heroes.
Because of its early emergence and fundamental importance we are
inclined to call this figure the *ur*-bachelor.

As an essay in the art of the dialogue, this exchange of verbal associations and fleeting images is as unsuccessful as the two "Conversations"
Kafka had published in *Hyperion* a year earlier. So blurred are the
outlines of the conversing figures that very often the "I" of the writer
seems to be speaking for the "You," the bachelor. At the beginning
they are to some extent distinguishable from one another: the "I" appears as a young man who still can think of his childhood spent in a
village, whereas the "You" is an older person who has been living in
the city for more than twenty years. The "I" has a profession, an un-
specified job which he seems to be using as a shelter to protect him
from the demands of the world. The bachelor, on the other hand,
resides both literally and metaphorically in the gutter, "stopping the
flow of the rain water" (*DI*, 23).

What little plot this conversation offers, centers on the young man's
wish to join a party which is in full swing in the brilliantly illuminated
house before them and the bachelor's attempts to continue their dialogue. The bachelor succeeds, but less by his harangues than by his
very presence, which seems to keep his listener spellbound. "I want to
leave," the "I" exclaims, "want to mount the steps, if necessary, by
turning somersaults. From this company I promise myself everything
I lack, the organization of my energies above all. My energies are not

satisfied with an intensification, which is the only possibility for this bachelor on the street" (*DI*, 24).

The young man seems to waver between the light and gay din within the house and the ominous solitude surrounding the bachelor. Young Kafka had not yet learned to resist completely the lure of society, especially in its festive aspects. "Description of a Struggle" starts with a party as bright and noisy as the one which awaits the young man here. But society has more to offer him than mere diversions; he hopes that it will help him to organize his energies, which still seem aimlessly wasted, as they often are before one makes one's choice.

All the bachelor holds out to him is an intensification, a sharpening (*Zuspitzung*) of his sensitivities. In this respect the *ur*-bachelor resembles an artist, and the conversation between him and the young man falls into the pattern of the traditional conflict between social usefulness and creative independence, a dilemma which has beset the imagination of young writers ever since Goethe showed its insolubility in his *The Sufferings of Young Werther*. Nor was Kafka blind to the fact that the artist must, in many cases, pay for his freedom by resigning himself to bachelorhood. He knew the biographies of such inveterate celibates as Franz Grillparzer and Gustave Flaubert and quoted them often and with sympathy.[10]

The *ur*-bachelor proves worthy of his descent from such illustrious ancestry by presenting his state as a general human condition; he would, his young listener recognizes, "be satisfied just to sustain his physique, which is indeed shabby, to protect his few meals and avoid the influence of other people; in short, to preserve only as much as is possible in the dissolving world" (*DI*, 24). The poverty of the bachelor's existence is set into direct relationship with a world in decline. Where reality itself dissolves, society has lost its attraction, and the requirements of life are reduced to the bare minimum of subsistence. An outsider in the true sense of the word, the bachelor "has only ground enough for his two feet to stand on, only as much of a hold as his two hands encompass" (*DI*, 26). His solitude is fundamental and his exposure to the world total. The rain that seems to fall incessantly on the scene of this conversation appears as a necessary concomitant to his lonely station in the midst of night and nothingness.

That Kafka in the *ur*-bachelor intended to draw an image of existential solitude can be seen from another observation that the young man makes about him: "This bachelor with his thin clothes, his art of prayer, his enduring legs, his lodgings of which he is afraid, and the other remnants of his patched-up existence now revealed after a long time—this bachelor holds all this together with his two arms and can never catch by chance any unimportant object without losing two others." He loses two objects when he tries to catch a third one. The former he possesses, they may be all that his two hands can hold on to, the last remnants of his human existence; the latter is being flung at him from somewhere outside, perhaps even from above. He calls this third object unimportant, as it very well may be if what his hands encompass is all that life has to offer him. In view of this sacrifice one wonders why he is so eager to catch this third object. Or is it only unimportant as long as it is not caught? Does it reveal its full importance only when it has become one's possession? In order to catch an object one has to stretch out one's arms and perform a gesture similar to that of a praying man who raises his arms when he asks for a blessing.

Here one must interrupt the argument with the objection that Kafka does not tell us that this enigmatic object descends on the bachelor from above. Nor must one forget that he called it "unimportant." And yet he has mentioned "the art of prayer" as one of the bachelor's properties. This can hardly be understood as a reference to Kafka's own life, for we know from his "Letter to His Father" (*DF*, 138–196) that he felt utter indifference toward any religious practice, if indeed he did not find it abhorrent (*DF*, 172 ff.). He was not what would commonly be called a believer, and this may superficially explain the lack of respect he shows for the third object. We may come still closer to the meaning of this "art of prayer" when we stress the artistic rather than the ritualistic aspect of the phrase. We find support for this shift of emphasis in one of Kafka's aphorisms written at a much later time, the often-quoted phrase: "Writing as a form of prayer" (*DF*, 312). He considered writing to be an almost religious act, a sacrifice, and prayed that his offering be accepted and his writing blessed. But the sentence also means that he was praying for the blessing of literature, that is, for an inspiration strong and sustained enough to allow him to produce what would be acceptable as a religious sacrifice.

Preoccupied with his inner experiences, he was tempted to let whatever he possessed slip from his hands, although he was thereby risking his social existence. The documents of Kafka's early life show him in a state of constant preparedness for the act of writing. While forcing him to sever his ties with others and casting a shadow over any joys a

companionable life might have held in store for him, this preparedness
provided him with the last, minimal foothold, the bachelor's "ground
enough for two feet to stand on." No other justification was needed if
one became a writer. To be sure, his devotion to literature did not
alleviate his misery but elevated it onto heightened states of awareness.
He was able to see himself as a bachelor and conceive in this figure an
image of the world in decline.

That he presented the bachelor in the shape of a clumsy juggler and
called the third and most desired object unimportant reveals how
constantly he harbored doubts about his calling and how ready he was
to turn against himself. He realized that at this late hour of despair
and dissolution it was no longer possible to raise art, or literature, to
the level of a religious expression, of a prayer. Even when his prayer
to be a writer was granted, his writings were not as blessed as he
expected them to be in his metaphysical longings. They were no
sacrificial acts, but literature, good literature perhaps, but at best still
literature. The *ur*-bachelor's "art of prayer" is one of Kafka's basic
paradoxes. Since it was insoluble, Kafka turned, like his bachelor,
against himself.

"He is," says the writer about the bachelor, "continually starved;
he has only the moment, the everlasting moment of torment, which is
followed by no spark of a moment of recovery; he has only one thing
always, his pain, but in all the expanse of the world no second thing
that could claim to serve him as a medicine" (*DI*, 26). Society has
nothing to offer him; he is opposed to it and by it; he is forever the
man in the gutter in front of a house where the "perfect bourgeois"
gives a brilliant party. He is compared to a "man in the waves on a few
planks of wood which even bump against and submerge each other,"
while the "gentleman and bourgeois . . . travels over the sea in a ship
with foam before him and wake behind, that is, making quite a splash
around himself" (*DI*, 25). The narrator stands between bachelor and
bourgeois; he has the choice between the rainy night and drinking
"champagne . . . up there under the chandelier." He still has to find
out where he belongs. Tongue in cheek, the bachelor even encourages
him to enter: "Try it anyhow, . . . often you can already recognize
yourself, if you pay attention, in the face of the servant at the door"
(*DI*, 23).

On the surface the narrator's choice is nearly identical with the
conflict between "artist" and " bourgeois," "spirit" and "life," so persuasively set forth in Thomas Mann's "Tonio Kröger." (Mann's short

story was published in 1903, and in the following year Kafka wrote to
Max Brod that he had already read it twice [*B,* 31]). Proud of his
decadence, Tonio Kröger seeks his bearings between his genteel origins
and an almost Nietzschean scorn of philistinism. He professes his contempt of the banality and futility of life's ordinary awards:

Only the irritations and icy ecstasies of the artist's corrupted nervous system are artistic. The artist must be unhuman, extra-human; he must stand
in a queer aloof relationship to our humanity; only so is he in a position, I
ought to say only so would he be tempted, to represent it, to present it, to
portray it to good effect. . . . It is all up with the artist as soon as he becomes a man and begins to feel.[11]

Yet if Tonio is disgusted with life, he is also horrified by literature:
"Literature is a wearing job. . . . It is a curse." Having to withdraw
from life, the artist has to renounce love as well. Or, rather, he is being
rejected by a life which seems to share, and thereby confirm, the doubts
he has about his own virility: "Is an artist a male, anyhow? Ask the
females! It seems to me we artists are all of us something like those
unsexed papal singers." [12] But Tonio Kröger does not stop here. The
ultimate sacrifice the artist has to make for the sake of his art is his
very existence, for he is not permitted to "pluck a single leaf from the
laurel tree of art without paying for it with his life." [13] Needless to say
Tonio Kröger is, and remains, a bachelor.

The young Kafka must have discovered for himself quite a few similarities between his own meditations and Tonio Kröger's devastatingly
elegant dissertation on the art of the writer. Yet his bachelor is no
"*bourgeois manqué.*" Instead his bourgeois side, like his artistic side,
is exposed to the bachelor's existential predicament. It is easy even for
the early Kafka to see through the sham security of the bourgeois,
who is ignorant of his destiny, and hence pathetically ridiculous. "This
gentleman and bourgeois," says the writer in the conversation with a
bachelor quoted from the diary of 1910, "is in no less danger" than the
bachelor. "For he and his property are not one, but two, and whoever destroys the connection destroys him at the same time" (*DI,* 25).
And how could this connection remain untouched in a world which is
so openly described as dissolving? Kafka's world is filled with bachelors,
married and unmarried ones, those who are conscious of their fate and
those who are blind to it. Since he cherishes self-awareness above all,
the writer in this conversation has no choice but gradually to merge
with the figure of the bachelor. Even the quotation marks, which had
served to set the two speakers off from one another, disappear in the

end so that the unity of the "I" and the "You," of the young man and the bachelor, is established typographically. The bachelor has entered the thoughts of the young man. Society has receded from the scene; the festive house has vanished into the night. In view of the solitude with which he had surrounded the bachelor, Kafka considered the antithesis between the bourgeois and the artist as arbitrary and artificial. It was this existential point of view which prompted Kafka to say in his letter to Brod in 1904: "The new in 'Tonio Kröger' does not lie in the discovery of this antithesis (thank heaven for my not being forced any longer to believe in this antithesis, it is intimidating) but in its . . . infatuation with antitheses in general" (*B*, 31).

Literature when conceived of as an "art of prayer" was not susceptible to this or any other kind of infatuation. That does not mean to say that Thomas Mann remained unaware of the metaphysical implications of his craft and did not see the redemptory powers with which literature is endowed. Lisabeta Ivanovna, Tonio's painter-friend, reminds him

of some things you very well know yourself: of the purifying and healing influences of letters, the subduing of the passions by knowledge and eloquence; literature as the guide to understanding, forgiveness, and love, the redeeming power of the word, literary art as the noblest manifestation of the human mind, the poet as the most highly developed of human beings, the poet as saint.[14]

But Thomas Mann approached the domain of the sacred with irony, which is as much as to say that he stayed willingly and consciously outside it until the end of his days. Kafka, on the other hand, incessantly sought to enter it and, being unable to discover an entrance, tormented himself and finally decided to destroy his work.

Because of his "art of prayer" the bachelor retires from life. He devotes himself to the practice of utter cleanliness, in the way he lives as well as in the manner he writes. Of a bachelor conceived much later, Blumfeld, Kafka says, "Blumfeld . . . cannot stand dirt in his room; to him cleanliness is essential; and several times a week he is obliged to have words with his charwoman who is unfortunately not very painstaking in this respect" (*DS*, 100). Yet the cleanliness of Kafka's bachelors is not merely a carry-over from his own life. It cannot be completely attributed to the pedantry of a man who is forced to live by himself and has consequently developed his sensibility to a point where it has degenerated into a compulsion. Nor is it solely a symptom of hypochondria. Fundamentally its origins are not physical at all but

moral. The cleanliness of Kafka's bachelor does not stand for purity,
a purity to be expected from one who has dedicated himself to prayer
as an art. It is his defense against its opposite, dirt. Outwardly and
inwardly the bachelor is engaged in a battle against filth precisely
because he knows that his existence, that is, his art, is in constant
danger of being corrupted by it. The early newspaper article, "The
Aeroplanes at Brescia" (published in *Bohemia*, September 28, 1909),
shows Kafka observant of life's dirt and quite willing to put up with it.
Rather lightheartedly he mentions the "dirt which is just there, that's
all, and about which no more is said, dirt which will never change any
more, which has made itself at home, which in a certain sense makes
human life more tangible, more earthly. . . . Who, one must ask,
could still have anything on his mind against this dirt" (*PC*, 300)?
Below the slightly forced display of irony we notice here a preoccupation with the word "dirt," repeated over and over again, as if the writer
enjoyed wallowing in filth.

In retrospect, however, this condonation of uncleanliness changes to
downright obsession against it. In one of his letters in *Letters to
Milena*, one probably written early in 1921, he relates his first sexual
experiences. He was initiated by a shopgirl who worked opposite the
Kafka apartment in a dress shop. It was in 1903 or 1904, at the time of
his earliest literary attempts. "Even before we got to the hotel all this
was charming, exciting, and horrible." But whereas charm and excitement seem to have prevailed during the first night, horror won out in
the one and only repetition of this particular adventure. The girl was
good-natured and friendly and yet

she had become (from my point of view) my bitter enemy. . . . I won't
say that the sole reason for my enmity was the fact (I am sure it wasn't)
that at the hotel the girl in all innocence had made a tiny repulsive gesture
(not worthwhile mentioning), had uttered a trifling obscenity (not worthwhile mentioning), but the memory remained—I knew at that instant that
I would never forget it, and simultaneously I knew, or thought I knew,
that this repulsiveness and dirt, though outwardly not necessary, was inwardly however very necessarily connected with the whole thing, and that
just this repulsiveness and obscenity (whose little symptom had only been
her tiny gesture, her trifling word) had drawn me with such terrible power
into this hotel which otherwise I would have avoided with all my remaining
strength.

And as it was then, so it has always remained. My body, sometimes quiet
for years, would then again be shaken to the point of not being able to bear

it by this desire for a small, a very specific abomination, for something slightly disgusting, embarrassing, obscene (*LM*, 163–164).

The fascination with dirt and obscenity may very well have been the enigmatic depth the *ur*-bachelor claimed to have discovered in the core of his personality: "And this depth I need but feel uninterruptedly for a quarter of an hour and the poisonous world flows into my mouth like water into that of a drowning man" (*DI*, 25). This depth which threatened to engulf him and barred him from normal intercourse was necessary to complete the image he formed of himself as a bachelor. Surrendering to it, plunging into it even "for a quarter of an hour," showed him the unsaintliness of his being, his unworthiness to engage in the "art of prayer." It was this depth that lured, drew, and drove him toward the dirt the very thought of which filled him with horror. In perpetual danger of being drowned by it, he developed as one of his symptoms the feeling of nausea, of "being seasick on dry land." Unable to attribute this conflict to the fickleness of human flesh in general, he remained spellbound by the pollution of his own hands, which he had meant to keep clean for the sacrificial duties of literature. Since he had forfeited the blessing, there remained only the curse. And in order to give the seemingly private record of his first nights its full symbolic value, he adds in this letter to Milena: "Even in the best that existed for me there was . . . some small nasty smell, some sulphur, some hell. This urge had in it something of the Wandering Jew being senselessly drawn, wandering senselessly through a senselessly obscene world" (*LM*, 164). The image of the bachelor as the Wandering Jew is the exact opposite of the writer absorbed in the "art of prayer." The letter to Milena is not meant so much to represent the self-incrimination of Kafka the Jew as to betray, exaggerated to the extreme, his inability to enter the holy of holies, a literature endowed with the power of redemption. Being a late witness of a late and skeptical age, Kafka's bachelor-writer saw himself hopelessly deprived of this power. Unredeemed, unredeemable, like the Wandering Jew, he projected the dirt which he dreaded in himself onto the world through which it was his curse to travel until the time of the Second Coming. But for Kafka's bachelor the Redeemer had not yet come the first time.

No wonder, then, that the *ur*-bachelor of 1910 is already suicidal. He "has teeth only for his own flesh and flesh only for his own teeth" (*DI*, 24). Instead of redeeming the world the bachelor consumes himself. Consequently, the bachelor's suicide is not conceived of as one determined act serving to put an end to life's unbearable condition, but as this condition itself, dragging on indefinitely. Like the wanderings of the Wandering Jew, it seems to last for ever. This suicide is, in the final analysis, identical with existence for the bachelor. Perpetually frustrated in the "art of prayer," forbidden to acquire progeny, and repudiated by his ancestry on account of his barrenness, he "has only the moment." There is "nothing before him and therefore nothing behind him" (*DI*, 25). Relating the phrase to the succession of generations, this "therefore" indicates that his childlessness ("nothing before him") has caused the bachelor to suffer also the loss of his heritage ("nothing behind him"). The torment of this everlasting process of self-negation is accentuated by the bachelor's good memory. Indeed, "the memory of this man has suffered as little as his imagination" (*DI*, 26). Here the bachelor's image has merged with that of the writer. Memory and imagination are the precondition and the guarantee of a writer's productivity, as they are of all creativity. What can distinguish a writer more than a memory that has remained intact and an imagination uncurtailed by the passing of time? Past and future are equally open to this bachelor; he strides freely from the one to the other; the curse of the Wandering Jew, however, prevents his ever stopping to reap the fruits that memory and imagination have produced.

So strong is the bachelor's memory that it permits him to catch a glimpse of the time when it all began, when he first became aware of his suicidal nature and his curse. This was a moment "which no one can know today, for nothing can be so annihilated as that time." And yet, he still realizes that he became a bachelor when "he felt this depth lastingly, the way one suddenly notices a boil on one's body that until this moment was the least thing . . . , yes, not even the least, for it appeared not yet to exist and now is more than everything else that we bodily owned since our birth" (*DI*, 25–26). The key word is "depth" which compares to a boil and which, in strange perversion of its original meaning, points to an abode of filth and obscenity in his own soul. When he discovered this "depth" in the recesses of sex, the bachelor "went astray." Since then he has been engaged in a ceaseless escape from an equally unending temptation. At that time, which his memory tried in vain to "annihilate" or suppress (for it has suffered as little as his imagination), the bachelor-writer entered the maze of his peregrinations.

To a Christian conscience this "depth," this "boil," translates easily into an allegory of original sin. But Kafka was just as little possessed of a Christian conscience as the Wandering Jew. Thus the boil, the metaphorical symbol for the "depth" of his guilt feelings, is and remains an image of sickness, the sickness, we may venture to guess, which confines the bachelor of 1913 to his bed in the corner of an empty room.

The paradox of his existence makes the *ur*-bachelor of 1910 the model of Kafka's principal figures. He "stands once and for all outside our people, outside our humanity," like Josephine, the Singer. "He is continually starved" (*DI*, 26), a description which anticipates the figure of the Hunger Artist. "He can live only as a hermit or a parasite. He is a hermit only by compulsion, once this compulsion is overcome by forces unknown to him, immediately he is a parasite who behaves insolently whenever he possibly can" (*DI*, 28). This foreshadows the metamorphosis of Gregor Samsa, who was changed from a recluse into a parasitic insect. The bachelor has less hold on life "than the trapeze artist in a variety show, who still has a net hung up for him below." Such a net will be conspicuously absent during the trapeze act in "First Sorrow." Finally, in the moment the writer decides to side with the bachelor, he is heard to cry, "We are outside the law, no one knows it and yet everyone treats us accordingly" (*DI*, 27), an expression of an idea so basic to Kafka that it anticipates the principal figures of *The Trial* and *The Castle* and their predicament. These figures are united by their common origin in Kafka's diary of 1910; they all stand for the bachelor and the bachelor will represent them all. The very incoherence of the early diary entry allowed Kafka enough space to store in it most of the themes he was later to develop.

Still, in 1910 Kafka was not yet completely identified with the image he had created. The diary conversation with a bachelor concludes:

Of course, nothing in the world can save him any longer and so his conduct can make one think of the corpse of a drowned man which, borne to the surface by some current, bumps against a tired swimmer, lays its hands upon him and would like to hold on. The corpse does not come alive, indeed is not even saved, but it can pull the man down (*DI*, 28–29).

Kafka had created the bachelor to express his self-destructive tendencies. The twenty-seven-year-old writer sees himself as a "tired" man in mortal danger of being destroyed by his own creation. By 1913, in the "Meditation," the process of Kafka's identification with the bachelor has been completed. Here the duality between "I" and "You," writer and bachelor, biographical material and its symbolic expression, has been overcome. The conversation has turned into a description. The writer has stepped out of the picture, and attention is focused on one figure alone, the bachelor "standing there with a palpable body and a real head, a real forehead, that is, for smiting on with one's hand."

Nine years later, two years before his death, Kafka looked back on his life and his work and called his youthful remarks about the bachelor "clairvoyant" (*DII*, 207—January 22, 1922). More precisely he referred to the sentence in "Meditation" containing the bachelor's lament that he had to model himself "on one or two bachelors remembered from one's childhood." Now, in this late diary entry, he identifies one of these exemplary bachelors as his mother's brother, Rudolf Löwy.

Like Kafka himself, Uncle Rudolf was quiet, shy, and excessively modest. At odds with his father, he was loved by his mother; first a hypochondriac, then really ill. Although he lived the monotonous life of an official and showed little external sign of development, inwardly he was unable to hold himself in check and thus was continuously on the verge of insanity. Ostensibly Kafka tries here to prove the truth of his bachelor figure—the clairvoyance of his writer—by reducing the image to the life material from which it sprang. Still there is one fundamental difference between model and image, which he must concede, although, in typical ambivalence, he refuses to say whether it worked in his favor or to his disadvantage. Uncle Rudolf "had less artistic talent than I, he could therefore have chosen a better path in life for himself in his youth, was not inwardly pulled apart, not even by ambition" (*DII*, 208). This reconfirms our previous conclusions: the misery which the bachelor feels is the reverse side of the author's dedication to literature. Both were a necessary outlet for Kafka's feeling of congenital guilt, and as such they are equal to the "art of prayer" of the bachelor in the conversation of 1910. The paradoxicality of Kafka's narrative work can be traced to these basic contradictions in the nature of their central figure, the bachelor. Yet what was and remained his personal problem becomes the secret of his heroes. Both his problem and their secret are insoluble. It can only be stated and restated in the flow of images that surrounds the image of the bachelor, just as an eddy centers around its vortex.

To produce this flow of images Kafka had to be a writer; to become a writer he had to remain a bachelor. Eventually bachelorhood was identical for him with a life spent in the continuous contemplation of life's paradoxical nature. Whether they admit it or not, the bachelors in his books are concerned with the all-encompassing presence of this paradox. The comedy as well as the tragedy of their actions results from their attempts to solve it; their defeat stems from their incapability of realizing that this paradox hovers over them as Fate hovers beyond the heads of the heroes in the plays of antiquity. From their concern with the paradox they derive their unjustified claims and their innate dignity. They are not only the paragons of modern man's universal presumption ultimately arising from modern man's cosmic insecurity; they are also martyrs, especially if we understand this word in its original sense of witnesses. The less everyday life seems to matter to them, the more they feel the matters of this life resting upon their shoulders. For life does not easily dismiss those who, for reasons obscure even to themselves, cannot help bearing testimony to its enigma. On January 19, 1922, Kafka entered in his diary:

The infinite, deep, warm, saving happiness of sitting beside the cradle of one's child opposite its mother.

There is in it also something of this feeling: matters no longer rest with you unless you wish it so. In contrast, the feeling of those who have no children: it perpetually rests with you, whether you will or not, every moment to the end, every nerve-racking moment, it perpetually rests with you, and without result. Sisyphus was a bachelor (*DII*, 204–205).

CHAPTER III

The Breakthrough

1912

Crisis

ON August 13, 1912, Kafka met Felice Bauer in Max Brod's living room. We know from his diary that he observed every minute detail of her appearance before he sat down: "By the time I was seated I had already formed an unshakable judgment" (*DI*, 268–269). On September 23 he entered in his diary:

This story, "The Judgment," I wrote at one sitting during the night of the 22nd-23rd, from ten o'clock at night to six o'clock in the morning. . . . The conviction verified that with my novel-writing I am in the shameful lowlands of writing. Only *in this way* can writing be done, only with such coherence, with such a complete opening out of the body and the soul (*DI*, 275–276).

With one stroke he brushed aside his previous literary exercises after having experienced the fearful bliss of authentic inspiration.

On October 6 Kafka read to Brod "The Judgment" and "The Stoker" (*FK*, 128).* Two days later Brod wrote to Kafka's mother

---

* As the first chapter of *Der Verschollene* (*Amerika*), "The Stoker" will be discussed at greater length within the context of the novel. Here it is worth noting, however, that Kafka produced evidence of its existence only under the impact of his crisis.

about Franz, who had toyed with the idea of committing suicide because duties at his father's factory, in addition to his office work at the Workers' Accident Insurance Institute, had kept him from writing (*FK*, 91–94). On October 28 Brod noted in his diary that "Franz has written a twenty-two-page letter to Miss F., and is troubled by worries about the future." On November 3 Kafka read to Brod and Oskar Baum, another Prague writer-friend, the second chapter of *Der Verschollene*, the continuation of "The Stoker." Brod adds, "He is completely in love with F., and happy" (*FK*, 128). This is followed on November 9 by a letter, the draft of which was discovered among Kafka's papers. In this letter he tried to break off his correspondence with Felice Bauer: "I could not help but make you unhappy by my writing, and I myself am past all help. . . . I was fully aware of [this], and in spite of [it] I tried to cling to you, I should deserve to be cursed for it anyway, if I were not cursed for it already" (*FK*, 140). This, in turn, was followed by "The Metamorphosis," which he read to Brod and Baum on November 24 (*FK*, 128).

The relationship with Felice Bauer developed into an engagement twice; each time it was broken after a prolonged struggle, for these first months had set the pattern of their friendship. The image of marriage had entered Kafka's mind and clashed headlong with the image of bachelorhood. Eight years later when he described the affair to Milena, he spoke of the "most voluntary assurances" which he had given Felice. "I know nothing more desirable than marriage in itself" (*LM*, 54). Yet it was not marriage in itself he was contemplating at this crucial time, but the commitment to another, real, person. The assurances he gave Felice were undermined and counteracted by his reservations, mostly about himself. The "judgment" he formed on first seeing her cannot have concerned *her* character, which was still hidden from him; it must have been a judgment of himself. The eye that saw her was at the same time turned inward, probing his capabilities, fathoming his hopes and anxieties, and leading his mind toward a decision. Reflecting the incompatible claims he made on himself, marriage, and life in general, this decision must have been a crucial one.

The problem of bachelorhood, paradoxical as it was in itself, was for Kafka only one aspect of a greater problem. He had to remain single in order to become a writer. Solitude was a prerequisite, almost a symbol, of the *littérateur's* existence. On the other hand, marriage meant for Kafka not only the crude and loud family life he was forced to share in his father's house, but also the ideal of a good life, which found its fulfillment not in the raptures of any creative act but in the natural equilibrium of the family, where generation followed upon generation. The industrial revolution and big city life had reduced this ideal to a literary wish dream—the longing of refined and decadent people for a robust and primitive life.

Kafka's concern about marriage was nourished by literary sources, most of which recorded the frustrations involved. Franz Grillparzer's lifelong "engagement" to Katharina Fröhlich and Søren Kierkegaard's broken relationship with Regina Ølsen became the mirrors in which Kafka reflected, and distorted, his own dilemma. Yet most of all he was impressed by a phrase of Gustave Flaubert, which was written down by the writer's niece, Caroline Commanville, in her *Souvenirs*. On one of their walks together they had visited a friend and had found her surrounded by a crowd of happy children. On the way home Flaubert remarked: "Ils sont dans le vrai," implying that he, having sacrificed to literature all joys of an ordinary life, was in the wrong.[1] Brod reports that Kafka was fond of repeating this sentence (*FK*, 98). While Kafka dreamed of a bachelorhood so radical as to be unattainable, he also suspected that this bachelorhood was a profound error. He demanded from himself an asceticism which excluded marriage as a matter of course, yet he desired also a truth which could be found only in the fulfillment of matrimony and fatherhood.*

Kafka's asceticism, which he embraced as a precondition of artistic creation, and his search for an ideally happy life as the head of a family (which was a literary idea as well) crossed each other in his meeting with Felice Bauer. The situation which he created with his "unshakable judgment" at first sight was a dilemma: either way was open to him, but only at the price of renouncing the other. Whatever the judgment was, it had to be self-contradictory because of the paradoxical situation which made it necessary. Neurotically mistrustful of *any* decision, Kafka entered upon a crisis which was to last for five years.

Kafka's bachelorhood was produced and sustained by his literary

* Brod has recently added a footnote to this dilemma, which, if its truth could be established, would be a good illustration of life emulating literature. Kafka may have had an illegitimate child, a son, born in 1914 or 1915, who died in Munich in 1921. In any case, the mother never revealed to Kafka that he was the father of her child (*FK*, 240–242). The mystery of this story is enhanced by Kafka's diary entry: "Wrap your cloak, O sublime dream, around the child" (*DF*, 210). The entry occurs shortly before August 20, 1916; his "son" would have been one or two years old at this time.

inclinations and ambitions. Its *raison d'être* was the responsibility which he felt toward himself as a writer and toward his writing. In comparison, his wish to marry and have children was literary afterthought. Therefore, it is not difficult to guess the direction in which he allowed his crisis to drive him.

Approximately one year after his first meeting with Felice Bauer, in July or August of 1913, he composed in his diary a "summary of all the arguments for and against my marriage." Characteristically, among the seven points he wrote down there was only one argument entirely in favor of marriage, and this was formulated in the negative: "Inability to endure life alone. . . . The relationship with F. will give my being more strength to resist." The other six points all argue with more or less conviction for bachelorhood: "I must be alone a great deal. What I accomplished was only the result of being alone. . . . I hate everything that does not relate to literature, conversations bore me (even if they relate to literature)." The argument which seems to have been most important of all to Kafka was that he feared to lose himself to a wife: "The fear of the connection, of passing into the other. Then I shall never be alone again." These arguments show that Kafka felt it emotionally necessary to his life as a writer to remain alone, but his last point indicates that there was also a financial reason against marriage: "Alone, I could perhaps some day really give up my job. Married, it will never be possible."

To be sure, in another of his arguments Kafka observed that while he was seeing Felice he was more lively in the presence of others, especially his sisters: "Fearless, exposed, powerful, surprising, seized [by emotion] as I otherwise am only when I write. If through the mediation of my wife I could be like that in the presence of everyone." At first glance this statement seems like an affirmation of marriage, yet the German original of the word "exposed" (*blossgestellt*) has a second meaning of "compromised" and "denuded." Thus his innate ambiguity toward life in general penetrates even his attitude toward his own creative urge and forces him to reject a wife as an intermediary: "But then would it not be at the expense of my writing? Not that, not that" (*DI*, 292–293)! In his decision about marriage Kafka reminds us of a man casting dice to determine his fate; only he had loaded the dice well in advance. The mere mention of literature turned what had begun as a timid affirmation of marriage into a frantic flight from it.

The initial shock of this crisis enabled him to create in dramatic succession stories in which he projected his doubts and fears onto figures exposed to situations which were as insoluble as his own. Since the word *Urteil*, with which he concluded his diary report of the first meeting with Felice Bauer, reappears as the title of the first of these stories, it could be possible that he wrote the story to accuse himself of having abandoned his asceticism for the sake of marriage. " 'The Judgment,' " he said later, "is the spectre of one night," and the fact that he wrote it down "merely the verification, and so the complete exorcism, of the spectre" (*J*, 34). But as he took himself to task for having jeopardized his future as a writer, he discovered in his self-indictment a literary quality hitherto denied him. To use the figurative language of his diary: in the very process of prosecuting the bachelor for the loss of his purity, he found the bachelor's "art of prayer" grown beyond expectation. For in this crisis he succeeded in breaking through the disjointed style of his early works and created for the first time a coherent tale distinguished by concentrated imagery. Suddenly he was able to distill from his personal situation visions of a more than personal significance. Piercing through the surface of his private experience, he saw beyond it a multitude of layers and facets receding into an ultimate enigma. To recreate this multiplicity with suitable images, he produced a language that was both simple and insolubly complex. Of such a language he had dreamed when he jotted down in his diary as early as February 19, 1911, "When I arbitrarily write a single sentence, for instance, 'He looked out of the window,' it already has perfection" (*DI*, 45). Now he had found and sustained this perfection in the basically unfathomable transparency of his language. He was overcome by an ecstatic elation. "How everything can be said, how for everything, for the strangest fancies, there waits a great fire in which they perish and are resurrected" (*DI*, 276). Everything could be said. These stories were free from the remnants of realism which had bound his earlier works. Now naturalistic detail was elevated to the level of a vision, as if it had been exorcised by the eye of a seer. To be sure, this seer only succeeded in penetrating reality in order to perceive a deeper-seated evil beyond it.

Kafka's new style expressed the complexity of his personal situation without revealing it. Immediately and enthusiastically he recognized this style as a medium thoroughly his own. He adhered to this opinion even when growing resignation forced him to qualify his initial enthusiasm. These stories still counted when, toward the end, he wrote his testament.

"The Judgment"

The autobiographical relevance of "The Judgment" is self-evident: Georg Bendemann is a man engaged to be married. The first paragraph of the story reads like a joyous hymn on a bachelor's break with his past. It is a Sunday morning and spring. The ghettolike environment of the bachelor's lodging is burst open; Georg's room is his own and faces toward a river, a bridge, and tender green hills. The very character of the building, which is airily constructed, reflects the mood of the bridegroom. In this setting Georg is about to inform a faraway friend of his engagement (49).*

The letter is long and divulges its message only at the very end:

I have got engaged to a Fräulein Frieda Brandenfeld, a girl from a well-to-do family, who only came to live here a long time after you went away, so that you are hardly likely to know her. There will be a better time to tell you more about her later, for today let me just say that I am quite happy and as between you and me the only difference in our relationship is that instead of a quite ordinary friend you will now have in me a happy friend. Besides that, you will acquire in my fiancée, who sends her warm greetings and will soon write you herself, a genuine friend, which is not without importance to a bachelor. I know that there are many reasons why you cannot come to see us, but would not my wedding be the right occasion for giving all obstacles a go-by? Still, however this may be, do just as seems good to you without regarding any interests but your own (53).

The first thing the observer recognizes in the words of this bridegroom is Georg's feeling of discomfort. He refuses to describe Frieda Brandenfeld in detail beyond remarking that she is a young woman of means. She arrived in town long after the friend left, and Georg seems relieved to think that the companion of his youth cannot possibly have met his future wife by accident. He claims to be only "quite" happy, as if to assure the faraway man that the new bride has not usurped his place. The very wording of the letter divulges more of Georg's uneasiness about his impending marriage than he himself is ready to admit. Georg Bendemann has taken over this ambivalent attitude toward his fiancée directly from Franz Kafka.

Ambivalence results in ambiguity, and ambiguity leads to contradictions. For example, when Georg protests the genuine friendship his

---

* Numbers without letters in this chapter refer to "The Judgment" and "The Metamorphosis" in the American edition of *The Penal Colony*.

bride feels for the friend, he comes close to hypocrisy. Frieda had told him earlier in a conversation which led to the composition of this letter, "Since your friends are like this, Georg, you should not ever have got engaged at all" (53). The bride realized, with more insight than her groom, that it must have been their common bachelorhood which united the two friends. Since this bond is to be severed now because of her, she insists on Georg's informing the friend of the change. She wishes him to be present at the wedding so as to confront him with an accomplished fact, to preclude any future misunderstanding, and to face squarely any threat that this friendship may hold for her happiness. Georg, on the other hand, is doing his best to forestall the friend's visit without openly contradicting Frieda's wishes. Thus he mentions first the obstacles which stand in the way of the outsider's return. He senses the danger which the meeting of his future with his past might bring, and the consideration he shows for his friend's wishes hardly disguises his own apprehension. "He would probably come," he tells Frieda, "but he would feel that his hand had been forced and he would be hurt, perhaps he would envy me and certainly he would be dissatisfied and without being able to do anything about this dissatisfaction he would have to go away alone. Alone—do you know what this means" (52)? In its heart-rending simplicity the last sentence betrays Georg's fear that the friend's reappearance may lure him back into the bachelor's solitude from which he hopes to escape with Frieda's help. Thus he invites him, but suggests at the same time that he stay away.

Like his creator, Georg Bendemann has an exaggerated respect for the written word. He seems to feel that by putting his invitation down on paper he has reached a turning point. He stays at his desk a long time, staring out into the street, oblivious of the beautiful spring day and insensitive to the happenings outside. Then, with the letter in his pocket, he goes to his father's room, although it flashes through his mind that there is no actual need for such a visit.

The way to his father's room leads Georg into the interior of his house as well as of his own mind. When he enters, he is struck by the darkness which prevails. The room produces and reflects claustrophobia: its one window is shut against the day, its view barred by a "high wall on the other side of the narrow courtyard" (54). Outside the house there is the freedom and peace of Sunday; inside, the deadly darkness of a prison or a tomb. Georg notices the various mementos of his dead mother, the enormous newspaper in the old man's hand,

and the disorderly remains of the breakfast on the table. These properties emphasize the counterpoint upon which the story is built: the son is about to enter life; the father has withdrawn from it since his wife died and he gave up the active leadership of the firm. The son is breaking out of his bachelorhood; the father seems to have surrendered to the second, even more painful, bachelorhood of the widower.

Old Bendemann's hair is unkempt, he himself only half-dressed; when his gown swings open his unclean underwear becomes visible. With his toothless mouth he utters platitudes saturated with impotent aggression; unable to concentrate on his thoughts, he repeats phrases; he gives them a peculiar stress only when the conversation turns to Georg's friend. He seems merely to ramble on, dwelling on the little slips and gaucheries of his son's behavior which offend him: "I beg you, Georg, don't deceive me. It is a trivial affair, it is hardly worth mentioning, so don't deceive me. Do you really have this friend in St. Petersburg" (56)? On the surface this question is imbecile talk. Yet Georg, who has suddenly noticed that his father is "still a giant of a man" (54), seems deeply disturbed by it. He rises in embarrassment and changes the subject. The sensitive spot of his existence has been touched by the father in a cruel and absurd fashion.

Who is this friend whom Frieda wants to see, whose existence the father questions, and whom Georg would like to eliminate from his life without being able to do so? Whatever we learn about him is negative: he is absent, nameless, unmarried, unsuccessful, and ailing. Dissatisfied with his achievements at home, he had "actually taken refuge in Russia" (49). There he lives in an ever more painful isolation. On his last visit home he had told stories about life in Russia, especially the Russian Revolution. "For instance, when he was on a business trip to Kiev during a riot [he] saw a priest on a balcony who cut a broad cross in blood on the palm of his hand and appealed to the mob" (57–58). This event, possibly patterned after a historical incident—the role Father Gapon played in the October uprising of 1905—adds a new, positive dimension to the figure of the friend. It unites the elements of social revolution (the mob and the riot), religious fervor (the priest), and self-sacrifice (the cross cut in the palm). It seems to have impressed the friend to such an extent that he decided to stay in Russia forever. He declined later invitations to come home under the pretext that the political situation was too uncertain for him to return. Georg, the practical businessman, dismisses this argument as a "lame excuse" (51); and he is quite justified in taking this attitude since the uncertainty of the political situation would suggest an early return to any man led by the principles of common sense. There remains only one explanation for the friend's perseverance, namely, his interest in the scenes of upheaval he has witnessed, perhaps even his sympathy with them. The full beard he had worn during his last visit showed his desire to look like a Russian monk. Even his lack of success can be understood in a symbolic way as an attempt to embrace a kind of evangelical poverty. Then the land he has adopted would be a Tolstoyan Russia. In any case the friend is not only a mysterious but a highly ambiguous character.

In his letter of condolence on the occasion of the mother's death the friend had once more invited Georg to join him in the faraway country. But his invitation had arrived at exactly the moment when Georg had decided to embark on the career which culminated in his engagement. He had sacrificed whatever ideals he might still have cherished to the pursuit of self-advancement; now he is prepared to throw his bachelorhood into the bargain as well. The friend, on the other hand, has preserved the bachelor's purity in a land of social unrest, has worked counter to his interests, and has removed himself from all that Georg would call reality.

The climactic scene of "The Judgment" is played between three bachelors: the absent friend, the father who has relapsed into the state of bachelorhood, and Georg who is on the verge of leaving it. The theme is rich in autobiographical implications, but its treatment leads determinedly beyond the realm of Kafka's personal experiences.

Superficially it is old Bendemann who holds the center of this tragicomical act. He rises up with as much authority as he can muster to make a series of accusations against his son which include fickleness, dark practices in the family business, neglect of his mother's memory and of his father's well-being, and crude sexual desire, which led him to this offensive engagement. After accusing him, the father sentences his son to death. In this scene Kafka displays his newly acquired mastery: not only is the son forced to accept the judgment, the reader also is compelled to approve of it. He does so by treating the dialogue of the two Bendemanns with the utmost economy as well as by accompanying it with images which are as unforgettable as they are ambiguous. One example will suffice. While Georg carried his father to the bed, "the old man was playing with the watch chain on his breast." This gave Georg "a dreadful feeling. . . . He could not lay him down on the bed for a moment, so firmly did he hang on to the watch chain" (58). Does this image indicate the father's childishness, his playful contempt of the son, his weakness and helplessness, or the firm grip he has on Georg? Is he clinging to the "time" of Georg's life in order to extend his own? Or does he attempt to separate Georg from the "time" of his life, that is, to kill him already here? The silent gesture is as opaque as it is portentous, and it remains unexplained.

The same is true of the vague and inexplicably dramatic conversation which ensues. After having questioned the friend's existence, old Bendemann flatly declares: "How could you have a friend out there! I cannot believe it" (57). But with a sudden change of mind (which is an indication of the same fickleness for which he blames the son), he reverses himself completely. "Of course I know your friend," he admits. "He would have been a son after my own heart. This is why you have been playing false all these years. . . . And this is why you had to lock yourself up in your office . . . just so that you could write your lying little letters to Russia" (59). This contradiction does not spring from the old man's insanity,[2] nor is it meant to be a cruel game,[3] a prosecutor's trick in the cross-examination of a criminal. The father pronounces a paradoxical truth while deceiving and bluffing the son. Undoubtedly the friend exists, a small businessman, somewhere in Russia. Likewise he has undoubtedly assumed a symbolic function for both Georg and the old man. On the level of the symbol the friend can no longer be said to have a real existence. Independent of this real existence he lives during this scene in Georg's conscience and in the vengeful sentiments of his father. Precisely because he is absent from the scene as a person is he able to fill it with his imaginary presence.

Yet there is still another meaning underlying old Bendemann's self-contradiction. He denies the friend's existence because he stopped being Georg's friend at the very moment when Georg decided to embark on a career of success and marriage. Young Bendemann's letters to Russia were false, not only because of their insincerity, but because they were directed to a wrong address, a spectre of Georg's past. The engagement letter is the final renunciation of this friendship, a fatal blow as real and at the same time as illusive as old Bendemann's death sentence, which thus appears as a punishment for the letter. (Did Georg not sense the importance of his communication to the friend when he lingered at his desk for such a long while?)

But in the same measure in which Georg has abandoned his bachelorhood, the friend has grown in old Bendemann's mind to personify all the virtues of the bachelorhood Georg has forfeited. This he indicates by saying the friend would have been a son after his own heart. In the father's contradictory terms of speech the more the friend ceased to exist for Georg, the more his ideal image survived in old Bendemann. Triumphantly the father admits that he has communicated with the friend. He has written him letters, but on the symbolic level of the story their correspondence was that of two communicating vessels which are really one. Old Bendemann, who during this scene changes from a debilitated oldster to an undisputed authority over his son's life and death, is aided in this metamorphosis by the faraway friend and the idea of bachelorhood that he represents. "Your friend has not been betrayed after all!" old Bendemann cries. "I have been his representative here on the spot" (60). The word "representative" is well chosen. Coming as it does from the father's commercial sphere (in German *Vertreter* is commonly used to designate a traveling salesman), it indicates that the authority of the friend transcends that of the father just as the power of the head of a firm is greater than that of an agent. Therefore we may assume that the final judgment is pronounced by the father on behalf of the friend and the bachelorhood that Georg has offended.

Spellbound by the father, Georg is unable to see that the old man has received his authority through this "communication" with the friend. He argues and fights on the grounds of reality, which are quite inferior to those of his opponents. Therefore he is doomed to fail.

Only once does George come close to understanding the role the friend is playing in this struggle. Upon the father's assertion that the friend knows everything about him a thousand times better than he does himself, he answers, "Ten thousand times!" He says so, Kafka adds, "to make fun of his father, but even in his mouth the words turned into deadly earnest" (62). Unconsciously Georg credits the friend with extraordinary knowledge of his life and its motivations. In trying to deride and brush off one of his father's arguments, he establishes involuntarily the friend's authority as well as the power of his representative, the father.

Georg overlooks this small insight, which might have brought him to a more profound understanding of his plight. Forgetting the friend, he turns aggressively outward, against the father. "So you have been lying in wait for me!" he exclaims. With the hauteur of a judge who has already formulated his opinion, the father overrides this quibbling. "You probably wanted to say this sooner," he observes casually. "Now it does not fit any more" (62). Now, that is, after Georg had gained a faint glimpse into the true, the symbolic, nature of his friend and, closing his eyes again, has missed his last chance.

The final judgment which the father proclaims consists of two parts. The first one is a psychological diagnosis: "So now you know what else there was in the world besides yourself," old Bendemann declares. "Till now you have known only about yourself." Here a clear case of human guilt is stated. Georg's offense consisted in his self-centeredness. Egoism made him insensitive to the events which led to this catastrophe: his betrayal of the bachelor-friend, his worldly ambitions, his self-promotion, his love-making with Frieda, his loss of purity. Thus far the father has been dealing with realities, although in a horrifyingly exaggerated fashion. The second part of the judgment, however, is a paradoxical statement which can only be appreciated on a metaphysical level. "An innocent child, yes, this you were, truly," old Bendemann decrees, "but still more truly have you been a devilish human being" (62). Here innocence and wickedness are no longer presented as consecutive stages in Georg's development from child to man. Rather the judgment, leaving psychology behind, speaks of the close interconnection in every human being of good and evil, of promise and betrayal—of the devil entering the world of divine creation.

The verdict which follows the judgment likewise contains a paradox. "I sentence you now," the father says, "to death by drowning." Carrying out this sentence, Georg accepts the double role of executioner and condemned assigned to him by his father and, behind the father, the friend. Only the language of paradox can make his suicide both a murder and a sacrificial death.

To end the story in style, Georg's last words, "Dear parents, I have always loved you, all the same," reveal that he considers the conflict even at its fatal conclusion as a family affair, and not a moral argument. In other words, he remains deaf to the metaphysical depth of the judgment and succumbs simply to old Bendemann's suddenly resuscitated will. The fact that there is insufficient justification of the judgment and its execution on the realistic level infuses the whole story with the atmosphere of an uncanny, if not absurd, ballad.

Georg's choice of the same bridge for his suicide which appeared in the beginning as a symbol of his connection with life demonstrates the economy of Kafka's imagery as well as the irony he was able to derive from seemingly insignificant details. For now "an unending stream of traffic was just going over the bridge" (63).* From a Sunday, when in Kafka's Europe the streets were deserted, Georg has moved through the timelessness of his encounter with the father to a Monday, when life resumes its business, the charwoman climbs up the stairs to begin the work of a new week, and cars and pedestrians move from one bank of the river to the other, unendingly and happily ignorant of the personal incident of George Bendemann.

Perhaps one could see in the last sentence a symbolic resumption of the city's commerce which had been temporarily halted by Georg's activities. Perhaps Kafka even meant this city to represent the world, a generalization that offered itself easily to him. It is as if this unending stream of traffic had only waited for the moment of the son's plunge into the river to proceed again according to its own rules and dynamics. On this level the judgment of the father and its execution by the son assume the dimensions of a universally valid tragedy. The harmony of the world is restored by the death of the hero. By reinstating the disturbed peace through his sentencing of the son, the father gains superhuman stature. Indeed, no ordinary modern man could plausibly blame another for the devilish traits in his existence and derive from them, in all finality, a death sentence.

"The Judgment" moves constantly in two spheres, the realistic and the superrealistic, the psychological and the metaphysical; but these two spheres have not been satisfactorily integrated. In old Bendemann, Kafka seized a likeness of his father and treated it as an Oedipal tyrant very much the way the expressionists used to treat their father images; he strove to elevate it to a godlike figure endowed with omniscience, omnipotence, and the authority of absolute jurisdiction. Being a child of the twentieth century, the writer could not muster the strength to accomplish this design. Thus he left old Bendemann suspended between earth and heaven, a figment of his imagination, a fearful wish

---

* Brod quotes Kafka as commenting upon this sentence: "When I wrote it, I had in mind a violent ejaculation" (*FK*, 129). This autointerpretation has given ample food for thought to psychoanalytically minded Kafka scholars. There is, however, a linguistic side to it. German *Verkehr* means both "traffic" and "sexual intercourse." The disreputable ambiguity inherent in this word is borne out by a diary entry of October 9, 1911, which registers in grueling detail a dream visit Kafka paid to a brothel. Leaving the woman, the dreamer catches sight of the opening of the staircase, "on which there was a small amount of traffic" (*"auf der ein kleiner Verkehr stattfand"*) (*DI*, 90). Using his gift of free association again, Kafka may easily have been tempted to mystify Brod with a pun.

dream, an expression of his psychological insecurity as well as of his never-fulfilled desire for a genuine metaphysical orientation.

Kafka himself was quite unclear about the significance of the story, which, he wrote, "came out of me like a real birth, covered with filth and slime" (*DI*, 278). On the one hand he used images in the ambiguous sense of psychoanalytical symbols. One example is the play with the word "cover." Having been laid in bed by Georg, old Bendemann covers himself up. Thereupon he asks craftily, "Am I well covered up?" And when the son innocently reassures him that all is well, he exclaims: "No. . . . You wanted to cover me up, I know, my young scamp,* but I am far from being covered up yet" (58–59). Unmindful of the fact that it was he who drew the blankets over his own shoulders, old Bendemann reads into the word "cover" the meaning of "bury." This is a conscious and rational act of translation. He interprets the gesture, which he wrongly ascribes to the son, foisting an ulterior motive upon it. Thereby he betrays his own aggressions instead of exposing Georg's hostility and disqualifies himself as a judge. Yet Kafka cannot have intended this play with the word "cover" to be understood only psychologically or psychoanalytically, for at the same time the father begins to concede the friend's existence, which is a thoroughly unpsychological turn pointing to the symbolic meaning of the story.

From this moment on, the family conflict changes into a highly unrealistic ritual. Furiously stepping up the hitherto tranquil tempo of the tale, Kafka transforms Bendemann, Sr., into a prancing, leg-kicking, finger-stabbing, primitive war god whose wrath subsides only when, in majestic and solemn words, he pronounces the verdict. He stands erect in his bed, "his one hand lightly [touching] the ceiling" (59); which is a rather theatrical trick to produce the illusion of superhuman physical size. The newspaper which he had been reading shortsightedly when Georg entered his room turns out to be so old that even its name is entirely alien to the son (62). Thus he adds an extraordinary longevity to his gigantic appearance, outgrowing the son in time as well as in space. In this metamorphosis of old Bendemann, Kafka has pushed psychology aside and resolutely replaced it with mythmaking. The father's words, "Do you think I did not love you, I from whom you sprung?" (61), have patriarchal pathos. In

* The highly idiomatic German word *Früchtchen* ("little fruit") connotes also the rottenness of Georg, who has proved himself unworthy of his origins in the Bendemann family tree.

waiting for his son to come and be approved before he goes on his way, he appears likewise as a descendant from those archaic fathers who had the power to bless and to curse. Yet nowhere in Kafka's story do we find any indication that this father could have forgiven this son. It was Kafka's misfortune that he could only imagine the curse of existence. There was no blessing in the world as he saw it. This mythical father figure, this nearly divine old Bendemann, turns out to be a very subjective demon.

The father's authority collapses, and old Bendemann crashes down on his bed as soon as the son has rushed out of the room. Old Bendemann held absolute power only for this one son, and the judgment, which has the ring of a universal statement on the condition of man, buries under its weight the judge as well as the judged. By killing the last Bendemann at his father's bidding, Georg puts an irrevocable end to the Bendemann family.

Only the friend remains, unseen, untouchable, and undefeated. While reading the proofs of the story on February 11, 1913, Kafka attempted to define the character of this figure: "The friend is the link between father and son, he is their strongest common bond," he notes, and proceeds:

Sitting alone at his window, Georg rummages voluptuously in [this consciousness of] what they have in common, believes he has his father within him, and thinks that everything is peaceful. . . . In the course of the story the father . . . uses the common bond of the friend to set himself up as Georg's antagonist. . . . All they have in common is built up entirely around the father, Georg can feel it as something foreign, something that has become independent, that he has never given enough protection, that is exposed to Russian revolutions, and only because he has lost everything except his view of the father does the judgment, which closes off his father from him completely, have so strong an effect on him (*DI,* 278–279).

As a typical Kafka commentary this diary entry is apt to complicate and obfuscate the basic relationships around which the story is constructed. Yet it singles out the friend and describes him as inscrutable, which is the way Kafka deals with all the central images in his work. It strikes us that the friend is just as invisible as the court in *The Trial* and the master of *The Castle.* Like them he is superficially based on one of Kafka's life experiences (the diary of February 12, 1913, mentions a certain Steuer of whom Kafka kept thinking while creating the friend), and like them he is far removed from any such concrete prefiguration. (The diary adds the ironic fact that the same Steuer, "when

I happened to meet him about three months after I had written the story, . . . told me that he had become engaged about three months ago" [*DI*, 279]). Thus the model bachelor himself betrayed his bachelorhood.

The friend has been described as a "symbolic projection of Georg's better side, his Kafka nature," [4] or a symbol "of the spiritual in Georg," [5] or an image of "Kafka's writing." [6] But he is both more and less. Even if we define him as the embodiment of whatever Kafka understood by a "bachelor's purity," the existential purity which was endangered by his meeting Felice Bauer, we move from the universal meaning of the story back to its psychological motivations and reduce the stature of the friend from the metaphysical to the merely interesting and ephemeral.

Yet Kafka aimed at the metaphysical when he created the friend. He made him a witness of revolutions and almost a martyr to his convictions. At the height of his struggle with the father Georg envisages the friend as "lost in the vastness of Russia, . . . at the door of an empty, plundered warehouse . . . among the wreckage of his showcases, the slashed remnants of his wares, the falling gas brackets" (59). The friend's presence on the scene of destruction might easily cause his death. But this death would then be a true sacrifice for the sake of humanity's progress, a tragic act, whereas Georg's own death, in the final analysis, is caused only by the whim of a middle-class father intent on settling his account with an obstinate son. The friend is surrounded by the vastness of Russia as if it were infinity, whereas Georg is conditioned, limited, and finally brushed aside by the soulless life of a modern city. Georg is condemned by his father, whereas the friend is hallowed by a "Father," the image of the Russian monk holding up his bleeding hand in a gesture of revolt, defiance, and self-sacrifice.

"The Judgment" does not convey any clearly discernible message beyond the warning against the loss of bachelorhood. But even if the story resists unequivocal interpretation, it still rests firmly on an existential statement—the father's (and the friend's) condemnation of the son. In this verdict Kafka uses successfully, for the first time, a paradox to express the insoluble contradictoriness of human existence. Yet this paradox is only convincing as an aphorism, independent of the plot of the story. On closer scrutiny we cannot establish a poetic truth that would justify this judgment on the evidence provided by Georg's life. Part of the enigma presented to us by the story is due to this artistic imperfection.

Being hypersensitive to his own weaknesses, Kafka produced a veritable wealth of clues from his own life to decipher the undecipherable. Like a New Critic he discussed the linguistic derivation of the protagonist's name, establishing once and for all the fashion in which he was to choose the names of the heroes in his books: "Georg has the same number of letters as Franz. In Bendemann, 'mann' is a strengthening of 'Bende' to provide for all as yet unforeseen possibilities in the story. But Bende has exactly the same number of letters as Kafka, and the vowel *e* occurs in the same places as does the vowel *a* in Kafka." He might have added that the stem "Bende" is reminiscent of the verb *binden* ("bind"), thus alluding to the inextricable involvement of the two Bendemanns with each other and with their fate.

He treated the name of the bride in a similar way: "Frieda has as many letters as F[elice], Brandenfeld has the same initial as B[auer] ("peasant"), and in the word 'Feld' ("field") a certain connection in meaning as well" (*DI*, 279).

Like a lay analyst, he furnished life material to elucidate the symbols he had created.

After I read the story at Weltsch's yesterday, old Mr. Weltsch went out and, when he returned after a short time, praised especially the graphic descriptions in the story. With his arm extended he said: "I see this father before me," all the time looking directly at the empty chair in which he had been sitting while I was reading.

My sister said, "It is our house." I was astonished at how mistaken she was in the setting and said, "In this case, then, Father would have to be living in the toilet" (*DI*, 279–280).

And like a patient in the beginning of psychoanalytical treatment he doubted the material he himself had produced.

If we are correct in assuming that in "The Judgment" Kafka had intended to create a new myth of the father at a time when the image of the father had been thoroughly deflated by a generation of parricides and deicides, then he defeated his own purpose by commentaries and interpretations of this kind. They only prove that he himself was puzzled by what he had succeeded in creating during a few nocturnal hours of creative trance. Whether he sincerely attempted to solve the problems he had posed while writing "The Judgment" or whether he poked fun at the listeners who identified themselves all too easily with these products of his imagination, we are unable to decide today. But we can realize that he understood where the artistic weaknesses of this story lay when we observe that in the very next narrative he replaced the aphoristic nucleus of his tale with a genuine and fully integrated image.

"The Metamorphosis"

The transformation of the commercial traveler Gregor Samsa into an enormous insect is completed in the first sentence of "The Metamorphosis" or, rather, before it. Like an analytic tragedy, the story shows but the last stages of the hero's ordeal; yet the crucial element of analytic dramaturgy—the posing of the guilt question and the gradual discovery of its answer—is neglected here. The reader finds himself in the unenviable position of a detective who is confronted by a culprit in safe custody but who is obliged to search for the culprit's guilt (a situation very similar to his attitude toward Joseph K. in *The Trial*).

To continue the metaphor, the last act of this play is confined to the interplay between the animal and its human opponents, the insect's inglorious end, and the final relief of the humans. This is the only act we see. At least on the surface Gregor's metamorphosis is taken for granted; the question why he was changed is never openly posed. When once drawn into the magic circle of the tale, the reader is forced to accept its premise as unquestionable, a process which is facilitated by the narrator, who continually shuttles back and forth between the world of the transformed and that of the ordinary figures, between suprarealism and realism.

"The Metamorphosis" is unique among Kafka's animal stories in that Gregor is a human in the form of an animal and not an animal who has been humanized. He does not mirror the world of the humans by way of a travesty—as does the ape in "A Report to an Academy" or the mouse in "Josephine the Singer." Moreover, if he was intended to serve as an allegory of Kafka's own existence, this intention is continuously disturbed by Kafka's insistence on the insect's *being* Gregor in addition to *representing* him. Even in the beginning the shock of the metamorphosis is increased by Gregor's rational reaction to it, and his death cannot fail to remind the reader of Georg Bendemann's submission to the verdict of his father.

The story stands out among Kafka's shorter narratives by being clearly divided into three parts. The first part shows Gregor in his relation to his profession, the second to his family, and the third to himself. This rather schematic structure is not aesthetically disturbing because the three parts are united by Gregor's fate, which is and remains an enigma. In spite of the symmetry and precision of its structure it is basically endless; the actual conclusion is a rather un- convincing addition.

The first part is as strictly limited in time as it is in space (Gregor's room). The alarm clock ticking on his bureau symbolizes the infinite and irrevocable circle of Gregor's professional life as a traveling sales- man, to which he has sold himself. "It was half-past six o'clock and the hands were quickly moving on, it was even past the half-hour, it was getting on towards a quarter to seven" (69). Here time tells itself. The insect's attempt to leave his bed, that is, his gradual awareness of his transformation, is continually accompanied by statements of time. "The alarm clock had just struck a quarter to seven" (70). " 'Seven o'clock already,' he said to himself: 'Before it strikes a quarter past seven I must be quite out of this bed,' " for the office "opens before seven" (73). The monstrosity of the scene—an insect preparing for a salesman's trip—is heightened and parodied by the cold mechanism of the passing of time. "In five minutes' time it would be a quarter past seven—when the front door bell rang" (74). The General Man- ager appears. The firm did not allow more than ten minutes before sending out after its missing employee. With uncanny and inhuman regularity, reflected in the incessant ticking of the clock, business moves in to reclaim the fugitive. To escape from the compulsion of his drab and strict job, Gregor may well have changed into an insect during his "agitated dreams" (67) of the past night. "The Metamor- phosis" then, would be an escapist wish dream come true.

However, Gregor is more than a cog in a capitalistic machine. There is a very human side to his relationship with the firm. His parents once borrowed money from the boss and staked Gregor's services as a guarantee for the sum advanced to them. "If I did not have to restrain myself because of my parents," he muses, "I would have given notice long ago. . . . Once I have saved enough money to pay back my parents' debts, . . . I shall cut myself completely loose" (68–69). Nobody can deny that he is a slave, but even slaves are men. If his animal shape were but a dream, then he would have paradoxically sacrificed his humanity in his attempt to escape slavery by his change into an insect.

"The Metamorphosis" is set at the end of one epoch in history and at the beginning of a new one. The boss's personal involvement with his salesman's family bespeaks the still patriarchal attitude of a liberal economic system when at the same time Gregor suffers from the uniformity of life inherent in the organization methods of later capitalism. The employer is both close to the employee and far removed from him. This ambiguity—a characteristic of the changing times—is depicted in the image of the boss perched on top of his desk (a standing desk?), "talking down to the employee who, moreover, has to come quite near because the boss is hard of hearing" (69). (An interplay of "closeness" and "height" recurs in Kafka whenever one of his heroes has to face authority.)

This proximity is also the reason why the boss seems to be taking Gregor's absence as a personal offense. Why else would he dispatch the General Manager, his next-in-line, to search for the tardy servant? What Gregor interprets as persecution could also be considered an indication of his indispensability, if only he were surer of himself. However, Gregor's weakness and insecurity must be known to the General Manager, who plays skillfully on them to spur him on. Speaking through the door, he says, "The boss did hint to me early this morning a possible explanation for your disappearance—with reference to the collection of cash payments which were entrusted to you recently—but I truly almost pledged my word of honor that this could not be so" (77). The grotesquely funny contradiction of the General Manager's "truly" and "almost" reveals in one stroke that he, too, is weak-willed and oscillating. "Truly" he offers his trust to the employee, to snatch it away from him with the next word, "almost."

Obviously Gregor has some reason to complain about his job. At the same time we are given the incidental information that Gregor had been promoted a short while before. Now he is approaching the status of those elevated salesmen whom he envies because they are able to "live like harem women" (68). But he shrinks back from the progress which would lead him closer to his long-desired freedom. The General Manager goes on prodding him, "For some time past your work has been most unsatisfactory" (77). Gregor craves success and runs from it at the same time. Thus he circles around in the treadmill of his job, strives forward toward his independence, then turns around to head in the opposite direction as soon as he comes closer to his aim. He is in perpetual motion and yet he does not move from the spot. His professional life is a self-imposed labyrinth.

Eventually he succeeds in silencing the Manager and even to putting him to flight. He does so by appearing before him in his present shape as an insect, ostensibly to reconcile the superior and to promise improvement. His last speech before the ever more frantically receding Manager is a model of tragicomedy, an early example of Kafka's style at its best. He embarks on a jeremiad on the sad lot of the traveling salesman, pulling out all the stops of the soft and hard sell, from the rhetorical question to the pathetic flourish. He is quite oblivious to the fact that he is no longer offering any merchandise but himself, and begs to be kept on in a profession which he has just been cursing. In this tirade he speaks not only for himself, but for the whole tribe of traveling salesmen. So engrossed is he in his words that he completely forgets his appearance. The General Manager, however, escapes this sight with an "Ugh!," relinquishing his cane, hat, and overcoat.

At this point the proposed theory that Gregor's metamorphosis represents an escape from reality collapses. If Kafka had been solely concerned with Gregor's incapability of breaking away from the law that determines his life, that is, his flight from day to dream, he would have interrupted himself here. It would have been superfluous and even detrimental to the poignancy of the story to continue the description of Gregor's meanderings. No better image could be found to portray man's inability to escape himself than the insect pleading to be retained as a traveling salesman. Yet Gregor goes on circling around a dead center, first in full view of the family on top of the staircase, then, having been steered back by the indignant father, within the four walls of his room. The circle of time, described by the hands of the alarm clock, is repeated in space by the insect's desperate gyrations.

The second part is characterized by a gradual dissolution of time. The first had lasted one hour, from half-past six to half-past seven in the morning. It was limited by Gregor's awakening at its start and the "deep sleep, more like a swoon than a sleep" (87) to which he succumbs at its end. With another awakening in the dusk of the same fatal day Gregor resumes the wanderings of his body and mind. But now we have left the sphere of everyday; the orderly march of time has been suspended; the alarm clock has vanished from the chest. Twilight fills the room, indefinite adverbs of time like "soon," "later," "daily," blot out the passing of days and nights. At one point we are informed that we have proceeded to "about a month after Gregor's metamorphosis" (98); only a few paragraphs later Gregor realizes "that the lack of all direct human speech for the past two months . . . must have confused his mind" (102). His very life is now undergoing a metamorphosis:

the distinct rhythm imposed on it by his professional activities has given way to a shapeless vagueness, such as is experienced by prisoners, the sick—and Kafka's bachelor. From now on the story will seem like a parody and refutation of the ideal of the bachelor.

Gregor is both diseased and caged. His sister enters his room "on tiptoe, as if she were visiting an invalid" (90), and he himself calls the time since his transformation an "imprisonment" (94). These phrases point to the interesting contrast that whereas time dissolves, space closes in on him. Previously Gregor could still look through the window into a world shrouded with an apparently endless rain; and whenever the fog cleared up a little, he could see "on the other side of the street . . . a section of the endlessly long, dark gray building opposite —it was a hospital" (82). Now he is locked up in his room as if it were a cell. To be sure, "the electric lights in the street cast a pale sheen here and there on the ceiling . . . but down below, where he lay, it was dark" (88). It will remain dark until his death. He is now doubly encased, by his "hard, as it were armor-plated, back" (67) as well as by his room. Both images point back to a preordained solitude.

Nobody can change this solitude any more. The family can only adjust themselves to it and, by so doing, allow us to measure their own humanity. At the beginning of the story the individual members of the Samsa household were introduced by the insect's reactions to their voices heard from behind his locked door. The mother's voice was "soft" (70), the sister's "low and plaintive" (71), but the father accompanied his summons by knocking with his fist against the door. The mother's softness is Gregor's comfort and the insect's despair. She is the first to catch sight of him after the metamorphosis, and she collapses. (The narrator's evil eye does not fail to notice the black humor of the situation: fainting, she sits down on the coffee table, upsets the coffee pot, and sends the brown flood gushing all over the carpet.) For the rest of the story, however, she appears more and more as her husband's appendage; literally Gregor's mother becomes more and more a Mrs. Samsa (and is mentioned as such in the text).

Among all the figures in the breakthrough stories Mrs. Samsa is most closely modeled after life. Here Kafka has recaptured his own mother's selflessness and the superficiality of her understanding of him. But above all he seems to have suffered from the idea that his mother had surrendered to the father all her love. "It was true," he says in the "Letter to His Father," "that Mother was illimitably good to me but all that was for me in relation to you, that is to say, in no good relation. Mother unconsciously played the part of a beater during a hunt" (*DF*, 157). That Georg Bendemann's mother had to die before "The Judgment" begins can now be seen in proper perspective: it was an act of grace as well as of shame.

Compared with Bendemann, Sr., Samsa, Sr., behaves very much like an ordinary being, conditioned and limited by his environment. Wisely Kafka used restraint here, for a realistic reproduction of the father was bound to heighten the contrast between man and animal. The father's aging during the heyday of Gregor's activity, his sudden recovery after the metamorphosis, when it falls upon him to resume his role of provider, and his display of relief after the fate of the insect has been decided are all realized on a thoroughly human plane. His mulishness, his self-assertiveness, and his brusqueness have little in common with old Bendemann's more-than-human stature; they are characteristics he shares with many a *petit bourgeois* father of his generation, which was, we must never forget, still a generation of pre-Freudian parents. There is a great distance between old Bendemann's archaic and unexplained wrath and old Samsa's thoroughly understandable reactions. This distance indicates how far Kafka has succeeded in traveling toward a solid mastery of his craft in a surprisingly short time.

If Samsa, Sr., is more acceptable logically than Bendemann, Sr., he is nevertheless of the same ilk—the family of Kafka fathers. (Even more than Bendemann's, his name resembles the name of Kafka.) Immediately after his metamorphosis Gregor overhears his father explaining the state of the family's finances. Tongue in cheek the narrator remarks that this statement "was the first cheerful information Gregor had heard since his imprisonment" (94). It turns out that the resources of the family have not been completely exhausted by old Samsa's bankruptcy; the self-abandonment with which Gregor had applied himself to salesmanship was, to say the least, overdone. Furthermore, the father has set aside certain small sums from Gregor's earnings which have never been fully used up. In other words, he has exploited Gregor's sense of duty, trusting that the son's ingrained submissiveness would prevent him from demanding a clear account. If Gregor's change into an insect was meant to dramatize certain parasitic traits in his character, we realize now that these traits are inherited. The "good news" does not fail to produce some resentment in the insect: "True, he could really have paid off some more of his father's debts to the boss with the extra money, and so brought nearer the day on which he could quit his job" (96). The father, on the other hand, could easily answer Gregor by mentioning his failure to live up to the higher responsibility granted him when he was entrusted with the collection of cash payments. This was advancement, too, and would have brought the day of his liberation nearer. Discussions of this sort, however, are hopeless because, as we have seen, the weaknesses of father and son are complementary. Perhaps Gregor's transformation is an image of this particular hopelessness.

The most complex and decisive character in the Samsa household is the sister, Grete. The assonance between her name and Gregor's is indicative of a deep-rooted familiarity between them. While he was a human, she was the only member of the family with whom he had entertained human relations worthy of the name. After the metamorphosis she is at first the only one to interpret it as Gregor's, and not the family's, misfortune and the first to master her horror and enter the insect's room. Her humaneness seems to be in tune with her artistic talent; she "could play movingly on the violin" (95). Naturally her music is soon forgotten by everybody, including herself, since Gregor's transformation has forced her out into the world of commerce. Like the father, she supports the family now. Thus she serves as a provider to the animal in addition to being his nurse, messenger, interpreter, and an expert in all his dealings with the family. This has given her an undisputed authority in all matters concerning the welfare of her brother and determines her behavior in the first open family crisis.

It is she who has contrived the plan of removing the furniture from Gregor's room. The idea of this change seems to originate in her intuitive understanding of the insect's needs: she wants to give him "as wide a field as possible to crawl in." She "got the idea in her head" (101), and since she too has inherited certain dispositions from her father, she sticks to her plan doggedly. At this moment the mother's objection that emptying his room "would not necessarily be a service to Gregor, . . . considering that he had been used to his furniture for so long," meets with the insect's wholehearted approval. He clings to the room and its objects as to the last remnants of his identity. However, so great is Gregor's submissiveness and belief in Grete's wisdom that he soon comes to prefer her council to his own predilections and interests. And yet it is his very identity that he endangers by accommodating himself to Grete's design. Soon it turns out that even the mother wants to keep the room in its present state, "so that when he comes back to us he will find everything unchanged" (102). "When he comes back" can only mean that he is absent at the present moment and that the insect creeping over desk and cupboard is not Gregor. Eventually Grete will complete his condemnation by arguing for the removal of the insect himself on precisely the same grounds: "You must just try to get rid of the idea that this is Gregor. The fact that we have believed it for so long is the root of all our trouble" (125). The mother, certainly, has never believed it. She takes refuge in fainting fits whenever the insect catches her eye.

In spite of his vacillations Gregor decides to fight for his identity. This struggle is carried out in a very strange way. In the second paragraph of the story we have learned that there hangs in Gregor's room a cheap print of a woman "with a fur cap and a fur stole, . . . holding out to the spectator a fur muff into which the whole of her forearm had vanished" (67). As the mother inappropriately informs the General Manager, Gregor has spent several evenings cutting out a pretty gilt frame for this picture. Excepting a cashier in a milliner's shop, who is mentioned in the same breath with a chambermaid, "a sweet and fleeting memory" (114), Gregor seems to have been a model celibate. His hidden desires have taken refuge in his affection for this print, although the reproduction reveals in its vulgarity how deeply the standardization and commercialization of modern life had penetrated the bachelor's unconscious. For the insect, the print becomes the one of his possessions to which he is determined to adhere both physically and metaphorically. He creeps up to the picture and covers it with his body when mother and sister threaten to remove it. The body of the animal covers the body of an animallike woman who is clad threefold in fur. A ludicrously dissonant variation of the main theme of metamorphosis is developed here when the insect presses himself against the glass. While Gregor notices that it "gave a good surface to hold onto and did his hot belly good" (105), the reader sees that the insect sits on the picture as if he were possessing the woman in it. Gregor is at the same time united with the picture of the fur lady and separated from his dream object by the glass. The fulfillment and simultaneous frustration of love are rendered here by a convincing paradox.

Gregor's defiance precipitates the crisis. We are not surprised to see the mother taking refuge in another of her swoons. The father joins the battle, plunging the insect into an unprecedented panic. He deserts the picture, the image of his love and his identity, and runs before his father, "stopping when he stopped and scuttling forward again when his father made any kind of move. In this way they circled the room several times." Again the image of the circle is chosen as a symbol of the inextricable self-involvement of Gregor's fate. With the consistency that characterizes Kafka's inspiration at its best, he now chooses a round object to put an end once and for all to Gregor's aimless circular wanderings: "It was an apple; a second apple followed immediately; Gregor came to a stop in alarm; there was no point in running on, for his father was determined to bombard him. He had filled his pockets with fruit from the dish on the sideboard" (109). One of the missiles penetrates his armor-plated back and later causes his death by rotting in his body. The deadly bullet appears at first completely unexpected and unrelated to the actual setting of the scene. "It was an apple"; it comes shooting out of the blue, from nowhere or the armory of a whimsically unfathomable fate. Kafka takes his time to establish the provenance of these eerily flying projectiles: only after four main clauses and one dependent clause, running parallel to the victim's gradual recovery from his shock, are we told the origin of these apples in a dish on the sideboard. So cogent, however, is their choice that we never quite wake up to the scurrility of the drama performed before our eyes—the chase of an insect with apples. They seem quite naturally to belong in the imagery of this story; their roundness corresponds with the circles Gregor was running in when they stopped him.

As images these apples are also related to the Tree in the Garden of Eden, Paradise Lost, love, cognition, and sin.* These are mere associations, to be sure; yet as such they are meant to turn our glances in the direction of a vague and veiled religious background, just as Gregor's exclamation "The Devil take it all!" (68) and his invocation of the "Heavenly Father" (69) had pointed to a deeper meaning at the very beginning of the story. The use Kafka makes of these innuendoes in this story is no more than a literary play with the religious connotation of his images, but it suffices to render the scene transparent and its meaning still more ambiguous. Kafka does not divulge the ultimate meaning of the scene but forces us to accept it as inevitable without even asking why. The same is true when he beckons us to turn away from religion and look in the direction of psychoanalysis. The second part is concluded with the "complete union" of the parents. With failing eyes Gregor can still see how the mother, her clothing

---

* Similarly Joseph K., in *The Trial*, bites into an otherwise completely superfluous and unrelated "fine apple" (*T*, 12) immediately after having been arrested.

loosened by the sister, embraces the father, "as she begged for her son's life" (110).

The deathblow Gregor received during this battle was accompanied by another, more subtle, wound. Grete has become a turncoat. From a Good Samaritan, a "sister" in the Christian sense of the word, she has changed into the father's daughter. By taking over his gestures and glances, she has visibly joined forces with him. "You, Gregor!" she cries at the sight of the insect squatting on the picture, and Kafka adds, "This was the first time she had directly addressed him since his metamorphosis" (106). She still acknowledges his identity; moreover, she uses it to burden him with the full responsibility for his fate in this catastrophic scene. His advocate becomes his chief prosecutor, and in the end almost his executioner.

The title of the story might apply to Grete with greater justification than to Gregor, for it is her metamorphosis which is developed in the course of the narrative, whereas we have to accept Gregor's as an accomplished fact. More and more she plays herself into the foreground: the end will show her transformation completed, very much to the detriment of the story. Again Kafka seems to have allowed some biographical material to interfere with his literary purpose. There is some evidence of his having been haunted by ideas of incestuous love. On September 15, 1912, he enters in his diary the news of his sister Valli's engagement and adds, "Love between brother and sister—the repetition of the love between mother and father" (*DI*, 272–273). In "The Metamorphosis" he was still playing with psychoanalysis as a child plays with fire and, like the child, he was not so much interested in the fire as the play. Much later he called the story "an indiscretion," asking facetiously, "Is it perhaps delicate and discreet to talk about the bed bugs in one's own family?" But, he added more seriously, "Samsa is not merely Kafka" (*J*, 35). In this "not merely," in the transformation his experiences underwent on their way to becoming literary images, we may hope to find some further help toward understanding the story.

Without Grete's support Gregor succumbs completely to decay. He appears now as "an old dung beetle" (116). This name he is called by the charwoman, who in the meantime has emerged from one of Kafka's limbos, where the social underworld seems to have joined forces with his primal fears to generate a universal nightmare. This "dung beetle" also carries in its back the wound with the rotting apple, which is the symbol of guilt as well as of cognition. Gregor has never been closer to

an understanding of his human failure than when he is in the shape of
a hurt animal which perishes in its own filth. Deserted by his sister,
released from the very last social contacts, he has now the chance to
turn inward. Yet he misses even this last opportunity. Whatever attempt
at introspection he might have undertaken is thoroughly blocked by
his resentment of the others. Sinister designs of revenge are forming
in his mind. "Although he had no clear idea of what he might care
to eat he would make plans for getting into the larder to take the
food that was after all his due, even if he was not hungry" (114). Previously the insect had been constantly disturbed by the human reactions
and reminiscences that were a hangover from his life as a man. Now
the extremity of his suffering offers him the prospect of deeper humanity. Yet his thoughts continue to wander on the surface and to
erupt in outbursts of true beastliness. Lacking in appetite, he is nevertheless obsessed by the idea of food. His fight against the family has
been reduced to a struggle for nourishment—a losing battle, for even
the choicest food of the humans cannot be his nourishment any longer.

He realizes his plight in one rare lucid moment. This occurs at the
climax of the third part when Gregor faces the family for the third and
last time. Again indefinite time has passed; the rain which seems to
have lasted since the first day is still "lashing on the windowpanes,"
but now it is "perhaps a sign that spring was on the way" (116). This
is an editorial "perhaps"; in the insect's mind time floats as an inert
and amorphous mass. The space of the scene has shrunk even
further: the insect's room is now serving as a receptacle of many odd
things "that it was no use trying to sell but that should not be thrown
away either. All of them found their way into Gregor's room. The ash
can likewise and the kitchen garbage can" (117). The reason for this
additional iniquity is the appearance in the Samsa apartment of three
roomers. Serious, silent, and nameless, they dominate with their full
black beards all the space that was previously at the family's disposal.
The family itself has been crammed into the kitchen. This new development seems also to be a consequence of Gregor's transformation.
(But was it necessary now, when both father and sister add their
earnings to the family savings?) In the insect's mind a dark guilt feeling turns to envy and self-pity. Listening in on the meal of the lodgers,
he says to himself: "I am hungry enough, . . . but not for that kind
of food. How these lodgers are stuffing themselves, and here am I dying
of starvation" (119)!

One evening the roomers invite the sister to play the violin before them. It is a chamber concert in the most ironically literal sense of the word. When Gregor decides to intrude upon the privacy of this concert and to expose himself to the unsuspecting roomers, his first impulse is a feeling of utter spite. He is going to take his revenge on the family for the ash can and the garbage can. His next emotion is one of disgust with the serious gentlemen. They obviously come from the same province of business for business's sake that was also the territory of Gregor, the traveling salesman. Their behavior is typical: first they allow the music to titillate their nerves; soon, however, they get bored with it. They display the signs of earnest practicality disturbed by useless and unprofitable art.

And yet Gregor's sister was playing so beautifully. Her face leaned sideways, intently and sadly her eyes followed the notes of music. Gregor crawled a little farther forward and lowered his head to the ground so that it might be possible for his eyes to meet hers. Was he an animal, that music had such an effect upon him?

This question is as rhetorical as it is consciously misleading. Of course he isn't an animal, since only a man can be transported by beauty in such a subtle way. This answer, in turn, leads to one of two conclusions: either Gregor's soul has never been touched by the transformation of his body or the metamorphosis has been suspended in this transfigured moment. In either case Gregor's identity as a man has been secured. And yet he remains what he has been. Moreover, a glance at the lodgers (and through them into Gregor's past, which they represent) suffices to show that it is all too human to use music as a pastime and to turn away from it with indignant words and gestures as soon as one has lost interest in it. (The parents are still listening raptly but only to satisfy vicariously their own vanity, as the end of the story will prove beyond doubt.) But the insect listens. It is as if this music were showing him the way to the "unknown nourishment he craved" (121). To be sure, this nourishment cannot be human food if the roomers are human. The metamorphosis had been necessary to inspire this yearning in him, for Gregor, the salesman, had been apathetic to the magic of sound. Although he had toyed with the idea of sending the sister to the Conservatory, "despite the great expense it would entail" (95), he was no friend of music. He weighed its value in cash, and he may have decided to incur this "great expense" partly out of spite, because the parents would have opposed it. There was a first faint sign of rebellion hidden behind this idea, for the rest of his earlier history as a man was completely free of the desire for anything subtler than the fur lady on his print.

Even in this moment of dedicated listening he cannot accept music for what it is; he has to translate it into images of concrete possession which is all that he understands. He confuses the player with the play when he decides to lure his sister into his room and never let her go, "at least, not so long as he lived." Like a primitive man, he hopes to get hold of music, the "unknown nourishment," by arresting Grete and her fiddle. He is as insatiable as he is unable ever to learn his lesson. "His frightful appearance would become, for the first time, useful to him, he would watch all the doors of his room at once and mew and spit at intruders. . . ." His confusion finds its expression in a hopelessly mixed metaphor: he sees himself as a kind of St. George, wresting away a virgin from a multitude of potential dragons (his name, Gregor, associates, however vaguely, with the name of the saint). At the same time he has also been changed into the monster, mewing and spitting flames to protect his sister-love.* He is resolved to possess the sister; he would "raise himself to her shoulder and kiss her on the neck, which . . . she kept free of any ribbon or collar." Once his conquest of the sister is complete, then, but only then, will he confide to her "that he had had the firm intention of sending her to the Conservatory, and that, but for his misfortune, last Christmas—surely Christmas was long past?—he would have announced it to everybody" (121). Even here, in this feverish wish dream, he feels compelled to make sure that Christmas is long past, as if with its passing his obligation also has been abolished. He not only wants to possess what cannot be possessed, he also refuses to pay for it. Christmas has passed, that is sure, and with it the day when the Redeemer and man's hope for salvation was born.

We have arrived at the vertex of the story, which, thanks to Kafka's masterful counterpoint, is also the low point in the insect's development. We feel the icy breath of an existence fatally gone astray. The question of Gregor's guilt and the reason for his transformation face us once more. Does his guilt lie in himself, in his possessiveness, of which he remains unaware to his end? The sister, he thinks, should stay with him without constraint and "of her free will" (121); that is,

---

* His name is identical with that of the hero in Hartmann von Aue's *Gregorius,* who committed an act of incest and atoned while suffering a miraculous metamorphosis. In 1902 Kafka had registered as a regular student in Professor Detter's course on Hartmann von Aue at Prague University (cf. Klaus Wagenbach, *Franz Kafka* [Bern: Francke, 1958], 100, 243).

he concedes her free will only as a sign of unconditional surrender. Does his guilt consist in his inability to reach beyond himself, in his desire to grasp and digest the "unknown nourishment?" Is this nourishment identical with music? If so, has he been transformed because he had tried to dedicate himself to the unknown by proxy, by sending his sister to the Conservatory instead of attending it himself? Did he want to use her as his emissary to the high unknown? Should he have become a musician, thus partaking of the "unknown nourishment?" Could he have avoided the metamorphosis by renouncing his hated job and embarking on a profession he loved? Would he have found salvation in the pursuit of music? Is music here an image of art in general or of the "art of prayer" in particular, that is, of literature? Is the *ur*-bachelor's paradox repeated in the paradoxical image of a man turned insect?

This whirl of questions leads us back to Kafka's bachelor and the "depth" of his guilt feelings, which he was eager both to reveal and conceal. Gregor's solitude points to this depth; so does the dirt to which the insect belongs and finally returns in the shape of a dead dung beetle. The bachelor's depth seems to be reflected by Gregor's metamorphosis in that both are paradoxes of human existence, knowing of neither cause nor effect. If we have seemed to discuss Gregor's transformation without ever coming closer to its reason or meaning, then we have been following the structural principle Kafka used in this narrative. This principle is: motion without origin or aim, its image the circle.

We have traced this circle through Gregor's human and animal stages. It ends in the state of inanimate matter.

The rotting apple in his back and the inflamed area around it, all covered with soft dust, already hardly troubled him. He thought of his family with tenderness and love. The decision that he must disappear was one that he held to even more strongly than his sister, if that was possible. In this state of vacant and peaceful meditation he remained until the tower clock struck three in the morning (127).

We misunderstand Gregor, as he has misunderstood himself throughout his life, when we read into his mood of forgiveness a "liberating cognition" or a "reconciliation of Gregor with himself and the world." [7] The insect cannot be measured by the standards of a classical hero who accepts his own destruction in order to redress the balance of the universe by sacrificing himself. Gregor's meditations are not only "peaceful" but "vacant." He agrees to his own demise as he once had submitted to the yoke of his job and, again, to the father's concealment of his savings. We have no reason to believe that anything but his deadly weakness prevents him from still another relapse into rebellious wrath. Whatever the "unknown nourishment" symbolizes, it would have passed through him without nourishing him, as did, of late, the food actually offered him. "Just see how thin he was," Grete remarks, pointing at his corpse. "It is such a long time since he has eaten anything. The food came out of him again just as it went in" (128–129).° This is a cruel but striking epitaph. Grete likens him here to a lifeless object. He has not really lived; existence, physical and metaphysical, has moved past him and left no trace. The metamorphosis has failed to change him. He dies, as he lived, a thing. The salesman has been dealing in things; the insect has clung to things; love and music he has craved as if they were things. Resigning himself in his last words to an animal existence, this human being reduces himself to impersonal matter. He does not die, he is put out. The charwoman sweeps "it" away.

Kafka succeeded in creating so complex and inexplicable an image that not even Gregor's "thingness" can be construed as his ultimate guilt. We would moralize unduly if we assumed that his preoccupation with the material side of life has caused his metamorphosis and eventually transformed him into a heap of useless matter. The content of the story contradicts any such moralizing: Gregor is never offered an alternative to his fate. He is given neither a choice between good and evil nor a genuine opportunity to repent or atone for his absorption in the superficial realities of his existence. He is condemned without accusation and judgment, and ultimately he remains in the dark about the reasons of his punishment. He and his readers are forced to accept it unconditionally.

Kafka's story describes the invasion of the material world by a power which resides beyond empirical experience. Empirical experience can only register this invasion and, as the Samsa family tries to do, come to terms with it. "Even the unusual must have its limits," Blumfeld, the elderly bachelor, thinks in one of Kafka's later fragments, when two small, blue-and-white-striped celluloid balls descend upon him out of nowhere (*DS*, 112). But in Kafka's world only the empirical has limits; the "unusual," the unempirical, is at liberty to

---

° This is borne out by the narrator's earlier remark: "Gregor was now eating hardly anything. Only when he happened to pass the food laid out for him did he take a bit of something in his mouth as a pastime, kept it there for an hour at a time and usually spat it out again" (117).

transcend these limits wherever and whenever it pleases. It chooses its victims, but the criteria for the choice remain obscure; the selection is grotesquely cruel in its arbitrariness. Why was Gregor Samsa chosen and not one of the three lodgers whom he resembles so closely? No answer is given. Yet in this arbitrariness there is a hidden element of universality. Precisely because Gregor Samsa is an average man, his incredible fate could befall any average man among the readers of this tale. So far does Kafka's skill as a narrator extend that the extraordinary begins to look commonplace.

Because of Gregor Samsa's commonplace character it is difficult to agree to the description of "The Metamorphosis" as a fairy tale in reverse, i.e., an "anti-fairy-tale," which shows "the world as it ought not to be." [8] Gregor's craving for his sister, Grete, has not been taken from the old legend of Beauty and the Beast and reprinted here, so to speak, in reflected face. Gregor is no enchanted prince, languishing in the shape of an animal for his redemption. Nor is he the opposite, the legendary pauper, whose sufferings are rewarded by a happy end. The concept of the fairy tale does not apply to him. He is a modest and mediocre salesman who had the misfortune to awake, one morning, in the shape of an insect. There is no tragic plunge from the noble and unique in this transformation. Quite the contrary, the metamorphosis appears consistent and strangely appropriate to Gregor's thoroughly unheroic character. The beast into which this nonhero has been changed remains as nondescript as Gregor was when he still functioned as a human salesman.

Moreover, even if Kafka intended "The Metamorphosis" to be an anti-fairy-tale, he would have had to suggest the power which transformed Gregor. Witch or magician, fairy or fate, this power would have had to appear in order to indicate the means by which it could be either placated or exorcised. Furthermore, the outlines of the desired order in the world would have had to become visible if the tale was to be considered as an image of "the world as it ought not to be." Such an outline appears indeed in the very last pages of the story, after the insect's death, but it left Kafka, and leaves the attentive reader, dissatisfied. The epilogue of "The Metamorphosis" shows the Samsa family on their way to recovering their physical health. But the power which transformed Gregor Samsa is infinitely more than an image of bodily disease. Nowhere does Kafka encourage us to interpret Gregor's insect shape as an expression of his physical or even mental disorder. The principal law of the force which caused his metamorphosis is its incomprehensibility. It can only be described by not being depicted at all. Its image is a blank space yawning amidst the everyday reality of the Samsa household.

The thoroughly negative quality of the transforming power seems to have been imparted to the animal itself. In the first sentence of the original, Gregor is introduced by two negatives as *ungeheures Ungeziefer* ("enormous vermin" [67]). Apart from the repeated negative prefix *un-*, the German word *Ungeziefer*, like its English equivalent, "vermin," is a generic term, a collective noun denoting all sorts of undesirable insects. Kafka never divulges the kind of insect into which Gregor has been transformed, nor does he specify its form and size. In the beginning he is flat like a bedbug, so thin that he can find accommodation under the couch, and yet long enough to reach the door key with his teeth. It would stand to reason that he was changed into precisely that animal which he—and other European salesmen— dreaded most when they entered the dirty and cheap hotels open to them on their route. And yet there is no direct textual evidence to support Kafka's later claim that in "The Metamorphosis" he was talking "about the bedbugs in [his] own family" (*über die Wanzen der eigenen Familie—J*, 35). Whatever vague contours the animal possesses are blurred in the course of the story by the "dust, fluff and hair and remnants of food" (120) which have assembled on its back. When the charwoman finally calls him "an old dung beetle" (116), she does not, as one critic maintains, pronounce an entomological classification,[9] but simply adds an insult to Gregor's fatal injury. By his metamorphosis Gregor Samsa has been turned into an untouchable in the most literal sense of the word.

What Kafka could not describe by words he likewise wished to keep unexplained by pictorial representation. When Kurt Wolff, the publisher, submitted to him a sketch of the title page which showed Gregor as a beetle, Kafka remonstrated: "The insect proper cannot be designed. Not even from far away is it possible to disclose its shape." As a substitute he suggested a drawing of the parents and the sister in the lamplit room, "with the door to the completely dark next room wide open" (*B*, 136). This complete darkness is the proper description of Gregor's fate as well as of the animal shape into which he was transformed. The *un-*, the dark, the void, are the only designations Kafka could find for the mystery at the center of the tale. Gregor's

metamorphosis is the image of his own negative possibilities as well
as of the incomprehensibility of the power that changed him into an
insect.

The epilogue shows the Samsa family on an excursion into the
open country. The insect has been removed, the charwoman dismissed,
the triad of lodgers given notice. Nature itself seems to conspire with
the rejuvenated Samsas. The trolley in which the family travels alone
"was filled with warm sunshine." Sinister past has given way to a
future of freedom and light. Now it appears that the prospects of the
family are "on closer inspection . . . not at all bad." The tale that had
begun with Gregor's "agitated dreams" is ended by "new dreams," in
which the parents anticipate a life of petty-bourgeois comfort in an
apartment better than the old one, "which Gregor has still selected."
Most obvious, however, is Grete's change. The parents are struck by a
sudden outburst of vitality, which seems to have changed her into
a completely different girl. "In spite of all the sorrow of recent times
. . . she had bloomed into a pretty girl with a good figure" (132).
Now she is joining the regenerative forces of nature and thereby com-
pletes *her* metamorphosis. Precisely because Kafka has devised this
end as a counterpoint to Gregor's transformation and precisely because
this counterpoint concludes harmoniously, it appears as a somewhat
forced adaptation of the now hackneyed antithesis of "art" and "life"
to the paradoxical nature of Kafka's new style. But Gregor cannot be
accepted as an artist, however frustrated. His metamorphosis is not
counterbalanced by Grete's awakening to normalcy, however trivial.
Neither the warm sunshine of an early spring day nor the social rehabilitation of a middle-class family nor the successful passing of a
young girl's puberty can make us forget the unknown which reached
through Gregor into life as it is known to us. So persuasively has Kafka
impressed the image of the insect upon reality that the ordinary world
itself seems to have changed. After Gregor's metamorphosis Kafka's
reality will never be the same.

CHAPTER IV

Parable and Paradox

"A Country Doctor" and

"In the Penal Colony"

THE years between 1914 and 1917 saw Kafka at the peak of his literary mastery. He finished "In the Penal Colony" and read it to Franz Werfel, Max Brod, and Otto Pick on December 2, 1914 (*DII*, 98). Eleven days later the diary mentions the "exegesis" of the "parable 'Before the Law,'" (*DII*, 101) which originally was to be included in "A Country Doctor." There is evidence that the bulk of *The Trial* was likewise finished around this time.[1] This is supported by the fact that the novel is thematically interconnected with "In the Penal Colony." On August 20, 1917, Kafka submitted to Kurt Wolff, the publisher, the complete collection of the *Country Doctor* stories (*B*, 158–159). The book appeared in 1919, which was also the year of the publication of "In the Penal Colony." *

---

* "In the Penal Colony" was published separately by Kurt Wolff, as was "The Stoker" (1913), "The Judgment," and "The Metamorphosis" (the last two in 1916). In English the story "In the Penal Colony," along with two of these stories and the *Country Doctor* collection, is to be found in the volume, *The Penal Colony*. Since "The Stoker," the third, is identical with the first chapter of *Amerika*, it is not included in the *Penal Colony* volume.

In his personal life, too, these were years of great importance. It was the time when Kafka tried to come to terms with the "unshakable judgment" he had pronounced after seeing Felice Bauer for the first time in August of 1912. Twice, in 1914 and in 1917, he entered upon formal engagements with her, but each time the engagement was broken off—the first time after two months, the second time after half a year. The beginning of this period is marked by an external catastrophe, the outbreak of the First World War, and its conclusion is sharply accentuated by a personal one, the medical diagnosis confirming the suspicion that he was suffering from tuberculosis.

During these years Kafka consolidated the literary gains that he had made. He discovered a second reality behind the reality he experienced. With a still trembling and yet often highly skillful hand, he created symbols which through their paradoxical form expressed the inexpressible without betraying it.

More and more consciously drawing on the tradition of the parable as it had come down to him through the ages, Kafka refined and perfected the form until it served to express his own religious uncertainties and metaphysical longings. He was not the first to use the parable as an expression of the religious crisis which had befallen the Western world. As early as the middle of the nineteenth century Heinrich Heine had ventured to speculate that "modern poetry is essentially distinguished by its parabolical character. Anticipation and reminiscences are its main content." [2] It was the same Heine who in 1826 had lyrically, ironically, and playfully asserted, "Dead is our Lord up there." [3] Yet it was Friedrich Nietzsche (an admirer of Heine's "divine wickedness" [4] because he believed it to be a malice directed against the Divine) who actually created the sort of parable the older poet had had in mind. In the one hundred twenty-fifth aphorism of *The Joyful Wisdom* (1882) Nietzsche tells of a "madman" who runs to the market place in broad daylight, a burning lantern in his hand, crying incessantly, "I seek God! I seek God!" He is a Diogenes twice reversed, a lunatic rather than a philosopher; he is looking not for a man but for God. In the market place the man encounters disbelievers who scorn both him and the God he seeks. Thereupon the "madman" is heard to cry: "Where has God gone? . . . I mean to tell you! *We have killed him*—you and I. We are all his murderers. . . . God is dead! God remains dead!" Eric Voegelin, who uses this aphorism to demonstrate the reemergence of Gnostic ideas in modern science and politics, has pointed to the paradox that lies hidden in this absurd anecdote: "The new Diogenes is looking for a God but not the dead one. Rather he searches for the new God among the very people who have killed the old one, this new God being none other than Nietzsche's Superman." [5] Indeed, the madman is the pathetic spokesman for the late-nineteenth-century nihilism which had stirred in Heine and which, two years after the writing of this parable, produced Nietzsche's *Zarathustra.* He strays "as though through an infinite nothingness" looking for a consolation that no one can give him. He has come too early; his time is not yet.[6] And with a gesture of true symbolic grandeur the madman takes his lantern and smashes it on the ground.

Like its predecessor, the Biblical parable, this anecdote has a metaphysical direction. It could have been written only by a man with a profound longing for the transcendental world and an equally profound disappointment at what he found here in its stead. The modern parable differs, however, from its model in that it no longer carries a clear-cut message but is built around a paradox. When, in the Gospel according to Luke, the prodigal son feeds on the hulls that the swine eat while his father is fattening a calf which will satisfy his son's hunger,[7] the images of the hulls and the calf stand clearly for the son's fallen state and the father's forgiveness. No such accepted imagery is at Nietzsche's disposal. Instead he has to improvise and parody, to turn tradition upside down and invent as tragically paradoxical a figure as his mad Diogenes. Moreover, since the Biblical parable is told within an established religious context, the figures of prodigal son and forgiving father easily extend to include such vast abstractions as Everyman on the one hand and God on the other. This built-in symbolism is likewise denied to Nietzsche. A clergyman's renegade son, he so emphatically turned his back on his origins, both physical and spiritual, that he grew to become the prophet of the modern "deicides," to borrow another phrase from Voegelin.[8] His insight that God is dead is an abstract idea negated. To translate it into communicable language was an undertaking as paradoxical as the idea he wanted to express.

Basically all modern parables are "fantasies," as Dostoyevsky's Alyosha calls the parable of the "Grand Inquisitor" when it is told him by his brother Ivan Karamazov. Here at least the intention is clear: Ivan improvises his tale to make Alyosha think twice about surrendering to a religion against which he, Ivan, rebels. And yet the story of a resurrected Christ who is apprehended, berated, and almost burnt at the stake by the Inquisitor is so involved, multifaceted, and, in the

final analysis, inexplicable that Alyosha at one point exclaims, "Your
fantasy is in praise of Jesus, not in blame of Him . . . as you had
meant it to be!" As with Nietzsche's aphorism this parable is resolved
by a silent gesture, the kiss Jesus presses on the "bloodless, aged lips"
of the Inquisitor. Alyosha repeats this gesture when he kisses Ivan.
But what for him is a naïve and spontaneous *imitatio Christi* appears
to his brother as a trick of literary "plagiarism." [9] Here even the simplest
symbol has ceased to function unambiguously.

Throughout Ivan's parable Christ remains silent and leaves the talking—prophecies, harangues, and contradictions—to his opponent, the
Grand Inquisitor. Generally speaking, the appearance of the supernatural in the modern parable occurs below, behind, and beyond the
spoken word. These parables are statements of man's awareness of
the supernatural; but instead of bridging the gap between the empirical
and the mysterious they reveal and perpetuate this gap in an insoluble
enigma. They are admissions of man's ignorance with regard to the
metaphysical. From this ignorance Nietzsche defiantly derived the
joy of what he called his "wisdom"; Kafka, more modestly and maturely,
simply tried to live with it. "I try to be a real pretender for grace,"
he said to Gustav Janouch. "I wait and see. Perhaps it will come—
perhaps it won't. It is possible that this quiet-unquiet waiting is already
the harbinger of grace, or grace itself. I do not know. But this does
not disturb me. In the meantime I . . . have made friends with my
ignorance" (*J*, 93). Kafka's parables are not the fruit of wisdom but
the professions of this ignorance.

In his short story "An Imperial Message" Kafka describes the failure
of a messenger to carry the Emperor's last words from his deathbed
to his subjects. Through subtle allusions we are given to understand
that this testament carries the weight of a religious revelation and that
the potentate now dying is none other than the Supreme Being. But
we are never told the actual wording of the imperial message; to us
the Emperor remains as silent as Dostoyevsky's Christ. Nor does the
messenger ever reach his destination. The capital city, "the center of
the world, overflowing with the dregs of humanity," will forever lie
between the imperial sun—which is now setting—and the "lone individual, the meanest of his subjects . . . you." By addressing the story
to an imaginary reader, Kafka seems to imply that the Emperor's testament was meant for everyone who comes across his story, and that
everyone misses it since it remains undelivered. "But you sit by your

window and dream it when evening falls" (158–159).* Describing the
fate of the parable in a time depleted of metaphysical truths, the
imperial message has turned into the subjective fantasy of a dreamer
who sits at a window with a view on a darkening world. The only
real information imparted by this story is the news of the Emperor's
death. This news Kafka took over from Nietzsche, in whose parable he
could have found also the image of the extinguished light, the setting
sun. By smashing his lantern, Nietzsche's lunatic Diogenes indicates
the breakdown of instruction and the Twilight of the Gods. Similarly,
the priest in Kafka's *The Trial* entrusts a small lamp to Joseph K.
before he tells him the parable "Before the Law." After K. has thoroughly misunderstood this tale and come to the conclusion that "lying
has turned into a universal principle," Kafka mentions again the lamp
which "had long since gone out" (*T*, 276–277). This is the darkness
which spreads in Werfel's "*Gottesfinsternis*" and "drops again" in W.
B. Yeats's vision of the "Second Coming." [10] The resultant gloom is
perhaps a reason for the obscurity of many a modern parable.

What we have called Kafka's mastery consists primarily in his way
of presenting the opaque content of his parables—the admission of
his ignorance—in narrative structures as clear and as cutting as crystal.
Both "Before the Law" and "An Imperial Message" are distinguished
by their utter simplicity. Yet both are the centerpieces of longer stories
neither of which can be called clear or simple: the first, of *The Trial*,
the second, of "The Great Wall of China" (*GW*, 148–173). By publishing them out of context in the *Country Doctor* collection and
holding back the larger structures to which they belonged, Kafka
repeated the practice he had established with the publication of "Meditation." If we consider that the *Country Doctor* collection also contains
the fragment "A Dream," which is an alternative reading of the end
of *The Trial*, we cannot escape the conclusion that Kafka was serious,
at least at times, in wishing the long stories to be destroyed and forgotten. On the other hand, his skill as a writer had now reached such
a peak that the parables "Before the Law" and "An Imperial Message"
are self-contained pieces apart from their larger contexts. It is safe
to say that Kafka's intentions and achievements would have survived
—perhaps even less marred by misunderstandings—if *The Trial* and
"The Great Wall" had never come to the attention of his readers.

* Numbers without letters in this chapter refer to the Schocken edition of *The
Penal Colony* which was cited in the Key.

Not all the stories written during Kafka's middle years are equally perfect examples of their kind. When he submitted the list of the *Country Doctor* stories to Kurt Wolff, Kafka included also a sketch with the intriguing title "The Bucket Rider." It begins: "Coal all spent; the bucket empty; the shovel senseless; the stove breathing out cold; the room inflated by frost; the trees outside the window rigid with rime; the sky a silver shield against him who asks for help. I have to have coal" (184). If, as Brod says, the coal famine of the winter of 1916–1917 was the background of this story (318), then Kafka extended it admirably into an image of the cosmic cold gripping the world as he saw it. The fire has gone out; fuel, energy, and vitality are wasted; the sky, bare as the earth, protects the void above against any intrusion from the emptiness below. As a statement of man's forlornness in a wintery world this beginning is lyrically perfect. To continue it and give it the form of a Kafka parable, he had to search for a central paradox. The vision of a man riding on a bucket instead of carrying it offered itself to him. From this idea he proceeded to develop dialogues between the Bucket Rider on the one hand and a coal dealer and his wife on the other—dialogues which are grotesque without having much bearing on the exposition of the story. A universal insight is reduced to a marginal gloss. This gloss may have added some local color—the piece was first published in the *Prager Presse* on December 25, 1921—but it leads nowhere. And nowhere is precisely the place to which the Bucket Rider retires after his mission has failed. " 'You bad woman,' " he cries out to the coal dealer's wife. " 'I begged you for a shovelful of the cheapest coal and you refused it to me.' And with this I ascend into the regions of the ice mountains and am lost forever" (187). Yet in a continuation not published in the *Prager Presse* edition Kafka destroys the image of the Bucket Rider by allowing him to realize his failure and to return to a normalcy turned upside down by his new surroundings: "My riding has lost its meaning, I have dismounted and am carrying the bucket on my shoulder." Nothing is left except another lyrical image of a dehumanized universe: "White, frozen plains of ice, streaked into slices here and there by the tracks of skaters since disappeared" (*DF*, 50). This is an absurd story, not a paradoxical one, and Kafka knew well why he excluded it from the final selection of the *Country Doctor* stories. His decision, however, was not considered binding by the editor of the American edition, where "The Bucket Rider" appears as the last of the *Country Doctor* stories, although it came third on the original list Kafka sent to Wolff.

Even the published *Country Doctor* collection contains a few tales which not only remain inexplicable on account of the opaqueness of their content but are basically unintelligible because Kafka failed to master their form. The title story is a case in point. The balladlike beauty of "A Country Doctor" is obvious in the wild upsurge of the visions and their ebbing and fading away at the end, the build-up of the narrator's tempo, and the frightening intensity of the individual scenes. Some basic details—the strange, savage groom squatting in the dark gateway, the pitiful and yet uncanny relatives of the young patient, the background chorus spilling over with nonsensically compelling ditties—these vignettes of horror stand out all the more sharply because they are incoherent fragments. As a whole the story is not the literary presentation of a nightmare; it is its literal transcription. It remains biographically relevant because it illuminates the conflicts which propelled Kafka into his more accomplished work; but it does not deliver even the message that there is no message to be delivered. It does not stammer because Kafka had decided to reject coherency; it stutters because the language failed Kafka. Its fragmentariness is not a structural principle but an artistic deficiency. The reader who finds himself unable to fathom its meaning need not blame himself for his lack of understanding.

The fact remains that Kafka singled out "A Country Doctor" by selecting it as the title story of the collection. He may have been prompted to do so by the directness of its statement. Like "The Bucket Rider," it describes the "frost of this most unhappy of ages" (143). Moreover, it expresses the helplessness of a man whose profession consists in helping, a paradox with which Kafka could all too easily identify his own situation. There may have been still another, even more personal reason. He dedicated the volume to his father. In the "Letter to His Father" Kafka recalls the older man making remarks "which must positively have worn grooves in my brain, like: 'When I was only seven I had to push the barrow from village to village.' 'We all had to sleep in one room.' 'We were glad when we got potatoes.' 'For years I had open sores on my legs from not having enough clothes to wear in winter'" (*DF*, 158). This winter landscape of pain and poverty returns as the scenery of "A Country Doctor." The fatal misunderstanding between the doctor and his patient may have been meant to reflect the equally hopeless relationship that existed between the two Kafkas. That Kafka was not averse to such mystifications can be considered characteristic of his personal style. It means little for the understanding of his work as literature. What matters is that the plight of the Country Doctor may be taken as a fairly direct statement of a theme on which the other stories in this volume are variations in counterpoint. Naked and old, betrayed and wandering astray, a scarecrow scared rather than scaring, the Country Doctor offers a prime image of humanity's dehumanization.

The process of dehumanization, which began with Gregor Samsa's transformation into an insect, continues in many directions in the *Country Doctor* stories. Kafka almost seems to be at his greatest ease and artistic best when he deals with less-than-human beings which inevitably turn out to possess more-than-human qualities. The title story itself produces a couple of unearthly horses which suddenly stick their heads through the windows and stare at doctor, patient, and reader alike. There is a battle charger turned advocate ("The New Advocate") and an ape aping the human race ("A Report to an Academy"). This ape is able to speak and commands an epistolary style which resembles Kafka's—too much, perhaps, for the good of the story. The jackals in "Jackals and Arabs" have reached a similar level of verbal sophistication. Here, however, an ironic contrast is intended—and achieved—between their pretended demand for purity and their actual desire to have the throats of all Arabs slit.* Conversely, there are humans whose main characteristics are borrowed from the animal kingdom. In "An Old Manuscript Page" the nomads do not have a language of their own but "communicate with each other as jackdaws do." (Since this "jackdaw" is the translation of Czech *kavka*, Kafka can be presumed to allude to his own writings when he mentions their screeching, which "is always in our ears.") These nomads are further distinguished by their habit of tearing morsels with their teeth out of the flesh of a living ox. They resemble their horses, who "devour flesh; often enough a horseman and his horse are lying side by side, both of them gnawing at the same joint, one at either end" (146). The nomads are harbingers of death, a trait ascribed to jackdaws by an old and widespread European superstition. Like beasts of prey they

---

* These jackals may be distant cousins of the "red-eyed desert cat" which bites Absalom's child to death in A. Goldfaden's "operetta" *Sulamith*. Kafka saw the play performed by Yiddish actors on October 13, 1911 (*DI*, 95–96), and may have remembered the image at the beginning of 1917 when, according to "Wagenbach," he wrote "Jackals and Arabs." The jackals, by attacking the Arabs, who are racial cousins of the Jews, would then become the image projection of Kafka's introverted hostility toward everything Semitic.

actually kill any animal—one is tempted to say any *other* animal—that crosses their path.

Ostensibly Kafka uses images taken from the animal sphere to illustrate the human one. This is the technique of the fable, a predominantly didactic device which has survived from Aesop's time to that of George Orwell's *Animal Farm*. The essential trait of the genuine fable is its message, which is spelled out or at least unmistakably suggested. Judging from the many and often contradictory interpretations that Kafka's fables have inspired, there is no unequivocal maxim which could be derived from them. They do not indicate anything beyond the bewildering fact that the creatures of this earth—man and animals alike—have left the stations assigned to them. They have confused their properties and exchanged their characteristics. Have the carnivorous nomads become horses? Or do the horses imitate their masters when they gorge themselves on raw meat? Has the ape become human by writing to the academy? Or is this august body made up of monkeys, since they as well as the readers themselves have no difficulties in understanding the creature's speech?

Kafka's speaking animals have lost the innocence traditionally ascribed to nature without gaining human stature, whatever this stature may be. Take the report-writing, handshaking, schnapps-drinking, pipe-smoking ape in "A Report to an Academy." After his capture he was put into a cage. "The whole construction was too low for me to stand up and too narrow to sit down in" (176). This painful and highly symbolical attitude the ape tries to remedy by his humanization. As he explains it at some length, he does not seek freedom but only a way out. He had known freedom as "a spacious feeling: . . . on all sides" when he still roamed through the primeval forest, and he knows that his capture has ended it once and for all. Human freedom, on the other hand, is despicable to him, since it is nothing but the "self-controlled movement" of some trapeze artists whom he had an opportunity to watch in the variety theaters where he performed. He is a realist looking for expediencies. His way out leads him into an in-between sphere which is both human and beastly, and consequently neither manlike nor animallike. His ties with "Mother Nature" are severed, but nature still clings to him. In the middle of his report he has to admit that even his idea of ceasing to be an ape by finding a way out originated in his belly, "since apes think with their bellies" (177). Having finally reached the "cultural level of an average European" (183), he still keeps returning to his consort, a half-trained chimpanzee. His humanization has led him no further than the realization that his companion "has the insane look of the bewildered half-broken animal in her eye," a look to which he is unable to face up. A moralist, that is, a traditional fable writer, would have used this final meeting between two apes for a mirror effect. The ape would have discerned his own downfall in the eyes of his consort and accepted whatever conclusions were still open to him. He may have tried to return to his native forest or he may have despaired and died from the sorrows of exile. Kafka's ape is different. He has adjusted to being neither beast nor man and has learned to live in his thoroughly bastardized condition. "I do not complain, but I am not satisfied either. . . . On the whole . . . I have achieved what I set out to achieve. But do not tell me that it was not worth the trouble. In any case, I am not appealing for any man's verdict, I am only imparting knowledge, I am only making a report" (184). The moral sphere of decisions, which are based on verdicts and eventually lead back to them, is relinquished; in-between figures like this ape are simply reporting on the one and only subject of interest, themselves.

But the ape's education affects his human teacher even more than it does himself. Instead of humanizing the ape, it all but turns his instructor into a simian: "My ape nature fled out of me, head over heels and away, so that my first teacher was almost himself turned into an ape by it, had soon to give up teaching and was taken away to a mental institution." With a certain dry glee the ape adds, "Fortunately he was soon let out again" (183). For other humans are none too different from this simianized man who had tried to humanize an ape.

The process of dehumanization is, with many variations, the unifying theme of the *Country Doctor* stories. It extends to the sketches which concentrate on humans. The "frail consumptive equestrienne" who whirls along in the circus on an "undulating" horse is connected to the world of the animals by her surroundings ("Up in the Gallery"). She is presented to the reader in one long and beautifully modulated sentence that translates the artistic act it describes into stylistic artistry. But the girl herself is soulless, a puppet, an automaton. So are the spectators, "whose hands are really steam hammers." The marionette character of this circus scene prompts the young visitor up in the gallery to burst into tears suddenly and unconsciously; "without knowing it" (145) he seems to understand that he is the lone human being in a universal puppet show, a show given by puppet riders and puppet horses for the benefit of the puppets in the audience.[11]

Schmar, who kills Wese before an urban background which may have been borrowed from a De Chirico painting, is likewise a marionette, which, with grotesque detachment, slits open the belly of another marionette. The story is called "A Fratricide," but there is no indication that Schmar and Wese are actually brothers. All the murderer calls his victim is "old nightshade, friend and beerplacecompanion" (169). They represent humanity, one part of which is murderously set against the other for no apparent reason except that humans are, after all, inhuman. The same can be said of Pallas, a "man of private means" (168), who, sheltered by his privacy, witnesses the scene and is satisfied with its outcome.

The reader is never told the actual reason for this assassination. A semblance of clues may be found, however, in the linguistic roots from which the figures' names are derived: Schmar may hark back to a Hebrew stem denoting "to watch, to be on guard"; Wese from a German one which appears in words like *gewesen* and *das Wesen*, "been" and "being." Alertness seems to have turned murderously against existence itself. Moreover, watchful Schmar, a bachelor, slaughters Wese, a married man. Is Kafka's Jewish heritage revolting against the German language in which it had to express itself? Or is the bachelor seeking revenge on the representative of marriage, the man who leads the good life denied to the Hebrew celibate who has become an assassin? Acoustically, if not logically, an archenmity seems to exist between Schmar and Wese, between the sharp and hissing monosyllable and the trochaic dissyllable evenly balanced on its two bright and open vowels. Beyond mere allusion and play with words and sounds, the reader will not be able to discover any convincing motif for the fratricide.

An atmosphere of vague generalization informs this scene, which is reminiscent of German expressionist movies like *The Cabinet of Doctor Caligari*. In its theatricality, its not quite successful stylization of the acting personages, and the hard and coldly pathetic cadence of its language this story is one of the very few examples that can be cited when Kafka's relationship with expressionism is discussed. Yet even here distinctions have to be made. German Expressionism— especially the Prague school, Franz Werfel, Max Brod, and Paul Kornfeld—is aimed at the spiritual rehabilitation of man, whereas Kafka's "A Fratricide" intends to debunk the myth of human dignity. "Why

aren't you simply a bladder of blood so that I could stamp on you
and make you vanish into nothingness," muses Schmar, bent over
Wese's corpse. "Your heavy remains lie here, already indifferent to
every kick. What is the meaning of the silent question you are asking"
(169)? This being a Kafka story, there are of course innumerable
answers which can be given. Since "A Fratricide" is a melodrama
among marionettes, even the living Wese is little more than a bag full
of blood, a doll whose hollowness was turned inside out and made apparent by the murder. Schmar's question may be a rhetorical one in the
sense that no answer at all is possible.

Man turns into a lifeless thing when time and space cease to function as frames of reference. The grandfather in the story, "The Next
Village," changes into a wondrous monster, a strange specimen resembling a mandrake root when he reflects: "Life is astoundingly
short. To me, looking back over it, life seems so foreshortened that I
scarcely understand, for instance, how a young man can decide to ride
over to the next village without being afraid that—not to mention
accidents—even the span of a normal life that passes happily may fall
short of the time needed for such a ride" (*PC*, 158). This and a short
introductory sentence are the entire text of the parable. It has been
said that it was fear that caused Kafka to tell this remarkably tranquil
tale. This fear, in turn, is nothing but Kafka's response to the superhuman demands made on him by his conscience, a truly holy terror
which in the end is able to produce "the gods, the songs, the archi-
tectures, and the institutions." [12] There is little evidence in the rest of
the *Country Doctor* stories to justify such a romantic interpretation.
Before the startled eyes of a child one of Kafka's metamorphoses takes
place: the realities of time and space which the young listener is just
about to discover withdraw from his ancestor while he speaks. A living being whose lips are still moving freezes into a marionette of old
age and timelessness.

Only a short step leads from man seen as a marionette to man seen
as a number. A distinct parallelism unites the two stories. "Eleven
Sons" and "A Visit to a Mine." Both are basically plotless enumera-
tions of nameless figures. In the latter, ten engineers correspond to the
eleven sons. The sons are joined by their father, the engineers by a
servant employed at the head office of the mine. Moreover, "A Visit to
a Mine" is told by an on-the-scene narrator, who may or may not be
an eleventh engineer. [In any case, what he says betrays his deep concern with the happenings in the mine.] Like the father who passes his
sons in review before the reader, the narrator of the "Visit" rounds

out the number of persons appearing in the two stories. In either instance it is a cast of twelve.

The father boasts: "I have eleven sons" (161). He is the inscrutable center of the family circle. As a matter of course, this central position is taken by the narrator of the "Visit"; yet the mystery of the story seems to have been passed on to the servant, who appears "with one hand tucked behind him, the other in front fingering the gilt buttons or fine facecloth of his uniform" (157). In a never-explained way this servant seems to hold the key to the mystery of the mine:

He keeps bowing to right and left as if we had saluted and he were answering, or rather as if he assumed that we had saluted him, he being too high and mighty to see any salutes. Of course we do not salute him, yet one could almost believe, to look at him, that it is a great distinction to be a servant in the employ of the mine's headoffice.

He is and stays an "unsolved riddle" (157–158), just as is the father, whom we vainly expect to reveal the secrets of his eleven sons and to tell us the reason for his recital. But nothing like it happens. The reader is left to wonder at the symbolism of the number twelve, which in one case indicates the members of a family, in the other a group held together by their professional activities.

The father of "The Eleven Sons" comments on the character traits by which he distinguishes one brother from the other. Yet in the end he shows his own image mirrored elevenfold by the sons with whom he has surrounded himself.[13] Similarly the engineers are silhouetted individually or in couples against the background of the mine, but only their work habits and attitudes are outlined in any detail. They are caricatured by the droll and yet awe-inspiring servant who seems to sum up in his figure all their characteristics. He is the last to vanish into the darkness of the pit; he follows the sequence of the engineers as the father preceded his sons.

Counting from the first son to the eleventh, joining the servant to the ten engineers, Kafka appears to be intent on individualizing them. Yet the progression of numbers obliterates any essential distinction between one figure and the other. One could speculate that Kafka chose the magic number of twelve in analogy with the hours of the day or the months of the year. Followed by the servant, the engineers, at least, pass out of sight as hours and months do: "Besides, our shift will soon come to an end; we shall not be here to see them coming back" (158). Moreover, as the hours and months run full circle to begin anew, so may the sons as well as the group assembled in the mine have been intended to symbolize entities which can be multiplied *ad libitum, ad infinitum,* and *ad absurdum.* Man is certainly cheaper by the dozen. Whatever human individuality is attributed to the single figures is minimized by the roundness of the figure twelve, which, on a clock dial, is identical with zero. In a kind of latter-day magic Kafka adds dozen to dozen to show the namelessness and facelessness of dehumanized humanity. He abstracted his sons and engineers from those areas of human society which contributed most to his own isolation and despair: family and profession, the latter aptly depicted as a dark and dangerous mine.

In this fantastic world of numbers, marionettes, apes, and other inhuman or semihuman figures emerges a being which originated in a completely extrahuman sphere, the thing Odradek ("The Worries of a Family Man").

Some say the word Odradek is of Slavic origin, and try to account for it on this basis. Others again believe it to be of German origin, only influenced by Slavic. The uncertainty of both interpretations allows one to assume with some justification that neither is accurate, especially as neither of them provides an intelligent meaning of the word (*PC*, 160).

Wilhelm Emrich, whom a long study of Kafka has taught to mistrust such seemingly well-meant warnings and to explore the very regions the author declares inexplorable, resolutely asked for the meaning of the word Odradek. He discovered the Czech and generally west-Slavic word *odraditi,* which means to "dissuade someone from doing something." Etymologically the word is connected with the German *Rat* ("advice"). The Slavic influence, then, would appear in the prefix *od-,* which means "off" or "away from" as well as in the diminutive suffix *-ek.*[14] Thus Odradek appears as the little dissuader, a messenger from an unreal world imposed upon the family man's reality. By its arrival alone it poses a problem, but it refuses to offer any information toward a solution. It is, however, willing to betray its name. If the family man had been possessed of Professor Emrich's curiosity and acumen, he might have heard in this name the silent but distinct message, "Do not enter the realm from which I came." The writer himself describes the apparition:

At first sight it looks like a flat star-shaped spool for thread, and really it does seem to have thread wound round about itself; to be sure, they probably are only old, broken-off bits of thread, knotted and tangled together, of the most varied sorts and colors. But it is not only a spool, for a small wooden crossbar extends from the middle of the star, and another small rod is joined to it at a right angle. With the help of this latter little rod on one side and one of the extensions of the star on the other, the whole thing can stand upright as if on two legs.

This is a piece of nonsense delivered in the jargon of a technical expert. It pokes fun at the machines whose inhuman shapes and functions Kafka had to study and describe during his working hours at the Workers' Accident Insurance Institute. It ridicules them by emphasizing their absurdity. The description of Odradek is reminiscent of certain surrealistic constructions found on Paul Klee's canvases or among Alexander Calder's stabiles. At the same time Odradek has too portentous an air to be dismissed simply as the product of a free flight of fancy. In other words, it is, as its name indicates, forbidding as well as amusing. On the surface the image of Odradek may, like many other images of Kafka's, embody a characteristic of its creator. The family man's dry comment, "The whole thing looks senseless enough, but in its own way perfectly finished" (160), can be read as the good-humored self-indictment of a writer who puts artistic perfection above everything and could never completely convince himself that even his most accomplished work made sense.

Wherever Kafka intended to reveal the interpenetration of super-reality and reality, he described reality with painstaking exactitude. Odradek is depicted with almost scientific accuracy, but this "thing" does not live, nor is it able to die: "Anything that dies has had some kind of aim in life, some kind of activity, which has worn out; but this does not apply to Odradek" (161). Senselessly moving from nowhere to nowhere, Odradek succeeds in bestowing a high degree of immediacy upon the nebulous spheres from which it has materialized.

The mystery of a second reality surrounds Odradek. The surface of our everyday reality is pierced by messengers from another reality which have nothing to announce except their names, and through their names their existence and the existence of a preternatural sphere beyond the dehumanized one which men inhabit.[15] This second reality bristles with the "frost of this most unhappy of ages," through which the country doctor is carried by his ghost horses; it is senseless and inscrutable, like the sky that refuses to reveal the future to Wese when he walks into the knife of Schmar; it is as devoid of the Divine as the first reality is empty of the Human. It materializes in Odradek as well as in the warders who arrest Joseph K. in *The Trial* and the officials who prevent K. from entering *The Castle*. These too are dis-

suaders, signposts of the unknowable signifying "Keep out," and yet
they stir the human imagination and whet man's appetite for the forbidden by their appearance. They spread confusion in the minds of
Kafka's heroes because they themselves were born out of confusion,
at a moment when an orderly universe became chaos. Their emergence
in the human sphere is a symptom that the cosmic order has broken
asunder: in a sane and safe universe Odradek would never have been
allowed to appear and frighten the family man. Looking for an orderly
world and its master, Kafka was anxious to discover what was wrong
with reality as it appeared to him. But the *Country Doctor* stories do
not contain more than the most general hints. "A false alarm on the
night bell once answered—it cannot be made good—not ever—" is the
closing line of the title story (143). The "Old Manuscript Page" ends
in a similar vein: "This is a misunderstanding, and because of it we
perish" (147). Because the human and the superhuman, the first and
the second realities, have lost their orderly relation, they now inter-
penetrate, albeit in an act of collision. The results are "false alarms"
and "misunderstandings." The dehumanization on the human side has
led to a despiritualization of the transcendent sphere. In vain does
man try to snatch a last seam of the robe of the vanishing Divine,
just as the Divine tries once more to appear—and frighten the Human.

The relation of the first to the second reality is also the theme underlying "In the Penal Colony." Here Kafka came as close to the metaphysical world as he was allowed to do by his personal situation, for
he always fled from the Divine just as violently as he sought his own
redemption in it. Next to "The Metamorphosis," "In the Penal Colony"
is the longest short story Kafka wrote during his best years. It is also
outwardly the most conclusive. Although it was written in 1914, it was
not published until 1919. In its center emerges another "thing," an
execution machine. The first sentence of the story introduces the
machine as "a peculiar piece of apparatus" (191), a formidable understatement indeed. Although this device is as dead as it is deadly, its
presence so dominates the story that the human figures around it must
be relegated to minor roles; they are not even accorded the privilege
of having proper names.

The machine sits in a deep hollow surrounded on all sides by bare
slopes which isolate it even from the rest of this small island, the site
of a Penal Colony for an unidentified but unmistakably European
power. The machine itself, in its slow, meticulous execution of the

detailed instructions given it, suggests the inevitability of fate. The lunar landscape surrounding it and the sea cutting off the island from the civilized world fortify this impression.

The apparatus seems to rise from the interior of the earth; at the same time it points to the "glare of sunshine poured out" over the valley (219), so that its parts "almost flash out rays" (195). Actually and metaphorically depth and height are united in this death-dealing contraption. It consists of three parts: the Bed, the Harrow, and the Designer. An officer, who appears to be the master as well as the servant of the machine, explains its function with passionate detachment:

On the bed here the condemned man is laid, . . . face down, quite naked, . . . here are straps for the hands, here for the feet, and here for the neck, to bind him fast. Here at the head of the bed . . . is this little gag of felt, which . . . is meant to keep him from screaming and biting his tongue. Of course the man is forced to take the felt into his mouth, for otherwise his neck would be broken by the strap. . . . Both the Bed and the Designer have an electric battery; the Bed needs one for itself, the Designer for the Harrow. As soon as the man is strapped down, the Bed is set in motion, . . . the movements are all precisely calculated, . . . they have to correspond precisely to the movements of the Harrow, . . . the shape of the Harrow corresponds to the human form; here is the harrow for the torso, here are the harrows for the legs. For the head there is only this one small pike. . . . When the man lies down on the Bed and it begins to vibrate, the Harrow is lowered onto his body. . . . As it quivers, its points pierce the skin of the body which is itself quivering from the vibration of the Bed. So that the actual progress . . . can be watched, the Harrow is made of glass. . . . In the Designer are all the cogwheels which control the movements of the Harrow, and this machinery is regulated according to the inscription demanded by the sentence. . . . Whatever commandment the prisoner has disobeyed is written upon his body by the Harrow (194–202).

Taken by itself, the machine is a very simple device: it communicates the guilt of the accused to him by engraving it into his flesh. A popular German adage says: "He who refuses to hear must feel," feel the pain of punishment. Moreover, there exists an etymological connection between "hearing," "listening," and "obeying" (*hören, horchen,* and *gehorchen*) so that Kafka could rely on his German readers to understand intuitively the meaning of his machine: he who disobeyed was bound to feel the consequences on his own body. Translating a proverb into an image, Kafka followed an old convention related to the technique of the fable. Pieter Brueghel used a similar technique when he painted adages current in the Netherlands of his time and filled them with a strange, half-allegorical, half-realistic life. In Kafka's own time European children were still fond of acting charades, which often represented proverbs by living figures, whose message was to be guessed by the onlookers.

Ostensibly the execution is as uncomplicated as the machine. The torture is scheduled to last for twelve hours. (We may note here another appearance of the mystic number twelve. It is in accord with his previous uses of this number to suppose that Kafka intends the twelve hours of punishment to represent an eternity of torture.) "During the first six hours the condemned man lives almost as before, he only suffers pain" (203). Kafka is true to his masochistic view of life when he minimizes the importance of physical suffering. For the condemned man the turning point arrives about the sixth hour, when "insight dawns upon the most stupid. . . .* Nothing more happens than that the man begins to understand the inscription, he purses his mouth as if he were listening" (204). This is, of course, the time when the needles of the Harrow have sunk deep enough into his flesh to start the actual killing. Insight and death are interdependent; together they form the "work" which is to be "completed" during the second six hours. During this time a "look of transfiguration" appears on the face of the sufferer, and the spectators of the execution can now "bathe [their] cheeks in the radiance of a justice which was achieved at long last and was already beginning to fade away" (209). At the end of the period the corpse is automatically cast into a pit, whereupon it is buried.

The simplicity of this machine and its workings is deceptive and proves to be superficial as soon as one questions its purpose. Although the dying man seems to be listening at long last, he is given no chance to obey the command which has reached him too late. He is allowed no second thought, given no opportunity to regret and repent. Without regard for the gravity of his crime a sentence of death is proclaimed as his only means of atonement. Not even the argument most frequently used by the advocates of capital punishment can be said to apply here; the death inflicted by this machine does not serve to deter others from crime. Far from being a grave and ominous event, the execution assumes the character of a popular rally with a definitely

* The poignancy of the German phrase "Verstand geht dem Blödesten auf" defies translation.

festive air; [16] small children are assigned the most favorable locations to "bathe" in this spectacle as if it were the source of a miraculous power. The revelation of a supranatural force seems to appear in the death pangs of the executed man and to vanish as *rigor mortis* freezes his face. There is a certain similarity between the thing Odradek and the execution machine; although both are described realistically in great detail and with much ironic gusto, both serve as messengers from a world far beyond any reality we know.

The mystery expressed by the execution machine is the mystery of the law. As will be seen, this obvious link between "In the Penal Colony" and *The Trial* is more than a superficial one. The law which is executed by the machine has its foundation in a logic well outside the patterns of civilized justice. It seems to us an unjust law, but actually it is related to the justice practiced by primitive tribes and martial courts. Accordingly it is a very primitive verdict that is about to be written into the body of the sinner before us: "Honor your superior" (197). But this primitiveness is just as deceptive as the simplicity of the machine itself. The paradox of this brand of justice is revealed as soon as we consider the question of the guilt which pro-voked this judgment.

The culprit is a private soldier assigned to a Captain. He must serve his superior both as an orderly and as a servant. It seems that he has to perform the latter duties during the day, the former at night. At night he must get up every hour and salute the Captain's door. Apart from the blatant uselessness of this routine, it robs him of the sleep necessary to allow him to satisfy his master during the day. Yet he "must be alert in both functions" (198). Consequently, the unfor-tunate private, "a stupid-looking, wide-mouthed creature with matted hair and bewildered face" (191), has taken the line of least resistance to solve this dilemma: he is found asleep on his master's doorstep when the Captain makes a random check. The superior disciplines him on the spot. Thereupon the soldier catches hold of the officer's legs, crying: "Throw your whip away or I'll devour you." The threat of the insurgent is just as self-contradictory as the offense of which he has been accused: he menaces his master with destruction and yet he remains squatting on the floor. How else could he have shaken the legs of the Captain? The Captain consequently does not take the menace seriously; he simply reports the incident to *his* superior, the officer in charge of the Penal Colony and the execution machine. "The Captain came to see me an hour ago," the officer explains; "I wrote down his statement and appended the sentence to it." There is to be no hearing. "If I had first called the man before me and interrogated him, only confusion would have ensued. He would have told lies, and had I succeeded in exposing these lies, he would have made up for them by new lies, and so forth" (199). To the question "Does he know his sentence?" the answer is given: "There would be no point in telling him. He will learn it on his own body" (197). Clarity, straightforwardness, elimination of possible mistakes, dispersion of all and sundry doubts, distinguish this process of law. "That was all quite simple," the officer sums up (199).

The monolithic simplicity of this system of justice rests on the basic assumption that "guilt is never to be doubted" (198). The officer's guiding principle is echoed later in *The Trial* by the assertion of Titorelli, the court painter, that he had never once experienced a single acquittal (*T*, 192). The Prison Chaplain who remarks in the Cathedral scene of *The Trial* that his court's "proceedings . . . gradually merge into the verdict" (*T*, 264) might just as well be talking about the Penal Colony and its law-enforcing apparatus. K.'s retort to Titorelli, "One single executioner could replace the whole law court" (*T*, 193), takes form in the figure of the officer who serves the Penal Colony simultaneously as judge, jailer, and hangman. In the second sentence of this tale the reader is informed of the accusation; its wording is made known to him in no uncertain terms; he is left to wonder only at the absurd conditions that brought about this action and at the frightening effectiveness of its execution. The verdict of the machine, with its individual message for each victim despite a common manner of execution, corresponds to the door in the parable "Before the Law," which, although intended for only a single individual, leads to a law assumed to be universal.

"In the Penal Colony" and *The Trial* are closely related by their conception of the paradoxical nature of law. They are, however, sharply distinguished from one another by the fact that K.'s guilt in *The Trial* remains unknown, whereas the soldier's offense in this story is more than clearly stated. Since "In the Penal Colony" and *The Trial* are in this way complementary, we may derive from the soldier's guilt certain conclusions concerning the guilt of Joseph K. in the novel. K.'s crime may have been to disobey a self-contradictory demand of a very general nature. Like the soldier, K. may have been expected to do more than he could possibly perform in his simple middle-class world; like the soldier's guilt, his crime may also reflect the primitive cruelty of the authorities persecuting him.

In the novel it is Joseph K. who doubts the system of law which persecutes him. The inarticulate half-wit in the short story could not be entrusted with an intellectual task of this magnitude. Therefore Kafka has provided a doubter in the person of the Explorer who chances upon the soldier's execution and eventually rescues him, seemingly also by chance. Although nameless like the condemned man, he is more readily accessible to the reader's mind. At times he even appears to function as the narrator's double; on the surface the story is told from a point of view only slightly removed from the attitudes and opinions of the traveler. And yet Kafka can be identified as little —and as much—with this Explorer as he is with his antagonist, the officer; he hides behind them and gains many an ironical twist from the distance which still separates him from both figures.

The traveler is a European, and his mind is conditioned by a civilization beyond the sea. He travels "only as an observer," though he presents himself as a man of considerable social, perhaps even political, influence. For he "had recommendations from high quarters, had been received (in the Colony) with great courtesy, and the very fact that he had been invited to attend the execution seemed to suggest that his views would be welcome." Although he is firmly resolved to use the visitor's prerogative and remain aloof, come what may, he cannot deny from the very beginning "the injustice of the procedure and the inhumanity of the execution" (206). He is gradually drawn into the proceedings, ironically for no other reason than that he is an outsider and therefore a disinterested party. Precisely because he is "conditioned" by European ideas, he is called upon to pronounce judgment upon the machine and the legal system it represents. And since he is "basically honest and unafraid" (216), he condemns the machine with the self-assurance of a man nurtured by tolerance and humanitarianism.

His judgment in turn shatters the basis on which the machine and the law of the Penal Colony are constructed. With the cryptic words, "Then the time has come" (217), the officer sets the condemned man free and proceeds to sacrifice himself in his stead. This sacrificial death ruins the machine.

The teeth of a cogwheel showed themselves and rose higher, soon the whole wheel was visible, it was as if some enormous force were squeezing the Designer so that there was no longer room for this wheel, the wheel moved up till it came to the very edge of the Designer, fell down, rolled along the sand a little, stood upright on its rim and then lay flat. But a second wheel was already rising after it (223).

In the hour of its destruction the inhuman machine seems to acquire human life; the wheel stands upright—a feat as unnatural as the upright stance of the thing Odradek; it only loses its "life" when its frame breaks down over the corpse of the officer. With the point of the great iron spike extending from his forehead, the victim fails to show even the slightest trace of the promised redemption. If his death was meant to be a sacrifice, then his offering was not accepted. The words he had instructed the Designer to imprint upon his body were: "Be just" (219)! The officer's death and the breakdown of the machine together mark the termination of the reign of justice as the officer understood it.

This machine, whose composition and decomposition are described with equal perspicuity and love, is Kafka's prime symbol during these years. If his purpose was to concentrate in one universally valid image the process of dehumanization characteristic of the time of the First World War, then he found it here in this symbol of man's self-destructive ingenuity.[17] If he sought to make externally manifest the hidden legal process of *The Trial*, then he found his symbol in this "peculiar piece of apparatus." If, finally, he attempted to catch a glimpse of a transcendent existence behind the rationalized and organized reality of twentieth-century civilization, then his invention of a machine which combined the streamlined glamor of technology with the barbarous primitiveness of a divinely justified martial law was a real stroke of genius. Here, too, the mysterious penetrates the world of experience solely in order to pronounce its principal taboo: "Do not enter." But even the destruction of this monstrous thing leaves a mark on the civilized earth; even when it has disappeared, its ghost lingers on. It continues to haunt the island and succeeds in putting the Explorer to an ignominious flight.

The execution machine may be understood as an image of the tortures to which Kafka, the writer, subjected himself. Apart from translating a proverb into a symbol, it may also express Kafka's belief that writing, his writing, had a deadly quality. When the officer spreads out the sheet of paper with the instructions for the Designer, the Explorer is unable to see anything on it but "a labyrinth of lines crossing and re-crossing each other, which covered the paper so thickly that it

was difficult to discern the blank spaces between them" (202). This
is an accurate description of Kafka's own manuscript pages, which
resemble hieroglyphics of an unknown language, beautiful and terrifying at the same time. The word "labyrinth" indicates a basic structural
design that Kafka has used as a ground plan for many of his works,
especially, as we shall see, for *The Castle*. The two commands the
Designer inscribes— "Honor your superior" and "Be just"—are exactly
the orders to which Kafka, the metaphysical anarchist, and his main
figures give perpetual offense. The word Designer (*Zeichner*) is itself
ambiguous; the verdict it designs can also be understood as the basic
design of many of Kafka's own writings, quite apart from the innumerable drawings (*Zeichnungen*) with which Kafka adorned the margins
of his manuscripts, cryptic ciphers of the message which the writer
knew very well he could not convey by words alone.

The Explorer can admit only that this "labyrinth of lines" is "very
artistic" (*sehr kunstvoll*), when he is asked his opinion about the
judgment in this particular *trial* (throughout "In the Penal Colony"
Kafka alludes to these themes and titles). Being honest, the Explorer
adds, "But I cannot make it out." Here Kafka seems to touch upon
the inherent difficulty any esoteric work of literature—and certainly
his own—holds for its readers. (The word "deadly," so appropriately
describing the script of the Designer, may have been repeated by
Kafka, when in sinister moods he passed judgment on his writings.)
For the initiated the meaning is obvious—what could be simpler to
understand than the command "Honor your superior!" inscribed upon
a lazy mutineer? For the outsider it remains unintelligible, unreadable,
and thoroughly confusing. The officer experiences as reality what for
the Explorer is at best a successful artifice. In other words, the officer
still belongs to a system of belief—whatever the merits of this system
and the creed of this belief may be; the Explorer, a child of the enlightenment, can only see but does not believe. The difficulty that Kafka's
writings, and "In the Penal Colony" in particular, offer the reader
stems from the fact that Kafka himself has taken a stand somewhere
between the officer and the Explorer.

Unlike Kafka's writings, the script used by the Designer contains an
unambiguous message. But this message points parabolically beyond
itself into regions beyond reality. Literally these regions open only
to him who is forced to leave reality, that is, to die. "Yes," answers the
officer, "it is no calligraphy for schoolchildren. You have to keep
reading it a long time. . . . Of course the script must not be simple;

it is not meant to kill a man straight off" (202). The condemned man is not allowed to penetrate the mystery of the written word until his spirit is about to leave his body. "The spirit becomes free only when it ceases to be a support," Kafka noted in his "Reflections" (*DF*, 42). Ironically, it may be added, the moment of insight and "transfiguration" arrives only when the eyes fail. The spiritual freedom Kafka contemplated was a freedom *from* the body and its reality. If, as Brod maintains, Kafka was a figure "pointing the way," [18] then the way he pointed had to cross the valley of death before it could reach the heights of freedom. At least this was the mystique to which he subscribed in 1913 when he entered in his diary: "The immense world I have in my head. But how to free myself and free it without being torn to pieces. And a thousand times better to be torn to pieces than retain it in me or bury it. This, indeed, is why I am here" (*DI*, 288). That the task he performed was a deadly one became apparent to the writer during his working hours, which were spent, as he said, "with . . . a complete opening of the body and the soul." In these hours of ecstatic agony he resembled the victim at the mercy of a torture machine. On August 6, 1914, he wrote:

Thus I waver, continually fly to the summit of the mountain, but can hardly maintain myself up there for a moment. Others waver too, but in lower regions, with greater strength; if they are in danger of falling, they are caught by a kinsman who walks beside them for this very purpose. But I waver up there; it is not death, alas, but the eternal torments of dying (*DII*, 77).

Struggling between life and death, he also experienced the mystical transfiguration of the dying victim. More than once he mentions the sensation of a "great fire," in which even "the strangest fancies . . . perish and are resurrected" and he himself soars "carrying [his] own weight on his back" and moves "as if [he] were advancing in water" (*DI*, 276). In his own body he reenacted the rituals of creation and creator's self-sacrifice, both of which were as tormenting as they were inspiring.

The script of the Designer is certainly more than a code for Kafka's literary work. The German word *Schrift* connotes both "script" and "writing"; it also stands for the Holy Scriptures. Toward the end of his life Kafka said to Gustav Janouch: "It is not by chance that the Bible is called the Scriptures (*die Schrift*)" (*J*, 97). Accordingly he created in the torture machine of "In the Penal Colony" a metaphor of what religion meant to him. To be sure, writing appeared to him as "a form of prayer." But this description takes account of the human attitude only. It is the metaphysical side—the answer, as it were, which man's prayer could expect to be given—that he referred to in the following aphorism: "A belief like a guillotine—as heavy, as light" (*DF*, 44). Pointedly Kafka uses here the indefinite article, *a* belief. For it was not belief in general but only a particular form of it which he likened to a cold and mechanical instrument of death. Unfortunately this particular form of belief was his. Heavy and difficult (*schwer*) before the believer becomes completely aware of the deadly judgment, it becomes easy (*leicht*) afterward when the blades of the guillotine or the Harrow of the torturing machine have done their duty and the victim's spirit is freed from the body it previously had to support. The "labyrinth of lines" which contains the judgment has reminded many a reader of a page printed in Hebrew, just as the grave and final cadence of the officer's commandments may have been borrowed from the Decalogue. But Kafka is far from equating the torture machine with Jewish belief. This is clear if only for so simple a reason as that its purpose radically contradicts the ethic of the Sixth Commandment: "Thou shalt not kill." The paradoxical character of this image consists in the fact that it expresses only a belief, a way of writing, a personal conflict, and yet seems to possess a parabolical, that is, universal, validity. Instead of showing man as a killer of God, it represents God as a hunter and slayer of men.

In its primitiveness the torture machine points to an archaic stage of religious development. This stage appears, in the mind of the officer, as the golden age of the human race, an epoch of superhuman order imposed upon a world guilty by its very existence. No bond or covenant could possibly be concluded between this law and mankind. Instead their relation was one of magic. The Bed of the torture machine is an altar, on which a man is slaughtered in honor of the monstrous idol, Law. If the idol is merciful—and it seems to have been merciful in the past whenever its appetite was sated—it performed a miracle in return and transfigured the victim. In spite of its mechanical sophistication the apparatus seems to be a relic from the times of primordial savagery. Its destruction appears as the precondition for the dawning of a new age, which is more human as well as more rational.

But appearances in Kafka are deceptive. The Penal Colony was the work of the old Commandant, a legendary figure who invented the machine and even drew the patterns for the Designer. We need not

stray too far afield from Kafka's intentions to call the old Commandant
the Archdesigner. "Did he combine everything in himself?" asks the
incredulous Explorer. "Was he soldier, judge, mechanic, chemist, and
draughtsman?" "Indeed he was," the officer replies without a moment's
hesitation (196). This Commandant, who united in his person the
functions of Lord of Hosts, Supreme Judge, and Creator, had died a
long time before, leaving responsibility for the machine to the officer.
But the officer has been allowed only the burden of the old Commandant's heritage; the authority has passed on to another man. A
managerial type, the new Commandant has turned away from the
administration of justice, as his predecessor understood it. He has
focused his interest on the economic and political rehabilitation of
the island and does his best to transform the Penal Colony into a
civilian one. With his appearance life on the island has acquired an
atmosphere of democratic liberalism. While allowing the machine to
disintegrate in its hidden valley, he opens the Colony to the world
by improving its port installations. Politically the new Commandant
has destroyed the autocratic regime of the old one by appointing
a commission of all the senior officers. To his annoyance even the Penal
Officer has been made a member of this body. Moreover, the transient
visitor from abroad, the Explorer, is expected to express his opinion
before this commission, a polite gesture, obviously intended to better
public relations and create international good will. The officer cannot
help interpreting this diplomatic nicety as a clever move by which
the new Commandant intends to undermine his position still further:

He has calculated it carefully: this is your second day on the island, you did
not know the old Commandant and his ways, . . . perhaps you object on
principle to capital punishment. . . . Now, taking all this into consideration, would it not be likely (so thinks the Commandant) that you might
disapprove of my methods (211)?

Thereupon the officer goes to work on the mind of the Explorer, trying
to swing him to his side by brainwashing him. Falling prey to his prejudices and illusions, he finally comes close to seeing in the Explorer
a defender of the faith, his own faith, of course. At the end of a
tortuous monologue he all but entrusts to the Explorer the final verdict
over his system of justice. (With an equally grotesque misjudgment
the jackals in "Jackals and Arabs" heap all their grudges and hopes on
a traveler from the "far North": "Master, you are the one to end this
quarrel which divides the world. . . . And so, master, . . . by means

of your all-powerful hands slit the Arabs' throats through with these scissors" [152–153]! The scissors as an instrument for cleansing the world bear a remarkable similarity to the torture machine as well as to the "guillotine" representing Kafka's belief.)

But the officer's plea for the Explorer's intervention is not only a sign of his utter failure at psychology, it is also a sin against the very system for which he stands. As a matter of course the officer has denied the condemned man all legal assistance and outside help; now, having nonsensically maneuvered himself into the position of a defendant, he clamors for the very help he had refused to grant. Thereby he offends the law under which he has been operating and indicts himself, even before the Explorer—and through him the new Commandant—have rejected the executioner, and with him his system. The commandment "Be just!" through which he dies, can only mean: Be as just unto yourself as you are to others! It is this justice unto himself which the officer practices when he allows himself to be strapped down on the Bed of the machine. The judge has proved to be guilty himself, and the law is forced to turn against its most faithful executioner. With him the law eliminates itself. It is the end of the trial.

And yet this end of the trial indicates neither the end of the law nor the victory of the new era. Kafka carefully keeps his distance from the new Commandant just as he did from the old. The new Commandant never enters the scene. Whatever we learn about him is colored by the officer's irate words. It cannot be denied that he brought a note of moderation to the island as well as introduced a feminine element. Indeed, the new Commandant seems to have surrounded himself with ladies, who follow him wherever he goes, dampen any loud word uttered in his presence (212), and disturb the execution by stuffing "the condemned man with sugar candy before he is led off." One does not have to be partial to the officer's way of thinking to notice an objective incongruity in his caustic observation that the condemned man "has lived on stinking fish his whole life and now he has to eat sugar candy" (207)! We are, after all, still on a primitive island. Even the officer has begun to succumb to the ladies' luxurious-ness; under the collar of his uniform he has tucked two of their delicate handkerchiefs, confiscated from the condemned soldier to whom they had been given first (192, 220). All this means that the standards on the island have been confused through the ladies' presence. Adoringly they call the new Commandant's voice "a voice of thunder" (212), an attribute incompatible with his mild attitudes and probably borrowed from his gruffly masculine predecessor. By the repeated turn of the phrase, "the Commandant's ladies" (207, *et passim*), the officer furthermore seems to imply the existence of romantic bonds between the new executive and his entourage. Finally there is a fragment belonging to "In the Penal Colony," which shows the new Commandant "blithely" ordering his laborers to prepare the way for the "snake, . . . the great Madame. . . . She is a snake without peer, she has been thoroughly pampered by our labor and by now there is nobody to compare with her. . . . She should call herself Madame at least" (*DII*, 179). Kafka never disclosed what he had in mind when he drafted this obscure alternative to his story. But the snake, whose way the new Commandant was to prepare, inevitably evokes the image of the serpent in the Garden of Eden, whereas "Madame" is a euphemism for the keeper of a brothel. Here as elsewhere in his stories Kafka uses women as symbols to show how the order of the law is being weakened by the temptations of sex. The company he keeps is meant to discredit the new Commandant not only in the eyes of the Explorer but in those of the reader as well. Even if the new Commandant is to remain the Colony's master after the close of the story, the effectiveness of his command has been called in question.

Nor does Kafka take an altogether favorable view of the other exponent of modern civilization, the Explorer. To positivistic readers the Explorer will appear as one of their own. Austin Warren describes him as "a naturalist, a scientist who shares the humanitarian views of his secularist generation but who, as a social scientist, is capable of intellectual curiosity and a suspension of judgment." [19] This "suspension of judgment" seems to have lured the officer into entrusting the Explorer with the final decision in the matter of the machine. In his despair he chooses as his advocate the self-styled spokesman of progressive enlightenment. But on closer examination we see that this does not describe the Explorer altogether accurately. He cannot conceal from himself his ever-growing fascination for the infernal apparatus. At first he is attracted by the technical perfection of the mechanics of the machine. Hardly has the officer begun to demonstrate the instrument when the Explorer feels "a little captivated" (195). When the machinery is tentatively set into motion, he forgets the deadly purpose of this brilliant technical performance. His only annoyance at this point is caused by a disturbance in the wheels: "If the wheel had not creaked, it would have been glorious" (203). When he becomes conscious of the conflict between the "glorious" play of the instrument and the horrifying end served by this play, he settles for a compromise: he remains opposed to the system but admits that he has been "touched" by the "sincere conviction" of the officer (217). He is determined to preserve his neutrality even when events take an unexpected turn and the officer prepares to take the soldier's place. "He knew very well what was going to happen, but he had no right to obstruct the officer in anything. If the judicial procedure which the officer cherished was really so near its end, . . . then the officer was doing the right thing; in his place the Explorer would not have acted otherwise" (220–221). Unlike the officer, the Explorer has no absolute norm he feels bound to follow. In a sense deeper than the one suggested by Warren his judgment is indeed suspended; it has no basis and no aim. He decides to let this exotic ritual take its course, all the more so as he sees it as the last of its kind.

Ultimately the Explorer is only a practicing cultural relativist. With the hauteur of the civilized man he observes the behavior pattern of a group of people alien and inferior to his own. What seemed at first to be a deeply felt attitude—his hostility to the machine and the system supporting it—was only a conditioned reflex, the defense mechanism of positivist rationality faced by the archaic and irrational.

The end of the story proves this point, perhaps even too drastically. Followed by the rescued soldier and his guardian, a fellow soldier, the Explorer reaches the beach and starts bargaining with the ferryman to row him to the steamer.

By the time [the two soldiers] reached the foot of the steps the Explorer was already in the boat, and the ferryman was just casting off from the shore. They could have jumped into the boat, but the Explorer lifted a heavy knotted rope from the floor boards, threatened them with it, and so kept them from attempting the leap (227).

Since, after all, it is the Explorer who saved the soldier from death, he might be expected to show some signs of enduring interest in him. Now he is offered an opportunity to give concrete proof of the humanitarianism for the sake of which he rejected the machine before. But the Explorer remains unmoved, and by missing this opportunity reveals a sluggishness of heart which parallels the premeditated cruelty expressed by the torture machine; man does not matter in either case. And yet there is a distinction to be made. The mind which devised the machine was a primitive one, still untouched by the idea of humanitarianism. The Explorer, on the other hand, represents the processes

of dehumanization which corrodes any civilization in the hour of its
decline. Prehumanitarianism and posthumanitarianism meet in this
story. The bewildered and wordless human creature, the soldier, is
neglected by both.

This Explorer appears as a caricature of twentieth-century materialism: he is indifferent to the drama he happens to have witnessed,
dazzled by the achievements of technology without regard for their
primitive origins and savage ends, and willing to pay lip service to
progressive and liberal ideals but incapable of applying them even to
the simplest action. Unlike any other Kafka figure, he is allowed to
return home. From the ease with which he refuses help to the survivors
of the ghastly scene we can conclude that he will not find it difficult
to wipe the nightmare from his memory. For him Western civilization
will remain intact in spite of the mechanized barbarism he has experienced somewhere on the fringes of his culture.

Kafka seems to pass judgment on the Explorer during this last scene,
but we cannot accept this judgment as final because he was never
satisfied with this ending. When, in a letter to Kurt Wolff, he called
the last two or three pages of the story "wretched" (*Machwerk*) (*B*,
159), he probably was annoyed at the obviousness of the conclusion:
how could he allow the Explorer to escape? The letter is dated September 4, 1917; less than a month before he entered in his diary several attempts to continue the story in a different vein. One of these sketches
contains the vision of the "Great Madame" quoted above; another
shows the executed officer, "the spike protruding from his shattered
forehead," as he appears in the Explorer's imagination, carrying the
traveler's baggage. "A conjuring trick?" the Explorer asks. "No," the
ghost officer replies, "a mistake on your part; I was executed on your
command" (*DII*, 181). Here the Explorer is resolved to report at home
what he has seen on the island; he will bear witness; he betrays
sympathy, a tendency Kafka abandoned because it was neither in con-
formity with the character of the Explorer nor with the air of annoyance which, as Kafka knew very well, pervades the whole story. During
the officer's self-execution the traveler found the presence of the soldier
and the guardian annoying (222). (The German word *peinlich*
includes also the nuance of "painful.") The same word reappears in
a letter to Wolff, who had found fault with "In the Penal Colony" as
a whole on account of its *Peinlichkeit*. "To explain my last story,"
Kafka wrote,

I only want to add that it is not unique in being painfully annoying. Rather, our time in general and my own time in particular were and continue to be likewise very annoying, and my particular time even more so than time in general. God knows how deep I would have gotten this way if I had continued to write or, better, if my circumstances and my condition had permitted me to write, as I, all my teeth buried in all my lips (*sic!*) had wished to do (*B*, 150 [October 11, 1916])!

Had he continued to write, the end would have been even more excruciating.

Even as the story now stands, it contains intimations of the future Kafka had in mind for his Penal Colony, and perhaps for the world at large. Early in his explanations the officer mentions the old Commandant's followers: during his lifetime

the Colony was full of [them] . . . there are still many left but none will admit it. If you were to go to the teahouse today, on execution day, and listen around, you would perhaps hear only ambiguous remarks. All of these would be made by partisans, but under the present Commandant and his present doctrines they are of no use to me (208).

The teahouse is one of "the first houses of the Colony"; it lies between the harbor installations of the new Commandant and the torture machine of the old. The Explorer stops there on his way to the sea. Being a sensitive observer, he immediately comes under the spell of "historical reminiscences" and feels "the power of past days." He notices the "cool, damp air"—the air of a tomb—which emanates from the interior. Soon he learns that "the old man," that is, the old Commandant, is buried here. He is shown a gravestone hidden under a table. Its inscription reads: "Here rests the old Commandant. His followers, who now must be nameless, have dug this grave and set up this stone. There is a prophecy that after a certain number of years the Commandant will rise again and lead his followers from this house to reconquer the Colony. Have faith and wait!" At first the letters of this inscription are as illegible as the "labyrinth" of the script of the Designer. Only after the Explorer has gone down on his knees is he able to decipher this writing, the last in a story dedicated to the imagery of *Schrift*. Although the Explorer has a perfectly rational excuse for bending his knees, the reader cannot help feeling that here at last he pays his involuntary respect to the spirit of the old Commandant. When he rises up again, the bystanders catch his eyes.

They are "poor humiliated folk, . . . strong men with short, glistening, full black beards, . . . probably dock laborers." The Explorer does not hear any of the ambiguous remarks that the officer had predicted, but he notices on their faces a smile, "as if they too had read the inscription, had found it ridiculous and were expecting him to agree with them" (225–226). This is, of course, only the Explorer's ready-made explanation. A silent smile is the epitome of ambiguity; it may also be understood as a sign of amusement caused by the foreigner's obvious skepticism. It may even be the smile of an expectancy that is sure of its eventual fulfillment.

In view of the fact that Kafka experimented in the fragments with the idea of allowing the executed officer to reappear, this last interpretation would seem plausible. In this case the bystanders are partisans of the old Commandant, as the officer predicted. They form a group quite apart from the officer, who, we learn, is ashamed of the lowliness of this burial place and has made several attempts to exhume the Commandant's remains. As partisans they have gone underground and have buried their master in their midst. One of them may have inscribed this "testament" on the tombstone. Perhaps they even know the exact number of years after which their leader will return. In any case it is the "good message" of the "testament" which unites the meek and oppressed dock laborers into a flock of disciples. There may even be among them fishermen who were forced into their new profession by the new Commandant's reforms. The smiling presence of these disciples changes the teahouse into a cleverly camouflaged sanctuary. In this light it can no longer be viewed as a somewhat exotic counterpart of a European coffeehouse, where rumors are also bred and many divergent sects convene. Its atmosphere is now more unified and assumes the air of a sacred shrine. Following this trend of thought to its conclusion, we may compare the teahouse with another old inn from which another old belief, Judaism, proceeded into the world, rejuvenated, as Christianity. The execution machine may be likened to the Cross, the suicide of the officer to a sacrificial death. The words on the tombstone, "Have faith and wait!" acquire an almost evangelical ring. The imagery of the story as a whole suddenly seems to carry definite overtones of Christian symbolism.

But as soon as we take the inscription on the old Commandant's grave seriously, a strictly religious interpretation of "In the Penal Colony" becomes untenable. The faith that the old Commandant's followers are admonished to preserve cannot be anything but belief in their master's rigorous martial law. This law is no more to be identified with Judaism than Christian hope is to be derived from the old martinet's return to the Colony. The prophecy promises the recapture of the island, and from all the intelligence we have gathered about the old Commandant's attitude we may safely infer that the conquest will be by force. There will be violence, bloodshed, and the blind execution of an inhuman law. So well has Kafka succeeded in identifying the old Commandant with his infernal machine that the reemergence of the one is bound to be followed by the reconstruction of the other. The war of recovery will be fought and won under the sign of the torturing machine. The chances are that many a one who is now hoping for the old Commandant's return will find himself strapped one day to its Bed, the Harrow ready to imprint his offense upon his body.

The prophecy of the teahouse scene reopens the story of "In the Penal Colony" and extends it into an infinite future. The promised return of the old Commandant is intended to hint at a second coming of the execution machine and its deadly writing. The real hero of the story, the "peculiar piece of apparatus," survives in spite of its ruin, unconquered and unconquerable. Kafka did not find an end to the visions of horror which haunted him.

CHAPTER V

Der Verschollene

The Innocence of Karl Rossmann

AS early as July 10, 1912, Kafka wrote a letter to Max Brod containing some vague allusions to the story which he later was to call *Der Verschollene* ("The Boy Who Was Never More Heard Of") and which was published posthumously as *Amerika*. The letter read, in part:

The novel is as great as if it had been sketched across the whole sky (also as colorless and as uncertain as this day), and I get entangled in the first sentence that I want to write. But I have found out already that I must not be deterred by the hopelessness of what I have written and I profited considerably yesterday by this experience (*B*, 96).

On September 30, 1915, he compared in his diaries the hero of this novel, with which he still seemed to be occupied, and the hero of *The Trial*: "Rossmann and K., the guiltless and the guilty, both executed without distinction in the end, the guiltless one with a gentler hand, more pushed aside than struck down" (*DII*, 132). Two years later, on October 8, 1917, while reading Dickens' *David Copperfield*, he commented on the first chapter of his story:

"The Stoker," a sheer imitation of Dickens, the projected novel even more so. The story of the trunk, the boy who delights and charms everyone, the menial labor, his sweetheart on the country estate, the dirty houses, *et al.*, but above all the method. It was my intention, as I now see, to write a Dickens novel, but enhanced by the sharper lights I should have taken from the times, and the duller ones I should have gotten from myself. . . . [Dickens] gives one a barbaric impression because the whole does not make sense, a barbarism that I, thanks to my weakness and wiser for my being his epigone, have been able to avoid (*DII*, 188, 189).

We do not know the name Kafka would have given his novel eventually. Nor do we possess any certainty about Karl Rossmann's ultimate fate. For Kafka's plan to have him "executed" is contradicted by Brod, who remembers, "From what he told me, I know that the incomplete chapter about the nature theatre of Oklahoma . . . was intended to be the concluding chapter of the work and should end on a note of reconciliation" (277).* Kafka's natural hesitation in deciding upon conclusive endings for his stories has, in the case of *Der Verschollene,* an outward and objective reason. He had begun to write the novel sometime in 1911 or 1912, in any case before the breakthrough, and the meeting with F. B. in August 1912. Thus he had to apply the vastly enhanced and refined creative powers that this crisis had produced in him to the completion of a plan whose derivative character became more and more clear to him and whose vastness was, as he early recognized, imperiled by his uncertainty about it. Indeed, he seems very soon to have become aware of the incompatibility of the material at hand with the new means now at his disposal.

The diary entry of September 25, 1912, is followed by the final version, still untitled, of "The Stoker" (*DI*, 330). Its appearance here leaves us uncertain whether he composed this first chapter of *Der Verschollene* after the breakthrough or only recast older material to fit a new style. Although he continued his work on the novel proper, Kafka acknowledged the independence of "The Stoker" by agreeing to its publication in Kurt Wolff's series *Der Jüngste Tag,* where it appeared in May 1913. His decision to release the manuscript may be taken as an indication that he had given up the hope of finishing the longer story of which it was a part. He treated "The Stoker" as he was to treat the parable "Before the Law," which in his will he condemned as part of *The Trial,* while he allowed it to "survive" independently as one of the *Country Doctor* stories. Just as "Before the

---

* Numbers without letters refer to the 1946 American edition entitled *Amerika.* As will be seen from the following interpretation, especially pp. 124–129 and p. 162, the name *Der Verschollene* seems more appropriate to me. Wherever the context permitted me to do so, I have used this title instead of *Amerika.*

Law" contains in essence a statement about Kafka's relation to the
world of metaphysics, so does "The Stoker" in an exemplary way probe
his attitude toward the physical world, even though it was a reality
he had never experienced.

Kafka with the Red Carnation

Recent investigations have focused on Kafka's interest in socialist
ideas and their application to the capitalist setting he provided for
Der Verschollene. Theodor W. Adorno remarks with unconcealed
satisfaction that the insight "into economic tendencies was not so alien
to Kafka as the hermetic method of his narrative techniques would
lead us to assume." [1] Wilhelm Emrich calls his chapter on *Amerika*
"The World of Modern Industry" and sets the tone of his interpretation
in the following sentences: "The novel belongs to the most clairvoyant
poetic revelations of modern industrial society known in world literature. The secret economic and psychological mechanisms of this society
and their satanic consequences are pitilessly bared in it." [2]

Kafka encountered socialism when he attended high school. His
classmate, Hugo Bergmann, remembers that at the age of sixteen years
Kafka demonstrated his radical political convictions by displaying in
his buttonhole a red carnation, the traditional party flower of European
socialists. [3] It is now difficult to establish with any degree of certainty
whether this adolescent gesture was meant to convey Kafka's sympathy
for socialism or his protest *against* home and school. In any case he
has documented his resistance against the social aspirations of his
father and the sham civilization of Prague's German Jewry in the
"Letter to His Father," tracing it back to the time of his youth. On the
other hand, he fails to mention there any positive interest in social
and political problems. At the same time he was passing through a
period of agnosticism, reading Darwin, and, "with uncommon enthusiasm," Haeckel's materialistic *Riddles of the Universe*. [4]

The student Kafka could not have behaved more normally. Curiosity
led him to explore the intellectual movements which excited young
people around the turn of the century. He did not differ from the rest
of his intelligent contemporaries who sought a way out of the stifling
atmosphere of their homes and the rigid formalism of their schools,
a way that was to lead them into a freedom still unknown. Trying to
discover their own identity, these young Jews of Prague took the road
to social and political freedom, which, in the beginning of the nine-

teenth century, the young German Jews Heinrich Heine and Ludwig Börne had taken—to their inevitable disappointment. Young Kafka's typical behavior contradicts his image of himself as a man who was an outcast from the beginning, deserted by everyone.

More significant and problematical is the attraction which the anarchist *Klub Mladých* ("Club of the Young") had ten years later for Kafka, then an employee of the Workers' Accident Insurance Institute. At the meetings of this club he met Jaroslav Hašek, the future author of *The Good Soldier Schweik*. Hašek was an eccentric rebel, possessed of a black humor, and Kafka could not have helped sensing the affinity of their personalities. He was present when Hašek, tongue in cheek, gave an election speech for the "Political Party of Moderate Progress within the Law," [5] and must have been fascinated by the game the seemingly debonair anarchist made of authority. There Hašek—in the final analysis as self-destructive a character as Kafka— tried to outwit, bluff, bypass, and stultify the powers that be, pointing the way not only to his own Schweik but to Kafka's protagonists from Georg Bendemann in "The Judgment" to the K.'s in *The Trial* and *The Castle*. Of course, all this was much less a profession of socialism than an anticipation of the sabotage in which the Czechs were to excel during the First World War. Hašek was to describe the practice and Kafka the metaphysics of this sabotage in their later books.

Kafka was by nature unable to become a member of *any* party, precisely because his temperament was anarchic. He had the evil eye of a born critic and the desperate courage to utter his criticism even when it was most inappropriate to do so. In his books he criticized the invisible authorities of the universe by taking the secular powers to task. He would have suffered under any regime and would have revolted against it. Both he and Hašek would have ended up in prison if socialism had materialized in their day and age.

In his later years Kafka was quite aware of the dangers socialism was to generate once it changed from an idea to reality. Sometime after 1920 he went for a walk with Gustav Janouch. They met a group of workmen who were marching with flags and banners to a party meeting. Kafka said:

These people are so self-possessed, so self-confident, and in high spirits. They rule the streets, and therefore think they rule the world. In reality, they are mistaken. Behind them already are the secretaries, officials, professional politicians, all the modern sultans for whom they are preparing the way to power.

To Janouch's question, whether he did not expect the Russian Revolution to expand, he answered: "The wider a flood spreads, the shallower and dirtier becomes the water. The revolution evaporates, what remains is the mud of a new bureaucracy. The chains of tormented mankind are made of red tape." Kafka's own world was governed by corrupt officials, deceived deceivers in the employ of an inaccessible central agency. This is what he meant by calling communism a "religious matter": "These interventions, revolts, the blockade—what are they? They are short preludes of the great and cruel religious wars, which will rage across the world" (*J*, 71). He did not justify these wars by calling them religious; rather did he express his doubts in the secularized religions of his day which would result in wars, the outcome of which would be the replacement of one cruel bureaucracy by another. He was haunted by the intellectual's fear of history: "The war, the Revolution in Russia, and the misery of the whole world appear to me like a flood of evil. . . . Historical events are no longer determined by the individual but by the masses. We are shoved, rushed, swept away. We are victimized by history" (*J*, 72).

As a student of law and, for the greater part of his life, an employee of the Workers' Accident Insurance Institute, Kafka could not remain blind to the political problems of his age. After all, he was not only an inspired writer but an intelligent man. Resentment of the working conditions which drained his energies and prevented him from fulfilling his true vocation and writing books is a natural reflex. But to interpret his works by the laments and complaints of his diaries, letters, and conversations and to suggest that Kafka's visions were directed against the *Zeitgeist*, the "imperialist period," the "stage of late capitalism," or the "world of modern industry," carries the danger of overlooking his peculiar relation to reality. The social world, which he at times gently derided, at others cruelly distorted, served him only as the material which he manipulated arbitrarily to express what he could not express by sheer imitation in this or any other material.

The reality in *Der Verschollene* is secondhand material. Besides Dickens it is taken from Benjamin Franklin's *Autobiography* and, perhaps, from the beginning of Edgar Allan Poe's *The Narrative of Arthur Gordon Pym* and some chapters in Ferdinand Kürnberger's *Der Amerikamüde*.[6] Because of the tenuous and derivative nature of this material Kafka was unable to come to grips with it. It crumbled under the touch that was eager to penetrate and transform it. Then, unexpectedly, we are introduced to visions which are completely

Kafka's own and show the mastery of his mature style. Even "The Stoker" abounds with suprarealistic details and indicates the direction Kafka, "wiser for his being an epigone" would have given the whole book had the original plan allowed him the necessary freedom. To mention the red carnation Kafka displayed in 1900 means little more than to indicate the distance he had progressed from his youthful socialism (however hypothetical it may have been) when he entered the first chapter of *Der Verschollene* in his diaries in 1912.

The Reality of Amerika

As Karl Rossmann, a boy of sixteen, who had been packed off to America by his poor parents because a servant girl had seduced him and gotten herself pregnant, stood on the liner which was already slowing down as it entered the harbor of New York, he saw the statue of the Goddess of Liberty, sighted long before, as if it had been illuminated by a suddenly increased burst of sunshine. The arm with the sword rose up as if recently stretched aloft, and round the figure blew the free winds (1).

Als der sechzehnjährige Karl Rossmann, der von seinen armen Eltern nach Amerika geschickt worden war, weil ihn ein Dienstmädchen verführt und ein Kind von ihm bekommen hatte, in dem schon langsam gewordenen Schiff in den Hafen von New York einfuhr, erblickte er die schon längst beobachtete Statue der Freiheitsgöttin wie in einem plötzlich stärker gewordenen Sonnenlicht. Ihr Arm mit dem Schwert ragte wie neuerdings empor, und um ihre Gestalt wehten die freien Lüfte.

These first two sentences of *Der Verschollene*, so densely packed with information, allude to the images and situations which dominate the rest of the book. Karl Rossmann's name establishes him as a relative of his author and Kafka's other principal figures. The inevitable "K" emerges, if only as the initial of his Christian name. The "mann" in Rossmann recalls the name Bendemann in "The Judgment," where it appeared as "a strengthening" of the first part "to provide for all the as yet unforeseen possibilities in the story." Karl Rossmann's possibilities lie indeed in the prospect of his becoming a *Mann*. Ross ("horse"), on the other hand, is an animal name, as is Kafka's own. Looking closely, one will discover a pronounced difference between K. in *The Trial* and Karl Rossmann. K. is as old as Kafka was at the time when he wrote the novel, but Karl is thirteen years younger than his author. It may be no coincidence that his sixteen years (mentioned in the German original as the third word of the sentence, preceding even the boy's name) correspond exactly with Kafka's age during his "socialist" period. Thus the author is able to look upon his figure with the eyes of a benevolent but highly critical older relative.

Karl is about to observe New York, "the most modern New York," as Kafka later wrote in a letter to Kurt Wolff (*B,* 117). Actually the first two sentences contain not so much the panorama of the city opening before the boy's eyes as a fixed image suddenly apprehended. The liner has slowed down and the light is "suddenly increased." The feeling is that of a flash photograph; the stream of life is interrupted by the light and recorded forever in its startled suspension. The vivid lifelessness of this passage suggests that Kafka wrote it while actually contemplating a photograph of New York. At the same time an atmosphere of something beyond reality is achieved by the stylistic paradox of a motion which has become motionless.

The Statue of Liberty has been changed into the monument of a goddess. However much impressed poor immigrants are by F. A. Bartholdi's creation, few have surrounded it with an aura of divinity. Karl Rossmann, however, not only elevates Liberty to Olympian status, he replaces the torch in her hand with a sword, the attribute of Justice. America, the promised land, changes into a Paradise Lost, guarded by a divine messenger brandishing the weapon of wrath. Since Rossmann had "sighted" the statue "long before," this change must have occurred in the very moment when all movement stopped. With a shock of recognition Karl perceives his past and future in this instant of petrified astonishment. To be sure, he has come to the "Land of the Free," and freedom, tolerance, and enlightenment are aptly represented by Liberty's torch. Yet Karl owes his arrival on these shores to a punishment; he has been "packed off by his parents"; the sword of justice has pointed the way to his voyage. The reappearance of the fearful weapon high over the port installations of New York is bound to discourage his hopes of an easy release from justice into the green pastures of America's freedom. All he finds free are the winds blowing round the figure of the goddess. To him, however, she promises nothing but a series of tests and trials. The question posed by the novel is whether he will be able to pass under the sword.

Since it is highly improbable that Kafka mistook the torch in the hand of Bartholdi's Liberty for a sword, and this slip—if it was a slip —could not possibly have escaped the attention of his friends and his publisher, it is safe to assume that he willingly and consciously gives us here a glimpse into the method with which he approached the reality of this America. Had he intended to unmask the American concept of freedom and criticize American democracy by baring its inner workings,* his imagination would have endowed the goddess with a less awe-inspiring attribute. The Sword of Liberty, however, is not drawn against the social injustices bred by America's capitalism; it is pointed against Karl Rossmann's conscience.

However, even "The Stoker" is, like the rest of the novel, a work of transition. Kafka was not yet able to blend realism and vision completely. His first sentence is phrased in the composed cadences of an objective narrator, whereas the second—the metamorphosis of the Statue of Liberty—reflects the subjective reaction of a perplexed boy. The first sentence compresses a vast amount of information into a sequence of long, beautifully controlled, and intricately intertwined periods; the second is artless, not quite coherent, and inconclusive. Kafka abandons too quickly the point of view of the narrator and assumes too readily the role of his hero to be able to persuade us that the shift was fully intentional. A certain erratic quality prevails throughout Kafka's first novel. Sometimes the knowing author seems to address the reader; at others he speaks to the protagonist, who is, and is meant to be, ignorant in matters of reality, and in most other matters.

Moreover, Kafka included in this novel insights which he could have found neither in his literary sources nor in the reality of his own everyday life. The following description of Uncle Jacob's business has been quoted as perhaps Kafka's most poignant disclosure of the structure of high capitalist economy:

It was a sort of commission and despatch agency such as, to the best of Karl's knowledge, was probably not to be found in Europe. For the business did not consist in the transference of goods from the producer to the consumer or to the dealers, but in the handling of all the necessary goods and raw materials going to and between the great manufacturing trusts. It was consequently a business which embraced simultaneously the purchasing, storing, transport and sale of immense quantities of goods and had to maintain the most exact, unintermittent telephonic and telegraphic communication with its various clients (42).

Where did Kafka learn about the function of the commission trade? Was it really as "strangely empirical" as Theodor W. Adorno has characterized it? [7] Commercial customs like these Kafka could have encountered neither in his father's retail store nor in the economy of Old

---

* As Bertolt Brecht did, in 1929, in St. Joan of the Stockyards.

Austria in general. His "empirical" method originated in his imagination, which created symbols of modern life's dehumanization by enlarging and accentuating the symptoms actually offered him by reality. Afterward reality caught up with Kafka's fantasies. Similarly he used the comparatively insignificant iniquities he had to suffer in his professional life to produce images of universal injustice, images which, after his death, materialized in the jurisdiction of the totalitarian states and in the hypertrophy of their bureaucracies. Yet Kafka the novel writer was not concerned with prophecy but with the literary validity of the images he produced.

Undoubtedly *Der Verschollene* is imbued with social compassion. But this feeling is relived as a memory, the recollection which the almost thirty-year-old Kafka shared with sixteen-year-old Karl Rossmann. He tried, admittedly not always successfully, to stay aloof from the enthusiasms and despairs which sway his adolescent hero. He did so primarily by showing time and again how Karl's intercessions in favor of wretched people bore no other results than the increased misery of all persons concerned, not excluding Karl himself.

Young Rossmann feels as young Kafka may have felt. The narrator, on the other hand, knows and tells his story from the vantage point of the disillusionment that all knowledge entails. The basic design of *Der Verschollene* is that of an apprenticeship novel—the education of a hero in the knowledge his author believes that he possesses. Hence it stands to reason that in this novel Kafka would be concerned with the development of Karl Rossmann rather than with the "baring" of the "secret economic and psychological mechanisms" of American society, let alone their "satanic consequences." Not the reality, present or future, of a civilization far away from Kafka's Prague, but the growth, both personal and intellectual, of Karl Rossmann is the theme of this first novel. The title *Amerika* is a misnomer, and Brod, who chose it, bears the blame for it. The book itself deals with "The Boy Who Was Never More Heard Of," an individual.

Der Verschollene

Karl Rossmann is an underdog of sorts. We have been told that his parents are poor, a statement that is qualified by the context in which it appears, since we learn at the same time that they employed a maidservant, Johanna, who seduced the boy. Even in the good old days before the First World War no one who was really destitute could

afford domestic help. Obviously, then, Karl stems from the outer
fringe of the European petty bourgeoisie, who enjoyed calling themselves poor in comparison with the middle and upper brackets of their
class. Typically enough the Rossmanns live in a big city, Prague (121),
and when they have their family picture taken, they insist that the
furniture of their apartment, easy chair, picture book, and all, be
included (93). This milieu has obviously colored Karl's personality.
His thriftiness, mistrust of chance acquaintances, and general appre-
hensiveness bear witness to the narrowness of his upbringing. He has
even accepted his banishment from Prague without much fuss. He
seems to subscribe to the conformist morality of the lower middle
classes, whose members believe that the ways of life will be smooth as
long as one succeeds in avoiding any rough edges. Having met one of
those rough edges in the person of Johanna, he is fully prepared to
be removed from the scene of the scandal.

He is a thoroughgoing petty bourgeois in his assertion that he "had
no feelings for Johanna Brummer," who is, after all, the mother of his
child. His recollection of the seduction scene and the sexual act are
described in detail with the directness of a nightmarish fairy tale,
representing an early example of Kafka's mature prose style. The
maid

pressed her naked body against his body, groped with her hand between
his legs, so disgustingly that he shook his head and neck free from the pillows, then thrust her body several times against him—it was as if she were
a part of himself and for this reason, perhaps, he was seized by a terrifying
feeling of helplessness.

One cannot sin more innocently. A tragic paradox is presented in his
realization that he cannot muster any feelings for a human being
whom he has accepted in his embrace as a part of himself. Therefore he bursts into tears; he is still a child and is to become a father;
he has become a father and remains incapable of shouldering the
responsibility for the conscious-unconscious act in which he, a child,
begot a child. His situation is the strongly accentuated image of the
confusion prevailing in many boys' adolescence.

He tries to suppress his memories of Johanna "in the throng of an
ever more receding past," and yet is struck by them again in the very
moment when his destiny takes a turn for the better. His uncle, the
opulent American senator Jacob, has taken an interest in the boy; he
has hastened to meet Karl, for the maidservant had advised him of the

boy's arrival behind Karl's back and without consulting his parents. This example of disinterested love should have the power to move his heart. His parents had packed off their son "irresponsibly unprovided for," had simply turned him out "just as you turn a cat out of the house when it annoys you," to use Uncle Jacob's stark description of the situation. The servant, on the other hand, had thought of him, had hatched plans "with much loving care for the father of her child," and had carried them through, regardless of her own security and the welfare of her child. "With somewhat simple but well-meant cunning" she has interfered with Karl's destiny and succeeded in improving his lot. And yet the boy sticks stubbornly to his insensitive attitude: "This had been very good of her and he would repay her later, if he could" (25–27). As he had previously tried to dismiss "the whole business with a wave of the hand" (4), he now refuses to acknowledge the full debt of gratitude he owes the woman. Neither Karl's class consciousness nor the after-effect of the trauma he suffered when he was seduced can fully account for his obstinate apathy. A residue of mystery remains.

Although we learn the little we know of the servant only by sharing Karl's memories and listening to the uncle's highly prejudiced remarks, we cannot fail to notice that her nature, too, is somewhat contradictory. The only objective intelligence we ever obtain of her is her name. Brummer, however, means "meat fly" or even "horsefly." As a horsefly molests the horse (*Rossmann*), she has circled round Karl, has followed and irritated him, and finally thrust herself on him in the manner of a parasite. And yet it is also she who prevents him from coming "to a wretched end, immediately, in one of the little lanes in the harbor of New York" (25). Johanna, one may conclude, is as little a parasite as Karl is, or ever will be, a man. This contradiction between name and character, between outward appearance and inner nature, is itself contradicted by our awareness that Johanna has, cunningly and almost cruelly, used Karl in her bed, and that Karl is, throughout the book, most assiduously intent on proving his masculinity. As deeply ambiguous as the names they carry are the characters themselves, and so is the guilt to which the sword of Liberty pointed in the first sentence of the novel.

Karl was a boy of fifteen when Johanna overpowered him; does his guilt originate in his lack of resistance against the seduction or only in his inclination to forget and suppress the past for the sake of the present, a technique with the help of which many weak natures protect themselves from the realization of their identity? Or is, conversely, his reluctance to be himself and to face reality the reason for his childish behavior in Johanna's arms? Kafka does not give an answer to these questions; rather he seems to pose them in order to allow them to fade away in the boy's unknown past. At the same time he uses this unsolved problem as the basic pattern of Karl's behavior throughout the book. As the boy allowed himself to be seduced by the servant, so will he accept invitations later on, will comply with requests for his assistance, and will follow recruiting posters. Others will warn and try to deter him, his own recollections will get in his way, and the voice of foresight will ring in his ears; and yet he will, innocently and guiltily, surrender to everybody and everything beckoning him to follow.

In the postscript to the first German edition of *Amerika* (1927) Brod has established the image of Rossmann as a paragon of guilelessness. He calls Karl "good, honest, and indefatigable" and refers to his "childlike innocence and touchingly naïve purity." [8] In his biography of Kafka he modifies this picture of untarnished brightness by admitting Karl's "infantilism." However, in the boy's retarded development he sees only a reflection of Kafka's own state of mind. This, in turn, relates Kafka to the great German tragedian Heinrich von Kleist, who committed suicide in 1811: "Infantilism is no weakness in [Kleist's] case," Brod exclaims; "it is only a more honest, a more serious comprehension of the fatal fundamental constellation of existence. . . . What a number of moving situations Kleist and Kafka [in *Amerika*] found to work up this one eternal situation in which someone has fallen into the most shameful disgrace, in which every outward circumstance tells against him, and in which nevertheless with the utter self-surrender of a clear conscience he demands that we do not condemn him" (*FK*, 35). Brod's reinterpretation of the Freudian term "infantilism" is highly dubious. So is his undertaking to carry it across the nineteenth century and apply it to so un-Kleistian a personality as Kafka was. Confusing author and figure, Brod furthermore projects onto Karl a "clear conscience," which Kafka, as his personal documents show, possessed just as little as does his hero. Only if we accept the term "infantilism" in its broadest meaning as a state of immaturity where dark feelings of guilt are pressing for the clarification a riper age may bring, can we apply Brod's diagnosis to Rossmann.

Nevertheless, the image of Karl, the innocent boy, has survived. Emrich believes in Rossmann's "guiltlessness" in order to be able to blame all guilt on the corrupt society of capitalist America. "Karl's struggle for human 'right,' for true justice, renders him useless to this world, in spite of his untiring work and his honest industry. For all his good and selfless actions are perverted to evil in the eyes of his associates to whom good actions seem downright incomprehensible, unthinkable, or silly." [9] Yet Kafka's America is both more and less than a frame of reference by which the human qualities of the hero, Karl's "goodness," could be determined. Like Uncle Jacob, the European immigrant who made good in the New World, Karl's American acquaintances defy any sociological stratification. More often than not they are fringe and border cases, such as the vagabonds Robinson and Delamarche or Brunelda, who has come to live with these tramps, forsaking her wealthy husband for no apparent reason whatever. A distinct fairy tale and adventure story atmosphere surrounds these Americans until in the end, in the Oklahoma theatre, mere allegory takes over, much to the detriment of the novel's plausibility. Caught between the realism of his sources and the symbolic quality with which he wanted to endow his story, Kafka created brittle, tragicomic marionettes. Their humor is neither completely of this earth nor of the realm of fancy.

The stage, however, on which these personages operate, is thoroughly symbolic and represents the most successful image that Kafka created in his first novel. (This may have been the reason why he abandoned the manuscript so late, and apparently quite reluctantly.) He knew, of course, America's description as a "land of unlimited potentialities." The word "unlimited" defines the fate of Karl Rossmann as well as it describes the scene on which it is enacted. New York rises above Karl's boat; highways connect coast with coast; motor cars race along them "as if an exact number were being expected in another distant place" (105); a hotel grows as if it were a tropical tree, is now five stories high (112), soon after, however, at least seven (149); trains roar across bridges, and whatever goes on in their tiny compartments fades "into insignificance before the grandeur of the scene outside" (276); a web of human relations is spun and just as easily torn asunder; and fate is like the wind that bloweth where it listeth. Moving without aim or peace, Kafka's America is the image of a dynamo which has no other meaning than its own circling around an invisible center. At the same time the world as such is seen as *perpetuum mobile,* and life a chase along an infinite arena. It is not surprising that this last image actually appears as the "Clayton Racecourse" (252), the scene of the novel's final chapter.

The paradoxical task Kafka set for his hero (and himself) is to mature in an environment which is constantly changing, growing, and decreasing; to hold his ground in a world which passes incessantly from one phase to another, thereby denying him any foothold; to disentangle guilt and innocence where the moral law of the jungle reigns; to be accepted where everyone is just as welcome as he is redundant. For him the Statue of Liberty holds the promise more of licentiousness than of freedom. Yet he will never be able to escape the sword of justice that this statue brandished for him. As a self-styled attorney of the accused Stoker in the first chapter he encounters justice; he will find himself in the dock when the case of Robinson is tried (sixth chapter); he will again be interrogated and cross-examined by authority when he finally applies for a position with the theatre of Oklahoma. The trials and tribulations through which Karl passes reveal Kafka's two model situations: man both guilty and innocent before the law and man seeking acceptance both on sufferance and by right. These themes he will develop fully in other works. "The Stoker," almost certainly based on older material, adds to these situations a third situation, quite unique in Kafka—the hero as defender of what he deems to be innocence. Kafka himself seems to have realized the autonomy of this chapter when he wrote to Kurt Wolff on April 4, 1913: "It is a fragment and will remain so; this future provides it with most of its finish (*Abgeschlossenheit*)" (*B*, 115).

"The Stoker"

The chapter's fragmentary character, visualized by Kafka as its main claim to perfection, establishes "The Stoker" as a paradigm for *Der Verschollene* as well as for *The Trial* and *The Castle*. But the role Karl seems to be playing loses much of its exceptional character as soon as one is able to discard the cliché of his innocence. It is true that he says to the Stoker whose defense he has undertaken: "You have been unjustly treated, more than anyone else on this ship; I know this well enough. . . . Now you must get ready to defend yourself, answer yes and no, or else these people can't have any idea of the truth" (31). Taken by itself, this exhortation is a declaration of the principles harbored by a pure heart. Unfortunately it is also Karl's farewell to the Stoker, after which he abandons his defense and follows his uncle into security and wealth. In the double meaning of the word, Karl "betrays" his good intentions here.

Karl had met the Stoker immediately after his return from the sunlit deck to the bowels of the boat. His way "down endlessly recurving stairs, through corridors with countless turnings," (2) leads him by chance to a door, against which he hammers with his fists only to discover that it is not locked. The Stoker, whom Karl finds behind it, is a huge man; again Kafka uses a low ceiling to give the impression that the figure under it is oversize. He is an anonymous German stoker on a German boat, subjected to the persecution of a Roumanian Chief Engineer, who, in contrast to him, has a name, Schubal.* In dark allusions he blames the conditions, "the way things are run" (5), for a fate from which, we are made to feel, he never will be able to escape. "Don't you put up with it!" Karl replies excitedly, and Kafka adds, "He had almost lost the feeling that he was on the uncertain board of a ship, beside the coast of an unknown continent, so much at home did he feel here in the Stoker's bunk" (6). Here social injustice seems to inspire the young idealist to protest and rebellion. Yet certain reminiscences may also have contributed to his unexpectedly violent reaction. He finds himself on the Stoker's bunk,† more precisely, he had "scrambled" into it (3), just as he had found himself in Johanna's bed before. The Stoker too had overpowered him physically: "Then the man suddenly seized the door handle and pulling the door shut he swept Karl into the cabin" (2). Both Johanna and the Stoker are huge, crude, inarticulate, surly, enigmatic, and gauche. Both are religious in the way of European lower classes: a crucifix hangs in Johanna's room and a Madonna in the Stoker's. Both the kitchenmaid and the Stoker tend a fire which benefits others. They prepare the food and heat the boilers; they are tolerated because of their services but deprived of the privilege of enjoying the fruits of their labor. They do not even "begin to earn [their] pay," (6), as the Stoker puts it in a rare outburst of irony.

With a masterly twist Kafka constructed the chapter so that the reader learns the details of the seduction scene only after Karl's encounter with the Stoker. When Karl hears about the Stoker's profession and is delighted, "as if this surpassed all his expectations" (4), we are led to believe that this excitement is due to Karl's interest in all things technical. Rereading the story, we recognize its reflected face. The flashback flashes truly back and reveals the very personal reasons underlying Karl's susceptibility to the sufferings of others, the ego-

---

* This name may be assonant to the German designation of a rogue, *Schubiack*. In certain parts of Germany *Schubiack* means also "a man who stands in everybody else's way." See Friedrich Kluge, *Etymologisches Wörterbuch der deutschen Sprache*, 11–16 (Berlin: De Gruyter, 1957), p. 682.

† Kafka says *Bett* for bunk and bed.

centric roots of his altruism. He wants to compensate the Stoker for the iniquities inflicted upon Johanna. Hence he decides to address no less an authority than the Captain, who occupies the same station in the organization of the boat as did his father in the family at home. Yet the Stoker shows little enthusiasm as this suggestion: "Oh, get away with you, out you get, I don't want you here. . . . How could I go to the Captain?" Whereupon he sits down and buries his face in his hands (6).

In this passage the narrator detaches himself from his adolescent hero. Kafka, the employee of the Workers' Accident Insurance Institute, knew well and took into account the apathy and hopelessness of the working masses. With obvious irony he allows Karl to incite the Stoker to an individual revolutionary action, such as he may have remembered from the days of his interest in the Prague anarchists. Karl is a young petty bourgeois, who, driven by private guilt feelings, goads a proletarian into action. His exhortation sounds empty to the Stoker; it does not indicate compassion but a thorough ignorance of the ways of the world. Only after prolonged resistance does the Stoker yield to Karl and suddenly and illogically decide to follow him to the Captain.

Karl has now taken the lead; this distinguishes the Stoker episode from his experience with the kitchenmaid. This time he is no longer misled and seduced; he has seized command and bears the responsibility for it. No longer is he swept away by an occurrence beyond his control. He himself is directly responsible for an event which, but for his action, would never have happened. The scene with Johanna may have been nothing but a predicament; the visit, with the Stoker, in the Captain's office is a test.

In the office two trials are going on simultaneously. The one concerns the Stoker, who, in spite of the Captain's initial sympathies, is eventually defeated. Clearly he has overstepped his mark and is now out of bounds. Alone with Karl he has been eloquently confused; now he is confusingly silent. When he finally begins to talk, he reveals in his accusation against Schubal his own hardened and seditious character, and once he is in full swing, he commits the additional blunder of questioning the Chief Engineer's professional competence, and hence the good judgment of Schubal's superiors, including the Captain. Having thus put himself most drastically in the wrong, he turns against his advocate, Karl, and pours his grievances and threats out over him. The eventual entry of Schubal, "fresh and gay in his shore-going clothes," is but a visual representation of the foregone conclusion of the case.

For the dispute is already settled by the contrast in the appearance of the two opponents. Schubal does not look at all "like the kind of person that would attend to machinery" (18), that is, like the underworld figure which had emerged from the Stoker's violent descriptions. Karl's client, on the other hand, stands "his legs a-sprawl, his knees uncertain, his head thrown back" (20), his former explosiveness congealed into fierce grimaces, his previously towering shape shrunk—defeated and admitting his defeat.

The second trial concerns the principle of justice itself. (We are still on board the boat, and in the mind of Karl the goddess of Liberty still stretches her sword over the scene.) "May I be allowed to say," he begins his plea, "that in my opinion an injustice has been done to my friend the Stoker?" After the friend's failure to explain himself, he tries to be helpful: "The Captain can't do justice to what you are telling him." Even when he is under fire from his own client, he persists: "I know . . . that you are right, you are right, I have never doubted it." And even when his case is lost by Schubal's entrance upon the scene, Karl stubbornly and childishly perseveres in his hope that this very confrontation "would achieve, even before a human tribunal, the result which would have been awarded by a higher tribunal" (12–19), thus invoking the supreme justice of God.

Yet the case is lost for justice by the simple fact that Uncle Jacob makes his identity known and offers Karl his protection. The boy, to be sure, resists, but his protests have a faint ring compared with the shame his action has heaped upon the Stoker's head. Not only did Karl's assistance seal the fate of his client, but he himself is now the one who has profited from it. As a poor and forgotten steerage passenger he had offered a helping hand to a man as victimized by fate as he was; by doing so he has found his uncle and an unexpected way to escape this fate. He still hopes to use his own advantage for the sake of the other: "What will happen to the Stoker now?" he asks, throwing in the weight of his newly acquired social rank. (The narrator adds, revealingly: "In his new circumstances he thought he was entitled to say whatever came into his mind.") Thereupon the senator: "The Stoker will get what he deserves." Karl's rather brash rejoinder, "But that's not the point in a question of justice," is brushed aside by the uncle's stern warning: "Don't mistake the situation; . . . this may be a question of justice, but at the same time it is a question of discipline. On this ship both of these, and most especially the latter, are entirely within the discretion of the Captain." The silence that ensues is broken only by the Stoker muttering a nonsensical approval of his own condemnation. Karl, standing before the Captain, does not dare to defy his paternal authority. As he had allowed his father to ship him off to America, protesting only vicariously against this verdict by taking the Stoker's case to the Captain, so does he now leave his friend and client at the discretion of the master of the ship. He thinks: "There is hardly any time left . . . but I cannot do anything without offending everybody. . . . The Captain is certainly polite, but this is all. In matters of discipline his politeness ends" (29–31).

Here he takes a deep fall indeed. At the height of the Stoker's trial when he still fancied he could win, he had lost himself in a daydream:

If only his parents could see him now, defending the good in a strange land before well respected men and, though not yet triumphant, dauntlessly resolved to gain the final victory! Would they revise their opinion of him? Set him between them and praise him? Look into his eyes at last, at last, these eyes so filled with devotion to them (20)?

His wishful dream of maturity reveals the degree of dependence with which he still clings to his parents. What has been initiated as an act of rebellion was also meant to rehabilitate him in the eyes of those against whom he had protested. Disregarding reality, he was bound to fail. But now he fails in public, "before well respected men," in full consciousness and charged with full responsibility. Had he won his case, he would have proved, at least to himself, the injustice of Schubal, the Captain, and his father. Losing it, he seems to justify his father's crass decision to banish him. Here the parallelism between the episodes with Johanna and the Stoker is perfected.

Nonetheless, Karl shows his client a sign of tenderness he had denied to the mother of his child: he goes over to the Stoker, pulls his right hand out of his belt, holds it, and plays with it. The play with the fingers of the beloved is one of the few erotic symbols that Kafka has included in his store of imagery.* Thus he declares to the Stoker his love but also his resignation. He will allow himself to be separated from him as he was separated from Johanna, whom he did not admit having loved, even in his innermost thoughts. In a last and desperate gesture of opposition he kisses the Stoker's hand, "that cracked, almost lifeless hand, pressing it to his cheek like a treasure which he would soon have to give up" (31). The erotic overtones are stronger in the German word *Schatz* than in its English equivalent, *treasure*. Yet they

---

* Cf. the love scene between K. and Leni in *The Trial*, 137.

suffice to indicate the pattern his fate will follow from now on. He will have to leave what he treasures: the uncle, the Manageress, and Therese. Or does he only treasure what he is compelled to abandon? An undefined compulsion, distinct behind and beyond Kafka's narrative, will expose him to situations in which he induces those who love him to "pack him off," as once and for all his parents did when they sent him to America. He will always magnify what he has lost and minimize what he has gained. Thus he doubts, while following Uncle Jacob into prosperity, "whether this man would ever be able to take the Stoker's place" (34).

With the senator he descends the short ladder that leads him from the steerage of an immigrant boat to the promises of the "land of unlimited potentialities." This downward movement is likewise indicative of his future career: from the room Uncle Jacob has prepared for him in his city palace he will descend to take to the highways; he will step down from the senator to the company of the vagabonds, Robinson and Delamarche; he will be thrown down from the pinnacle of the Hotel Occidental, which he has explored to the very roof, to the bottom of the slums through which he is chased by police; he will forfeit the company of the generous Manageress and of mild Therese to associate with that monstrous bundle of flesh, Brunelda. The trend of *Der Verschollene* is so thoroughly determined by this downward motion that in spite of Brod's recollections and assertions little is left to the imagination of the reader intent on figuring out for himself whither Karl will be plunged after having gloried in the picture "of the box reserved in the theatre for the President of the United States" (271–272) and having crossed the "high range of mountains" in the last chapter of the book (276).

Descending with Uncle Jacob in the first chapter, he "bursts into violent sobs" (33). He sheds more than the tears of a boy who has failed an examination. "It is the root of men's guilt," Kafka said much later to Janouch, "that they prefer the evil which lies so temptingly close at hand to the moral values which seem so difficult to obtain." When Janouch asked whether this was not inevitable, he answered: "Man can act otherwise. The Fall is the proof of their freedom" (*J*, 65). This seems to be Kafka's explanation for the sword of Justice which he put in the hand of the Statue of Liberty.

The Road into the Interior

The way from the deck of the boat, where Karl acted as attorney, to the Head Waiter's office in the Hotel Occidental, where he has to stand trial himself, is both long and short. Topographically it leads from the city residence of the senator to the country estate of Mr. Pollunder and thence to Rameses, a distance to be covered by a day's journey. Karl spends about two and a half months in his uncle's house, if we equate his stay there with the time it took him to master English (122). After having been expelled by his uncle, he works for two more months in the hotel (172) until catastrophe strikes there too. Both time and place remain somewhat vague, due partly to the unfinished state of Kafka's manuscript, but partly also to the surrealistic tendencies of Kafka's narrative manner.* Symbolically, however, it is clear that he has not moved far away from his port of disembarkation and from Liberty's sword.

Although, in its end result, his road has not led him far, it has carried him steeply up and down, not once but twice. Before being thrown out for the second time by a relative, he experiences an immense rise in his fortunes. Uncle Jacob compares the first days of a European in America to a "rebirth" (35), and Karl indeed opens a child's eyes to the new reality awaiting him. Next to the streets of the big city, the details of which Kafka cautiously veils in the haze of a dreamlike vision, it is the desk in his room, "such as his father has coveted for years," which impresses him most as a sign of the magnitude and complexity of his new life:

For example, it had a hundred compartments of different sizes, in which even the President of the Union could have found a fitting place for each of his papers; there was also a regulator at one side and by turning a handle you could produce the most different combinations and permutations of the compartments to please yourself and suit your requirements. Thin panels sank slowly and formed the bottom of a new series or the top of existing drawers promoted from below; even after one turn of the handle the top was quite changed, and the transformation took place slowly or at a nonsensical speed according to the rate you turned the handle around.

---

* Both these reasons ultimately invalidate H. Uyttersprot's painstaking investigations into the realities described in The Trial and Amerika (Eine neue Ordnung der Werke Kafkas? Zur Struktur von "Der Prozess" und "Amerika" [Anvers: De Vries-Brouwers, 1957]).

Rather than marvel at this "strangely empirical" insight into the future of American automation, one may be struck here by the skill Kafka displays in turning, with a few sentences, a good old European desk into a fantastically useless contraption, reminiscent, but for its complexity, of the thing Odradek in "The Worries of a Family Man." Yet Karl is "vividly" reminded by it of the crèches on display in the market place at home at Christmas time, and when he surrenders further to his memories, the image of his mother reappears to "cover his mouth with her hand" (36–37), holding him back and frustrating his desire to explore the miracles expanding before him. His "rebirth" has not given him the strength to sever the ties that bind him to the past. More and more the place of his parents is occupied by the uncle, who, for instance, advises him against using the regulator of the desk, pointing out the sensitivity of the mechanism and irritating Karl, who dismisses his remark as quite inappropriate.

Gradually we are being prepared to accept the break between uncle and nephew as an inevitable repetition of his original banishment from home. Mr. Pollunder, a business associate of the senator, has come to invite Karl to his mansion in the country. The uncle opposes this visit without giving any reasons. (The image of the mother keeping Karl back and shutting his mouth might be remembered here.) Uncle Jacob: "You see . . . what a lot of trouble this visit of yours has caused already." This is countered by Karl: "I'm very sorry . . . but I'll be back again in a minute," as he prepares to rush away and get ready to leave (46). In this display of impatience Karl proves to be a typical Kafka hero. Not only is he deaf to his uncle's words, he also disregards the senator's gesture of disgust when he sees that his warnings are in vain. ("As if without will, he drummed on the arm of his chair.") And when, in a last attempt at reaching a compromise, the senator sets the limit of one night to the visit so as not to upset the studies of his nephew, who later on will be able to accept "such a kind and flattering invitation even for a long time" (47), Karl takes a childish pride in his uncle's apparent self-contradiction. The senator has gone when Karl, ready for the journey, returns to be picked up by Pollunder.

Uncle Jacob's misapprehensions are fully justified by Karl's experiences in the country. Once more he risks being seduced and getting lost—becoming a *Verschollener* in the dark labyrinth of this house which is "a fortress not a mansion" (67), half a Castle in the Gothic tradition and half a "Burrow" (68), which in Kafka's ambiguous German is the other meaning of *Bau* ("building"). It was not only care and

foresight which prompted the senator to keep Karl away from Pollunder's mansion, but what he calls, in his farewell letter, his "principle." He had introduced the nephew to this principle in the first hour
of their acquaintance when he set the idea of discipline against the
boy's craving for justice. He had reiterated it after a few days when he
advised Karl "to take up nothing seriously. He should certainly examine
and consider everything, but without committing himself" (35). Thus
he offered the boy the chance of quiet growth under his guardianship.
When Karl rejects this tutelage by following Pollunder to his "fortress,"
he dismisses him, for the sake of discipline. Yet he pays his nephew the
respect of considering Karl's decision a principle: "Against my wishes
you decided this evening to leave me; stick, then, to this decision all
your life. Only then will it be a manly decision" (85). The stern but
far-from-hostile tone of this exhortation is dictated by the uncle's
realization that Karl is still lacking in manliness and that it was this
deficiency which brought about their break. As if to prove this point,
Karl, "suddenly realizing the true situation," takes the messenger, Mr.
Green, to task for having delivered his message too late: "On the
envelope you gave me it was merely stated that I was to receive it
at midnight. Why then, on the strength of this letter, did you keep me
here when I wanted to leave at a quarter-past-eleven?" Mr. Green,
however, followed the instructions he had received; the inscription on
the envelope specified midnight as the time of delivery. Karl may
blame his uncle for the rigidity of his disciplinary measures and for his
fondness for round figures, like midnight, but he cannot blame the
executor of these measures for ulterior motives behind his tardiness:
"It says on the envelope: 'To be delivered after midnight.' . . . Does
not the inscription quite plainly convey that midnight was to be the
final term for me? And it is you who are to blame that I missed it"
(84–88). Not Green but Karl commits an act of deception here, one of
those tiny, hardly visible slips which our unconscious is so fond of
producing to deceive our conscience: the final term on the envelope
said "at midnight," the moment when the day of their separation was
complete and the break perfected. The absence of the senator at Karl's
departure, many hours earlier, indicated that he considered the matter
closed. Karl, however, transforms the final term into a mere deadline
when he changes its wording from "at" to "after" midnight. What was
originally a decree of separation, whimsically dated perhaps in the
manner of a businessman, becomes now an ultimatum. But for Green's
ill will it would seemingly have been possible to undo what he had

done and to rush back into the arms of his uncle, still open to welcome him. Cunningly Kafka has done his best to discredit the messenger in order to induce the reader to accept Karl's accusations and exculpate the boy. By doing so, the reader will miss the ironical point that Kafka is trying to make here: the senator, though an arbitrary, unpredictable, and authoritarian personality like all the paternal figures Kafka has created, is nevertheless vindicated by Karl's reaction. The farewell letter contained as a kind of blessing the uncle's charge for the boy to be a man. Karl's behavior on receiving it, however, is that of a child who shifts the blame from his shoulders by throwing it on an unimportant person such as Green. What appears as "deception" to Karl is nothing more than the execution of the will of authority.

Does Karl, as his critics maintain, "really" love his uncle, the senator? [10] When his conscience is stirred in Pollunder's house, he imagines his return:

how in the morning . . . he would surprise his uncle. True, he had never yet been in his uncle's bedroom . . . , but he . . . would . . . rush into the room and surprise his dear uncle, whom until now he had known only fully dressed and buttoned to the chin,* sitting up in bed in his nightshirt, his astonished eyes fixed on the door. . . . Perhaps he might breakfast with his uncle for the first time, . . . perhaps as a result of such informal breakfasting . . . they would meet oftener than simply once a day, . . . perhaps his uncle was lying in bed and thinking the very same thing at the moment (57–58).

At the time of this innocent daydream the uncle has already dismissed Karl. But is this fantasy as innocent as it sounds? We recall the scene in "The Judgment" when Georg Bendemann surprises his father in bed and, full of filial loving kindness, covers up his father, which is interpreted by the latter as the son's hidden wish to bury him. The repentant nephew here plans an intrusion into the senator's privacy, and his intention to surprise him in his nightshirt reveals, beneath its manifest tenderness, a surprising amount of aggression. Is it "merely the lack of a frank interchange of confidences that had made him a little refractory, or better still, mulish towards his uncle" (58)? Or is it not rather that he is prepared to exchange these confidences only on his own terms, sitting at the bedside of the old man, imposing his will on his uncle, whose sleeping attire is bound to reveal his weakness, instead of allowing the expected confidences to influence him? Inasmuch as Uncle Jacob has served him as a father image, he is quite prepared to de-

---

* The German *zugeknöpft* also denotes a high degree of formal restraint.

throne this image in spite of the piety with which he surrounds this act of unconscious iconoclasm.*

On the boat he had acknowledged the uncle as his relative only after the senator had denigrated his parents by some vague and sinister hints (24). Now he considers him with his parents, who have similarly rejected him. The successful immigrant to America and the old people beyond the ocean belong to the past from which the boy tries to escape but which nevertheless catches up with him.

Of all the props Kafka uses in his book it is the old traveling box which establishes Karl's connection with his past, as well as his identity. He had left it on the deck of the boat, in the charge of a man with the improbable name of Franz Butterbaum, before he descended to meet the Stoker (1–3). Along with Karl's other possessions this box contains a piece of Veronese salami, which is known to spread a penetrating smell of cheap spices, especially if kept for a protracted span of time in rooms that lack ventilation. Talking to the Stoker, Karl wishes he could offer it to him, "for such people were easily won over by the gift of some trifle or the other; Karl had learned this from his father" (7). Yet Karl forgets both box and sausage while he defends the Stoker and leaves the boat without them. Symbolically speaking, this augurs well because he seems to be prepared now to begin a new life unburdened by the relics from his past.

Mr. Green, however, delivers the box together with the uncle's farewell. Fittingly it had been Schubal, the villain, who had delivered the ominous object, thus reestablishing the connection between Karl and his past. In the inn on the road to Rameses Karl opens the box again and notices that "the Veronese salami . . . had bestowed its smell on everything. If he could not find some way of eliminating this smell, he had every prospect of walking about for months enveloped in it." In other words, Karl resents the smell which reminds him of home and which grows stronger the further his home recedes from him.

Yet his own identity is tied up with this very smell. In the box, from which "not the slightest thing was missing," he finds "in the secret pocket of his jacket . . . his passport" (91). Put together, the images of the passport, the sausage, and the box form the symbol of Karl's past

---

* An archetypal pattern of this scene may be found in Genesis 9:22 and 25, where Ham sees the nakedness of his drunken father Noah and is cursed by him. The image of "Noah in his drunken state" was as unconsciously suggestive to Kafka as was the punishment visited upon the son who has observed the human frailty of his creator. See pp. 27 and 54–55 above.

that adheres to him wherever he goes. "Nothing good comes out of your family," the uncle writes him (85), and he must know this, for despite his protestations to the contrary he is a member of this family.

The final irony of Karl's encounter with his uncle consists in the fact that Karl seems to have proved to the well-principled senator that he was no better than the rest of his family and therefore deserved to be disposed of. Yet by "packing him off" as Karl's father had done, the uncle establishes his own identity with the Rossmann family. In Karl's imagination he will now merge with the "throng of the past" and gradually be forgotten in a faint smell of Veronese salami.

With the recovered box in his hand, Karl is standing now in front of the Pollunders' home. The sentence with which Kafka concludes his adventures in New York and the neighboring countryside is not lacking in irony: "So he chose a chance direction and set out on his way" (88). A choice is an act of deliberate decision, and the direct opposite of a surrender to the contingencies of the moment, which is connoted by the phrase "a chance direction." Combining these two disparate elements in one seemingly innocent and simple sentence, Kafka illuminates the confusion still reigning in Karl's mind. He pretends to possess the freedom of choice, while he slides, half-consciously, down the lanes of the next adventure opening before him. Thus he leaves his uncle, associates with the vagabonds, Robinson and Delamarche, and enters the Hotel Occidental.

A Sentimental Education

The Hotel Occidental is a place full of contradictions. The name of the town, Rameses, an Egyptian name, and the name of the hotel immediately confront East with West. This does not necessarily mean that the hotel serves as a "symbol of Western civilization"; [11] it may, much more literally, allude to the image of sunset and the idea of decline. The Hotel Occidental in Rameses unites ascent and descent and symbolizes the choices offered to Karl.

In the Hotel Karl is met first by the Manageress Grete Mitzelbach from Vienna (121) and then by the secretary, Therese Berchtold from Pomerania (127). The Manageress' family name is as ambiguous as the name of the Hotel. Mitzel is the Austrian diminutive of Maria and points to the maternal place she is going to occupy in the boy's life. Accordingly she leads him at once to the large, cool storeroom and provides him with food. Yet her family name may just as well have been borrowed from Muzenbacher, the surname of the heroine of Old Austria's best-known and most successful piece of pornography.[12] "Then come with me, my boy," she invites him. The German phrase, "Dann kommen Sie mit mir, Kleiner," is the formula with which Viennese streetwalkers accost prospective customers with the exception of the formal *Sie*, which may be meant as an encouragement to the adolescent. Maternal compassion distinguishes her; she assumes the role of the great mother during the boy's stay at the hotel and appears as the very exemplar of disinterested helpfulness. Yet after the boy has been dismissed, he sees his principal adversary, "the Head Waiter, surreptitiously seizing her hand and fondling it" (179). Since Gregor Samsa's mother yields to his father in a similar way in the moment of the son's humiliation in "The Metamorphosis," Kafka may have recorded in both scenes his deep-rooted aggressions against the maternal principle in general.

In Therese, the Manageress' secretary, Karl meets the first and only human being who could accompany him on his road to maturity. Her family name, Berchtold, is etymologically related to "brightness." Her Christian name, Therese, the saint, is appropriately chosen for one who seems devoted to mystical suffering.

The account of her mother's death is a powerful anecdote, one of the few truly conclusive pieces of prose Kafka ever wrote: the walk of the immigrant woman and the five-year-old child through a New York blizzard, the image of little Therese ducking playfully under the gusts of snow and ice, their straying through corridors as forbidding and inhuman as the world outside, the last few kisses bitter with the blood the mother has coughed up—all this is seen with the eyes of a child stricken with awe and yet overcome by the giant beauty of the frozen city. The mother hurries along, "as if following a mirage," brushing the rime from the railing of a bridge as the sun rises over the building where she has been promised work as an unskilled laborer. Leaving the child behind, she climbs the scaffolding, knocks down a heap of bricks, and plunges to her death.

A shower of bricks came after her and then, a good while later, a heavy plank detached itself from somewhere and crashed down upon her. Therese's last memory of her mother was seeing her lying there, . . . her legs thrown wide, almost covered by the rough plank atop of her, while . . . a man shouted down angrily from the top of the wall (138–143).

A curse is her eulogy, a piece of crude wood her tombstone. Even by her desperate death did this proletarian woman disturb the progress of industrialized society and violate its rules; and yet it is hard to observe any "satanic mechanisms" in Therese's tale. This piece of prose shows "the world of modern capitalism as an inferno," to use a phrase by the communist critic Georg Lukács. Yet it refutes the continuation of the same phrase: "and the impotence of the human faced by this infernal power." [13] For Kafka has succeeded here in conquering the hell by changing it into a permanent image of tragic beauty. Slowly building up to the fatal climax by visions of despair and delusion, Kafka has bestowed upon this death scene the air of inevitability, the solemnity of a nonsensical ritual. He has Therese tell the fairy tale of misery in sentences of a deadly clarity, which by comparison reveals as pale blue the romanticism of Hans Christian Andersen's "Little Match Girl." If social surrealism can be achieved at all, then Kafka has succeeded in producing it here. He has done so by mirroring the horrors of social injustice while disconnecting one splinter of reality from the next, mixing them, and presenting them anew in kaleidoscopic formations and ice-fern-like constellations, as they may have appeared to the child Therese. The novella is connected with the framework of the entire story by its narrator; the cadence of disinterested compassion in which it is told is also used to characterize the nature of its actual narrator, Therese.

"As soon as I saw you, I felt I could trust you" (129), she informs Karl. So she comes, during his first night in the Hotel, to sit down beside the sofa where he sleeps. The parallelism of this situation with the seduction scene at the beginning of the book forces itself upon the reader's mind: Therese takes the initiative as did Johanna. Yet Kafka also uses the evident contrast between the two situations to reveal the chances offered Karl's development by Therese: she does not drag the boy into her bedroom but visits him and sits down next to him; she talks and explains herself, whereas the kitchenmaid acted in a stubborn and horrifying silence; she gives him time and cleverly allows him to continue on the way on which she has started him, whereas Johanna simply buried him under her weight. Thus her promise, on parting, that she would come up in the morning and wake him possesses symbolic ambiguity; this time, however, this ambiguity holds a bright prospect. Karl seems to have understood her fully. "You are so clever at wakening people," he says. "Yes, some things I can do" she replies (130).

She introduces Karl, who is employed as an elevator boy, to the higher regions of professional life by correcting his exercises in commercial correspondence. Here, however, in the middle of an idyl the like of which he had never experienced before, the first frictions occur. He knows better, as he did in the house of the senator. He corrects Therese's corrections, quoting "his great New York professor in his support" (144). At that time, we may remember, the "professor" was not at all great but a young teacher who did not instruct him in commercial correspondence but, much more generally, in the elementary use of the English language (39). If the Manageress is approached to settle their dispute and decides in Therese's favor, then Karl brushes off her verdict as "not definitive, since Therese was her secretary." Rather than admit that he was wrong, he imputes partiality to his protectress. Not even in a moderate climate of sympathy and encouragement is he capable of submitting to authority.

The climate changes rapidly, however, with the reemergence of Delamarche and Robinson, the tramps who have remained in the outside world. Therese warns him against them as Uncle Jacob had cautioned him against Pollunder. The results are similar. "Karl realized that he really had been influenced by Therese in coming to the conclusion that [Delamarche] was a dangerous man; . . . he was only a tramp corrupted by ill-luck and easy enough to get on with." Upon her entreaties to shun the company of the men, who, after all, had once broken into his box, he promises "not to speak to Delamarche unless I can't avoid it" (146). Here he leaves himself a loophole through which he is to fall headlong.

In the evening of his fall Therese gives him an apple. The all too obvious symbolism of this gesture is mitigated by the direction Karl's new decline takes. He is far from becoming another Adam. He neither falls in love nor tastes the fruit from the tree of knowledge. As far as Therese is concerned, she has shown him that her "life was a bitter one" (129) and that the bitterness of one human life may in some small way be able to mitigate the bitterness of another. This is the meaning of her offering herself.

Karl's Trial

Therese has long since gone when Karl finally gets around to eating the apple, which "gives out a strong fragrance as soon as he bites into it" (147). Standing up on high, under the very roof of the Hotel, he looks down into a light shaft, into which Robinson is going to vomit a few moments later. At its bottom the shaft is surrounded by the windows of the storerooms, the domain of the Manageress, which also will be polluted by the stream "pouring from Robinson's mouth into the deep" (150). Behind the storeroom windows Karl sees "hanging masses of bananas gleaming faintly in the darkness" (147), the image of a lush and lascivious underworld inviting him once more to plunge down into guilt and punishment. These bananas symbolically antici- pate Brunelda, "the magnificent singer" (149).

The offense he now commits is superficially a petty one. To whisk Robinson away as well as to help him, Karl has abandoned the elevator which was in his charge. To be sure, he begged "the lift-boy whose work he had taken on that night . . . to oblige him in return for a little while" (153), but he failed to report the change to the Head Waiter, and thereby violated the regulations for the elevator. Intent on justifying himself before the irritated Head Waiter, he defends himself: "It's just the regulations one never needs that one forgets about." Dis- missing the law he has transgressed as insignificant, Karl hopes, as Kafka informs us, "that this would appease authority" (160). Karl is neither as naïve nor as arrogant as his thoughts and words would tend to suggest. Subjectively his desire to come to terms with his superior is as sincere as was his attempt to show his uncle affection by surpris- ing him in his bed. Objectively, however, he once more rebels against discipline by asking for justice, but this time it is justice for himself. Hopelessly entangled in the web of conscious urbanity and unconscious aggressions, he allows his words to contradict his thoughts. The gau- cheries of his speech reveal what his intellect tries to keep from realiz- ing. In other words, he produces one of his many slips. By spelling out Karl's cerebrations and connecting them with the unconscious origins of his words and deeds, Kafka creates an irony all his own, gently deriding his hero as well as the reader who takes these motiva- tions at face value.

Karl's case is aggravated by the fact that he has stowed Robinson away in one of the dormitories reserved for the elevator boys. There the tramp is discovered in a state of complete drunkenness, "carefully tucked up in one of the beds" (170), incriminating Rossmann and finally getting into a general brawl with the other inmates. Karl will need the good will of his judges to vindicate himself. This good will, however, he expects as his prerogative. "It is impossible to defend one- self when there is no good will" (174), he tells himself; and since he is obviously not meeting with the ideal conditions he deems necessary for his trial, he refuses to cooperate. He stops answering the Head Waiter. The sort of authority which he is willing to accept must be distinguished by the understanding it provides rather than by the claims it is entitled to make—a schoolboy's utopian dream of authority. He does not think of engendering the good will that he so urgently needs. How he could proceed he is told by the Manageress, who bases her insight on feminine intuition: "When things are right they look right, and I must confess that your actions don't" (175). Of course, she puts appearance before essence, outward semblance before inner truth. She has come to help him, with, as she puts it, "the best of prejudices in your favor" (175–176). (This is, at least in German—*mit dem besten Vorurteil für dich*—a contradiction in terms, since *Vorurteile* have a general tendency to be negative.) Seasoned by her years of service, she realizes that the universe of the Hotel Occidental could not persist by abstractions like Karl's conception of good will. Yet even if this good will must not be presupposed as a universal principle, it can still be counted on as a customary expediency. "Many cases have occurred when this kind of thing was pardoned," Karl has been told by the elevator boy who had taken his place. "You must think up a good excuse" (156). That is, you must arrange things to look right, as the Manageress suggests, independent of the inherent rightness of your cause.

If Karl had been a fighter for abstract justice as was Heinrich von Kleist's Michael Kohlhaas, who prefers the destruction of the universe (and himself) to tolerating a break of the universal law that binds all creatures under a stellar system of absolute imperatives, then he could have neglected the Manageress' advice as a treacherous example of meretricious compromise. But the Stoker episode has proved him to be no fighter. Thus he has to depend on the good will of his associates and is rationally quite prepared to do so. The Head Porter, who has taken over the prosecution from the Head Waiter, accuses him of being the only boy "who simply refuses to give me a greeting" (160). This time Karl is resolved to make the best of a bad bargain. He refrains from voicing the obvious protest that no elevator regulation on earth requires a greeting of the Head Porter. He is willing to compromise "since he realized that though the Head Porter's reproaches could not do him any harm, his enmity could." To placate his influential adversary he says:

Sir, . . . I most certainly do not pass you without a greeting. I have not been long in America yet and I have just come from Europe where people are in the habit of greeting each other excessively, as is well known. And of course I haven't been quite able to get over the habit yet; why, only two months ago in New York, where I happened to be accepted into the higher circles of society, I was always being advised to drop my exaggerated salutations. And now you tell me that I do not greet you of all people. I have greeted you every day several times a day (161).

Toppling over itself, Karl's zeal defeats its own purpose. The adverb "certainly" and the phrases "as is well known" and "of course" do not belong to the vocabulary of an underling trying to ingratiate himself with authority. Nor is name-dropping—the reference to "higher circles" —the most timely device to placate a man whose honor has been hurt. He ends by giving his accuser the lie. When the Head Porter insists on Karl's duty to greet him "every time, every single time, without exception," Karl replies, "Every time?" Although the words are uttered "softly, in a questioning tone" (161), they reveal the obstinacy of one who knows better. Much later, when physically attacked by the Head Porter, his resources almost exhausted, he will cry: "Even if I actually did pass you without greeting, how can a grown man be so vindictive about such an omission" (188)! Here the reason for his resistance is literally extorted from Karl's unconscious. The child in him resents and tries to slight the grown man. Consciously, however, he argues like the man who, in a popular Jewish joke, is charged with having broken a pitcher and defends himself by saying, "First, I have never seen the pitcher before and, second, the pitcher was broken already."

We are witnessing a tragicomedy of errors, a macabre ballet of misunderstandings, a haunting repetition of the Stoker's predicament on board the ship. But the parts have been reversed. As the Stoker faced the Head Purser and the Chief Engineer, Schubal, Karl himself is now confronted by the Head Waiter and the Head Porter. As he once protected another man, he is now being defended by the Manageress and Therese, likewise in vain. He imitates the Stoker when he retires behind an obstinate silence. As the Stoker then "did his best not to look at Karl" (30), so Karl now does "not look at the Manageress . . . but in front of him at the floor," although he is aware that "it could only be construed as a bad sign" (170). If both scenes point to the rigidity of social institutions aggravated by the inhumanity of their functionaries, they also stress the asocial dispositions of the Stoker and of Karl. Both are prisoners, the former of the dreary circumstances of his life, the latter of the unresolved conflicts in his mind. And as the Stoker eventually seems to accept his guilt when he agrees with the senator (30), so does Karl, in one climactic moment, confess, "Well, I am to blame." Then, however, he pauses "as if waiting for a kind word from his judges." It is Karl's sophistication that distinguishes him from the simple Stoker. He may still be naïve enough to cherish hopes that his judges would "give him courage for continuing his defence" after he had complied with their wishes and admitted his guilt. Yet he also registers annoyance by prefacing his words with a condescending "Well." By inserting a pause afterward, he attempts to ascertain the effect his admission has made on the judges. May they not be swayed by it, allowing him to proceed unscathed by the trial? His expectations may be childish but they are the expectations of a very calculating child. "I am to blame," he continues, "only for taking the man to the dormitory." He has forgotten the original accusation, the breach of the elevator regulations, and the Head Waiter is quick to remind him of the money Robinson was promised by Karl, who thus incriminates himself. He feels victimized by appearances working to his disadvantage and remains convinced of his profound innocence. Yet he engages in a sham fight and, his bluff having been called by the Head Waiter, he uses his haste and confusion to excuse himself for having been "too peremptory in declaring himself innocent" (173). He occupies himself, as the Manageress remarks, "with small justifications," thereby glossing over his actual guilt, which may likewise be small but, regardless of its size, is "undeniable" (176) not only in the eyes of his maternal friend but in those of the reader as well.

By the parallel structure of the two trial scenes Kafka seems to underscore the boy's life problem and the task set him. Like any other young person, Karl has to find the balance between freedom and discipline, liberty and justice. The universal character of his conflict is stressed by the image of the Statue in the first chapter; here, in the sixth, it is expressed by an acoustic sensation. Immediately before the boy is dismissed from his service the clock strikes half-past six "and with it, as everyone knew, all the other clocks in the whole hotel; it rang forebodingly in the ear, like the double quiver of one great impatience" (175). The order in the big house had been disturbed; the clocks reestablish it in fearful harmony by striking the hour of Karl's dismissal.

With this almost mystical chorus of striking hotel clocks the story has imperceptibly moved into the sphere of the parable. Karl appears as the younger brother of Joseph K., and his case, so far presented more or less psychologically, as the forerunner of the metaphysical proceedings carried out in *The Trial*. Karl Rossmann, too, enacts a

paradox: in the name of justice, as he sees it, he refuses to take the
blame for a misdeed he has been rightfully accused of; having broken
the discipline, he demands freedom for himself, a claim which separates him even from those who love him. "You see," says the Manageress, "that Therese is silent too." And the narrator, following Karl's
glances, adds: "But she was not silent, she was crying" (176). Therese's
tears, however, are related to those shed by Karl when he had to part
company with the Stoker.

The Information Givers (Part One)

The parabolical atmosphere of the trial scene is maintained through
most of the chapter, the last chapter of *Der Verschollene* that Kafka
actually finished. On the way to the exit Karl once more has to pass
by the Head Porter's huge office, a box with walls made entirely of
glass panes. The Porter seizes him and holds him back. The following
exchange ensues: " 'But I have been thrown out,' said Karl, meaning
that nobody in the hotel had a right to give him orders now. 'As long
as I keep hold of you, you are not thrown out,' said the Porter, which
was also true enough" (180). It is even truer than Karl is able to realize.
The Head Porter is the master over all the doorkeepers, "in charge of
all the doors of the hotel, this main door, the three middle and the ten
side doors, not to mention the innumerable little doors and the door-
less exits" (186). He is, as Emrich has noted, akin to the doorkeepers
who wield the power in *The Trial*, since it is they who control the
passage through the gates of the Law.[14] As long as Karl explores this
America, he will move in the shadow of the sword, and authority,
carrying out the law, will continually cross his way. The Head Porter
keeps hold of him not only with the crude force of his arms but with
the spell cast by an ubiquitous symbolic image of Justice.

The Head Porter, powerful as the doorkeepers in *The Trial*, is also
as corrupt as they are. It is the misfortune of this adolescent boy that
he arouses desire in both women and men. (This, by the way, is the
only hint that Kafka gives us of his hero's attractive exterior.) Fat Mr.
Pollunder had come unduly close to him when he "put his arm round
Karl and drew him between his legs" (71). Now the Head Porter
covers the glass panes of his box with "black curtains reaching from
the roof to the floor" (184). Having thus isolated his victim from the
outside world, he betrays his intentions, which, whatever they may be,
are couched in the language of perversity: "Since you are here, I am

going to enjoy you" (186). He begins by tugging "at the most diverse parts" (187) of Karl's suit, ostensibly searching his pockets for stolen goods.* In panic fear Karl slips out of the sleeves, abandoning his jacket and in its breast pocket the passport, the symbol of his identity. He gains the open road but not freedom, for outside Robinson, suffering from a hangover and a thrashing by Karl's former colleagues, is waiting in a car. "Considering the figure he cut, would not Karl be best provided for in the darkness of the taxi" (191)? Tongue in cheek the narrator poses this rhetorical question. Karl answers the question in the affirmative, hurriedly as the situation demands, without the pause for reflection to be expected from one able to learn from past experiences. He seats himself beside Robinson and is driven into his next adventure.

Before thus revealing the treacherous nature of certain questions, Kafka has questioned the validity, perhaps even the possibility, of questions in general. He has done so by putting an Information Giver into the box of the Head Porter. As a matter of fact, "two providers of information" are sitting there "at two great sliding windows," dispensing answers on the most diverse subjects, facing "at least ten asking faces before them in the window opening." By using two men instead of one and designating them as underporters, i.e., subalterns of the Head Porter, Kafka stresses the transcendent, parabolical character of these figures, as he does with the two assistants of the Land-Surveyor in *The Castle* or the two celluloid balls dancing around "Blumfeld, an Elderly Bachelor." The underlings catch Karl's eye before the Head Porter begins his punitive action, that is, when there is still time for Karl to ask one question or another himself. One of the Information Givers is "a gloomy man with a dark beard surrounding his whole face"; his gloom and blackness are certainly not suited to the public relations work in which he is engaged.

Furthermore, his beard somewhat interfered with the intelligibility of his speech and . . . Karl could make out very little of what he said. . . . Additionally confusing was the fact that one answer came so quickly on the heels of another as to be indistinguishable from it, so that often an enquirer went on listening intently in the belief that his question was still being answered, without noticing for some time that he was finished already. You also had to get used to the Under Porter's habit of never asking a question to be repeated; even if it was vague only in wording and quite sensible on the whole, he gave an almost imperceptible shake of the head to indicate

* A humiliation to which Karl had once subjected his comrades Robinson and Delamarche, after they had opened his box (117–118).

that he did not intend to answer this question and it was the questioner's business to recognise his error and formulate the question more correctly.

Putting these Information Givers before Karl in one of the most improbable moments of the story, Kafka seems at first to intimate that his hero, too, would be well advised to recognize his error and formulate more correctly the question of where he ought to go. And since the story of Karl has risen here to the height of a parable, the reader may feel inclined to ask a similar question of Kafka himself. Where was he leading his hero, this innocently guilty Karl? Yet Kafka's parables are not meant to provide any clear information; the answers they give are multifaceted, as they have to be, since the writer must have felt, like his Information Givers, surrounded by a throng of "inquiring faces . . . who were continually changing," producing "a perfect babel of tongues, as if each were an emissary from a different country" (181–182). From the point of view of the Head Porter, however, the work of the Information Givers "is the stupidest of the whole hotel; you need only listen for an hour to know pretty well all the questions that will be asked, and the rest you don't have to answer at all" (184). This is the voice of authority speaking, one of Kafka's bored and blasé demigods looking down on the crowd of petitioners and supplicants, neglecting those whose demands are ordinary and treating with even greater contempt those whose demands are not. He who still hopes to receive an unequivocal answer to his question may share the fate of the enquirer in front of the window who, still listening, gradually becomes aware that he is "finished already." "He" is finished, says Kafka, not only his question; and the German word *erledigt* spans all the nuances between "dispatched" and "lost." The scene is summed up by the Information Giver's "almost imperceptible shake of the head," a gesture of negation. Inasmuch as Kafka will soon return from parabolical significance to the realities of an apprenticeship novel, this sign of negation expresses an exhortation for Karl to stop, reflect, and reformulate his claims. On the symbolic level, however, even this faint hope is dissipated. After all, we still find ourselves within the confines of the Hotel Occidental, and the decline connoted by this name heralds the darkness of a world where questions are drowned by silence, and answers, if they are given at all, are distinguished only by their unintelligibility.

Brunelda's Opera Glasses

Kafka did not finish the novel's penultimate chapter, called by Brod not quite convincingly "A Refuge." [15] Although Karl actually finds shelter from the police in Brunelda's apartment, he is exposed there to human wild life as haunting as all the experiences of his past. When the chapter breaks off, he is, however, sadder, wiser, and almost a man. This may have prevented Kafka from continuing, since a disillusioned hero would have fitted poorly in the highly illusionary world of the Oklahoma theatre, the scene of the last chapter.

Brunelda in her massive carnality succeeds where tender and soulful Therese has failed: she awakens the boy. Far from being attracted by her, he comes to understand and accept sexual love as a natural phenomenon. Waking up in the middle of the night, he gropes his way to "a sort of bed, on top of which, as he found out by feeling around cautiously, Delamarche and Brunelda were sleeping." Experiencing neither fear nor horror nor surprise, he is now able to register these simple facts of life with a dry "So now he knew where they all were" (242). Supported by Delamarche's cocky possessiveness and the feverish prattle of Robinson, Brunelda makes up for past omissions: she introduces Karl to the reality of human relationships in their grossest and most grotesque form. He, however, remains only an observer.

Surrounded by men, Brunelda lives only for her rank flesh, which she cherishes and protects, bathes and scents, nourishes and dresses. She is a relic of tropical primitivity surrounded by the depraved civilization of a slum street. Neither good nor bad, always eager to sate her never-diminishing appetites, she is reminiscent of Molly Bloom, who, while falling asleep, says yes to the murderously virile world of James Joyce's *Ulysses*.

To call Brunelda the "apex of Kafka's critical investigations into society" [16] is to misunderstand her nature and to misrepresent her function in the novel. She has left her husband because his wealth strangled her like the corset in which she is "too tightly laced" (216) when Robinson and Delamarche lay eyes on her for the first time. She follows the tramps because in their company she is at liberty to indulge in her whims and both figuratively and literally take off her bodice whenever she pleases (213). Robinson had touched her back on the first ocasion; Delamarche had boxed Robinson's ear (216); thus she decides for the stronger man. However, she has obviously not objected to Robinson's seeing her naked (212) and comforts the wretch, who is completely deranged by his lovesickness, as often and as intimately as Delamarche, her master, is willing to permit.

Brunelda's unabashed amorality dispels in one short day Karl's dark suspicions about the supremacy of sex which had haunted him ever since he saw the Head Waiter playing with the fingers of the Manageress; it does so by confirming them as stark reality. The question of trust and good will which he had posed to the Manageress and Therese has become obsolete in his new surroundings. Johanna Brummer and the Manageress had one thing in common: they served the fire of the hearth. The Manageress acted consistently by sending him straight from the hotel to the Pension Brenner (177), Brenner being the German equivalent of "burner." A mild domestic warmth would have awaited him there if the place had lived up to its name. Instead he has landed in a house of ill repute, in spite of Delamarche's jealousy. And it is indeed a brothel to which Karl moves Brunelda in one of the fragments belonging in the context of this chapter. To reach the "dark, narrow lane" where this ominous "Firm Number Twenty-five" is situated, he has to pack Brunelda in a cart, covering the whole bulk of her with a gray cloth. On the way he is accosted by a man who wonders what on earth is concealed beneath the cloth. Karl tries to brush him off. "But since this aroused still greater curiosity in the man, Karl ended up by saying: 'Apples.'" He may be thinking of the apple in Eve's hand or, rather, of the fruit Therese offered him once as a token of her affection. "'So many apples!' said the man astonished, repeating this exclamation many times. Finally he said: 'A whole crop.' 'What of it?' answered Karl." [17] The uniqueness of Therese's love is contrasted here with the multiplicity, the "crop," of sexual acts most willingly performed by Brunelda and as indistinguishable from the rest of her favors as one apple is from the other. But Karl could not care less. His "What of it?" (*Nun ja*) is an expression of complete indifference.

Yet there is another side to Brunelda. "She is certainly a singer, and a great singer," Robinson exclaims (217). Her very name is assonant with Brunhilde, and she certainly possesses the enormous measurements the Valkyries used to display on the Wagnerian stage at Kafka's time. Now, however, she has retired, for "although she is so fat, she is very delicate; she often has headaches and almost always gout in her legs" (215). Not even in private does she sing any more, and Robinson "had to turn one of her theatrical costumes into a curtain and hang it up instead of the old one" (214). In view of the role of the disenchantress which Kafka has assigned to her in the development of his hero, it is noteworthy that he chose an artist, albeit a retired one, to perform the task of disillusionment. Art is seen here not as the master but the *maîtresse* of life.

From the days of her glory she has kept opera glasses, and these she forces upon Karl when they watch a procession down on the street from the balcony of their house. She bends over him and tries, with the aimlessness of a carnivorous plant, to embrace the boy. "And sighing deeply she kept plucking restlessly and distractedly at Karl's shirt." But, Kafka hastens to add, she "was not thinking of him; she was occupied with quite other thoughts" (about what?—231). Although Karl tries to extricate himself from her embrace and leave the house at the earliest possible moment, he is momentarily spellbound by the happenings far down on the street. What fascinates him is the campaign of a candidate for the post of district judge. As Brunelda behind (and around) him has revealed to him the prostitution of love, so does the scene before him open his eyes to the corruption of liberty and justice. For the freedom of this election consists primarily in the distribution of free beer. Here if anywhere does Kafka come close to a satirical treatment of American democracy, and democracy in general. At the same time he transforms the mob scene into a ghostly—and most competently staged—ballet of beer-thirsty humanity. Moreover, he constructs a direct parallelism between Karl, who is hemmed in by Brunelda's embrace, and the political candidate below, who is just as tightly wedged in by the crowd of his voters scrambling for drinks. The unfortunate vote getter is perched on the shoulders of a supporter, who, "strong giant as he was, could not take a step of his own free will" (237). Karl, perched on the balcony above, has no free will either: "Delamarche was standing on his left, Robinson had now moved across to his right; he was literally a prisoner" (235). This parallel construction is more than a literary device, a stylization to mitigate the crass realism of a satirical mob scene; it carries a distinct meaning for the process of disillusionment going on in Karl: he, the former fighter for abstract justice, finds himself just as imprisoned as is the would-be judge, the prospective administrator of practical justice, down there on the street. Thus Karl receives an object lesson on what freedom and justice look like when they are allowed to materialize. Brunelda, still leaning against him and threatening to push him down through the flimsy railing, is apt to remind him of the real character of another abstraction, love. This time, however, Karl learns his lesson. When his neighbor, the student Joseph Mendel, offers a melancholy epilogue to the spectacle of democracy in action they have just witnessed, Karl seems wholeheartedly to agree. The candidate, says Mendel, "is not without ability, and as far as his political views and his political past are concerned, he would actually be the most suitable judge for the district. But . . . he will be defeated as dismally as any-

one can." Thereupon Karl and the student "gazed at each other for a
little while in silence" (250). Karl does not know better any more.
He has understood and is resigned to accepting Mendel's views as a
mature judgment.

Mendel—Kafka may have chosen the name because it sounds like
a pejorative diminutive of *Mann*, "man"—has no illusions whatever.
His words reflect the utter vacuity of a soul from which all hopes have
fled. He knows the mechanisms of life down to their smallest cogwheel
and is quite prepared to take the machine apart for the benefit of
Karl. But is he able to put it together again? His own state does not
suggest too high a degree of efficiency: during the day he serves as
"a miserable counter-jumper" in a department store (247); at night he
studies and is convinced that this additional drudgery is detrimental to
his career as a businessman: "Unfortunately the others . . . call me
'Black Coffee,' a stupid criticism which I am sure has damaged my
career already" (248). This image of human frustration has been
chosen by Karl as a mentor. He takes Mendel's advice and decides to
stay in Brunelda's service. Disenchanted, Karl becomes the successor
to the prime victim of delusion, Robinson.

At this point *Der Verschollene* ceases to be an apprenticeship novel.
Within the pseudorealistic framework of Karl's American surroundings
Kafka has given us no indication that Karl would surpass the dreary
example set to him by Mendel, whose student he is now to become.
Quite the contrary, "he did not have such high aims as the student;
perhaps at home he would never have succeeded in carrying studies
to their conclusion; and if it was difficult to do this at home, no one
could expect him to manage it here in a strange land" (251). The scene
in the fragment where Karl pushes Brunelda's cart to a whorehouse
supports these melancholy musings.

Brunelda has taught him too well. Among the many uncertainties and
improbabilities offered us by this fragmentary chapter there remains
at least the probability that Karl will never succumb physically to his
new mistress. (In the last sentence Karl, who hears her stirring in her
sleep, has bedded himself far from her.) A latter-day Circe intent on
turning into swine all men who come near her, she has tried to use
a most fitting magic instrument: to facilitate and intensify her embrace
on the balcony she offered Karl her opera glasses. Opera glasses are,
of course, destined to add to the illusion of the stage the further illusion of the spectator's propinquity to a scene going on at a considerable
distance. For the retired singer the glasses are a part of her past,

and she intends to distinguish Karl by passing them on to him. (Delamarche is not even being considered.) "How do you like it, my boy,"
she asks him, using the same prostitute's phrase, *Mein Kleiner*, with
which the Manageress had once addressed him. "Would you not like
to look through my glasses?" "I can see well enough," Karl replies. "Do
try, . . . you will see much better." If, however, he were to see the
street scene better still, he would only recognize sooner the sham character of the campaign and be all the more profoundly disillusioned. As
to Brunelda herself, her increased attention has the immediate effect
of increasing his resistance: "I have good eyes. . . . I can see everything." Yet with the word most mysterious in love and most direct
in sex—with the syllable "you," "uttered melodiously but threateningly"
—she overpowers him. "Now were the glasses before Karl's eyes and he
actually saw nothing" (233). Involuntarily showing him only emptiness
through her magic glasses, Brunelda has led him to the very bottom
of disillusionment. It is this nothingness that has taken the place of
his juvenile visions. While justice and freedom are discredited before
his eyes, he sees, "actually," the vacuum to which he has been awakened. Karl has reached nihilism as the last stage in his disillusionment.
From this no man's land, Kafka must have felt, he was only to be
rescued by a miracle.

This miracle Kafka tried to perform in the Oklahoma theatre of
the last chapter. In order to do so he had to change the scene so drastically that the very form of the novel was shattered. However hard
he tried to connect this last chapter with the preceding ones, however
skillfully he disguised its basically mystical nature by introducing
parodistic images and others which seem to parody even these parodies,
the original mold of the work was broken and could not be restored.

The Final Examination

The central image of this chapter, the theatre itself, is a case in
point. Boldly it introduces itself:

The Oklahoma theatre will engage members for its company today at Clayton race course from six o'clock in the morning until midnight! The great
theatre of Oklahoma calls you! It calls only today and never again! If you
miss your chance now you miss it for ever! If you think of your future, you
belong to us! Everyone is welcome! If you are an artist, report here! Here is
the theatre that can employ everyone, each at his place! If you decide in
our favor, we congratulate you here and now! But hurry, so that you

get in before midnight! At twelve o'clock everything will be shut and never opened again! Cursed be those who do not believe in us! Up and to Clayton (252)!

The actual message of this remarkable poster is drowned out in a hailstorm of exclamation points. Who is shouting here at the top of his voice? The theatre owner or the proprietor of the race course? A resident of Clayton or an Oklahoman? A lunatic or a philanthropist? A salesman or an evangelist or a proselytizer? Whoever it be, he blesses and curses in the same breath. His sentences have the same "melodious but threatening" cadence that struck Karl in Brunelda's approaches. And his insistence on the hour of midnight as a deadline conjures up the far-more-distant memory of the hour Uncle Jacob had set to banish Karl.

The nature of the Oklahoma theatre remains undisclosed to the very end. To one critic Clayton is the tomb (Clay-town) and Karl's eventual journey to Oklahoma, the "beautiful country," his pilgrimage into infinity.[18] Another, blind to Kafka's ironic sidelights and deaf to his parodistic overtones, translates the initiation rites to which Karl is subjected into the stages of his confirmation into the Catholic church: "In his reception one will be able to see the parable of man's redemption by love of Christ." [19] A third, whose senses are acute enough to register the effects of caricature Kafka was trying to produce, attributes them to a satire on the critical condition from which religion suffers in the modern world. On the one hand, "there is no institution other than the church that can promise a place, employment, as does the nature theatre"; on the other hand, however, he claims: "The church that attempts to win Karl Rossmann is the church in its contemporary situation: few join the fold." [20] A fourth, in the quest for a secular and philosophical Kafka, decrees: "There can be no doubt: This 'Nature Theatre' is a theatre on which the truth of the world is enacted, truth in every sense, as a critical unmasking and as a positive liberation." [21]

Conflicting as they are, these interpretations are united in accepting the allegorical nature of the Oklahoma theatre. Differences arise solely when it comes to recognizing the meaning of the allegory. A successful allegory does not allow for explanations which are mutually exclusive, whereas a genuine symbol can convey a multitude of meanings and still remain profoundly undisclosed. Not every image that refuses to yield its full meaning to rational investigation is *ipso facto* a symbol; it may simply be an opaque allegory. We are confronted by such a miscarried symbol when we follow Karl into the theatre. It seems that Kafka attempted unsuccessfully to regain the parabolical level of the trial scenes in the Hotel Occidental. He was not fully prepared to believe in the miracle that was to save his hero and was tempted to parody what he still, at least partially, believed. Because this last chapter consists of different layers which are not sufficiently amalgamated to impress us with their unity, we can hope to trace Kafka's intentions by outlining some of them.

Sham religious trappings cover the surface of this theatre, which is in reality a race track. The pathos of the posters is false. The din of the trumpets is confused and confusing. The trumpeters are angels who, on closer inspection, turn out to be women playing these very unfeminine instruments "very badly" (257). The pedestals which support them threaten to collapse any moment. When they are tired, these angels are relieved by devils, who are men dressed as satans. We cannot help agreeing with Karl's observation that "perhaps this display of angels and devils frightens people off more than it attracts them." Yet it is "the greatest theatre in the world"; it is old but, like the Hotel Occidental, continually growing, and some people who have already been in Oklahoma report that it is "almost infinite" (258). Blending the elements of a country fair with those of a mystical theatre of the world, a *theatrum mundi*, this enterprise does not extend into infinity, although its contours are certainly vague. The scene is set for the redemption of Karl; yet the actors appear to be mostly vaudeville comedians and circus artists.

It is impossible to perform a mystery play and an operetta simultaneously on the same stage. This, however, is precisely what Kafka is trying to do. A diary entry from the year 1911 may help to elucidate his failure. He comments on the performance of Grillparzer's late romantic love tragedy *Des Meeres und der Liebe Wellen:* "I had tears in my eyes several times, as at the end of the first act when Hero and Leander could not take their eyes away from one another." Here speaks a spectator who is ready to succumb to the magic of the theatre and, as a writer, willing to exploit its charms to redeem his hero as Faust is redeemed at the end of Goethe's tragedy. Then the diary continues, still concerned with Grillparzer's star-crossed lovers: "Hero stepped out of the temple door-way through which you saw something that could have been nothing else but an icebox" (*DII*, 243). With this Kafka shows that, like Karl Rossmann after his experiences with Brunelda, he will not be taken in by illusions of any kind. The theatre of Oklahoma has been imagined by a writer who wanted, as Brod

put it, to believe in "some celestial witchery" which would enable his
hero to find "a profession, a helper, his freedom, even his old home
and his parents" (277). But Kafka's imagination was too often deflected
and his vision disturbed by an "icebox in the background," a reminder
of reality which sufficed to negate the transcendence of his vision
and destroy its illusion.

Thus Karl, on the one hand, is admitted to the offices—"the more
there are the better" (260); but, on the other hand, the offices are in
"the stands where the bets are laid on ordinary days" (258) and the
prospective employee is not judged, as the poster had announced, by
his promise as an artist but by his physical strength (269). The successful applicants (and not one fails) are wined and dined by the
authorities in what appears to be an only slightly parodied version of
Lubberland (which is itself a parody of Paradise) (271), only to realize soon after that the lordly last supper has been offered the newcom-
ers as a bait to prevent them from defecting at the last minute (274).
Similarly Karl is given a photograph of the theatre building itself as
a harbinger of all the things to come. The picture shows the presi-
dential box, and Karl, who has not yet outgrown his admiration for
the powers that be, puts it beside his plate and keeps gazing at it.
Characteristically the picture presents an expanse of space so generous
that "one might have thought it was not a box but the stage itself."
The box, however, is conspicuously empty and its background appears
"like a dark vacuum glowing in a reddish dusk." It is the same nothingness into which Karl had peered through Brunelda's opera glasses.
Like this box the theatre as such seems to consist of a foreground
"literally bathed in light" (272) and a background occupied by nothing and nobody.

The theatre, then, indicates the two stages of Karl Rossmann's
development: the state in which he arrived in America, full of illusions
and hope, and his disillusionment, brought on by his experiences in
the service of Brunelda. The question arises which point in his development he has reached when he is inducted into the theatre. Standing
before the poster, he betrays a considerable awareness of reality. He
reflects:

There were so many posters; nobody believed in them any longer. . . .
Above all . . . [this poster] did not mention payment. If the payment were
worth mentioning at all, . . . this most attractive of all arguments would
not have been forgotten. No one wanted to be an artist, but everybody
wanted to be paid for his labors (252–253).

And yet he enters, attracted mostly, as he admits, by the welcome extended to all and sundry. The desire to be accepted at any price is still so strong in him as to overcome easily his more rational deliberations. And once he has emerged from the subway that carried him to Clayton and entered the race track, he surrenders to the course of events and slides from station to station, as he has always done.

In the employment bureau he is asked for his name. "He did not reply at once; he felt shy of mentioning his own name and letting it be written down. . . . So as no other name occurred to him at the moment, he gave the nickname he had in his last posts: 'Negro'" (264). This is the first and only time that the word "Negro" appears in Kafka's America. If Kafka had intended to emphasize political problems and to bare them critically, he would not have delayed mentioning the Negro question until these last pages. A trace of social criticism is contained in this name only in the very indirect and tenuous sense that it had been given to Karl recently as a sign of his profound degradation. But this trace is no more conclusive than a memory of waking reality that one carries over into a dream. The dream of acceptance and welcome, however, was born of the wish to rise beyond the depths of humiliation in which he, whose white color had been his only possession, was called black.

The name "Negro" emerges in Karl's imagination perhaps because it alludes to the type of work for which he is compelled to volunteer, illicit work, black work, *Schwarzarbeit*. "Is there perhaps an engineer here?" the personnel manager had asked. "Karl stepped forward. He thought that his very lack of papers made it imperative for him to race through all the formalities with the greatest possible speed." His impatience proves how little he has learned in all his tribulations, how much he is already a typical Kafka figure, how little he can hope for a happier end than the K.'s in *The Trial* and *The Castle*. With them he also shares the inclination to excuse himself by means of self-delusion. For Karl continues his train of thoughts. "He had also a slight justification in reporting, for he had once wanted to be an engineer" (262). With this reflection Kafka cleverly joins the last chapter of the novel to the first, where Karl had indeed informed the Stoker: "I have always had a passion for mechanical things and I would have become an engineer in time, that is certain, if I had not had to go to America" (4). Now he recalls his old dream in order to engineer at least his retention by the theatre. He is ready to accept all kinds of work, and since he is an unskilled laborer, whatever he accepts will be illicit work, *Schwarzarbeit*. "As soon as he had a place here, no matter how small, and filled it satisfactorily, they could have his name, but not now" (264). Having left his passport in the hands of the Head Porter, unable to acquire new identity papers in his plunge from one position to the other, he now decides on this temporary blackout until he has acquired a new identity by being accepted into the crew of this theatre.

But the theatre in turn has subjected him to an examination, a process that counteracts somewhat its assertion that everybody is welcome. Whatever Kafka may have intended to say here, whether this theatre was to represent a judge of the dead, a church, or an abstract court of truth, Karl is undoubtedly put into a situation of being tested. He does not seem to fare too well; from the office for engineers he is sent to a bureau for technicians, thence to an office for people who have been high school pupils, and from there to a bureau for European high school students (263). He is whittled down to his real measure, especially by being advised that even the office for people who have been pupils (*gewesene Mittelschüler*) is not yet the right place for him. Relegated to the category of European high school students, he is told precisely what he still is, a foreigner in America and a youth who has not passed his final examination in school. Twice before, in his speech before Pollunder (73) and during his second conversation with the Manageress (121), Karl has described this school as a Latin school or *Gymnasium*.* The final examination of Austrian Latin schools is called *Matura*. To pass his *Matura* and prove his maturity, Karl has been sent to this bureau, which is, as he recognizes, "probably" his "last refuge." When he catches sight of the Head of this office, he is

almost frightened by his resemblance to a professor who was probably still teaching in the high school at home. The resemblance, however, . . . was confined to certain details; but the spectacles resting on the man's broad nose, the fair beard as carefully tended as a prize exhibit, the slightly curved back, and the loud voice, that kept erupting unexpectedly, held Karl in amazement for quite some time (263).

---

* That he remembers it now as a *Realschule* (263) is probably due to a slip in his (or Kafka's?) memory prompted by the fact that this type of high school, with its emphasis on science, offers an education appropriate for one who claims to be an engineer. In the German original he furthermore declares, first (to Pollunder), that he has passed only four grades, then (to the Manageress), that he has attended five grades.

This vivid description fraught with memories, which all but identify the Head of the Bureau as the professor at home, underscores the similarity of the interrogation here and the final examination still in store for Karl there.

Here, at last, the student seems to pass, although in a most curious manner. "Accepted," says the clerk who, in contrast to his superior, has not been distinguished by detailed description. It is at this point that Karl gives "Negro" as his name. " 'Negro'? said the Head, turning around and making a grimace as if Karl had now touched the high watermark of incredibility." Strongly protesting the clerk's acceptance of this name as the correct one, the "professor" tries to control himself and pronounce the engagement clause, "but he could not go against his own conscience, so he sat down and said: 'He is not called Negro.' The clerk raised his eyebrows, got up himself and said: 'Then I am the one to tell you that you have been engaged" (264–265).

If the Head of the office is meant to represent Karl's past and the clerk his future, then the past has revealed both his deception ("He is not called Negro") and his lack of maturity (the "professor" "could not go against his conscience" and pass him at the *Matura*). The cleik, on the other hand, has committed both an act of insubordination (he offended his superior, the Head) and a mistake which is bound to be discovered when Karl's case is "looked into again" (269). The Head has declared Karl remiss in the task set him by Kafka's original design, that is, to grow up and be a man, and the glimpse the clerk allows us to get of the boy's future is far from reassuring. Yet if this examination is not a *Matura,* it is still a commencement: he is allowed to set out on a new career—under false pretences.

Thus he graduates from "Negro, the European high school student" (266), to "Negro, a technical worker" (269), a title which is displayed on an announcement board. He is likewise officially informed that his work will be "minor." This means manual labor, as he realizes when his informant, "a member of the tenth recruiting squad" (266), unabashedly feels the strength of his arm. Having reported as an engineer, he is now reduced in the last chapter to the status of an unskilled laborer, the same social level on which he had found his friend, the Stoker, in the first chapter.

Yet he is resigned to his low status. "As everything here was taking an orderly course, Karl felt that after all he would not have regretted seeing his real name on the board." Needless to say, he does not lift a finger to fulfill the promise he had given himself during the final examination. He keeps his name to himself. Yet fate catches up with him, instantly and ironically. Or, as Kafka puts it, "the organisation was indeed scrupulously precise," for an attendant waits to fasten a band around his arm. "There, right enough, were the words 'Technical Worker'" (269–270). The theatre has not accepted the false name, Negro, nor any other name. Karl has become nameless, an anonymous particle in an amorphous mass, to be shipped across the country and used for unknown ends. He is, as an attendant points out to him, "the last" (270), in the truest sense of the word.

He who has lost his name is forgotten and will never more be heard of. The magnificent scene of the following train ride cannot blind our eyes to the fact that this is Karl Rossmann's last journey. From now on the nameless one will be what he always was in Kafka's mind, *Der Verschollene*.

CHAPTER VI

The Trial against the Court

NO matter when Kafka conceived the idea of *The Trial* or began work on it, the book in its present form reveals the mastery of literary style which he achieved only after 1912. The novel shows an originality of design and a unity of structure which were still absent in many parts of *Der Verschollene*. Like "The Judgment" and "In the Penal Colony," *The Trial* is a projected vision of punishment. Yet the punishment, which materialized in the nightmarish details of the execution machine in the Penal Colony, is translated here into the all-encompassing image of a more than dubious justice.

Since Kafka's visions of punishment ultimately grew out of his own guilt feelings, one is tempted to connect *The Trial* with the crisis engendered by his relationship with Felice Bauer. According to Max Brod, his formal engagement to her was announced at the end of May 1914.[1] This announcement seems to have precipitated rather than mitigated Kafka's torments. Less than two weeks later the diaries contain the outlines of an arrest (or execution) scene which anticipates the first (or last?) chapter of *The Trial*.

It was about midnight. Five men held me, above their heads a sixth had raised his hand to grab me. "Let go," I cried and whirled around in a circle, shaking them off. I felt the presence of some sort of law, had known that this last effort of mine would be successful, saw all the men reeling back with raised arms, realized that in a moment they would throw themselves on me together, turned toward the door of the house, . . . opened the lock (it sprang open of itself, as it were, with unusual rapidity) and escaped up the dark stairs (*DII,* 59).

The pursuers of *The Trial* have appeared already, although they out-number the two warders and the two executioners of the novel. The man has already reached a door, the central image of the novel, al-though this door leads to an ordinary house instead of into the law. Even the law is mentioned. But it is only a provisional "law of sorts," and not yet the one law which remains unfathomable in spite of its uniqueness and omnipresence.

After this entry the genesis of *The Trial* is registered in the diaries in terms of the progress of Kafka's personal crisis during this summer. On July 23 the decisive meeting with Felice's family is called, "the tribunal in the hotel" (*DII,* 65). On July 27 he seems to have decided to break the engagement; he calls the farewell letter "a [last] speech from the place of execution" (*DII,* 66). The next entry refers again to the meeting in the hotel as "the tribunal" (*DII,* 68). One day later, July 29, both Joseph K. and the doorkeeper make their first appearances in a diary passage; the former is still described as the son of a rich merchant and the latter stands guard before the house of the Mer-chants' Corporation (*DII,* 71).

August 1914 seems to have been a manic period of intense literary activity, such as frequently alternated with Kafka's most dismal de-pressions. On the twenty-first the diary mentions no fewer than three stories with which he occupied himself at the moment. Kafka notes that he is resuming work on what is called here for the first time *The Trial* (presumably one of the three stories), adding, however, that the hope to finish it is "ridiculous." Yet "the effort was not entirely a fail-ure," as can be seen on August 29, in which entry grudgingly and with constant self-detractions, he acknowledges the steady progress of his work. "I must not forsake myself, I am entirely alone," he concludes (*DII,* 91).

On December 8, less than four months later, he notes the beginning of the chapter "Journey to His Mother," which was to remain a frag-ment (291–296).* On December 13 he blames himself for having written this day "only one page (the exegesis of the legend)" (*DII,* 101); this comment refers to the conversation between Joseph K. and the Prison Chaplain toward the end of the last finished chapter of the novel. Although this does not necessarily mean that by this time he

---

* Numbers without letters refer to the American edition of *The Trial* (1957).

had finished the book as it exists today, it indicates that he had already written the parable "Before the Law," which is the legend mentioned above.

When on New Year's Eve 1915 he gives an account of his activities during the past year, he has every reason to be satisfied with himself. He writes: "Have been working since August, in general not little and not badly." Of course he qualifies this rare acknowledgment of his own achievement by self-reproaches and the reminder that *The Trial* was still unfinished business. The novel was to occupy him for some time before he interrupted his work, allowing it to remain a fragment; yet in the five months since he broke with Felice he had succeeded in writing the bulk of the book.[2]

In spite of the correspondences between the novel and Kafka's life which have been discussed above, the novel is infinitely more than an autobiographical document in which Franz Kafka punished Joseph K. for the misdeeds he blamed himself for having committed. On the contrary, the points of contact between life and novel reveal and stress the distance Kafka now puts between experience and creation. To be sure, his initial, the "offensive letter K.," * serves as the family name of his hero. But by being reduced to this one letter, the rest of Kafka's name becomes unimportant just as the author's personal properties are consciously removed. K. is an Everyman. Kafka has given him only as many of his own individual characteristics as were necessary to prevent the figure from dissolving into the mist of abstraction. Kafka and K. are almost contemporaries: after a trial that lasted one year, K. is killed on the evening before his thirty-first birthday (279). He dies at an age very close to Kafka's own at the time when he wrote the novel. Yet this age has different meanings for the writer and his figure. For Kafka it is the time when he had to decide between bachelorhood and a marriage that threatened to render his vocation, literature, still more impossible than it had been before. But marriage plays no part in Joseph K.'s career. Fräulein Bürstner, Felice Bauer's counterpart in the novel, does not threaten K. with wedlock. On the contrary, she is (along with the other women in the novel) used as a symbol of his ever-more-alarming withdrawal from the reality of life. Only in the fact that marriage pointed the way to an ideal life for Kafka and that K. was patently missing this life is the coincidence of their ages re-

---

° On May 27, 1914, he entered in his diary: "I find the letter K. offensive, almost nauseating, and yet I write it down, it must be characteristic of me" (*DII*, 33–34).

vealing. That is to say, it explains very little that would not have become clear by the simple statement that K. is, after all, a Kafka bachelor.°

As the title indicates, *The Trial* is not focused on the fate of the bank clerk Joseph K. but on the proceedings to which he is subjected. These proceedings are Kafka's theme, and Joseph K. can claim to play the role of the protagonist only because the Trial needs him to become manifest. He is a *Mann ohne Eigenschaften* (in Robert Musil's phrase), a nondescript man, devoid of spectacular deficiencies and virtues. His personal tragicomedy stems from the fact that he, in his mediocrity, is called upon to respond to demands that even a character of impressive stature would find impossible to fulfill. Above all, Kafka does not seem to be interested in the psychological development of his hero during the year of the trial (as, on the level of the apprenticeship novel, he still had been in *Der Verschollene*). As a human character Joseph K. shows as little body and soul as the monolinear figures Kafka drew on the margins of his manuscripts. K. is a literary image, and not a portrait, let alone the self-portrait of his author.

Since the novel is told from K.'s human point of view, it is bound to give the impression that its action consists of K.'s idle attempts to discover his guilt. This, however, would lower *The Trial* to the level of a mystery story in which the crime has to be ferreted out, not the criminal. It also would reduce the Trial itself to a mirror "of the process which starts in any man who is suddenly forced to master and justify his life in its totality." [3]

It is the reality of the invisible Court of Justice that permeates the story with its presence, and K. is nothing but the visible object chosen by the Court to prove its claim to adjudge man. The Court's effort to prove K.'s guilt to him are at least as fruitless as K.'s own attempts to discover his crime. Not only does the man try to penetrate into the interior of the Court, the Court also does its best to reach the conscience of K., to present the case made against him as justified and to induce him to atone actively.† Yet K. and the Court miss each other. Both movements, K.'s quest and the Court's pursuit, run past one another and lead to nothing. The metaphysical world of the Trial and the everyday sphere of K. have lost their common meeting ground.

In his "Reflections" Kafka once coined a very enlightening simile for

° On the other hand, there are, as we shall see, certain questions of K.'s life that can only be answered with reference to Kafka's biography. It is more than likely that Kafka intended these problems to remain unsolved and his private experiences to stay untouched.

† If K. is exposed to the trial, then the Court is likewise exposed to the grasp of K. This double exposure distorts the picture.

the state of affairs, as he perceived it in *The Trial:* "The crows maintain that a single crow could destroy the heavens. There is no doubt of this, but it proves nothing against the heavens, for heavens simply mean: the impossibility of crows" (*DF*, 37). The tangible creature, the crow, and the absolute which it has become impossible for the creature to grasp, the heavens, appear as mutually exclusive. If the heavens (Kafka's plural serves to remove them still further from the realm of reality) desire to take possession of the crow, they have to materialize; that is, they must stop being heavens. From the first page of the novel to the last, from the corrupt warders who arrest K. to the grotesque gentlemen who execute him, the Court has to send emissaries who seem to deride the principles both of law and of its sanctity. Even the Chaplain who emerges from the mystical darkness of the Cathedral shows "truly Satanic" [4] traits. Law has to renounce its very essence, justice, in order to confront man, just as the heavens would have to give up their very nature and take shape if ever they intended to meet a crow. Another of the "Reflections" reads: "A cage went in search of a bird" (*DF*, 36). This aphorism includes the parabolical content of *The Trial*. In its desire to communicate with man the Court of Justice has to choose messengers and use a language which must appear to K. as hostile as a cage seems to a bird. The surrealistic absurdity of this cage image contains in a nutshell the paradox underlying the novel. And yet, in the final analysis, there is a great amount of truth in this simile. Just as it is highly improbable that the search of a cage for a bird could ever be successful, so little does the Court of Justice, seemingly equipped with infinite power and a like store of information, succeed in convincing K. of his guilt. It wins the Trial only by slaughtering an ultimately unconvicted victim.

No formal suit is brought in this Trial against the accused. But *The Trial* itself is the indictment of a world order in which, as K. puts it, the "lying" of the authorities has been turned "into a universal principle" (276). What begins with the arrest of K., will end with K. challenging, in the hour of his death, the powers behind his Trial. Here, however, it appears that K. has retained enough of Kafka's doubts and uncertainties to give this challenge the form of a question and to surround it, mercifully perhaps, with the haze of ambiguity.

The law of the Law

"Someone must have denounced Joseph K., for without having done anything wrong he was arrested one morning" (3). This first sentence of the novel points to the paradox of the Law. But it remains hidden from the reader until he hears the last words the Chaplain speaks in the Cathedral scene. Here, at the high point of what is to be considered the climactic chapter of the book, the clergyman formulates the law of the Law. His words contain the only statement about the Trial which is no longer the guess of an outsider, the gossip of a meddler, or the doubtful hint of an incompetent intermediary, but a declaration of principles made by the Court about itself. "Do you realize who I am?" asks the priest. K., impatient and tired from a long-winded conversation, replies, "You are the Prison Chaplain." The clergyman retorts, "This means I belong to the Court." Underscoring the authority of the initiated, he also reveals the close connection his chaplainship has with the prison and the Law. Then the priest adds: "So why should I want anything from you? The Court wants nothing from you. It receives you when you come and dismisses you when you go" (278).

This characterization of the Court is accurate but for one thing. In majestic patience the Trial has enveloped K.'s life; yet it still allows him to come and go as he pleases. "You are under arrest, certainly," he had been informed in the beginning, "but this need not hinder you from going about your business. Nor will you be prevented from leading your ordinary life" (20). In this respect, the Trial resembles the Cathedral, the scene of this revelation: the church is always there but only for him who enters of his own volition; its doors are open equally for those who come and those who go, as K. will realize when he leaves. It, too, wants nothing from him.

Although K. is not used to worship and this particular visit has been planned as a tour, he enters the Cathedral voluntarily. He even enters it twice: the first time he is driven through the portals by the rainy day outside. "The Cathedral Square was quite deserted. . . . On a day like this, this was even more understandable than at other times. The Cathedral seemed deserted too" (255). He has stepped in, automatically and unconsciously, while he was immersed in his thoughts. The moment of entry has not been registered in the narrative. Therefore he has to go back to the entrance and make the circuit of the building once more before the tale continues: "Since he was tired he felt like sitting down, went into the Cathedral again . . . and sat down" (256). Here he knows what he is doing; the language dwells on the act of his entrance (he "went . . . again"); and the tiredness which prompts him to do so is, as we have learned at the beginning of the chapter, no momentary feeling of lassitude but the exhaustion caused by his yearlong occupation with the Trial. Consciously he enters now upon the scene in which the Court is to disclose to him the Law of its actions.

But if it is the law of the Law to receive those who come, dismiss those who desire to go, and otherwise remain unmoved and unmovable, then the Court has broken this Law by the very act of arresting K. It has singled him out and separated him from the others; it initiated the action when it forced him to start on the way that leads to the Cathedral, and eventually to his execution. This Law is at variance with another law, which was announced by the tall warder in the hour of K.'s arrest: "Our officials, so far as I know them, and I know only the lowest grades among them, do not by any means go hunting for the guilty ones in the populace, but, as the Law decrees, are drawn toward the guilty and must then send us warders. This is the Law." The limitations and qualifications of this statement should not deceive us; they are due to the warder's desire to avoid any responsibility for what he has said, an attitude typical of the servants of this Court. The Law itself, which "must" dispatch its emissaries and is "drawn toward" the criminals it persecutes, has lost its supremacy. No longer does it rest impassively above the humans who come and go; it reacts, it acts, it arrests. When K. admits, "I don't know this law" (10), he refers of course to the "legal constitution" (7) of the country in which he lives. But the higher constitution under which, according to the Chaplain, the Law of this Trial operates is contradicted by this arrest. Even the Chaplain violates the fundamental laws by calling K.'s name as soon as he sees him, thus summoning him once more. And when K., who senses a contradiction between the spirit of the Law and its administrators, suggests to the priest: "You may not know the nature of the Court you are serving," the Chaplain cries, "Can't you see one pace before you?" Here the sovereign indifference of the Law gives way to its urge to seize the man, to direct him, to keep him back, and to impart itself to him. The narrator adds by way of elucidation: "It was an angry cry, but at the same time sounded like the unwary shriek of one who sees another fall and is startled out of his senses" (265–266). In this moment of terror the Law unmasks itself. Showing concern for K.'s despair, it also admits the responsibility for the arrest which caused him to despair in the first place.

This basic paradox, inherent in the nature of the Law, may contribute to our understanding of the intermediaries whom the Court uses in its attempts to communicate with K. These officials, attorneys, and women appear stricken with guilt of one kind or the other because the Law which they pretend to know or to represent has committed a crime: it is guilty of having violated itself. By contradicting himself the priest proves his association with the Court more clearly than by his robe or his words. Since *The Trial* never proceeds beyond the sphere of these intermediary figures (among whom the Chaplain is the most advanced in rank and the most confusing), it is their paradoxical nature rather than the nondescript character of K. which seems to have fascinated Kafka.

This novel, the imagery of which abounds with symbols of light and darkness, is steeped in twilight.[5] Twilight fills the offices, the Court, and the studio of Titorelli, the painter; it winds its way into K.'s room in the bank and changes it into a shadowy, tomblike chamber; it floats through the nave of the Cathedral before it is extinguished by the night of K.'s execution. Yet twilight presupposes a source of light, however veiled. The sadness which informs the imagery of *The Trial* originates in Kafka's realization that there is a sublime sphere of light desiring to reach man. But in order to do so, it is forced to renounce its own nature: light. Brod reports a conversation with Kafka on February 28, 1920, during which Kafka described the human world as "one of God's bad moods, one of his bad days." Thereupon Brod asked whether there still was any hope. Kafka replied, "Plenty of hope—for God—an abundance of hope—only not for us" (*FK*, 75). As long as we are primarily interested in K.'s guilt we shall find support here for the thesis that K. is condemned to his sinister fate because he is and remains unaware of the existence of this hope. If, however, we read *The Trial* as a statement about the separation which exists between the spheres of light and darkness, hope and torment, then the realization that there *is* hope but *not for us* can only increase the shadows of forlornness thronging upon a lost world. This does not mean that the light has ceased to shine, but it does indicate the still more tormenting thought that, although it shines, it will never be able to dispel the twilight.[6] The year of K.'s trial is only a "bad day" of the Court. Yet this day is lost, not only for K. but especially for the Court.

Joseph K.'s Guilt

K.'s guilt is relatively simple if we compare it with the guilt of the Court and its intermediaries. Yet it is equally paradoxical. The whole catalogue of his sins—which are mostly sins of omission—does not suffice to justify his arrest. He has been blamed alternately for his inability to love,[7] his "weakness in living" (*FK*, 179), and his mediocrity, which makes him a representative of modern middle-class society,[8] but he shares these negative characteristics with most of the characters he encounters. These other people, however, were not arrested. Nor can he be reproached for his ignorance of the laws governing his Trial.[9] Most of the Court's emissaries are just as unfamiliar with the intricacies of the Law as he is. Even the painter Titorelli, who prides himself on being versed in the ways of the Court, proves to have no more actual insight into its principles than a blind man could have into the scheme of colors. "In the Code of the Law," he says, "which I admittedly have not read, it is of course laid down that the innocent shall be acquitted, but it is not stated there on the other hand that the judges are open to influence. Now, my experience is diametrically opposed to this" (192). Only two explanations seem possible here: either the Law is lying, or the painter, who describes himself as "being in the confidence of the Court" (184), is just as ignorant of the Law as the tall warder admits to being during K.'s arrest. There is, of course, a distinction between the Law and the Court, but only a legal expert would be equipped to draw it satisfactorily. To K. it must seem that the net in which he finds himself entangled is woven of split hairs. If, on the other hand, the Law does not lie, then the utterances of its emissaries are nothing but opinions and, as the priest in the Cathedral says: "The text of the Law is unalterable, and the opinions are often enough only an expression of despair about this text" (272–273). How, then, would we be justified in basing K.'s guilt on his lack of familiarity with a Law about which even its messengers have only vague and highly subjective opinions?

In spite of this apparent guiltlessness, K. makes a confession of his guilt. On the way to his execution he realizes that "the only thing for me to do is to keep my intelligence calm and analytic to the end." In German he uses the word *einteilend*, which means "distributing" as well as "analytic." How does his intelligence distribute and systematize his guilt? "I always wanted," he confesses, "to snatch at the world with twenty hands" (282). This is not a metaphor: it is not introduced with an "as if" or "as it were." It is a stark exaggeration: he multiplies the number of his hands by ten. But Kafka was a realist of unreality. If he has Joseph K. refer to his fantastic "twenty hands," he uses an image which characterizes his state of mind rather than one which expresses his guilt or his awareness of it.

In this passage K. accuses himself of boundless ambition, of greed, and of ruthlessness when he disturbs the even proportions of the organized world with his grasp of twenty hands. Yet until his arrest his life has been a downright model of moderation, and this very moderation is considered by some of K.'s critics to be his guilt. He owes his career to the middle-class virtues of "diligence and reliability" (23), which he has proved during his service. "His talent for organization" is "highly praised in the Bank" (189). He usually remained behind the desk in his office until nine o'clock in the evening, then he took a short walk and ended his day at eleven o'clock, after having patronized a restaurant in the company of "mostly elderly gentlemen" (23). To be sure, one cannot help noticing the care he took to build up the right social connections as well as his pronounced status-consciousness. But these are characteristics of the average person who knows his limits yet is eager to get ahead. If he really begins to lose his balance during his Trial, and starts to fidget and grasp nonsensically into the void, then his "snatching at the world" is like that of a drowning man who is trying in vain to regain solid ground. It reveals no lust for life, but is, rather, a final symptom of the mental destitution to which he has fallen prey.

The tirade he adds to his confession continues and exaggerates the attitude which was expressed in the image of the twenty hands: "Am I to show now that not even a year's trial has taught me anything? Am I to leave this world as a stubborn man who has no common sense? . . . I am grateful for the fact that . . . it has been left to me to tell myself all that is needed" (282–283). This confession comes close to the type of statement made by political prisoners who have been brainwashed by their opponents. Yet Joseph K. has been neither beaten nor drugged physically. Exhausted and horrified, he follows the last advice his "calm and analytic intelligence" is able to give him. Having recognized in his conversation with the Chaplain that lying has become a universal principle, he tells the Court what, in his opinion, the Court expects him to say. But if he commits the sin of hypocrisy, he acts in self-defense. These lies are the last consequence of his Trial; they remain confined to his thoughts, are never uttered, refuted, or approved, nor do they contribute anything to our understanding of K.'s arrest or his execution.

In spite of the fact that there seems to be no actual source for K.'s guilt, he has been feeling guilty from the moment the proceedings against him began. Kafka has used here the contrapuntal technique of juxtaposition: at the same time that K. is protesting his innocence, there are distinct indications of his guilt feelings. K. does not notice them, but the reader is forced to stop and consider their sudden and unexplained emergence in the text.

When on the evening of K.'s arrest his landlady announces her intention to give notice to his neighbor, Fräulein Bürstner, in order to "keep her house clean," he explodes with the cry: "Cleanliness! . . . If you want to keep your house clean you will have to begin by giving me notice" (29). This eruption occurs without preparation and remains without immediate consequence. Nor are we given any motivation for it.

Much later K. answers Titorelli's question, "Are you innocent?" with an ostensibly unhesitating "Yes." The narrator intervenes at this point by enlarging on the firmness of K.'s reply: "Nobody else had yet asked him such a frank question. To savor his elation to the full he added: 'I am completely innocent'" (186). Yet when the painter begins to map out his strategy of defense, K. feels progressively more irritated by Titorelli's insistence on his guiltlessness. "The repeated mentioning of his innocence began already to annoy K. At moments it seemed to him as if the painter were offering his help on the assumption that the trial would turn out well, which made his offer worthless" (190). He registers the displeasure which he experiences whenever his innocence is mentioned by someone else. Doubts have emerged which are too strong to be easily dispelled by K.'s intelligence. A traumatic spot has been touched in his unconscious; yet K. uses whatever conscious energies he possesses to push back and suppress his misgivings about himself. Eventually the reader is led to the conclusion that the paradox of K.'s guilt consists in his inability and unwillingness to remember what this guilt really is. "I forget myself" (*Ich vergesse mich*), he exclaims when he reenacts his arrest during the first night of his Trial (35). To the very end of the novel he goes on forgetting himself and his guilt.

The Man from the Country

So far we have been discussing K.'s guilt primarily on the basis of our psychological insight into his character. Yet Kafka was not concerned with K.'s psychology when he wrote *The Trial*. The novel is a parable, and when we approach it on the more-than-realistic level suggested to us by its intention of being a simile of human existence, we may discover in its language a clue to K.'s apparently enigmatic guilt.

In the Cathedral the priest tells K. the parable "Before the Law." He tells it to prove to K. that he is deluding himself about the Court. He prefaces his tale with the remark: "In the Scriptures introducing the Law it is said about this particular delusion . . ." By pointedly stressing the scriptural as well as the legal character of the tale, the priest bestows upon it an indisputable authority. As evidenced by the "exegesis" which ensues, each single word of the parable carries decisive importance. The first two sentences run as follows: "Before the Law stands a doorkeeper. To this doorkeeper comes a man from the country and begs for admittance into the Law . . ." (267). Since K. is told the story so that he may learn through it the delusion under which he is laboring with regard to his Trial, the man from the country stands in the same relationship to the doorkeeper as does K. to the emissaries of the Court of Justice, above all to the priest. Yet what is the country from which the man has come? K., who is supposed to identify himself with the man, never poses this question. In the parable the qualification "from the country" is used to indicate the long distance the man had to cover before he reached the door of the Law; he has, the priest tells K., "equipped himself with many things for this journey" (268). Joseph K., on the other hand, has not changed his residence after his arrest; he has entered the Cathedral completely unequipped; and although he may have been born in the small provincial town where his mother still lives (291), he now behaves like a confirmed big-city dweller.*

Yet in spite of the fact that the description "the man from the country" hardly seems appropriate at first, it begins to fit K. as soon as it is translated into its Hebrew equivalent, *Am-ha'aretz*. Kafka was familiar at least with the Yiddish version of the word, *Amhoretz;* since 1911 [10] he had occupied himself intensively with Jewish and Yiddish folklore, and the expression actually occurs in the diaries late in November of this year (*DI,* 166). *Amhoretz,* however, is the nickname for an ignoramus. The *Am-ha'aretz* is just as unversed in the scriptures as he is ignorant of the social conventions in secular life. K. inevitably acts and reacts as an *Am-ha'aretz* whenever he comes near one of the messengers of the Court: in spite of the smooth manners which befit him as an average person, he appears both arrogant and submissive, both gauche and slick; he asks awkward questions, gives coy replies,

* Not even the projected "Journey to His Mother" materializes. The chapter devoted to this excursion was rejected and broken off after a few pages. See also pp. 338–339 below.

and exhibits a knack for doing the wrong thing or saying the wrong word at the slightest provocation. Before the Law he is a primitive whose mind grasps only what he can touch with his hands or otherwise take in with his senses. He is able to understand pictures such as the image of Justice represented as a goddess of hunt and victory which he finds in Titorelli's studio (182 ff.), but he is by nature unable to comprehend the legal and theological abstractions which form the Law of his Trial. If he were to possess the Bible, it would have to be one of the mediaeval *biblia pauperum,* which substitutes the picture for the word. When he enters the Cathedral, he actually carries instead of a prayerbook a picture book, an album for sightseers tucked under his arm. He misses what could not escape even so simpleminded an observer as his landlady, to whom his arrest appears as "something learned." Being an *Am-ha'aretz,* he considers the Trial at first "completely null and void" (26), then he translates it into accepted usage and calls it a "legal action" which "was nothing more than a business deal such as he had often concluded to the advantage of the Bank, a deal within which, as always happened, lurked various dangers which must simply be obviated" (159). An *Am-ha'aretz* is often recognizable by the clichés he uses to deceive others and himself about his ignorance.

In Biblical times, however, *Am-ha'aretz* did not mean an individual simpleton but the whole people of the Palestinian hinterland—the fishermen, shepherds, and craftsmen who were looked down upon by the dwellers of the mountain city, Jerusalem, living close to the Sanctuary.

This group included those at the bottom of the social ladder, the very poor, the uneducated—those too preoccupied with their struggle for a scanty living to observe the meticulous requirements of the Law. The Gospels intimate that this disinherited population was the object of Jesus' special solicitude. . . . Among them, according to some scholars, Jesus may have belonged.[11]

They too belong to the *Am,* the people bound by the Covenant; but *ha'aretz,* ("the country") claimed their services and barred them from easy access to the nation's spiritual center, the Law. Through the ages, the word *Am-ha'aretz* has retained vestiges of the tension between the priestly and abstract on the one hand and the profane and concrete on the other.

In the Cathedral scene, where the Law comes closest to revealing itself to K., Kafka may, perhaps even consciously, have used the image of a Catholic church and the figure of a Christian priest because he recognized in Christ the promise of a mediatorship between the country below and the Law on high. To be sure, this promise concerned Kafka, a Jew, as little as it became visible to his hero, K. Rather it was a ray of that "abundance of hope" which was "not for us." When, in the fourth Octavo Notebook, Kafka jots down: "We too must suffer all the suffering around us. Christ suffered for mankind, but mankind must suffer for Christ" (*DF*, 46, 97), the accent falls heavily on suffering, and redemption remains unmentioned. Kafka used Christian symbols in his Cathedral scene but he employed them solely as scenery and costume, as props in a play of his imagination, without being able to derive from them the good tidings of man's salvation. At first he may not even have been aware of the metaphysical depths he had touched here. Considerable time elapsed before the "significance" of the priest's parable "dawned upon" him (*DII*, 112). Whatever the deeper meaning of this story may be, the man from the country never enters the Law, and K. to whom the parable is told is bound to misinterpret even this simple fact.

K. is an *Am-ha'aretz* in that he is a man dedicated to the concrete activities of his professional life and has no patience with the lofty abstractions of the Law. Disturbed in his daily pursuits by his arrest, he is eager to win his Trial and resume his former active life. His controversy with the Chaplain, then, is an expression of the conflict between a mundane and a priestly life. Kafka himself was torn by a similar conflict, the incompatibility of his professional activities and his vocation as a writer. The conflict seems to have been inherited, for Kafka on his father's side was the offspring of a "man from the country," whose boorishness, ignorance, and unbelief he deplored in the "Letter to His Father." Kafka's mother was born a Löwy, who could retrace her descent to the priestly family of the Levites. Thus Kafka saw himself as a "Löwy with a certain basis of Kafka, which, however, is not set in motion by the Kafka will to life, business, and conquest, but by a Löwyish spur that urges more secretly, more diffidently, and in another direction, and which often fails to work entirely" (*DF*, 140). The Kafka in Kafka prevailed upon him to stand his ground in life and prove his worth to the father by conquering reality. The "Löwyish spur" drove him in the opposite direction and forced him to dedicate himself to writing, a "form of prayer." He never resolved this conflict; he thought he had failed both the Kafka and Löwy trends in his heritage and felt guilty on both counts.

Kafka's despair may be reflected in K.'s guilt. Conversely, K.'s guilt may remain undecipherable as long as it is sought within the confines of the novel. Since to K., the average man, writing is as alien as prayer, he is unable to remember a guilt which is not his at all but was enjoined upon him by his author. Kafka's failure to implant this guilt intelligibly in K.'s personality and life history forces us to break the story open and extend it into Kafka's biography, in other words, to commit an intentional fallacy. As usual Kafka exploits this failure to the best advantage. For within the parabolical framework of the novel K.'s guilt acquires the mysterious air of complete impenetrability. Remaining to the last undefined, it appears also all-encompassing, just as K., by remaining a nondescript Everyman, appears as universally typical. The parable, built around this paradox, is essentially circular. Its end points back to its beginning. Were Joseph K. to be strapped on the execution machine of "In the Penal Colony," the apparatus could engrave onto his body no other commandment than "Remember thy guilt." Thus the paradox is being kept intact and reigns supreme.

Only as long as we treat the paradox of K.'s guilt as the main subject of *The Trial* will Kafka's failure to motivate it remain a major flaw in the construction of the novel. It seems, however, negligible if we return from the paradox of K.'s guilt to the much more vexing paradox of the Law that violated itself by his arrest.

The Parable of the Doorkeeper *

If the paradox of the Law is accepted as the central point of interest for Kafka in *The Trial*, it follows that the central figure in the parable "Before the Law" is not the man from the country but the doorkeeper who denies him entrance. There is some textual evidence to support this assumption. The doorkeeper is introduced in the first sentence of the parable, the man only in the second. The language itself establishes his priority. The doorkeeper is described in detail, "in his furred robe, with his huge pointed nose and long thin Tartar beard"; even the "fleas in his fur collar" do not go unnoticed. The man from the country, on the other hand, remains as impersonal as K., to whom he is meant to serve as an example. The doorkeeper is mentioned twenty-three

---

* In this section, all quotations without references are taken from pp. 267–278 of the American edition of *The Trial* (1957).

times during the very brief narrative, the man only eleven times (in the German original, nine times), and of these only twice with his full title, the "man from the country." This word count betrays the priest's—and the Law's—intention to sidetrack K., to divert his attention from the man and direct it to the doorkeeper by means of his frequent appearance in the text.

The doorkeeper seems to have been there since time immemorial, just as does the Law which is introduced before the keeper ("Before the Law stands a doorkeeper"); the man on the other hand has to undertake a long and troublesome voyage to appear before the door. Human time and eternity seem to meet before the gate of the Law. A first discrepancy appears: according to "the very words of the scriptures" the Law has precedence over the doorkeeper, and yet the latter behaves as if the Law were there for his sake and not the other way around. He interferes between the man and the Law when he says that he cannot admit him at the moment. Immediately afterward he contradicts himself: he steps aside and grants the man entrance to the Law, which "stands open as always." Just as confusing is the next information he gives the man: "I am powerful. And I am only the lowest doorkeeper." Almost literally the doorkeeper repeats here the words that the tall warder had spoken to K. in the first chapter. Although he was powerful enough to arrest K., he immediately betrayed his insignificance before the higher grades of the Court's officials (10). The way that led K. from his arrest to the Cathedral is mockingly extended into infinity when in the parable the doorkeeper continues to enlighten the man: "From hall to hall, doorkeepers stand at every gate, one more powerful than the other. And the sight of the third of them is more than even I can bear." As was the case with the warder, the doorkeeper seems to impart this information to the man partly to impress him with the magnitude of the Law, but partly also to escape a full measure of responsibility. Visually we can grasp the double role he is playing when we realize that, while addressing the man, he has to turn his back upon the Law he represents. His words are spoken simultaneously with regard to the Law and with disregard of it. His actions betray a similar ambiguity: he interrogates the man but merely as a routine measure. He accepts his bribes but only "to keep you from feeling that you have left something undone," thus adding compassion to corruption. Finally he roars at the man whose hearing is failing him: "No one but you could gain admittance through this door, since this entrance was intended only for you. I am going now to shut it."

This amazing statement concludes the parable "Before the Law" just as the law of the Law is pronounced at the very end of the Cathedral scene itself. This structural parallelism establishes the correspondence between the doorkeeper and the Chaplain: they are both intermediaries between Law and man; they both act as deterrents rather than as helpers; and the priest is defending his own role when he subjects the doorkeeper to an "exegesis." It also relates, by way of a contradiction, the last words of the doorkeeper to those spoken by the Prison Chaplain. By pronouncing his final verdict, the doorkeeper speaks counter to the scriptural passage according to which the door is open "as always." Furthermore, he belies the principle, announced by the priest, that the Court "receives you when you come." Finally, an authority such as the Court described by the priest, which is prepared to dismiss the man who wants to go, does not need a door, and certainly not a closed one. Put into the context of the whole chapter, the parable shows that the doorkeeper is speaking and acting quite independently of the Law. His independence, however, works to the detriment of the man from the country.

Martin Buber has discussed at some length the contribution which Kafka has made to the "metaphysics of the 'door'": "Every person has his own door and it is open to him; but he does not know this and apparently is not in a condition to know." Expanding from the parable "Before the Law" to the whole of *The Trial*, Buber says that the novel describes

a district delivered over to the authority of a slovenly bureaucracy without the possibility of appeal. . . . What is at the top of the government, or rather above it, remains hidden in a darkness, of the nature of which one never once gets a presentiment; the administrative hierarchy, who exercise power, received it from above, but apparently without any commission or instruction. . . . Man is called into this world, he is appointed in it, but wherever he turns to fulfil his calling he comes up against the thick vapours of a mist of absurdity. . . . —it is a Pauline world, except that God is removed into the impenetrable darkness and that there is no place for a mediator.

Buber's reading reverses the point of view taken by most critics of *The Trial*. Whereas the story is usually analyzed with Joseph K.'s predicament foremost in the mind of the reader, Buber interprets the novel—and judges its hero—from the heights of the Law, the very Law that Kafka proclaims has been lost to the world. Textual evidence, however, suggests that Kafka was interested less in the Law and the man from the country than in the doorkeeper. The doorkeeper, in turn, stands for the other emissaries of the Court whom Buber calls, with great insight, "extremely powerful bunglers."[12] Bunglers conduct the Trial and stand trial in it.

The "exegesis" of the parable turns right away to the doorkeeper and occupies itself with him almost exclusively. "'So the doorkeeper deluded the man,' said K. immediately, who was strongly attracted by the story." He falls into the trap set for him by the wording of the narrative. With his first remark he misses the one dialectical advantage he had: by concentrating on the man from the country instead of the doorkeeper, he could have denied the relevance of the parable for his particular situation. He could have stressed the fact that the man from the country had come to the Law out of his own volition, whereas he, K., had been sought out and overtaken by the Court. However, K. is as spellbound by the doorkeeper in the parable as he had been fascinated before by the warders when they appeared in his bedroom. Quite generally, the parable serves as a symbolic master plan for the novel as such. The initial situation of the novel is repeated here; this time it is couched in the form of an intellectual exercise, rather than as a part of the plot. K. loses out both here and there.

Actively supported by K., the Chaplain now "interprets" the doorkeeper instead of the man. Accordingly K. fails to learn anything from this "exegesis" which he could not have gathered previously from his meetings with the other intermediaries. Like them the doorkeeper is simultaneously dutiful and negligent of his duty, both patient and impatient, compassionate and condescending, free and bound, a deceived deceiver, "extremely powerful" and yet "a bungler." He is the visible representative of an invisible authority which even he cannot comprehend fully, precisely because he is visible. He shows the same ambiguity that K. had noticed in his dealings with the warders, the Examining Magistrate, the lawyer, and Titorelli, who appear superior to him but have to obey a higher authority, deriving, on the other hand, a considerable degree of freedom from the fact that they are not able to comprehend fully the command under which they operate. Like the doorkeeper, they stand before the Law, turning their backs upon it, unaware of the radiance that streams forth from it. Yet they need not see it, since they take part unconsciously and mysteriously in the proceedings of the Court.

The Chaplain is prepared to support this paradox with a note from

the commentators: "The right preception of the matter and a misunderstanding of the same matter do not wholly exclude each other."
It is the one little word "wholly" that protects this statement from
any attack and renders it at the same time useless for K. It explains
that the doorkeeper can misunderstand the Law and still have the
right perception of the order he serves. The command given him may
even have been meant to be misunderstood by him. Only at the very
end of the "exegesis," when the figure of the doorkeeper has vanished
behind a multiple web of pettifogging sophistry, does K. voice the
claims of the man from the country, which are also his claims: "Whether
the doorkeeper is clearsighted or deluded does not decide the question.
I said the man is deceived." Now he has let go of the intermediary;
it is, at long last, the man who matters. Compare the introductory
statement, "So the doorkeeper deluded the man," with K.'s last formulation, "The man is deceived": the man has turned from object to subject, and the phrase has changed from a noncommittal active to a
truly tragic passive voice. K. adds imploringly, "You must not forget
that the doorkeeper's delusions do himself no harm but harm the man
a thousandfold." The priest has now been challenged and nothing
remains to this "interpreter" but to withdraw behind the authority of
the Law: "Whatever he may seem to us [the doorkeeper] is yet a
servant of the Law; that is, he belongs to the Law and as such is beyond
human judgment. . . . It is the Law that placed him at his post; to
doubt his dignity is to doubt the Law itself." This commentary means,
on the basis of K.'s past experiences, that the warders whose selfish-
ness and greed he had castigated vociferously (53 ff.) had acted under
the authority of the Court, although the same Court had also responded
to K.'s complaint and sent out the whipper to punish the derelict
servants (103 ff.). By the same token he rebels against the Law when
he questions the dignity of the Examining Magistrate, whose books
contain obscene drawings (65). Therefore he dismisses as a lie the
priest's concluding remark that "it is not necessary to accept everything as true; one must only accept it as necessary." This blatant
paradox contains the truth. Although it is not a truth that would profit
K. in his Trial, it reveals the true nature of the Court: K.'s arrest had
become necessary since it offered the Court the only opportunity to
communicate with him. By this "necessity" the Law explains the offense
it committed against itself. For its "truth" rests in itself, consists of itself,
is "beyond human judgment" but also beyond the Law's ability to communicate with man.

The words of the priest throw light on the Court and its proceedings. It is, however, a light that leaves K. in the dark about himself and his guilt. For this paradox Kafka has found a poignant image introduced shortly before K. is summoned by the Chaplain:

K. happened to turn round and saw not far behind him the gleam of another candle, a tall thick candle fixed to a pillar. . . . It was quite lovely to look at, but completely inadequate for illuminating the altarpieces, which mostly hung in the darkness of the side chapels; it actually increased the darkness (256–257).

The light shines to reveal the depth of the darkness. Hope is there for man to fathom his despair. Even the radiance that in the priest's parable "streams inextinguishably from the door of the Law" starts up only when "the man's eyes grow dim and he does not know whether the world is really darkening around him or whether his eyes are only deceiving him." One thing has become clear after the reflection of this radiance has played across his deadly tired eyes: "Now he will not live much longer." Also K.'s life is drawing to a close after he has perceived, in the words of the Chaplain, a ray of the mortifying light of the Law.

The light of the Law only illuminates the depth of the abyss in which it appeared to K.

The "Pass"

The parable "Before the Law" is concerned with the nature and function of the doorkeeper, its "exegesis" with his competence. In this figure Kafka seems to have crystallized the insights he had gained into his personal situation as well as into the decline of his era.* The figure of this doorkeeper is, however, so complex and his significance so vast as to suggest that Kafka drew for its creation on traditions which were alive, perhaps unconsciously so, at the very core of his artistic imagination.

The image of the man who seeks his way past the doorkeeper to the seat of light stems from Gnostic and hermetic doctrines, the Jewish variants of which Gershom S. Scholem has traced back to the second and third centuries A.D. In his *Major Trends in Jewish Mysticism* Scholem reports on the voyage the soul of man has to undertake in order to reach "God's throne-chariot (the 'Merkabah')":

* We have every reason to believe that this piece was written shortly after the outbreak of hostilities in the First World War.

The place of the gnostical Rulers (archons) of the seven planetary spheres, who are opposed to the liberation of the soul from its earthly bondage and whose resistance the soul must overcome, is taken . . . by the hosts of "gate-keepers" posted to the right and left of the entrance to the heavenly hall through which the soul must pass in its ascent.[13]

Of these seven planetary spheres and the seven heavenly palaces to which they lead, Kafka seems to have retained only the one gate which is guarded by his doorkeeper. At the same time he extended the traditional number, seven, into infinity by hinting at the countless and innumerable doorkeepers who line up behind the first. The doorkeeper who stands in the way of the man from the country is only the lowest, the utmost concession made by the invisible and unintelligible to the limited powers of human perception. That he stands before the Law, that is, that he represents without being responsible for what he represents, is the basic reason for his dubious character.

This dubiousness strikes Joseph K. as an intentional deceit and therefore as unconcealed hostility. But even the enmity of the doorkeeper is based on an old Gnostic convention. Since the soul expects opposition, Scholem recounts, it "requires a pass in order to be able to continue its journey without danger: a magic seal made of a secret name which puts the demons and hostile angels to flight. Every new stage of the ascension requires a new seal" but "all the seals and the secret names are derived from the Merkabah itself where they 'stand like pillars of flame around the fiery throne' of the Creator." [14] In the priest's parable the man from the country does not have a pass which would show a reflection of the light streaming forth from the door of the Law. But Joseph K. produces, during his arrest, such a document. To prove his identity to the warders he pulls out a drawer of his desk, finds his bicycle licence but puts it aside because "it seemed too trivial a thing, and he searched again until he discovered his birth certificate" (8). His birth, his being a man, is the last, the only certificate he possesses. However, this certificate does not support him anymore as it would undoubtedly have supported him in a more God-fearing generation. Man's claim to be protected by his heavenly father has been suspended. The fact that he too was born in the image of God does not provide Joseph K. with a pass acceptable to the officials of this Court nor offer him assistance in his Trial: "Here are my identification papers." "'What are your papers to us?' cried the tall warder now: 'You are behaving worse than a child'" (9). Worse than a child, that is, like somebody who has outgrown his childhood and yet pretends still to be a child. Superficially K. acts rationally; by producing his papers he announces his citizen's right in a country where, as he is well aware, "there was universal peace" and "all the laws were in force" (7). At the same time, however, he claims to belong to a realm where all men should enjoy equal rights as children of their divine Creator.

This scene is as ambiguous as symbolic actions are apt to be. Yet its profound meaning is reiterated pointedly when Joseph K. tells the priest in the Cathedral scene: "How can a man be called guilty at all? We are all simply men here, one as much as the other." Here he poses the crucial question of his Trial. Why, he demands, has he been singled out among all the people he had come to know before his arrest? The year's fruitless searching has at least led him to the realization that he is as guilty and as innocent as the rest of the human race. If he is guilty, all are guilty "one as much as the other." What distinguishes him and the other accused men from those who are free? "This is true," answers the Chaplain, "but this is how all guilty men talk" (264). The repartee is bound to leave Joseph K. completely dissatisfied; the priest has not revealed to him his personal guilt any more than did the warders. Again K. tries to identify himself as a man born in the image of his Creator. Again he is rejected. But this time it is a clergyman who refuses to acknowledge and to honor his birthright. In this refusal the Chaplain proves to be another doorkeeper, hostile to man and intent on preventing him from entering through the gate. Still worse, he stands no longer before the Law but within it. (Figuratively speaking, he has appeared to K. from within the Cathedral— which is the image of this Law—and vanishes back into the interior of the church.) That K. is rejected by the highest-ranking gatekeeper he encounters on his pilgrimage indicates the nihilistic turn the Gnostic vision has taken in Kafka's imagination. The Cathedral scene seals the break between The Law and the man. It may be read as Kafka's bill of particulars in which he indicts the Court for having summoned K. and then abandoned him to misery.

The Public Secret

Kafka started his cross action against the Law as early as the first page of the book and pursues it from K.'s arrest to his execution. The voices of defense and prosecution blend continuously so that neither accused nor accuser (nor, ultimately, the reader) can gain a clear impression of the proceedings. To the very end the Court insists on

K.'s guilt, K. on his innocence. Since the words "guilt" and "Law" hold contradictory meanings for the two parties involved—K. continues to consider the Court a civil authority, whereas the Law operates as if it were an agency of superhuman judgment—the trial remains perforce inconclusive. K.'s meeting with the Examining Magistrate soon after his arrest sets the tone for all that is to follow.

The first interrogation is the only direct contact he will ever be able to establish with the judiciary body of the Court. When he first encounters the lowest echelons of the judicature, he experiences as reality what he will later on gather from information inevitably distorted by hearsay and speculation. He summarizes the results of this first encounter at the end of the session in a piece of highly emotional rhetoric:

There can be no doubt that behind all the actions of this court . . . there is a great organization at work. . . . And the significance of this great organization, gentlemen? It consists in this: that innocent persons are accused of guilt, and senseless proceedings are put in motion against them, mostly without effect, it is true, as in my own case (57).

The session had been in vain. For little did he notice that behind the contradictions, obvious by now, of this Court's discipline and untidiness, authority and incompetence, a third and perhaps more profound paradox has been revealed to him: the workings of the Law are both secret and public.

He had already received a foretaste of this when he was arrested in the intimacy of his bedroom while being watched by the old lady opposite, "peering at him with a curiosity unusual even for her" (4). Following the progress of the scene from window to window, she is soon joined by an older man, whom she had invited to enjoy the spectacle with her. Finally the party across the street is increased by a man, "towering head and shoulders above them, . . . with a shirt open at the neck and a reddish pointed beard, which he kept pinching and twisting with his fingers" (15). If his arrest was meant to be a mystery, it certainly also served as a show to the neighbors, who thronged the window as if it were a box in the theatre. A little while later he meets, in the company of the Inspector, three young men who turn out to be subordinate employees in his Bank: "The stiff Rabensteiner swinging his arms, the fair Kullich with the deepset eyes, and Kaminer with his insupportable smile caused by a chronic muscular twitch" (21). Their appearance in this scene is inexplicable unless one assumes that the Court has invited them in order to discredit K. before his colleagues as well, thus calling in question the Inspector's assurance that the arrest was not to disturb K.'s business. Moreover, their names add a still more general importance to their presence. Together, the German Rabensteiner, the Czech Kullich,* and the Jew Kaminer represent the three nationalities of Prague, which is also the city of K. Thus Joseph K. is arrested *urbi et orbi;* his guilt is not only hidden; it is also assumed to be universal.

When the telephone rings in K.'s office to inform him that a short inquiry is to be held the coming Sunday, the voice that summons him is the perfect example of impersonality. "One" advises him; his attention is "being drawn" to this or that fact (39). And yet the caller seems to have read his innermost thoughts; he takes up a remark K. made to his landlady on the evening of his arrest:

In the Bank . . . I am always prepared, nothing of this kind could possibly happen to me there. . . . The general telephone and the office telephone stand before me on my desk, . . . and above all, my mind is always on my work and therefore on the alert, it would actually give me a pleasure to be confronted with such a situation there (26–27).

This pleasure is given him now. As if he had challenged the Court with his reflections, the voice calls him on his business telephone and proves to him that neither his presence of mind nor his matter-of-fact work habits were worth bragging about. At the same time the clandestine threat materializes before his superiors, his clients, and his clerks.

The interrogation is held on a Sunday, the day of the Lord, but in the shabbiest possible surroundings. The name of the street, Juliusstrasse, is reminiscent of Julius Caesar, his glory—and his assassination. It also evokes memories of the month of July, a time of summer, light, and rest. Yet this "Sunday was a gloomy day," and K.'s mind is overcast by the aftereffects of a celebration held the night before. This blue Monday feeling finds its objective correlative in the Court's street where shops are open, a fruit hawker almost knocks him down with his cart, and a phonograph "murders" a tune (43). K., who had been invited to spend this Sunday morning on the Assistant Manager's sailing boat, cannot help interpreting this scene as a degradation of both

* Paul Eisner identifies this name as the German spelling of Czech *kulich*, a little screech owl, a bird portending death according to European folklore. Since Rabensteiner also points to *Rabenstein*, in mediaeval usage the place of execution, both names give the impression of being *noms parlants*, indicating the sinister mission of their bearers ("Franz Kafkas *Prozess* und Prag," *German Life & Letters*, n.s. XIV [1960–61], 19).

Sunday and the Court. Above all he feels humiliated: to be summoned
to proletarian quarters such as these strikes him as an infringement on
his social status. Yet being naturally pliable, he soon adjusts to the
new situation and pretends to look for "a joiner called Lanz" (45).
His resentment and hurt pride break through again when he is officially
asked whether he is a house painter. "No," said K., "I am the chief
clerk of a large Bank" (50). This provokes an outburst of laughter in
part of the Courtroom. Nonplused, K. joins in the uproar, thus unconsciously and spontaneously ridiculing his own class consciousness.

The fact that this Court convenes in slum tenements is only superficially an "aspect of social criticism." [15] By removing the accused man
from his accustomed social surroundings, the Court seems to provide
for at least some measure of secrecy: the proceedings are less likely to
be noticed by K.'s upper-middle-class acquaintances. However, if any
consideration of K.'s status was in the mind of the Court, it was
thwarted by a strange coincidence: on the way to Juliusstrasse he is
observed by "the three clerks already involved in his case: Rabensteiner, Kullich, and Kaminer. The first two were journeying in a street-
car which crossed in front of him, but Kaminer was sitting on the
terrace of a café and bent inquisitively over the railing just as K.
passed" (42).

To his astonishment he finds a large audience present at the hearing
itself: instead of a police room or court chamber he enters what seems
to him an assembly hall. "A crowd of the most variegated people . . .
filled a medium-sized two-windowed room which just below the roof
was surrounded by a gallery, also quite packed." On the floor of the
hall two factions seem to face each other, each engrossed in negotia-
tions among themselves. The group in the gallery is distinguished from
them by even shabbier costumes as well as by their bent posture, "with
their heads and backs knocking against the ceiling" (47). These people
accompany the happenings in the hall with comments and critical
observations. Gradually K. is able to distinguish better between the
two parties on the floor: the right half participates in the hearing with
muttering and applause; among its members the declaration of K.'s
profession produces explosive laughter. The other party is less numer-
ous but impresses (and disquiets) K. with its continuing silence, the
importance of which he tries in vain to guess. Still later, he notices
a considerable interchange going on between the two factions; at the
same time all the people in the first row keep their eyes fixed on him,
independently of their allegiance to right or left. "They were without

exception elderly men, some of them with white beards. Could they possibly be the ones who had to decide" (52–53)?

For a long time K. is kept wondering whether the crowd in the hall consists of spectators, accused, witnesses, or an unusually large number of jurors. Most of them were in their best suits—after all, it is a Sunday —but since we are in a slum, even their best suits show considerable wear and tear. Had it not been for these clothes K. would have taken the gathering for a local political meeting.* Although the door of the assembly hall is closed and separates the crowd from the outside world, it seems to K. to extend into the street, to spread over the whole district, and to include the city itself. In this respect it really resembles the executive gathering of a political party representing the multitude of its constituents. The people show a basic unity, although among themselves they are divided into right and left, floor and gallery. This division into three groups is never fully explained; we may assume, however, that, like the three employees Rabensteiner, Kullich, and Kaminer, each part of the crowd stands for a far more important collective.

The Magistrate asks K. to step forward. A bystander jumps down from the platform, and K. takes his place. He does more than the Magistrate had asked him to do; his elevated position, which forces him "to brace himself to keep from knocking the . . . Examining Magistrate himself off the plaform" (50), induces him also to deliver a series of supercilious tirades. Protesting, swaggering, and lambasting the Court, he comes not one step nearer to recognizing the identity of the crowd before him. Only when he jumps down from the platform again—which he does "recklessly"—and physically regains an equal footing with the crowd, is he able to unveil their secret:

What faces these were around him! Their little black eyes darted furtively from side to side, their cheeks were droopy, as if they had been drunkards, their beards were stiff and sparse, and to take hold of them would be like touching one's own claws rather then clutching their beards. But under the beards—and this was K.'s real discovery—badges of various sizes and colors gleamed on their coat-collars. They all wore these badges, so far as one could see.

This close-up shows the assembly as a crowd of corrupt and degraded figures. But are they really depraved? The fact that their cheeks are droopy does not make them alcoholics. Their beards are both stiff and

* An earlier version says "socialist meeting" (320).

sparse, which is a contradiction in itself, but the contradiction dissolves into nothingness, for the hand that would clutch these beards would succeed only in gripping itself, grasping nothing but empty air. This unreality, which remains real enough to cause nausea in K., leads to the badges concealed behind the beards. They are of various sizes and colors, and as such point to factions or ranks existing within the gathering. The assembly as such is united against K., the only person on the floor of this hall deprived of any such distinction. But worse is still to come: "As he turned round suddenly he saw the same badges on the coat collar of the Examining Magistrate. . . . 'So!' cried K., 'you are all officials!' " (59). They are all members of the great organization which K. had prided himself on denouncing before them. The bystanders turn out to be colleagues of the Examining Magistrate, who, boastful and unworried, displays several of these badges, obviously an indication of his superior rank. One wonders why K. has failed to notice these insignia before. They are indeed distinctive marks of this Court in that they are at the same time public and secret. They signify the membership in an organization which is widespread, if not all-embracing (the crowd). The individual members may disagree about the ways and means of the Trial's execution (the badges are of various sizes and colors), but they are also unanimous about the proceedings themselves. Their bias is there to see, even when their badges are hidden; and when these badges are revealed, they still continue to conceal any information by which K. might gain insight profitable to the conduct of his case. He is not shown (or fails to notice) any detail on the Magistrate's badge; he does not read a word or observe an emblem which would indicate the origins or aims of the conspiracy formed against him. For all he notices, the badges could be empty buttons—perhaps they are precisely this.

The secret of his Trial goes further: it may even have been kept from the Examining Magistrate and the associates surrounding him. On entering the hall, K. had been told that the door must be shut after him; "nobody else must come in" (47). From this he concludes reasonably enough that he is the one for whom they have been waiting. Moreover, he is scolded by the Magistrate for being "an hour and five minutes" late (48). Beyond this we get no indication that K.'s preliminary interrogation is to be held here. Not even K.'s profession seems to be known to the Magistrate. This may, of course, be nothing but a trick played on K. by the official, who seems to be a malicious type. On the other hand, the Magistrate's ignorance is borne out later in the novel when

K. learns from his lawyer that "the proceedings of the Court were generally kept secret from subordinate officials. . . . Any particular case appeared on their horizon often without their knowing whence it came, and passed from it they knew not whither" (149). It is the higher irony of this Trial that it remains secret even to those who are charged with presenting it to the public.

Nor do the Magistrate's last words betray any knowledge of the course K.'s Trial is to take in the future: "I merely wanted to point out . . ." he says, "that today . . . you have deprived yourself of the advantage an interrogation invariably confers on an accused man." Although these words are as unrevealing (and, at the same time, as revealing) as the rest of the session, they do assume significance by their setting. K. has hastened to the exit, but the Magistrate has been faster. Running past K., he waits for him at the door, and it is here that he dresses him down. For a moment he stands, a hostile gate-keeper, before the door, preventing K. from leaving the Law as his parabolical colleague bars the man from the country from entering it. But "K. laughed at the door" (60), this door which leads both to the Law and out of it again. As he rushes out into the open, he takes another step in the wrong direction.

The Women

A shrieking voice interrupts K. at the climax of his last speech before the Examining Magistrate. As he looks about for the source of the disturbance his eyes fall upon a washerwoman. He recognizes her face, for it was she who had ushered him into the hall and had remained "a potential cause of trouble" ever since (58). But the shriek was not from her; it came from a man who was cuddling her in his arms in a distant corner of the room. This man is later identified as Berthold, a law student who collaborates with the Examining Magistrate (69). He is sitting, with his mouth wide open, "gazing up at the ceiling" (58), yet without betraying the reason for his shriek; it could have been either a mating call or a cry of pain, or both.

The character of this scene is unmistakably sexual, even if one disregards the following passage. It is a sentence which Kafka later deleted, probably because he did not consider it ambiguous enough: "All that K. could see was that her blouse was unbuttoned and hanging round her waist, that a man had dragged her into a corner and was pressing her body to his, she being bare from the waist up except for

her slip" (320). However unexplained the actual cause of the interruption may remain, its effect on K. becomes immediately clear. He
jumps down from the platform and stands eye to eye with the crowd,
thereby being put into a position to discover the badges behind their
beards. In a way the washerwoman has helped him to realize the
true nature of this interrogation. Later the woman tells him, "It did
not do you any harm to have your speech interrupted" (63); and K.,
considering the course the session has taken, is in no mood to disagree
with her.

The case of the washerwoman is still more complicated. She is not
what she first seemed to be; she is no washerwoman, but a young
mother who just happened to be washing her children's clothing when
K. met her. Her motherhood does not, however, prevent her from displaying her promiscuity openly. She is coveted both by the student
and his collaborator, the Examining Magistrate, and to the displeasure
of her husband, who is an usher at court, she yields to the desires of
both. She also offers herself to K., if only at first as a helping hand.
As a matter of fact, she had already assisted him, for when he asked
for a joiner called Lanz, she opened the door to the Courtroom and
allowed him to pass. Instinctively she had complied with his unexpressed wishes and responded to his lie with the understanding of a
silent accomplice. Then she entered the hall and enjoyed herself with
Berthold; afterward she has the cheek to assure K. that it all had
happened "because of you" (65). For all we know about her, she might
be telling the truth—a truth, however, iridescent with facets of lying
and deception. She is evasive, and in spite of her attractiveness, her
"sparkling black eyes" (47), she seems to terrify K. In the fear she
arouses she resembles her surroundings, the Law. Within the paradoxical jurisdiction of the Court there lies the province of the women, a
very special region distinguished by an even greater degree of ambiguity.

The role Kafka assigned to the women in The Trial amounts to a
separate appendix to his general indictment of the world. He allowed
them to continue "the great trial pending between the sexes," which
the dramatist Friedrich Hebbel had instituted in his plays seventy-five
years earlier.[16] The author of Der Verschollene did not know enough
about women and the author of The Castle knew too much to portray
them as inexorably as he did here, in his middle period. The women
accompany K. on his way into the interior of the Law as far as they
can and observe as much as they are allowed to, even though they

are "actually forbidden to do so" (65). They interfere with K.'s defense for personal reasons, like the washerwoman, but claim afterward to have acted for the good of the accused.

Leni, lawyer Huld's nurse, exemplifies Kafka's opinion of women. At first glance she seems to abound with affection and compassion. Traditionally, nursing is the vocation of women who wish to assist others by mitigating their sufferings. And yet Leni is utterly unable to help; her wards are pictures of misery and seem to fade away under her touch. The fact that these men are beyond hope and cannot ever be cured spurs her into action, but her only action consists of long-winded and inconclusive talk.

We never see Leni alone, because she is always busy caring for the lawyer or his clients. She even grants some of her attention to Block, the tradesman, though she quite candidly calls him "a miserable creature." Her candid remark is obscured by a sudden change in the line of her thought: she states that Block is still "one of the lawyer's greatest clients" (211, 212). This observation, aside from suggesting that materialistic motives lie behind Leni's urge to help Block, reveals how utterly inconsistent she is. She changes her mind even when she is talking about only one person. Nor should one be misled by the apparent honesty of her remarks. She is a compulsive gossip, who seems to forget and tangle up the thoughts which cross her own mind; thus one can never be sure she *really thinks* whatever she happens to be saying. Moreover, that trait which her master, the lawyer, calls her "obtrusiveness," i.e., her habit of "pestering" his clients, seems to have its source in a deep-seated aggressiveness. Huld's description of Leni hints that there is a sexual origin to her helpfulness: "A peculiarity of hers consists in her finding nearly all accused men attractive. She makes up to all of them, loves them all and is evidently loved in return." The lawyer enjoys Leni's affection only passively, "She often tells me about these affairs to amuse me" (229). But in telling about these affairs, she betrays the only emotion of which she seems to be capable, her sexual feeling.

Leni's appearance is described with the help of images which suggest that she is little more than a thing: her face is that of a doll (124), and her movements are lifeless like those performed by a marionette. Furthermore she seems to think of herself as a negotiable object: when she feels certain that she has succeeded in alienating K. from Elsa, the cabaret girl, she cries triumphantly, "You have traded me for her"

(138)! Since she is not aware of her own worth, she cannot appreciate the human value of the accused men who succumb to her seduction out of anxiety. K. also escapes into her embrace without being able to find any respite, let alone peace. For Leni just collects the accused; as a true collector, she is ever prepared to increase their number.

It is for the sake of adding another item to her collection that she urges K. to confess from the beginning of their acquaintance, "You cannot fight against the Court, you must confess the guilt." She is a very practical nurse; unconcerned with whatever truth K. may be willing or able to admit, she advises confession as an easy expedient: "Make your confession at the first chance you get. Until you do this, there is no possibility of your slipping from their clutches, none at all." She discloses her real motives, however, when she informs K. that even then he will be in need of assistance and "I shall see to this myself" (135). Although K. refuses to declare himself guilty, she still nurses his ills. Yet in the end she is ready to assault him physically when he announces his decision to dismiss the lawyer and escape her care. "But Block got in her way, and she requited him with her fists. Still clenching her fists, she chased after K." (228). It is impossible to overlook the sinister threat of this gesture which grotesquely belies the charity to which her role as a nurse has committed her; the helping hand is savagely lifted against her ward as soon as he dares withdraw from her tutelage.

Pursuing K. for the sake of possessing him in the most literal sense of the word, she is quick of hearing as far as the other persecutors of her victim are concerned. "They are chasing you," she tells K. when he informs her of his appointment in the Cathedral (255). By using the impersonal pronoun "they," she clearly detaches herself from the Court. "They" are the officials of the Law which Huld ostensibly serves. As the lawyer's confidante, Leni has time and again considered herself an integral part of the proceedings. But she abandons this position most easily as soon as the accused man ceases to be a part of her personal belongings. Losing K., she also recedes from the scene of the novel. The regret K. notices in her last words is not meant to convey pity for him. Rather it expresses the resentment of a collector who must yield a prized item to a superior bidder.

Because of her initials and the place she occupies in the novel Fräulein Bürstner is singled out among the women K. encounters during his trial. Kafka establishes her relationship with Felice Bauer by

abbreviating her name in his manuscript to F. B.; * although he fails
to describe Fräulein Bürstner's appearance, we might imagine her as
closely resembling the writer's fiancée: "Bony, empty face that wore
its emptiness openly. . . . Almost broken nose. Blond, somewhat
straight, unattractive hair, strong chin. . . . Looked very domestic in
her dress although, as it later turned out, she by no means was" (*DI*,
268–269). Making her appearance the night after K.'s arrest, Fräulein
Bürstner is the first to show him how deeply disturbed he is by the
summons he has received. So strong is the impact of K.'s encounter
with her at the end of the first chapter that it seems to accompany
him through most of his later experiences. Yet Fräulein Bürstner
doesn't reappear in person until K. catches sight of her, or a woman
closely resembling her, as he is led to his execution. F. B., who is connected with the beginning of K.'s trial as well as with its end, seems to
play a part second only to the actual proceedings of the Court.

In particular, Kafka seems to have carried over from Felice Bauer to
Fräulein Bürstner the look of domesticity, which on closer inspection
turns out to be misleading. When K. enters the Fräulein's room during
his arrest, it presents a model of tidiness, adorned with photographs
and other paraphernalia of petty-bourgeois comfort. But he is also
struck by a solitary white blouse dangling "from the latch of the open
window" (15). Later the garment disappears, having already served as
an allusion to its wearer's physique, if not to her sensuality. The impression is supported by K.'s observation later in the day that the
pillows on her bed "looked strangely high, they were lying partly in
the moonlight" (28). He seems to be puzzled rather than attracted by
her empty bed.

The contradiction between a well-ordered and highly disciplined
outer appearance and an air of sensuality and, perhaps, availability
is not limited to Fräulein Bürstner's room. Even before we meet her,
the landlady claims to have seen her promenading on the outskirts of
town in the company of various gentlemen (28). This accusation, a
scathing indictment of her morals according to the standards of
Kafka's time, is repeated later in the novel (94). It seems to have
made an impression on K. He tries to convince himself "that Fräulein
Bürstner was an ordinary little typist who could not resist him for long"
(100). In one of the unfinished chapters of the novel he imagines her
at Court, "her arms around two men standing beside her" (307). In

* F(räulein) B(ürstner) belongs to the family of F(rieda) B(randenfeld) in
"The Judgment." See p. 64 above.

other words, she may be just as promiscuous as Leni or the washerwoman and distinguish herself from them solely by hiding her secret
behind a prim and cool façade.

Coldness is the first impression she gives when she finally enters the
scene: "As she locked the front door she shivered and drew her silk
shawl round her slim shoulders" (30). Throughout the ensuing conversation she displays a strange mixture of coquettishness and frigidity.
She shows the mannerisms of a woman of the world, if not a *demi-
mondaine,* when she sits there, in front of K., "leaning her head on one
hand . . . while with the other she slowly caressed her hip" (34).
Yet she is intent on keeping up appearances and remarks in all seriousness when K. ventures to move a table: "I am so tired that I am letting
you take too many liberties" (35). She is also curious and allows K. to
reenact his arrest for her. When he does so, she remains insensitive to
the monstrosity of the scene and the terror by which its one and only
actor is struck. To his plea for assistance in his predicament she answers with the vaguest of generalities: "This may well be, . . . why
not? I like to make good use of my knowledge" (34). Finally she surrenders wordlessly to his embrace, neither offering resistance nor
answering his desperate approaches. A cross between misunderstood
woman and *femme fatale,* she remains passive to the point of heart-
lessness.

Her social status is ill-defined: her behavior is that of a well-to-do
and sheltered young lady, but her presence in the boarding house bespeaks her independence and betrays her solitude. She seems to be
intent on bettering her position and plans to join a lawyer's office in
the near future. But her work as a typist explains only in part the
interest she professes to have in matters of the Law. She admits to
being fascinated by the Court in a manner which she herself calls
"curious" (33). When K. confesses that he does not know the meaning
of his arrest, she is "extravagantly disappointed" (34). The Court itself
seems to be aware of her secret inclination: it implicates her in K.'s
case by shifting the scene of the arrest from his bedroom to hers. K.
is almost thrust toward Fräulein Bürstner by the inscrutable design
of the Law.

He does not ask for the satisfaction of his senses when he embraces
her that evening. Nor does he succumb to his sexual desire, which he
was able to control so successfully before his arrest. When he kisses
her "all over the face, like some thirsty animal lapping greedily at a
spring of long-sought fresh water" (38), he seeks to quench a thirst

which was unknown to him before and awakened only by the summons of the Court. What he seems to crave is a drink from the river Lethe that would make him forget the action the Law has brought against him. But Fräulein Bürstner frustrates his search for oblivion just as she had previously brushed off his plea for assistance. Her passive attitude is a parody of the Law which, according to the words of the Chaplain, receives him who comes and dismisses him who goes. And like the Law, she is not content with displaying signs of aloofness and neutrality—she is aggressive as well. When she acts, the measures she takes are directed against K. A few days after the arrest she sends a messenger across the corridor of the boarding house to refuse any further meeting with K.

This messenger, a Fräulein Montag, approaches K. on a Sunday, a day which must remind him of his first interrogation. Symbolically a connection between Fräulein Bürstner, her messenger, and the Law is intimated. Fräulein Montag obviously relishes the bad tidings, which she recites in a long-winded speech. Unattractive, "a sickly, pale girl with a slight limp" (92), she seems to take revenge on K. for the hardship she had to endure on account of her own shortcomings. She can hardly conceal the satisfaction a further victory over K. has given her; Fräulein Bürstner has invited her to share her room. As far as the typist is concerned, the implications are clear: she wants to forestall any future surprise visits on the part of K. The two women, at least in K.'s eyes, have become accomplices, just as the factions in the Interrogation Chamber had formed a conspiracy against him. Once his suspicions are aroused, he credits the messenger with an intention much subtler than simply barring his way to her friend's bedroom:

She had exaggerated the importance of the connection between Fräulein Bürstner and K., she had exaggerated above all the importance of the interview he had asked for, and she had tried at the same time so to manipulate things as to make it appear that it was K. who was exaggerating.

He recognizes "that Fräulein Montag had chosen a very good if somewhat two-edged weapon" (99–100). This two-edgedness, this ambiguity, unites the women of *The Trial* and the Court in a common front.

Kafka uses all his skill to hint at a secret agreement, directed against his hero, between the women and the Law. He does so to put one more obstacle in the way of K. and to lead him one more step astray. K. is unable to see that these women carry on their own trial against him, sometimes working for, sometimes against, the Court. Like parasites, they move along the edges of the wounds the Law has inflicted upon him. Even cold Fräulein Bürstner finds it hard to resist the charms of these wounds. Why else would she have allowed him to stay in her room in the middle of the night?

We would be justified in turning away in horror from these women —and their author—if Kafka had intended them to be only studies of neuroses in the female. But his critique of the opposite sex is profoundly metaphysical. In this attitude he is closely related to the Viennese philosopher Otto Weininger, who was born in 1880 and shot himself in 1903. Weininger's dissertation on *Sex and Character* had left a distinct mark on Kafka's generation, especially on those who, like Kafka, had learned to sympathize with the rampant misogyny of August Strindberg and were stimulated by Sigmund Freud's ardor to discover the mechanism at work below the threshold of consciousness.

It does not really matter how extensively Kafka read Weininger, even though the one reference he makes to the philosopher in his letters (*B*, 320) allows us to presuppose a more than fleeting acquaintance. A similar distrust of his own virility, a similar horror of the darker side of existence, especially of all things sexual, similar predispositions, and consequently similar experiences led Weininger to formulate a philosophical concept of the relation between the sexes which at times reads like a blueprint for the female figures in *The Trial*. The insecurity which caused both the philosopher and the writer to distort their images of womanhood almost certainly originated in the mistrust which the two men had in their own identity. Both were assimilated Jews trying to break away from what they considered the shallowness and rootlessness of the bourgeois liberalism that they experienced in the houses of their fathers. Outwardly they took different routes of escape: a year before his death Weininger was converted to Protestantism, whereas Kafka during the last years of his life drew closer to eastern European Jewry. Although they may have disagreed about the nature of heaven, Weininger and Kafka held strikingly similar views of hell, especially the inferno of sex.

Take for instance the blend of motherhood and promiscuity that is exhibited in the character of Kafka's washerwoman. It closely resembles Weininger's findings. After having established the categories of "the absolute mother" (if such a being existed) and "the absolute prostitute" (in whose existence he never expressed the slightest doubt), Weininger traces at least a formal resemblance between the two types. Both really do not demand individuality from their sexual complement. The one accepts any acceptable man who can serve to make her a mother, and once this has been achieved asks no more; on this ground only is she to be described as monogamous. The other is ready to yield herself to any man who helps achieve her sexual enjoyment; this for her is an end in itself. Here the two extremes meet.[17]

The meeting ground of Weininger's extremes is the psyche of Kafka's washerwoman. The assistance she offers K. is a model compound of the motherly and the meretricious.

Even more revealing is Weininger's analysis of the "compassion" which induces a certain female type to take up the calling of a nurse. If Kafka had not read *Sex and Character* before creating the figure of Leni, the nurse, he must have drawn on life material very similar to the examples the philosopher had in mind when he wrote the following passage:

It is very shortsighted of anyone to consider the nurse as a proof of the sympathy of women, because it really implies the opposite. For a man could never stand the sight of the sufferings of the sick; . . . a man would want to assuage the pain and ward off death; in a word, he would want to *help;* where there is nothing to be done he is better away; but it is only then that nursing is called for and that woman offers herself for the task. . . . *In the case of man, the choice between solitude and community is always somewhat of a problem.* . . . The woman gives up no solitude when she nurses the sick, . . . *for a woman is never in a condition of solitude,* and knows neither the love of it nor the fear of it. *The woman is always living in a condition of fusion with all the human beings she knows.* . . . This sense of fusion is part of the *sexual* character of the woman, and consequently it displays itself in the desire *to touch, to be in contact* with the object of her pity; the mode in which her tenderness expresses itself is a kind of animal sense of contact [Weininger's italics].[18]

This "animal sense of contact" manifests itself as a visible image in the physical anomaly Leni produces to complete her seduction of K.: "She held up her right hand and stretched out the two middle fingers between which the connecting web of skin reached almost to the top joint, short as the fingers were" (137). A cross between ducks' feet and cats' paws, Leni's hand indicates above all the soft and slippery touch with which she caresses K. in order to acquire him as her possession. "Now you belong to me," she exclaims while she pulls him down to the floor in her embrace (138).

Weininger, like Kafka, seems to have measured the female sex by
the standards of abstract truth. "I am not arguing," he maintains, "that
woman is evil and antimoral; *I state that she cannot be really evil;* she
is merely amoral and *vulgar* (*gemein*)." [19] Just as Kafka's women are
fascinated by a Law which ultimately claims to represent the truth
about the human race, so are Weininger's females attracted by the
truth, but "they do not know that the entire urge for truth has come to
them from the outside and has gradually been implanted in them." [20]
They may even say a word that will assume the weight of truth as soon
as a man appropriates it, but they will do so unconsciously, unwittingly,
and totally unconcerned with the deeper meaning contained by the
word which simply slipped across their lips. Weininger says, "Anyone
who has had anything to do with women knows how often they give
offhand, quite patently untrue and improvised reasons for what they
have said or done, *under the momentary necessity of answering a
question*." [21] Yet these reasons may reveal their relation to truth as
soon as they are accepted and understood by a man.

Woman's total lack of any relation to truth, and the conquest of
this truth by man's inherent moral drive, find telling expression in
The Trial. After K. has met Fräulein Bürstner—or a woman resembling
her—on his way to the execution, "he followed the direction taken by
[her], not that he wanted to overtake her or to keep her in sight as
long as possible, but only that he might not forget the lesson she had
brought into his mind" (282). Kafka never spells out what particular
lesson K. may have learned from his neighbor in the boarding house.
His behavior during the execution, however, suggests that he remembers the words Fräulein Bürstner had said to him near the climax of
their one and only conversation. Then she had said, "I can bear the
responsibility for anything that happens in my room, no matter who
questions it" (37). Groping through the darkness of his last hour, K.,
as we shall see, endeavors to follow the truth which the woman's
words had acquired in his mind since that crucial night. Taken by
themselves, these words were simply meant to say that the Fräulein
was ready to stand up against any gossip which might arise in the
neighborhood. They were born by the "momentary necessity" of justifying the nightly disturbance, by her desire to calm the man down
and be rid of him at the earliest possible opportunity. Even on the
level of a trivial expedient they were not completely true, as can be
seen from her subsequent invitation to Fräulein Montag to act as her
chaperon and thereby share the responsibility for her reputation. What-

ever real meaning or truth this phrase acquires at the end of the book
is bestowed upon it by K. It obtains its metaphysical direction solely
by the place it occupies in the memory of a man.

In the final analysis both Weininger and Kafka were interested in
womanhood as a metaphysical principle. To quote the philosopher
once more: "The question is not merely if it is possible to change
women into moral or even sacred beings. It is this: is it possible for
women honestly to wish to realize the problem of existence, the conception of guilt?" [22] In *The Trial* Kafka posed the question of guilt
as the problem of existence. He left the question open, as far as his
hero is concerned. With regard to the women K. encounters, he clearly
answered this question in the negative. It is a man whom the Court
chooses to state its case and to prove it. There is not one single woman
among the accused. Although the women are certainly no more innocent than K., they do not seem to be capable of being arrested. They
are excluded from the proceedings by order of the Court as well as by
their own incapacity to comprehend the truth of the Law. They are
put to use as instruments to weaken the resistance of the victims. They
conduct their own war of attrition against them and appear as the
guerrillas of Evil, operating independently from the Court and yet as
auxiliaries of its grand strategy of destruction. "One of the most effective means of seduction that Evil has," Kafka says in the "Reflections,"
"is the challenge to struggle. It is like the struggle with women, which
ends in bed" (*DF*, 35).

The Information Givers (Part Two)

The women operate on the periphery of the Law. As K. comes closer
to the center of the Court, he encounters three Information Givers.
Only the first of them is actually appointed by the Court. He has no
name of his own but is introduced by his general title. "This gentleman represents our Information Bureau. He gives the waiting clients
all the information they need, and as our procedure is not very well
known among the populace, a great deal of information is asked for.
He has an answer to every question" (86). Having already been fore-
warned by the Information Giver scene in *Der Verschollene*, we cannot help noticing overtones of irony in this advertisement.

On the Sunday after his first interrogation K. again pays a visit to
the Court only to learn that no sitting has been announced for this day.
When he decides on an investigation of his own (thus turning the

tables on the Court), he finds in the lobby a number of other people and is told that they too are accused men. "All of them are defendants." "Indeed," answers K., "then they are colleagues of mine" (79). K.'s meeting of his colleagues at this juncture destroys any illusion of grandeur he may have cherished about his being the one and only victim of the Court. By introducing him to the companions in his misfortune—only one of whom, Mr. Block, the Tradesman, assumes individual traits later on—Kafka denies K. any insight into the exceptional role he plays. He has been singled out and yet he is only one among many. The Everyman of the morality play is still allowed to be a hero, though a highly allegorical one; K., his modern counterpart, is only a protagonist insofar as the spotlight is centered on him rather than on his colleagues. Moreover, Kafka uses this scene to provide K. with a glance into his own future: all these clients "were carelessly dressed, though to judge from the expression of their faces, their bearing, the cut of their beards, and many almost imperceptible little details, they belonged to the upper classes." But now, "their backs . . . bowed, their knees bent, they stood like streetbeggars" (78, 79). In them the process of disintegration has reached a more advanced stage than in K., whose Trial is still young.

It takes a while for K. to become conscious of the shock his self-confidence has suffered. Upon the usher's "innocent" remark that he has not seen everything yet, he answers, "I don't want to see everything. . . . I want to get away . . . show me the way" (81–82). The usher promptly refuses to comply with the request, whereupon the Information Giver materializes out of the corridor's dusty darkness, "holding on to the lintel of the low doorway and rocking lightly on his toes, like an eager spectator." The latter movement is an outward projection of K.'s emotional state. A girl who has likewise emerged from the interior diagnoses, "A little dizziness" (83). (The German *Schwindel* also means "false pretenses" and may refer to the manner in which K. has sought access to the Court.) Now the Information Giver takes over with the suggestion that K. be led "out of these offices altogether" (85). The first "information" K. receives from this Clerk of Inquiries is the suggestion to leave. The advice finds him amenable, his head swims, and he signals the two helpers to take him under the arms. "Yet the man did not respond to his request but kept his hands in his pockets and laughed" (86).*

---

* His laughter relates this Information Giver to the *Schutzmann* in our model story, "Give It Up!" (see Chapter I above), just as K.'s dizziness harks back to

To stress the discrepancy between the Information Giver's appearance and his true function, he is dressed in a stylish suit which sets him off from the poorly attired clients as well as from the rest of the staff, who never seem to take off their shabby clothes. However, the smart suit, the gray pointed waistcoat, and all have been provided by his colleagues and not by the authorities. "We bought him this fine suit," the girl informs K. "Nothing more would be needed now to produce a good impression, but he spoils it all by his laughter." The laughter, then, is the second piece of "information" given K. by the Court through its appointed clerk.

The following exchange between the Information Giver and the girl impresses K. with its complete indifference; he notices that the two of them discuss him "as if he were an inanimate object." But "he suffered" it, "indeed he actually preferred it" (87). With this self-devaluation his downward path begins to show; it is appropriate that now even the Information Giver moves to lead him in the same direction—downward. As he is being helped along the corridor K. again catches sight of the other accused. He has come much closer to resembling them now; "the Information Giver was balancing [K.'s] hat on the tips of his fingers, his hair was in disorder and hung down over his sweat-drenched forehead." His derangement is thrown into bold relief by the Information Giver's genteel appearance, the purpose of which only now becomes fully apparent in all its cruelty.

K.'s dizziness has increased. "He felt as if he were seasick. He imagined he was on a boat rolling in heavy seas. It was as if the waters were dashing against the wooden walls, as if the roaring of breaking waves came from the depth of the corridor, as if the corridor itself pitched and rolled" (88–89). K. understands this feeling when he registers it as seasickness; he experiences the sensation of drowning. Characteristically K.'s feeling of being carried down to his destruction recurs in one of the alternate endings of *The Trial*, the *Country Doctor* story "A Dream." There K. descends the path to his grave "gliding . . . as if on a rushing stream" (*PC*, 170). The rationalization of this image may be found in the "Reflections": "A man was amazed at how easily he went along the road to eternity; the fact was he was rushing down along it" (*DF*, 38).

Delivered into the impersonal hold of the Information Giver and the office girl, tottering under their unsympathetic grasp, half-conscious,

---

the feeling of being "seasick on dry land," which Kafka had experienced as a young man (see Chapter II above).

and wholly paralyzed—"if they would let him go, he would fall like a piece of wood"—K. is forced to stop thinking, asking, and seeking justice for himself. He is given an opportunity to concentrate on his feelings. The Court seems to have translated the gist of the information it is prepared to give K. into this sensation of going down and drowning. Accusation and judgment are, so to speak, "engraved" in his body as if it had been exposed to the execution machine of "In the Penal Colony." Intellectually he is well out of the reach of words. Yet through the din that has arisen around him (he hears the blood rushing through his ears), he suddenly makes out "a shrill unchanging note like that of a siren" (89). The threatening tone is suggested by the sea and ship imagery preceding it; the changelessness of the tone points to the infinity which moments of danger—like those of drowning—are said to contain; and the communication value of the note is nil.

Since he is an *Am-ha'aretz*, K. is unable to recognize the metaphoric quality of this situation. He takes it literally. Having been thrown back on his physical sensations, he devotes his thoughts to them as soon as his powers of reflection return. He shuts the door to the Court behind him "with utmost haste" and asks himself, "Could his body possibly be meditating a revolution and preparing a new Trial for him, since he was withstanding the old one with such ease" (90)? Fear of physical sickness takes the place of recognition. Hypochondria prevents him from reaching a "more correct formulation of his question," which, according to *Der Verschollene*, is all the receiver of information can hope for in Kafka's world.

K. has visited the Court in vain. Even if K.'s physique were to be subjected to the "new Trial" of a disease—say tuberculosis, which was probably already menacing Kafka at the time when he wrote this novel—he would not be able to grasp the meaning of this "revolution" any better than the importance of his arrest. "Disease . . ." Thomas Mann has said, "First of all it is a question of who is sick . . . an average dolt, . . . or a Nietzsche, a Dostojevski." [23] Sickness has touched K., offering him a chance to refine his powers of perception, to inspire him; in other words, it bestows upon him a further resemblance to the author. Kafka, however, reveals the distance he intends to keep from his figure in K.'s final summing up of the event: "He did not entirely reject the idea of going to consult a doctor at the first opportunity, in any case he had made up his mind—and there he could advise himself—to spend his Sunday mornings in the future to better purpose" (90).

K. adheres to this resolution. He does not set foot in this Courthouse any more; nor does he solicit advice from anybody voluntarily. Both Dr. Huld, the lawyer, and Titorelli, the painter, are forced upon him, the first by his uncle, the second by the intimation of one of his clients, the Manufacturer, that the news of his Trial has spread all over town. He does not expect specific counsel from either Information Giver; rather he approaches them with the mistrust aroused in him by any person connected with the Law or the proceedings of the Court. Both counselors grant him certain insights—insights no more substantial or promising than the information he had received from their Court-appointed predecessor. And he reacts accordingly.

Neither the lawyer nor the artist is authorized by the Court; that is, to use Kafka's imagery, they do not wear the badges which distinguish even the usher in the Courthouse (75). Yet both are sought out by the authorities: a high-ranking official, the Clerk of the Court, sits in the shadows of the lawyer's bedroom when K. is first introduced there (130), and Judges are the painter's models (182 ff.). The two belong to the Court the way servants belong to a central European household: they consider themselves members of the family and speak about their masters with halfhearted deference, at great length, and without any inside intelligence. Actually they share with the Court nothing more than its ambiguity.

"We shall drive straight to Huld, the lawyer," announces the uncle. "You know his name, of course. You don't? This is really remarkable" (122). The word *Huld* connotes a religious category, "unfathomable grace"; [24] as such it is unknown to free-thinking K., who certainly cannot be expected to associate any kind of grace with the Law as he has experienced it. Yet on closer acquaintance this Huld turns out to be a veritable *Unhold,* a disgrace, a monster, who, harping on his disease, a weakness of the heart, denies freedom to any client who has once succumbed to his domination: "An accused man, once having briefed a lawyer, is required to stick to him, come what may" (153). Whenever K. visits Huld, he finds him lying in bed. His bed is his burrow and his fortress; when he goes to sleep it is "his habit to creep right under the feather quilt" (322); and when he is awake he is nursed by Leni, who caters to his curiosity and "vindictiveness" (215). Freely dropping the names of his friends at Court—"perhaps only one or two other lawyers could boast of the same connections" (147)—he seems actually to conspire with them. He never finishes his work on K.'s first plea and thus keeps his Trial in its preparatory stage, the lowest. His sluggishness is common knowledge among the clients; there is little left to them except to follow Block's example and hire five or six of these "pettifogging lawyers beside him" (216).

K. refuses to follow Block's way. He dismisses Huld, and, while carrying out his decision, he states his case against him:

> When I was alone I did nothing at all, yet it hardly bothered me; after acquiring a lawyer, on the other hand, I felt that the stage was set for something to happen, I waited with unceasing and growing expectancy for your intervention, and you did nothing whatever. I admit that you gave me information. . . . But this is hardly adequate assistance for a man who feels the Trial secretly encroaching upon him (232–233).

K. seems to have forgotten that his arrest had actually bothered him a great deal; nor can Huld alone be charged with the ever more threatening pressures of the Law to which K. feels exposed. Yet he is right in accusing Huld of doing nothing except holding on to him. So great is the power exerted by this figure that Kafka did not succeed in finishing this chapter to the point where the lawyer's actual discharge is completed.

And yet Huld does not lie to K. The "information" about the Court he imparts is supported by K.'s own experiences. Moreover it reads like the blueprint of the strategy Huld follows in the course of events:

> The only sensible thing was to adapt oneself to existing conditions. . . . One must lie low . . . and try to understand that this great organization remained, so to speak, eternally in a state of delicate balance, and that if someone took it upon himself to alter the disposition of things around him, he ran the risk of losing the ground under his feet and falling to destruction, while the organization would simply right itself by some compensating action in another part of its machinery (151–152).

These are abstractions, however, and K. finds it difficult to penetrate their meaning even though he is able to remember them to their last detail. What he remembers first and foremost is the picture that Huld has given him of the work which the lawyers are doing at the Court. This he did by enumerating a few examples of the esteem in which they are held. There is, for instance, the room assigned to them officially. It lies in the very top of the attic, one story higher than the interrogation chamber and immediately below the sky. It is lit by a small skylight; in order to reach it one lawyer has to hoist another on his back, a grotesque sight worthy of Pieter Brueghel's imagination. At the same time we become aware of the lawyers' physical smallness.

If the window is opened, one seems to be nearer to hell than to heaven: smoke from nearby chimneys "blows into your nose and blackens your face." ° To make things even worse, only a thin floor separates the lawyers' room from the clients below. Their precarious station is driven home to them by a hole "big enough to let a man's leg slip through" (145). One can easily imagine the lack of confidence caused in the minds of the accused men sitting there in the dusty and drafty corridor by the sight of a lawyer's leg coming down through the ceiling and dangling, helpless and isolated, over their heads.

The imperturbable majesty of the legal organization and the arbitrary humiliation of the lawyers, who seem to be punished in advance for the crimes of their clients, complement each other most paradoxically in the insights Huld grants K. On the other hand, the lawyer resembles the authorities of the Court closely enough to relish the torture his disquisitions and descriptions cause the accused. All he intends to achieve is, as he betrays in an exceptionally lucid moment, "a clean wound" (155). Incapable of bridging the break that exists between Law and man, Huld is only concerned with a "clean" presentation of this break, cleansed, that is, of all human sentiments and considerations. This strictly academic interest of the lawyer in his cases inevitably reminds one of the medical joke in which the surgeon returns from the operating theatre with the remark: "Operation successful. Patient dead." Huld is no advocate of grace before the Law, no healer of the men who are mortally wounded by the accusations of the Court. Taken by himself, he is a self-possessed artisan in the craft of keeping the wound sterile and the operation going. Against the background of the Law, however, he appears as an allegory, and a negative allegory at that. Surrounded by ambiguities and spreading them himself, he unequivocally signifies the impossibility of help.

Like the name Huld, the name of Titorelli, the painter, is a misnomer. It is Italian, a resounding blend of illustrous prototypes such as Titian, Tintoretto, Signorelli (plus a possible assonance with "titillation"). Yet the pictures he paints are primarily northern. The variety of motives that informs Italian art is likewise contradicted by Titorelli's output; a heathscape turns up on one picture after the other. His nature studies are, as a matter of fact, identical: "Two stunted trees

---

° This is an aspect already familiar to K. In the scene with the Information Giver the girl had opened such a skylight "to let in fresh air. Yet so much soot fell in that she had to . . . wipe K.'s hands clean with her handkerchief" (84).

standing far apart from each other in darkish grass. In the background was a many-hued sunset" (203–204). No human being appears on these canvases; the scene is plain, infinite, savage, and sinister; the trees are foresaken and frail; only a sunset enlivens the general dreariness with a spectacle of decline. This sunset reappears only slightly changed, as "a reddish shadow . . . which tapered off in long rays" around the edge of Titorelli's portrait of a Judge, his second motif. It seems to be his special theme.

Titorelli is not only a misnomer, it is also a pseudonym. "I do not know at all what his real name is," admits the Manufacturer, who has heard from him about K.'s Trial. "For years he has been in the habit of calling at my office; . . . he is almost a beggar" (170). Thus we are not surprised that we have to accompany K. to the slums again when he goes on another of his pilgrimages with the Manufacturer's introduction in his pocket. At first K. feels relieved to see that the painter lives "in a suburb which was at the almost diametrically opposite end of the town from the offices of the Court" (176). That his studio lies in an attic is easy enough to explain by the painter's profession as well as by his poverty. Only at the end of his visit does K. discover a door behind Titorelli's bed which leads straight into the offices of the Court. "There are Law offices in almost every attic," the painter comments. "Why should this be an exception" (205)? Under the bed, which stands before this door, he hides his paintings, covered with dust. This final discovery not only reveals the ubiquity of the Court, it establishes beyond doubt the double identity of the painter. (The Manufacturer had already warned K. that Titorelli is "certainly a liar" [170].)

He introduces himself as "artistic painter" (*Kunstmaler*—179), a redundancy which finds its explanation in his later remark that he also functions as a Court painter. But this fine distinction does not keep us from the realization that art, as well as all other creative undertakings, has become almost impossible in the neighborhood of the Law. As long as the painter limits himself to the representation of reality, his work is drowned out by monotony. Outside the Law his theme remains the forlornness of nature, a veritable *nature morte*. He is not blind to the paucity of his motifs: "It is my uninterrupted association with the gentlemen of the Court that left this imprint on me," he says. "I have many advantages from it, of course, but I am losing a great deal of my *élan* as an artist" (189).*

* The author of *The Trial* may even have indulged in self-parody when he

Among the advantages he enjoys he may count the undefined, but in any case lascivious, relations he entertains with the flock of adolescent girls who camp on his doorstep. When he first appears he seems to be "wearing nothing but a nightshirt" (178) and is almost mobbed by his female admirers. Ostensibly trying to turn them away from his threshold, he nevertheless responds to their jokes, the meaning of which remains hidden from K. Time and again "one of these pests" (180) hides out under his bed, addresses him from behind the door (187), or peeps at him and at K. through the cracks in the door (195). After K. has departed, the painter is again surrounded by the budding maenads (206). Kafka appears to be ridiculing the importance traditionally attributed to the "Eternal Feminine" for the creative process; the painter, who is vain, exhibitionistic, and uninhibited to the point of perversity, allows his artistic ego to be inflated by the attentions of these "ugly" brats (179). The girls in turn succumb to a double charm: they are tickled by the presence of an artist in their midst and, like the other women in the novel, aroused by the Law, which he, too, represents. (They have been in his room and know that a way to the Court leads through the painter's bed.)

Another advantage Titorelli enjoys as a Court painter is the hereditary character of this post: "I inherited the connection. My father was the Court painter before me." The creative abundance of a living tradition in art is guaranteed by the dialectics of generations following one another, the pupils trying to throw into the shade the achievements of their masters. In Titorelli's case these dialectics are replaced by a strict code of rules and regulations, handed down from father to son. "New people are of no use here. There are so many complicated, various and above all secret rules laid down for the painting of the different ranks of officials that a knowledge of them is confined to certain families. . . . Only a man who had studied them can possibly paint the Judges" (190). The monotonous realism of Titorelli's heathscapes corresponds to the orthodox traditionalism he has to display in his official portraits. His imagination frozen, the artist has become a lackey and a monkey of the Court.

To be sure, the Judge in Titorelli's portrait shows some likeness to his model. He is "a stout man with a black bushy beard." Yet K. is immediately struck by the resemblance of this picture to another Judge's

---

created Titorelli. With the painter he shares especially the scarcity of basic themes. The fear of "losing his *élan*" was also one of Kafka's perennial anxieties.

portrait he has seen in Huld's office. "Here too the Judge seemed to be on the point of rising menacingly from his throne, bracing himself firmly on the arms of it" (182). This kind of portraiture is free only as far as the object portrayed is human, and this, K. has learned, is not very far. Beyond this, it consists of clichés. K. is particularly interested in the Judge's seat—the throne—because Leni, explaining the Judge's picture in the lawyer's office, had pointedly remarked: "This is all invention. . . . Actually he is sitting on a kitchen chair, with an old horse-rug doubled under him" (135). Literally Titorelli echoes her words when he admits, "This is all invention," adding, "but I am told what to paint and how to paint it" (183). In the final analysis, however, this throne is also a copy of the Merkaba, the throne chariot of the divine, emptied of all meaning. A faint recollection of these time-hallowed origins seems to have survived in the imagination of the present Judges and their painter: "Every Judge," says Titorelli, "insists on being painted as the great old Judges were painted, and nobody can do this but me" (190). The sublime has come down to this Court distorted by vanity and deception. Where art has lost its spiritual center, the artist is left with nothing but a merely ornamental symbolism, inevitably accentuating the ugliness of any realistic detail which, like the Judge's face, may have intruded into the stylized surroundings.

Behind the Judge on Titorelli's picture still another figure emerges. Unable to identify it at first sight, K. asks the painter for its meaning and is informed that it is Justice. Slowly the conventional attributes of the allegorical figure, the bandage over the eyes and the scales in the hands, begin to take shape. With a veritable stroke of genius Kafka animates the apparition by showing how, step by step, K. grasps its meaning. Moreover, Titorelli resumes his work on the portrait in the presence of his visitor. While his work is in progress, the figure itself seems to be set in motion. The Goddess of Justice is flying, carried by wings on her heels. K. is struck by this obvious deviation from allegorical convention and takes the painter to task for it. "I comply with my client's instructions," Titorelli answers curtly, but adds, "Actually it is Justice and the Goddess of Victory in one." Being a visual type, with eyes quicker than his brains, K. immediately comprehends: "Not a very good combination. . . . Justice must stand quite still, or else the scales will waver and a just verdict will become impossible" (182, 183). Spellbound he follows the work of the artist, who now concentrates on the sunset around the edges of the picture.

This play of shadow bit by bit surrounded the head like a halo or a high mark of distinction. But the figure of Justice was left bright, except for an almost imperceptible touch of shadow; this brightness brought the figure right sweeping into the foreground and it no longer suggested the Goddess of Justice, or even the Goddess of Victory, but looked now exactly like the Goddess of the Hunt in full cry (184).

What K. witnesses is the pictorial self-revelation of the Law.

This image occupies a place in the Titorelli episode similar to that held by the parable "Before the Law" in the Cathedral scene. The picture even surpasses the parable in disclosing the Law's irrevocable hostility toward man. For one moment the countenance of the Law unveils itself—as an oversimplification.

Titorelli's actual words of advice, however, envelop the Law again with ambiguity. They draw a curtain before the picture he has shown to K. In this, the counsel of the painter corresponds to the "exegesis" the Chaplain adds to his parable; in both cases a seemingly clear metaphor is intentionally veiled by a commentary more complex than the image it explains. (It is as if Kafka had anticipated and derided Kafka criticism.) "The trial must be kept rotating all the time, although only in the small circle to which it has been artificially restricted" (201), is one of Titorelli's directions; he himself follows it in his discussion with K., thereby disclosing that even his counseling is part of the proceedings.

As Titorelli leads K. through the labyrinth of judicial mystique, he reveals nothing that he has not already shown K. much more clearly in the picture: "There are three possibilities: definite acquittal, ostensible acquittal, and indefinite postponement." Definite acquittals do not occur. "I have never encountered one case." The Goddess of Justice is the Goddess of the Hunt. The remaining alternatives are no more promising: ostensible acquittal results in an "ostensible, or more exactly, provisional, freedom," which can be terminated any time by a new arrest, whereas "postponement consists in preventing the case from ever getting further than its first stages." The assistance Titorelli offers K. is like the help rendered to the quarry by the hound. "Both methods," the painter concludes, "have this in common that they prevent the accused from coming up for sentence." Thereupon K. replies, "But they also prevent an actual acquittal" (191–202). Here K. has reached the limit of the information that the Court imparts to him.

The session with the painter draws to a close. The portrait of the

Judge has proved to K. that art is impossible in the vicinity of the Court, but the figure behind the Judge's throne has failed to answer his principal question, a question that concerns his own survival rather than a problem of aesthetics. To be sure, K.'s arrest can be explained if Justice is like a figure which storms through the world blindfolded. At the same time, however, such an image of Justice destroys K.'s hope that he will ever bring the Court to change its mind, revoke his arrest, and abandon its judgment. "If I were to paint all the Judges in a row on one canvas," Titorelli informs him, "and you were to plead your case before it, you would have more success than before the actual Court" (187).

Whether K. is now any more ready for "a free and voluntary condemnation of himself" [25] than at any other point of his predicament is a moot question since there is no evidence in the text. At least one can say that his eyes have been completely opened to the Law and its paradox. In this the painter succeeds where the priest fails.* The narrator himself indicates how important K.'s insight into the hopelessness of his case is by having him pronounce it "in a low voice, as if he were ashamed of his own perspicacity" (*als schäme er sich, das erkannt zu haben*—202). The word "shame" appears in the last sentence of the final chapter, giving it an unexpected turn in the direction of ambiguity.

The Last Shame

On the eve of his thirty-first birthday Joseph K. expects the end of his Trial. A full year has passed since his arrest, the circle closes, and K. is ready to let it close. A year ago the warders had insisted that he

---

* H. Uyttersprot goes so far as to call Titorelli the "most central figure" of the novel (*Eine neue Ordnung der Werke Kafkas* [Anvers: De Vries-Brouwers, 1957], 54). His argument remains valid as long as he bases it on the importance which the painter's information has for K. He overstates his case, however, when he uses his observation, which is a personal value judgment, in support of his suggestion that the Titorelli episode should follow the Cathedral scene rather than precede it because it is more important. Precisely because the parable is more ambiguous than the picture, Kafka may have deemed it more important—for the Court—and truer to the paradoxical nature of the Law. In any case the metaphysical implications of the Cathedral scene speak strongly for the preservation of the textual *status quo*. So does the topography of K.'s city. Fashioned after the model of Prague, it seems, like the Czech capital, to be dominated by its cathedral. Allowing our imagination to reign even more freely, we may suggest that there on Hradžany Hill Kafka found in the royal residence next to the Cathedral one of his inspirations for *The Castle*.

wear a black coat and had enforced their order against his objection: "The main session is not yet" (14); now he is voluntarily dressed in black. To his solemn attire he has added "a pair of new gloves that fitted tightly over the fingers"—gloves such as a host may wear who expects a ceremonial visit or a surgeon who prepares for an operation. K. seems prepared for any eventuality and preserves throughout the composure of a man who is ready for everything.

"So you are meant for me?" he asks the two men who enter his room unannounced. The initial "so" indicates the strange blend of fatigue, resignation, and disgust that has settled over his mind. The visitors seem to annoy K. more than one might expect, but the reason is not disclosed. One only learns that he is reminded of the theatre by their appearance, and that their puppetlike impassivity increases his uneasiness to the degree of nausea. "Tenth-rate old actors they send for me" (280), he says to himself, not yet willing to ask for the purpose of their mission. Have they come to accompany him to the main session of the Court, to free him, or to execute him? He is willing to let events take their course. "Perhaps they are tenors" (281), is all he thinks, "studying their heavy double chin" (Kafka's language cuts a sinister caper here by attributing only *one* double chin to the two men.°) Turning abruptly to them with the question, "What theatre are you playing at" (280)? he elicits no more than an astonished stammering from them.

It is a characteristic of the works which Kafka finished that they end in a subtle form of theatricality. Since he cannot envisage an absolute conclusion—either an unconditional condemnation or complete redemption—he resorts to effects quite opposed to his otherwise understated style. To be sure, most of his narratives are basically endless: they consist of an infinite sequence of tortured moments of metaphysical anguish and despair, produced by the absence of any metaphysical frame of reference. But when he reaches the end (of his strength and patience rather than of his tale), he is forced either to interrupt his work or to use costumes and masks. (Substituting theatricals for valid religious content, he reminds us again of his distant relationship with the author of the spectacular Salzburg *Jedermann*, Hugo von Hofmannsthal.) Kafka is, however, well aware of the incompatibility existing between these stage effects and his artistic

---

° Speaking of "double chins" in the plural, the English version misses this fine point.

integrity; therefore he detaches himself from the show by turning it into a parody as he did in *Der Verschollene.* °

Kafka considered three different conclusions for *The Trial.* In "A Dream" (*PC,* 170–172) Joseph K. attends and enacts his own interment. Two men, reminiscent of the two visitors in the actual novel, hold a gravestone, into which an artist, a vague counterpart of Titorelli, engraves K.'s name. This invitation lures him gently and irresistibly into the "impenetrable depths. . . . Enchanted by the sight, he woke up."

"The House," one of the unfinished chapters of the novel (304–309), moves in the opposite direction. K. has made friends with the painter; in a daydream he entrusts Titorelli with the task of accompanying him back to Court. But he must pay for this assistance by suffering caresses which border on homosexuality. (The artist's eroticism seems to be as all-embracing as it is insatiable.) Kafka takes up the water imagery which had suggested K.'s drowning at the end of his visit to the empty Court offices (89). But now a complete reversal seems to be imminent. He allows K. to ride on the crest of the wave, so to speak:

In the twinkling of an eye they were in the Law Courts and flying along the stairs, upward and downward too, without the slightest effort, gliding along as easily as a buoyant craft through water. And at the very moment when K. looked down at his feet and came to the conclusion that this lovely way of motion could not belong any more to the humdrum life he had led until now—at this very moment over his bent head the metamorphosis occurred. The light which until then had come from behind them changed and suddenly flowed in a blinding stream toward them (309).

This sudden change of light indicates a change of mind on the part of the Court. K. has broken through to the Law; the miracle has happened and the accused man faces the glory of forgiveness, shining upon his countenance.

However persuasive the imagery of these two variants may be, it is still the imagery of dreams. Kafka discarded it when it came to completing K.'s Trial. He decided in favor of the more than real reality with which he had informed the rest of the novel. (Had he decided differently, he would have run the risk of the whole trial's being misunderstood as a dream—an ambiguity not acceptable even to him.) Literally he had to stage K.'s execution, borrowing actors and props from the alien world of the theatre. By doing so, however, he seems to take

° In *The Castle* he maintained the artistic unity by leaving an open ending; he omitted any final scene.

sides in the proceedings. A Court whose executioners look like tenors, by tradition the silliest members in a European theatre company, condemns itself. The horror inevitably evoked by an execution is increased, almost beyond endurance, by the air of incompetence emanating from the executioners. They have come to murder K., not to carry out a judgment. The Court which sent them is once more compromised by the intermediaries it has chosen.

"He was repelled by the cleanliness of their faces. One could clearly still see the cleansing hand which had been at work in the corners of the eyes, rubbing the upper lip, scrubbing out the skinfolds at the chin." The cleanliness of his executioners cannot hide from K. the melancholy dirt he had noticed on the faces of the other officials; their puffed-up cheeks and apparent harmlessness relate them paradoxically to the pictures of the Judges he had seen in Huld's office and Titorelli's studio. As the radiance of the Law had indicated the depth of the night enveloping him, so the cleanliness of the visitors betrays the filth from which they emerged and the murky aims they pursue. K. has seen enough of the double face of this Court to be able to read his destiny in the cleansed dirt on the faces of these men. He stands still and cries, "Why did they send you, of all people" (281)? Here he has accepted the inevitable, but he still protests against the shameful confusion of the clean and the unclean which will accompany him, must accompany him, to the end, because this paradox contains the very essence of the Law.

The appearance of his executioners has once more revealed to K. the structure of the Law; founded on a paradox, it is built of contradictions. Therefore he decides to refrain voluntarily from any resistance. During the short span of his last moments he realizes that he can only preserve his dignity by divesting himself of any sign of theatricality. He gives up arguing, harping on his innocence, and the pathos he had previously displayed in his defense. He counters the melodrama of his execution by utter simplicity. As his so-called confession shows, he is willing to comply with the wishes of the Court; he allows it to execute a marionette.

Before leaving his house at the beginning of the chapter, he had gone once more to the window to take a look at the street. At one lighted window opposite "small children were playing behind bars, reaching with their small hands toward each other although not able to move themselves from the spot" (280). They form the exact counterimage to the greedy old people who watched from their windows the spectacle of his arrest. But the memory of his arrest lies as far behind him as this innocent and yet equally depressing scene where immature and imprisoned creatures try in vain to touch one another.

Fräulein Bürstner appears and vanishes again. He cannot ascertain whether the apparition is real. If the Court really produces Fräulein Bürstner in this dramatic moment in order to stir up K.'s old guilt feelings, then this legerdemain is lost on him. To be sure, a year ago he had poured out his frantic words and feelings before her. Now, however, he attempts to shoulder the responsibility for himself in its total, existential sense; he is strong enough "to do without her" (283) and let her disappear.

Wedged in by his companions, he sets out on his walk, "and the joy he caused thereby to the men, was transmitted to some extent even to himself" (282). He neglects an opportunity to shake off his companions and to call a policeman for help. He drags the men along until they have to run, breathless, beside him. For the first time he has taken the lead and is resolved to keep it.

The execution takes place in a quarry, on the border of the town, near the open country to which the man from the country now returns. He is as far from the bourgeois neighborhood of his office as he is from the belt of slums in which the Court is located. To be sure, the force of his executioners keeps him physically within the jurisdiction of the Law. Moreover, the Court is not satisfied with disposing of him physically; it reaches for his mind once more; over his head the executioners pass the knife from one to the other.

> K. now perceived clearly that it was his duty to seize the knife himself, as it traveled from hand to hand above him, and to plunge it into his own breast. But he did not do it. . . . He could not completely rise to the occasion, he could not relieve the authorities of all their work; the responsibility for the last blemish lay with him who had denied him the remnant of strength necessary for the deed (285).

As he has seen the executioners' true face behind their official masks, he comprehends now the meaning of the murderous ritual over his head. The Law expects from him a sacrificial death, a self-execution, which is, after all, only another word for suicide.* He has to "rise to the occasion" and do his duty; failing to commit suicide, he would

---

* The parallelism of this scene with the death scene in "The Judgment" is striking. Equally striking, however, is the difference between Georg Bendemann, who submits to authority, and Joseph K., who resists it, at least during the last minutes of his life.

disobey once more, prove guilty, vindicate his arrest, and justify his execution. But having assumed the responsibility for himself, he now
puts the responsibility for this "last blemish" squarely before the seat
of the Supreme Judge, "who had denied him the remnant of strength
necessary for the deed." By surrendering the responsibility for his
case to the Court, he assumes paradoxically the full responsibility for
himself as a free man. The Supreme Judge had summoned him without the "pass" the searching soul requires when it is called upon to
appear before its creator. In K.'s refusal to kill himself, in this biblically
simple sentence, "But he did not do it," Kafka has articulated K.'s final
revolt against the Law. With the strength of his weakness he resists a
superior opponent in the very last minute of the struggle. Not being
permitted to die as a marionette, he dies as a man.*

He also dies on the border line between extreme fear of God and
extreme skepticism. As long as he is able to think and speak, his words
will oscillate confusedly between these two poles. For language does
not travel far enough to reach these limits. Only by raising questions
can it point in their direction; only by ambiguities can it break the
silence of the inexpressible. The end of the novel abounds with both
questions and ambiguities.

Questions arise in K. when he catches sight of the top story of the
house that adjoins the quarry: "As a light flares up, the casements of
a window there suddenly flew open; a human figure . . . leaned abruptly far forward and stretched both arms still farther. Who was it?"
This sets off a veritable litany of questions which lead from the individual ("Was it one person only?") to the universal ("Or was it mankind?") and culminate in the outcry: "Where was the Supreme Court
to which he had never penetrated?" Only the most noncommittal figure
of speech, only a question, could be used to hint at the possibility that
there, "faint and insubstantial in the distance," the Law itself is extending its arms toward man—toward the man it has to kill because
it can neither convict nor acquit him. This possibility is, to a certain
extent, supported by the secret interplay of images which sustains the
novel as a whole. The casements which flare up "as a light" may reflect both the parabolical radiance streaming "inextinguishably from
the door of the Law" and the "blinding stream" of light flowing toward

* See the diary entry of July 20, 1916: "If I am condemned, then I am not only
condemned to meet my end but also to defend myself until I have reached it"
(*DII*, 161).

K. in his redemptory wish dream. However this may be, at the end of his questions K. "raised his hands and spread out his fingers."

It is at this point, in this mute gesture, that the ultimate ambiguity of the story sets in. On the one hand, spread-out fingers indicate a warding off, an attitude of rejection, and are the very image of self-defense. Rejecting the light before him, K. may want to preserve his humanity in an existential solitude, no longer persecuted by the Court, but freed from it by his death. On the other hand, spread-out fingers are a sign of worship, even of blessing. Seen in this light, he may accept his judgment here, affirm it, and welcome death at the hands of the Court. This ambiguity is carried through to the very last sentence of the manuscript. It reads: "'Like a dog!' [K.] said, it was as if the shame should survive him" ("'Wie ein Hund!' sagte er, es war als sollte die Scham ihn überleben"—286). Whose shame, and the shame of what? The shame that K. has to die like a dog or that the Court has to finish him off like an animal? The shame of a man who has lost his Trial or the shame of a Court which could not convince him of his guilt? A Court that taught him responsibility in order to be blamed for its own irresponsibility? Is it the primal shame of man who has to appear before his Supreme Judge as naked as he was born? (K.'s body too lies half-naked before the executioners.) Or is K. ashamed of his perception, as he was in Titorelli's studio, that is, of what his insight has revealed to him? That he has seen authority resorting to murder when man refuses to kill himself? That he has met a Court whose jurisdiction does not know of acquittals? That he has identified the Goddess of Justice with the Goddess of the Hunt? Is the shame which should survive him man's shame at the mercilessness of a Law and at the deadliness of a light still worshipped as divine?

We do not know, for Kafka did not know either. Like the Court, he can only accuse; like K., he can only answer accusations by cross accusations; the power of conviction is denied him. At this point Kafka himself turns into a man from the country, and so does the reader. In this process Kafka exemplifies the monstrosity as well as the grandeur of the Court against which he had instituted his *Trial*.

CHAPTER VII

The Bitter Herb

The Castle

WE still do not know exactly when Kafka began work on the manuscript of *The Castle*. In neither his diaries nor his letters does he mention the beginning stages of the novel. Max Brod at first set the spring of 1922 as the date based on the evidence at the following entry in his own diary: "On March 15, 1922, Franz read me the beginning . . ." Since it was customary for Kafka to acquaint his friend with his new achievements at a very early stage, Brod concluded that Kafka had started the work "not far" from the day of this reading (*FK*, 185–186). But when the *Letters to Milena* became known after the Second World War, Brod found parallels between Kafka's love affair and the erotic experiences of K., the Land-Surveyor. He believed he saw in Klamm, the most powerful official in the Castle, "an exaggerated and demonized image of Milena's legal husband, from whom she would not completely break away emotionally" (*FK*, 220). Comparing the impact this affair had on Kafka's creativity with his breakthrough nine years earlier, Brod revised his estimate and set the inception of the novel in 1921 to let it coincide with the experiences which supposedly inspired it. Elsewhere in his biography of Kafka he describes the fragment "Temptation in the Village" as "a preliminary study" for *The Castle*. This fragment, however, was entered in Kafka's diaries under the date of June 11, 1914 (*DII*, 48–58). The novel itself, Brod remarks on this occasion, "was not begun before 1917 at the earliest" (*FK*, 250).

Brod's estimate of 1921 has been generally accepted, but it is certainly possible that Kafka began work on *The Castle* at an earlier date. The interconnection of the imagery used in this novel and in *The Trial* of 1914 indicates that they may have been written in fairly close succession. On the other hand, the reading of March 15, 1922, recorded by Brod indicates that Kafka was then still at work. How deeply involved he was and remained for quite some time can be seen from a letter he wrote to Brod on July 5, 1922. Enlarging once more on his situation as a writer, he seems to refer directly to *The Castle* when he says:

Writing is a sweet and wonderful reward, but for what? At night it became clear to me with the distinctness of an object lesson given to a child that it is a reward for services rendered to the devil. This descent to the dark powers, this release of spirits which are bound by nature, these dubious embraces and whatever else may occur down there unknown to someone up here who is writing stories in broad daylight. . . . I am sitting here in the comfortable position of a writer, ready to accept all things beautiful, and must watch idly when my real Ego, poor and defenseless, . . . is being pinched, thrashed, and almost ground to dust by the devil. What right have I, who was not at home, to be startled when the home suddenly collapses; for do I know what has gone on before the collapse; have I not exiled myself, leaving the house at the mercy of all evil forces (*B*, 384, 386)?

Kafka was thirty-nine years old when he wrote this letter, and he had less than two years to live. There is a certain finality to the image of the house in which he had been free to live and which he, a voluntary exile, had abandoned to the dark forces set on its destruction. This image, an autobiographical statement, reemerges in the prehistory of K., the Land-Surveyor; it marks the point of departure from which Kafka's protagonist proceeds. The Land-Surveyor is also an expatriate, having left his home under no other compulsion than the lure of sinister powers in a faraway land. Homelessness is his fate. Although his home is mentioned only in a few scattered reminiscences, it appears as a place of peace, rendered even more peaceful by K.'s reminiscing. Yet he does not betray any nostalgia; he has firmly struck his roots in rootlessness. What happens to his home we are not told; it may even have remained unmolested by the demons who followed K.'s trail. Nor do we learn the ultimate fate of the Land-

Surveyor, for this novel also has remained a fragment. K.'s experiences
in the book make at least one thing clear: he is never going to go
home again.

It seems almost certain that Kafka was still occupied with *The
Castle* when he described his descent to the underworld to Brod in
the letter of July 1922. Indeed, the letter serves as an explicit statement of the atmosphere pervading the novel. The story is populated
by ghosts irrationally unleashed by unknown hands. Instead of love it
shows the dubiousness of embraces and abounds, quite generally, with
specters risen from the underworld of a highly agitated unconscious.

The horror of this ghostly scene is increased by the fact that the
Land-Surveyor seems to have sought it out of his own volition. The
protagonist has not been "packed off" like Karl Rossmann, nor is he
arrested like Joseph K.; he consciously chooses his fate. He goes to the
Castle wishing to be acknowledged as the Count's Land-Surveyor. To
be sure, he maintains that the Count is expecting him (5),* but having
lost his way, he does not know the village into which he has "wandered"
and seems unaware of the Castle's existence (4). Long spaces of the
novel are devoted to a discussion of the legal merits of K.'s case, but
whatever these may be, one fact remains undisputed: K. was not
forced to appear here. If he was called, he was also free to disregard
the call. Yet he responded to whatever real or imaginary voice he
heard. Thus K.'s attitude is immediately distinguished from the attitudes of Kafka's other central figures by a greater degree of independence. He decides to enter the Castle, and when he finds it impossible or
too difficult to achieve this aim, he concentrates on bringing about
a personal interview with Klamm, the Court Official in charge of Land-
Surveyors. As much as any man is free to exert his will, K. thinks,
speaks, and acts in freedom. Even when he has almost exhausted his
energies, he can say, "I came here of my own accord, and of my own
accord I have settled down in this place" (258).

In this respect he resembles the man from the country, who, like
him, has come to the Law of his own accord but will never leave it
voluntarily. At least in their complete inaccessibility the Law of the
parable and the master of the Castle are closely related, and we shall
not be surprised to meet the image of the door in all its ambiguity as
often here as we did in *The Trial*. The line of doorkeepers reappears
in the bureaucracy of the Castle, from the village elders up to Klamm.
Their corruption flavored with understanding is the same; of the offi-

* Numbers without letters refer to the American edition of *The Castle* (1954).

cials in the Castle it is also said that they "accept bribes simply to avoid trouble and discussion, but nothing is ever achieved in this way" (276). And it is more than probable that the final words of the door-keeper in the parable are just as valid for the more aggressive Land-Surveyor K. as they are for the passively stubborn bank employee Joseph K.

The Man from the Country as Land-Surveyor

Even in the literal sense of the phrase the Land-Surveyor is a man from the country. His home is a little town with a distinctly rural character: "A church stood in the market place, partly surrounded by an old graveyard which was again surrounded by a high wall" (38). His behavior and his speech are more down-to-earth than those of K. in *The Trial;* his profession, the surveying of land, brings him into closer contact with the soil.

From his little home town he has come with empty hands; he plans "to go back with something in his pockets" (8). He claims to have made great sacrifices in leaving but also has to concede the "impossibility of finding some other suitable job at home" (96). He even admits candidly to having a family, a wife, and children down there.* However, he introduces himself to the village as a genuine bachelor of the Kafka variety and does not seem to notice that this introduction of himself as a family man is apt to work against his desire, expressed soon afterward, to marry one of the village girls. It is quite possible that he fabricates the few allusions to his previous life in order to impress the villagers and officials in his favor, or at least that he invents for present advantage a past in which truth and fiction are inseparably interwoven. Yet if he lies, he is not smart enough to realize that his lies have shorter wings than his imagination. He speaks without considering the undesirable effects his words may have.

In a metaphoric sense also he is a man from the country. He comes close to calling himself an *Am-ha'aretz* when he confesses to being "ignorant" (72, and again 73), when he realizes that in the opinion of one of the village girls he knows "less about things than anyone else" (401), and when, finally, he is prepared to own that he knows nothing at all (409). His enemy, the landlady, compares him to a blind-

---

* This statement, which occurs in the first chapter during his conversation with the landlord, is omitted from the definitive American edition (see *Das Schloss,* German edition, 14).

worm, a faceless nothing creeping in the dust (72).* At a later point
she gives a very incisive thumbnail sketch of his character, saying, "If
only you would not always want to have things offered to you as if
they were for eating" (150). Like Joseph K., he can grasp intellectually only what he can clasp physically in his arms. Being aggressive,
he also wants to take in his possessions, to "eat" them, as a baby would.
When his "bride" Frieda is about to leave him, he asks her to provide
him with a meal (322) as if it were a substitute for her affection. Food
seems to be the best substitute for love. This is, of course, a small
child's psychology; by stressing it, Kafka seems to detach himself still
further from K. than he does from his other leading characters.

That K. has remained a child in many aspects is hardly a hindrance
for him, for he is often able to capitalize on his pitiful state, especially
in his relationships with women. Masterfully he exploits his helplessness in order to solicit assistance and uses his helpers one against another to achieve his aims. Even the landlady has to concede: "I cannot
stand him, but I cannot abandon him either; one simply cannot control
oneself when one sees a child that can hardly walk trying to go too far;
one simply has to interfere" (319). With the help of the childish and
childlike traits in K.'s character Kafka is able to endow his adventures
with the poignancy of a primitive epic.

As a man from the country, K. is attracted by pictures and falls prey
to them, especially to those he has imagined himself. At one time the
Castle appears to him as a ramshackle building "with battlements . . . ,
as if designed by the trembling hand of a child" (12), at another as a
man "who sat quietly there gazing in front of him . . . free and un-
troubled" (128). Ronald Gray has likened the images Kafka employs
throughout the novel to *Vexierbilder*, "the name deriving from those
pictures, originally so popular in the seventeenth century, where a
given set of lines and shading can be interpreted in two entirely different ways, according to the way in which they are sized up by the eye." [1]
On the Continent these *Vexierbilder* survived well into the twentieth
century, especially as the toys of children. It is as if the somewhat
infantile imagination of K. had permeated the landscape and even the
people confronting him.

The only aspect of the world which can change so facilely is its
surface; thus it is not surprising that K. concentrates on observing and
embellishing the external facets of his environment. A very important

---

* The English translation fails to do complete justice to the finality of K.'s
admission *"er habe kein Wissen,"* as well as to the landlady's mordant invective
when she calls the Land-Surveyor a *"Blindschleiche."*

role is assigned to people's clothing; an illustration of this is that the manuscript breaks off during a discussion of dresses (412). K.'s eyes continually wander between the surface of reality and the guise in which it appears to him—between skin and dress that is—yet it does not occur to him to penetrate beneath or beyond them. Again it is the landlady who pins his weakness down in a paradox. "Oh, what a person you are," she sighs in a deleted passage, "seemingly clever enough, but at the same time abysmally ignorant" (436)! She says *"bodenlos unwissend,"* (bottomlessly unknowing); it is the bottom, the foundation, of things which invariably escapes him.

Even his profession betrays his superficiality. This man from the country is no peasant concerned with seeds and roots and growth, but a surveyor of surfaces. He has abandoned his own soil to measure the fields of others, to draw up their limits, to arrange and rearrange their contours instead of tilling the earth.

He has already practised his profession at home, for he is expecting his former assistants (9). On the other hand, he quickly resigns himself to accepting the new helpers, Arthur and Jeremias, when they are assigned to him by the Castle. It soon appears that they have joined him without instruments and are completely unskilled in land surveying. "But if you are my old assistants you must know something about it," he insists. They answer with an extremely eloquent silence. Thereupon K. completely reverses his attitude: "Well, then, come in!" he says and takes them into the house (24). When he accepts these helpers from the Castle, K. commits one of those acts of overzealous adjustment to a new situation which discredit in advance any future claims he might derive from this adjustment. By overlooking their obvious professional incompetence, he all but exposes his own position as a daring bluff. And yet, during the entire course of events, he is never proved guilty of lying and of not being a Land-Surveyor. His competence is never fully established or categorically denied.

This sustained ambiguity finds a strong support in the subtle pun Kafka makes on the word Land-Surveyor.

The German for it is *Landvermesser,* and its verbal associations are significant. The first is, of course, [his] activity. . . . But *Vermesser* also alludes to *Vermessenheit,* hybris; to the adjective *vermessen,* audacious; to the verb *sich vermessen,* commit an act of spiritual pride, *and* also, apply the wrong measure, make a mistake in measurement.[2]

Using his *Vexierbild* technique, Kafka has, on the surface of things, shown us a man who may well be able to measure the land (*das Land vermessen*) and who is also perpetually engaged in overstepping his limits (*sich vermessen*) wherever he turns. In his relations with people and objects he continually applies the wrong measures, thus asking for the very calamities he is so eager to avoid. Although his demands are superficially modest, they are, in view of their never-clarified premises, also incommensurable and unmeasured.

His last dialogue with the Herrenhof landlady revolves around this pun on the word "measure" and its immeasurable paradoxicalities. "Did you not once learn tailoring?" the landlady asks, alluding to his interest in clothes (which are objects for which a measure must be taken). Upon his denial she wants to know what he really is. He reaffirms that his work is to measure the land. In order finally to convict him of his lie (or at least to give him further opportunity to confess), she asks him to elaborate. K. elaborates, but the explanation bores her as she had expected a recantation instead. Then she decides to resort to utter bluntness: "You are not telling the truth. Why don't you tell the truth?" Here she penetrates the surface and points to the origins of his plight. Instead of following her lead, K. commits the act of arrogance which is *Vermessenheit*. He answers her attack with a counterattack, "You don't tell the truth either," and is properly taken to task for the ignorance at the bottom of his arrogance. "Perhaps you are not impudent at all," the landlady says, "you are only like a child that knows some silly thing or other and cannot . . . keep it to himself" (411). Had he himself not admitted before that he had no knowledge? "You have none," the landlady had agreed; "very well then, do not arrogate any to yourself either" (*du sollst dir aber auch keines anmassen*) (410). Knowledge and truth are demonstrated to K. as absolute and primary values by which he can orientate himself, whereas he continues to operate with the relative and ancillary measurements provided by the word "measure" (*Mass*).

We can trace K.'s *Anmassung*, his arrogance, back to his youth. In one of his reminiscences he reveals that as a boy in the country he had challenged and conquered death. Climbing the wall of the churchyard, he had planted a flag on top of it; "he looked down and round about him, over his shoulder too, at the crosses vanishing into the ground; nobody was greater than he at this place and this moment. . . . The sense of this triumph had seemed to him a victory for life" (38). In this reminiscence we are able to observe the basic pattern of K.'s aggressive imagination. Yet likewise basic is the sudden change from a sham triumph to a painful and humiliating defeat; to the boy strutting on the churchyard wall the schoolteacher appears, reprimanding him and forcing him down from the scene of his glory. On his descent K. hurts his knee, just as in the novel any attempt the grownup K. makes to conquer the Castle inevitably results in an injury suffered either in his mind or on his body.

Yet he does not desist as long as his resources allow him to carry on his struggle. It seems that by his very nature this Land-Surveyor is less interested in drawing new border lines than in altering and obliterating the old ones. The audacity of this attitude attracts the village malcontents, the group around Brunswick, the cobbler. For them the surveying of land heralds the possibility of a new social and economic order; this is why the door of Lasemann, the tanner's, house is opened immediately to him, "the first door that had opened during the whole length of his walk down the village" (15). But the villagers are direly mistaken in their judgment of K. and his aims. His arrival in front of the Castle does not represent a "revolutionary act"[3] in the sense they would like to attribute to the activities of a Land-Surveyor. K.'s revolutionary activity, his *Vermessenheit*, aims at the interior of the Castle and is not to be satisfied by changing a few boundary stones in the fields around it. No villager can be his ally nor are the officials his real enemies. As the Law is Joseph K.'s true antagonist, so the Castle is the real adversary of the Land-Surveyor. The first sentences of the novel indicate that he had better not underestimate his opponent.

The Arrival

The story opens:

It was late in the evening when K. arrived. The village was deep in snow. Nothing could be seen of the Castle hill, mist and darkness surrounded it, nor was there even the faintest glimmer of light to indicate that a great Castle was there. On the wooden bridge leading from the highway to the village, K. stood for a long time gazing into the apparent emptiness above him.

Es war spät abends, als K. ankam. Das Dorf lag in tiefem Schnee. Vom Schlossberg war nichts zu sehen, Nebel und Finsternis umgaben ihn, auch nicht der schwächste Lichtschein deutete das grosse Schloss an. Lange stand K. auf der Holzbrücke, die von der Landstrasse zum Dorf führte, und blickte in die scheinbare Leere empor.

Here the first paragraph ends. The second begins:

Then he went to find quarters for the night (3).

Dann ging er, ein Nachtlager suchen.

K. stands on the bridge which separates him from the highway, on the one hand, and from the Castle and the village, on the other. The highway is still outside the Castle domain; the village is inside; he will have to submit to the jurisdiction of the Castle as soon as he enters the village. But whereas the village, nestling at the foot of the Castle hill, appears before him, the Castle itself remains invisible. It is mentioned first in conjunction with the hill on which it is built, but even the hill is hidden by mist and darkness. K. gazes into this darkness and attempts to penetrate it, but all he discovers is "the emptiness above him." A newcomer's eyes are usually sharper than those of the native whose vision is dulled by custom and dimmed by an all-too-great familiarity. K.'s first impression of the Castle as a void may more accurately represent its character than all later appearances.

K. arrives, but only on the bridge. There he stops, probably in the center. He is tired and the hour is late. The impending nightfall and the deep snow around suggest a rest in the nearest inn. And yet the wanderer stops, not only to catch his breath but, as the narrator stresses, "for a long time." His environment should goad him on toward a shelter for his tired bones, but simultaneously a deep-seated suspicion of the things to come prevents him from taking any further step. He is still free to choose between returning to the highway, perhaps even to his old home, and proceeding in the direction of the darkness which veils the Castle. Finally he decides to proceed, yet not because hunger and fatigue have urged him to do so but because he is attracted by the invisible Castle behind the visible village. Now his will is no longer free and no more choice is open to him. Kafka expresses this conscious-unconscious decision by omitting K.'s actual entrance into the village from his account. We are only told that the wanderer "gazes up" to the Castle and "then" goes to find quarters for the night. The decisive steps from the bridge to the village occur during the break which separates the first paragraph of the story from the second. They too remain invisible. While he takes them, however, K. succumbs to the spell of the Castle, a thoroughly negative spell as Kafka's treatment of the language indicates.

Stylistically *The Castle* is the best integrated of Kafka's major works. There are fewer dramatic highlights here than in his other narratives. The flow of the narration is sustained more evenly on one consistent level. The logic of the events is more convincing, although it derives from equally irrational presuppositions. As he did in *The Trial*, the narrator stands close to his hero, his eyes continuously fixed on him.

To a greater degree than in any other work events and conversations are recorded by the effects they have on the hero. Generally speaking, nothing is reported that is beyond K.'s immediate sphere of experience. This is consistent with the tone set for the rest of the story by its first paragraph: reality lies behind K. on the other side of the bridge, and before him opens a fallow and monotonous winter landscape, shadowy and treacherous, which he reflects rather than penetrates. As a result of this careful technique, the few instances in which Kafka steps back from his hero and speaks for himself carry special significance. In the very first paragraph the Castle is called "great" and the emptiness is described as "apparent." Certainly K. can have no idea of these qualities for to him not "even the faintest glimmer of light" is visible. A later and even more dramatic example occurs in the scene in which the secretary Bürgel speaks but is not heard by K., who has fallen asleep. If K. had heard Bürgel's remarks, he would have been able to enter the Castle, but the fact that K. does not hear tells us that this possibility exists only for Kafka, not for K. This can only mean that the Castle is both great *and* accessible—but not for K.

The negative quality of the Castle becomes even more obvious when, the next day, K. is actually able to see it. Introducing it to K., Kafka tells us what the Castle is not rather than what it is: "It was neither an old stronghold of knights nor a modern luxury building." It is not a real Castle but "a rambling pile of many small buildings closely packed together. . . . If one had not known that it was a Castle, one might have taken it for a little town." Although K. would not have recognized it without having been told beforehand that there was a Castle there, he is still not surprised at its appearance: "On the whole this distant view of the Castle corresponded to K.'s expectations." Had he anticipated this arbitrary agglomeration of ramshackle houses because it was the fitting complement to the needy village or because he could not imagine as his destination anything greater? Is what he actually sees nothing but a reflection of his own imaginings? Objective reality and K.'s personal reactions to it are already so closely interwoven that the great Castle is presented as a non-Castle, "a huddle of village houses," which can be called anything but great.

On stepping closer the Land-Surveyor is disappointed: "K. had a fleeting recollection of his home town. It was hardly inferior to this so-called Castle." The question arises in his mind why he has come here at all, since he seems merely to exchange, at the price of great sacrifices, one misery for another. He has to remind himself that he did not arrive here as a sight-seeing tourist but for professional reasons. Yet his next reflection leads him away again from such practical considerations and betrays something of the symbolic meaning of his wanderings: he compares the church steeple of his native town with the one tower rising over the Castle. The tower at home was "an earthly building" and obviously did not satisfy K., who on a childhood visit to the nearby churchyard had flattered himself with having conquered death. The very fact that this steeple at home stands out more clearly in his memory than does the Castle tower dominating the landscape before him seems to predispose him against the "earthly" steeple at home. He asks himself, and the tone of the question is scornful, "What else can we men build?" To be sure, the tower in front of him has nothing divine about it; it belongs, as K. takes care to determine, not to the chapel but to a house, "perhaps the main building." And yet, in accordance with the negative appearance of its surroundings, this tower offers a definitely unearthly look. It is in part "mercifully mantled with ivy" and shows a number of small windows, which glitter in the sun. This insignificant detail, this mirroring of the light in the Castle tower's windowpanes, gives the Land-Surveyor the sensation of observing "something insane." Having materialized out of nothing, the Castle, dilapidated and crumbling away stone after stone, is still able to reflect the light of heaven and thus, perhaps, to satisfy K.'s desires better than his home-town church.

On the other hand, this mirror effect impresses K. as an image of insanity. Again it is impossible to distinguish here between reality and K.'s reaction to it; yet in this impression the Castle seems to assume the role it is going to play with regard to K. (Or, conversely, K. assigns this role to his antagonist.) He is drawn to the Castle because, in reality and as an image, it lies between heaven and earth; but whatever heavenly light it reflects strikes him as a phenomenon bordering on madness.* Translating the image before him into anthropomorphic terms, as he is wont to do, he misses its deeper meaning in the process: "It was as if an afflicted inhabitant who ought to have been kept locked in the most remote room of the house had broken through the roof to present himself to the world."

The warning of madness to come is lost on K. He stops "as if in

---

* This image would even suggest insanity as a possible end for K. were it not for the fact that such a conclusion would reduce a parable to the level of a pathological study. It cannot be overlooked, however, that K. is driven ever closer to the end of his wits the further the novel progresses.

standing still he had more power of judgment." If he were to use his discrimination he could still take heed of the forbidding vision, the "afflicted inhabitant" of this Castle, and retreat from it. Being a man from the country, however, he allows himself to be distracted and surrenders to the power and the judgment of the Castle. He does not even see that "swarms of crows were circling" around this tower (11–12). According to German folklore, crows, like jackdaws, are harbingers of death.

The Labyrinth

K. has contemplated the Castle from the main street of the village. But this road "did not lead to the Castle Hill; it only made toward it and then, as if deliberately, turned aside; and though it did not lead away from the Castle, it led no nearer to it either" (14). The village is built along this street which, for very good reasons, "seemed to have no end" (15): as far as can be ascertained the road describes a circle. Along this street are located the various stops on K.'s way: near the bridge is the Bridge Inn where he spends his first night; then comes the school where he finds employment as a porter; and finally the Herrenhof Inn where he meets Frieda in the taproom and is able to espy Klamm.* The Herrenhof is also the scene of his meeting with secretary Bürgel, and it is here that the novel breaks off during his conversation with the landlady. Since the Herrenhof is also on the village street, K. at the novel's end has come not a single step nearer to his goal, the Castle.

He moves along a perimeter in the center of which the Castle Hill and the Castle itself are situated. It is his intention to leave the periphery and advance toward the center, but all kinds of real and imagined obstacles bar his way. He learns only a little about the region which separates him from the center, the realm of the "intermediate figures," the officials and the messengers; and whatever information he gathers is second hand, obtained by hearsay. Olga, for example, reports about the barriers which her brother, the messenger Barnabas, has encountered in the offices of the Castle:

He is admitted into certain rooms, but they are only part of the whole, for there are barriers behind which there are more rooms. . . . You must

---

* One of the reasons that led Brod to compare Klamm with Milena's husband may have been the fact that the latter, Ernst Pollak, used to patronize a famous Viennese coffeehouse, the Herrenhof.

not imagine that these barriers form a definite border line. . . . There are even barriers through which he is able to pass, and they look exactly like the ones he has never yet passed, and therefore one must not jump to conclusions and suppose that behind these latter barriers the offices are essentially different from the others (228–229).

The image presented by the offices—barriers which can be passed before others which protect a last inner chamber which remains inaccessible—is derived from the age-old pattern of the labyrinth. A possible ground plan for the interior of Kafka's Castle could be found on the late Renaissance wooden ceiling of the ducal palace in Mantua. There a deceivingly simple system of bars and passageways is organized around a center which dominates the whole design.[4] Another less classical model is the glass-covered round box in which a little ball has to be steered to the middle through winding runways interrupted by walls and intertwined with other corridors. This box, a favorite toy, must have come to Kafka's notice at a very early time in his life. The maze has proved attractive to the human imagination at various stages of its development, primarily the early ones and those when man was in search of a lost primitivity.

Although K. is never admitted to the interior of the offices, he succeeds at least in advancing into the Herrenhof, where the senior officials occasionally put up for a night. In the end he even penetrates the region of these sleeping quarters, seemingly an extension into the village of the Castle's secret:

In the hall they were met by an attendant who led them . . . into the entry and through the low, somewhat downward sloping passage. . . . Everything was on a small scale, but well and daintily appointed. The space was utilized to best advantage. The passage was just high enough for one to walk without bending one's head. Along both sides the doors almost touched one another. The wall did not quite reach the ceiling, probably for reasons of ventilation, for here in the low cellar-like passage the tiny rooms could hardly have windows (314).

This corridor, subterranean, carefully constructed according to a well-considered design, interrupted by a multiplicity of closed doors, is still only the fringe of a labyrinth.

That Kafka's tortuous ways of thinking predisposed him to adopt the labyrinth as a central image has long been recognized. One has only to think of the intricate script the execution machine produces in "In the Penal Colony," of the meandering interpretations of the Law in which both Titorelli and the Prison Chaplain indulge in *The Trial,* or of the "tormenting complications of the labyrinth" which, in one of Kafka's last stories, make up an unnamed animal's Burrow (*GW,* 94–95). The image of the maze must have suggested itself to Kafka with undiminished urgency during all the phases of his life. He would have had to invent it if it had not come down to him from tradition in untraceable ways.

But Hermann Pongs both oversimplifies and complicates matters unduly when he calls Kafka the "poet of the labyrinth." Pongs defines the labyrinth as "an effective image of a world out of joint" and uses it in opposition to what he terms a "symbolism of light." Comparing, not quite fairly, Kafka's world with the "universal mystery" of Goethe's *Faust,* in which the "struggle between god and devil, light and darkness" has been more fully presented, Pongs arrives at the judgment that Kafka's labyrinthine world is nothing but "some sort of shrunken form." [5] Throughout his disquisition Pongs sees in the labyrinth a dark and vague counterimage to the glories spread through the ages by solar myths.

Archeology, however, has shown that from its very inception the labyrinth was informed with the duality inherent in a universal image. C. N. Deedes, who has followed the shape and function of the labyrinth from its origins in Egyptian art to the European Middle Ages, concludes: "Above all, the Labyrinth was the centre of activities concerned with those greatest of mysteries, Life and Death. There men tried by every means known to them to overcome death and to renew life." [6] Even Gustav René Hocke, who seems to have inspired Pongs's Kafka interpretation, is ready to admit that for the earlier civilizations "the labyrinth was a metaphor unifying the calculable and the incalculable elements of the universe. The roundabout way leads to the center. Only the roundabout way leads to perfection." [7] This original duality of the labyrinth reappears in *The Castle,* stated, to be sure, as the basic paradox upon which the novel is built.

Hocke followed up the tradition of the labyrinth from the Middle Ages to the present day. His work, a *catalogue raisonné* of the suprarealistic achievements in European civilization since the late Renaissance, points to Kafka's native city, Prague, as a "focal point" of long standing for all types of "mannerism," that is, of exercises which lead the human mind beyond the classical canons of literature and art. [8] Under Rudolf II of Habsburg (1552–1612) Prague became a center of cabalistic thought as well as of astrological and alchemistic practices.

The labyrinth, being a Hermetic figure of prime importance, seems to have survived by some secret intellectual osmosis from those golden and gold-making days until it reappears in Kafka. Hocke at least points emphatically to the following aphorism in Kafka's notebooks (October 1917):

Seen with the terrestrially sullied eye, we are in the situation of travelers in a train that has met with an accident in a tunnel, and this at a place where the light of the beginning can no longer be seen, and the light of the end is so very small a glimmer that the gaze must continually search for it and is always losing it again; and furthermore, both the beginning and the end are not even certainties. Round about us, however, in the confusion of our senses, or in the supersensitiveness of our senses, we have nothing but monstrosities and a kaleidoscopic play of things that is either delightful or exhausting (*DF*, 66).

According to Hocke, of all the mysteries of the "mannerists" at least the "secret malady" of being spellbound by the darker sides of divinity has survived in Kafka.[9] This malady, then, degenerates in Pongs's view to "some sort of paralysis," [10] a diagnosis which is even at first sight contradicted by K.'s feverish activities with regard to *his* labyrinth, the Castle.

There exists in any case an atmospheric connection between the Castle of Rudolf II on the Hradžany Hill and the Castle of Kafka, who lived near Rudolf's palace during the winter of 1916–1917 in the small Zlatá ulička (the "Golden Lane"), supposedly the street of the Emperor's alchemists. Brod assures us that "Franz did not choose this quarter at all from any mystic or romantic inclination, except perhaps subconsciously" (*FK*, 156). No critic will be such a mystic as to postulate with conviction a direct relationship between the two castles; yet, considering the strange and devious ways in which the imagination of a writer often works, one cannot resist the temptation to reinforce Brod's all-too-timid observation, "except perhaps subconsciously."

With these qualifications in mind we may notice that the images of the Castle and the Labyrinth merge in the *Amphitheater of Eternal Wisdom* (1609) of the Rosicrucian and alchemist Heinrich Khunrath. This Amphitheater

represents the secret doctrine in the form of the dragon of Hermes, who lives in an impregnable fortress. It has twenty-one entrances which seem to invite the seeker to enter the sanctum, yet twenty of these ways lead him to closed compartments. The bewildered student of the occult may wander from one to the other without ever reaching the drawbridge of which Hermes is the watchman.[11]

With Hermes the watchman even the figure of a doorkeeper is added to what appears in outline and design as a labyrinthine castle.

The Czech polymath and Moravian brother Jan Amos Komensky (Comenius—1592–1670) leads us still closer to Kafka's Castle. His treatise, *The Labyrinth of the World and the Paradise of the Heart* (1623), contains, as its title indicates, a warning against black magic rather than an introduction into its secret practices. Its hero, a pilgrim, in the end resigns from the world, perhaps not quite convincingly, and commends his soul to his creator. Yet at the outset of his wanderings he meets an associate named Searchall or Impudence, who introduces him both to the world of the labyrinth and the world as a labyrinth. They are soon joined by a strangely hermaphroditic being called Falsehood. These two companions are emissaries from the same labyrinth through which they are going to lead the pilgrim. They correspond in function and to a certain degree even in character to the two assistants K. obtains from his Castle. Komensky's three wanderers climb a tower from which they view the maze of the world, which appears to them as a city: "I counted six principal streets all running from east to west side by side," says the pilgrim, "and in the centre of them there was a large, round square or market-place; behind it there stood to the west, on a rocky, abrupt hillock, a high and splendid Castle, at which almost all the inhabitants of the town gazed." This Castle of ultimate wisdom has a sister palace, dedicated to Fortune. Door images abound. Yet the most striking anticipation of Kafka is in the dim view Komensky's pilgrim seems to take of Land-Surveyors. He passes in review the conditions of man, his trades and avocations, and meets, between the philosophers and the musicians, "those who measured and weighed" the place.

Others, again, measured the hall itself; and almost everyone measured it differently. Then they quarrelled and measured afresh. Some measured a shadow, as to its length, width, and breadth; others also weighed it in a balance. They said generally that there was nothing in this world nor out of it which they were unable to measure rightly. But having watched this their craft for some time, I observed that there was more boasting than use.[12]

The combination of Castle, Labyrinth, and Land-Surveyorship, as well as the conception of "measuring" as an incommensurable boasting

(*Anmassung*), would suggest that Kafka was influenced, perhaps directly, by Komensky. The suggestion is supported by Kafka's interest in Czech literature, which makes it more than probable that he was familiar with the labyrinth of his predecessor. But even if we could establish beyond doubt that Komensky's allegory served as a source of Kafka's symbolic parable, we would have contributed little to our understanding of the later writer. After all, Komensky fully explains the meaning of his castles by giving them names. Kafka, on the other hand, confronts us with an unanswerable question in the very moment when he gives us, instead of the name of his Castle, that of its master, the Count Westwest.

Count Westwest

Brod's theological interpretation of the Castle in the postscript to the German editions * has been most eloquently contradicted by Erich Heller:

The Castle of Kafka's novel is, as it were, the heavily fortified garrison of a company of Gnostic demons, successfully holding an advanced position against the manoeuvers of an impatient soul. I do not know of any conceivable idea of divinity which could justify those interpreters who see in the Castle the residence of "divine law and divine grace." [13]

Ascribing a Gnostic heritage to the Castle officials, Heller has undoubtedly fathomed deeply the regions where Kafka gathered the material for his demonology. Yet he avoids touching upon the secret of the Castle's innermost chamber.

Georg Lukács enters there, somewhat brazenly, when he explains: "Kafka's god, the Senior Judges in *The Trial*, the real administration of *The Castle*, represent the transcendence of Kafka's allegories: nothingness." Presupposing the existence of a "real" master of the Castle and as a materialist disbelieving unreality, Lukács is quite consistent in eliminating this master once and for all from the pages of the book. "If a god is present here," he continues, "he is a god of religious atheism: *atheos absconditus*." [14] This characterization of the Castle's master as a hidden un-god is wittier than it is profound. It simply projects the "emptiness," with which the exterior of the Castle impressed K. at first sight, into the innermost center and replaces Kafka's warning qualification that this emptiness is only "apparent" with a certainty,

* To be found now on p. 484 of the second German edition.

the certainty of absolute negation. Negating the godhead absolutely, Lukács comes close to Brod, who posits it—closer in any case than it may be pleasant for either critic to realize: both are translating what appears to them as an allegory into conceptual language. If Lukács's interpretation proves anything to be true, then it is our suspicion that atheism is a theology turned upside down.

In order to gain at least a measure of the paradoxicality of this Castle we have, as usual, to consult Kafka's language. Again his choice of names is revealing—revealing, that is, of his intention to mystify his reader. The lord of the Castle is identified very early in the first chapter as "the Count Westwest." Emrich has observed that "this name could refer to the absolute end, the region of death beyond the sunset, but also to the transcendence, the conquest, of death." [15] Looking more closely, we can see Kafka at work playing a most intricate word game with the reduplication of the syllable "West." Assuming that "West," like the Hotel Occidental in *Der Verschollene*, is indicative of decline, then its repetition underscores the signs of decomposition that welcomed K. on his arrival: the crumbling of the Castle walls, the crows around the tower, the long stretches of darkness, the snow of winter. Yet the negative emphasis provided by repetition is counteracted by the law of logic according to which a double negation results in a reinforced affirmation. The West of the West may indicate the decline of the decline, that is, an ascent. Then Kafka would have alluded here to eternal life, would have attempted to say in his opaque way what a more believing soul, the Dean of St. Paul's, John Donne, expressed in the line: "And Death shall be no more; Death, thou shalt die." [16]

The secret of the inner chamber consists in the complete ambivalence it represents between life and death, descent and resurrection, heaven and hell. It is both; at least it seems to waver constantly between the poles of man's physical and spiritual existence. Kafka succeeded here in concentrating into two syllables all the uncertainties and indecisions, the doubtful expectations and hopeful fears, that the hero of *The Trial* poured out in the veritable flood of his last questions.

Kafka took great care to sustain this ambiguity throughout the imagery of the novel. There are bells in the Castle, as if it were a church. First "a bell began to ring merrily up there, a bell that for at least a second made his heart tremble . . . as if it threatened him with the fulfillment of his vague desire." The menace of having one's desire fulfilled is still the expression of K.'s personal ambivalence, a psychological remark indicating the state of a mind that feels threatened at the prospect of finding his wishes terminated by fulfillment. Yet K.'s subjective ambivalence is soon followed by the objective observation that the place of the merry bell was "taken by a feeble, monotonous little tinkle," the very opposite of the first. To blur the image still further, Kafka adds that this tinkle "might have come from the Castle, but might have been somewhere in the village" (21).

He uses this technique more subtly when it comes to K.'s entry into the Herrenhof. He describes the scene as follows: "The front steps had a balustrade, and a fine lantern was fixed over the doorway. When they entered, a piece of cloth fluttered over their heads; it was a flag with the Count's colors." K., eager to establish his future master's identity, could be expected to study the emblem of this flag or at least make a guess at the character of the Westwest family by observing the color scheme of the piece of cloth fluttering over his head. Exactly the opposite comes to pass. K. concentrates on the details of the door and the doorway, although "all the houses in the village resembled one another more or less" (43). The flag, however, is described as having colors without actually displaying any, and whatever heraldry Count Westwest may boast of in his coat of arms remains undisclosed.

Still more intricate is an exchange K. has with the village teacher. Asked whether he knows the Count, the teacher first replies in the negative, and when K. insists, adds in French, "Remember that there are innocent children present" (13–14). Superficially this uncalled-for admonition may heighten the "sinister, perhaps macabre and disreputable, or even infernal and obscene aspect" [17] of the Castle, since it implies that the Count is so depraved that his name must not be mentioned before infants. Yet it may also mean that K. tries to pronounce in vain the name of a superior being, violating something like the Third Commandment and committing a sin that innocent children should not be allowed to witness. Either interpretation may serve as a reason for K.'s taking this rebuke as a "justification" (14) to invite himself into the teacher's house: he may suspect that the teacher is the accomplice of an infernal procurer or that he is a piously reticent apostle of his most mysterious Lordship.

Kafka did not, could not, decide on the identity of the Castle's "afflicted inhabitant" whom K. had imagined. As usual, he left this question open. Thus the Count seems to be *both* sublime *and* satanic, someone *and* no one, and what K. actually perceives are mirrorings of his own doubts.

Mirrors

In *The Castle* Kafka introduces us to a greater number of characters than in any other story, and for the first and only time the female element prevails among them. These figures, female as well as male, are engaged in almost uninterrupted conversations about one another, and since their characters are highly unusual, they approach one another at the strangest angles and from the most unexpected directions. The distortions of reality generally characteristic of Kafka's style present themselves here as a matter of course. Moreover, these figures cannot avoid talking about the Castle; the Castle forms the continual background of their conversations; it colors their relations with one another and informs them with its own enigmatic presence, whether they are villagers or officials. It seems to speak through them all, but what it communicates is the insoluble puzzle of its existence. If the ground plan of this village is a labyrinth, then Kafka has complicated the wanderings of his hero still further by using K.'s dialogues with his antagonists as an elaborate constellation of mirrors reflecting the Castle, each other, and K., all simultaneously. One of the most perfect labyrinths is the mirror cabinet, and Kafka seems to use similar techniques to delay K.'s progress on a way where "deceptions are more frequent than changes" (296).*

While still at the beginning of his way, K. receives a letter from the Castle, which begins, "My dear Sir, as you know, you have been engaged for the Count's service" (30). The three words, "as you know," are the reflection mirroring K.'s wishes and intentions rather than the statement of an actuality; he has not been told by anyone before that he has been accepted. Noticing the letter writer's mental reservations, K. suspects a hidden trap: the letter, he observes, does not "gloss over the fact that if it should come to a struggle, K. had had the audacity to make the first advances; it was very subtly indicated and only to be sensed by an uneasy conscience—an uneasy conscience, not a bad one; it lay in the three words 'as you know'" (33). These three words disturb his conscience because they throw the responsibility for all future developments back upon him. As a whole, the letter does not really welcome him; it does not authorize his position; it only reflects his arrival.

* "Täuschungen sind häufiger als Wendungen." The German *Wendungen* ("turns") points still more distinctly to the labyrinthine nature of K.'s way.

The signature on the document is illegible, but Barnabas, the messenger, names powerful Klamm as the sender. Klamm's name certainly suggests "straits, pincers, chains, clamps, but also a person's oppressive silence." [18] Klamm also shares his initial with K., so that, theoretically speaking, the name of his so-called employer could be abbreviated to indicate the name of the Land-Surveyor. This does not mean to suggest that Klamm exists only in K.'s imagination nor that he merely embodies K.'s subjective ideas about the Castle officials. A real person appears to K. soon afterward, a man who is if anything the Land-Surveyor's extreme opposite: the epitome of bourgeois sedateness, a towering image of trivial virility.*

The identity of their initials does inidicate, however, that a basic and fundamentally inexplicable connection exists between them. That K. has no hope whatever to clarify this connection (which, of course, represents his relation to the Castle as a whole), he can see from Klamm's letter: printed beside the illegible signature it shows as the sender's official rank the designation "Chief of the Department X" (30). This "Department Number Roman Ten" is also the unknown department, since X stands for an undefined quantity in German as it does in English. K. is at liberty to replace this X with any figure he chooses, yet this X, the secret at the Castle's center, will never fit without a remainder in any of his calculations. The struggle upon which he enters is a struggle against an unknown, an unknowable opponent. It is also a struggle of letters, K. versus X, a cabalistic battle, and our man from the country is ill-advised when he solicits human help to gain it.

K.'s first move in this unpromising fight is the conquest of Frieda, the barmaid at the Herrenhof:

An unobtrusive small girl with fair hair, sad eyes, . . . but with a surprising look, a look of special superiority. As soon as her eye met K.'s, it seemed to him that her look decided something concerning himself, something which he had not known to exist, but which her look assured him did exist (47).

K. hardly notices Frieda's frame, nor does her appearance warrant any special attention. Her attraction for him lies in her eyes—Kafka resorts again to the rather primitive expedient of mentioning her eyes and looks six times in two sentences—or rather in the "something," existing

---

* It can be argued that, in Klamm, Kafka drew a likeness of his father; this would be another reason for K.'s and Klamm's names beginning with the same letter.

and not existing, which is mirrored in them. He is struck by the "decision," which he has projected into her looks and which her eyes reflect back to him, a decision, we may safely assume, made with regard to K.'s claims on the Castle. When she reveals herself as Klamm's mistress, he decides to win her as an ally in his fight, because of the "special superiority" he has noticed in her glances. "In your eyes," he says, "I read far more the conquests still to come than the conquests past" (50). These future conquests are to end his own struggles, and since Frieda's eyes seem to bear good tidings as to their outcome, he tries to seduce Frieda from her allegiance to Klamm to the serving of his own purposes. He succeeds, to a certain degree: their embrace, consummated "among the small puddles of beer and other refuse scattered on the floor" of the taproom (54) is a perfect parody of a Wagnerian *Liebestod*. What dies in this embrace, however, is primarily Frieda's relation to Klamm. After this night the Chief of Department X does not call her any more; the "special superiority" fades from her eyes, and with it any reflection of the Castle. When Frieda professed to be Klamm's mistress, her glance swept "triumphantly" over K. (48); now that K. has deflected her eyes and concentrated them upon himself, he has extinguished the triumphant view of the Castle in them and replaced it with his own image. For Frieda will not tire of reflecting his weakness in endless curtain lectures, a process during which he paradoxically develops an ever-growing affection for her. When Frieda is ready to leave him, K. actually seems to love her. Mirrors make bad allies.

K.'s first informant after his night with Frieda is not his new mistress but her "Little Mother" (56), Gardena, the landlady of the Bridge Inn. He learns that Gardena herself had entertained tender relations with Klamm; thus her conversation is inevitably tinged with nostalgia for past glories and present aversions to K., the intruder upon her cherished memories. He has to hear, by way of an introduction, that the landlady's "poor head cannot understand how a girl who had the honor of being known as Klamm's mistress—a wild exaggeration in my opinion—should have allowed you even to lay a finger on her" (65). Rather than informing K., the landlady offends him. The only intelligence he obtains consists in the doubts that Gardena casts on the relation that exists between Frieda and Klamm, a thoroughly negative sort of information since it suggests that K.'s strategy, which is based on this very relationship, is nothing but tomfoolery. A little while later Gardena declares, "You put me in mind of

my husband, you are just as childish and obstinate as he is" (67).
Instead of the desired picture of Klamm, K. is shown here his own
self-portrait, with which the likeness of the landlord is blended, to
K.'s disadvantage. His own image is tarnished as well as blurred in the
eyes of the landlady.

The further K. progresses in his wanderings, the less positive is the
information that he is able to gather about Klamm. Gardena, for
example, speaks about her long-lost lover in tones reminiscent of the
teacher's warning. "Don't use Klamm's name," the landlady says. "Call
him 'him' or something, but do not mention his name" (111). With
the utmost piety she speaks of a being with whom, after all, she has
enjoyed herself in a most human way: "The fact that he had ceased
to summon me was a sign that he had forgotten me. When he stops
summoning people, he forgets them completely" (108). She seems to
explain her own resignation to her fate, but she also mirrors here the
collapse of K.'s hopes which were to use Frieda as a decoy in *his* relations with Klamm.

Whatever intelligence K. succeeds in gathering is not only scarce
but contradictory. Olga, Barnabas' sister, calls Klamm rude: "He can
apparently sit for hours and then suddenly say something so brutal
that it makes one shiver" (254). Gardena, on the other hand, infers
"that he is terribly sensitive." But she touches on his secret, the letter
X, when she concedes, "How it is in reality, we do not know" (143).
Erlanger, his secretary, maintains that "Klamm's job is, of course, the
biggest" (353); yet K. never learns in what this job actually consists.
He only finds out some duties which Klamm shirks: he does not read
any protocols (150) nor does he wait for messages from the village; he
is downright irritated when a messenger approaches him (157). Thus
we are not surprised in the end when we hear that Barnabas, who has
been assigned to Klamm as a messenger and receives his instructions
by word of mouth, doubts that the official referred to as Klamm in the
Castle is really Klamm (229).What could be called Klamm's protean
nature [19] is also the effect produced by the mirrors of the labyrinth,
which distort and refract everybody and everything that presents itself
to them.

There is, however, one thing in which all the accounts about Klamm
agree with one another: "He always wears the same clothes, a black
morning coat with long tails" (231). Only what is arbitrarily change-
able remains rigidly unchanged—his solemn and sinister attire, which
truly befits a secretary of Count Westwest. Klamm's toilet harmonizes

with the monotony surrounding the Castle; its funereal character agrees with the general mood of decline, the dark cloth being, so to speak, an expression of the darkness, the unknowable, which it covers. Yet it would be a mistake to draw any conclusions from Klamm's coat about his real nature. "Woe to him," says an old adage from the cabala, "who takes the mantle for the law." [20] This mistake, however, K. made when, looking through the peephole in the taproom, he mistook Klamm's orderly appearance and bourgeois propriety for human qualities against which he could pitch his energies. Klamm's "mantle" hides a secret which is just as impenetrable as the Law of *The Trial*.

The law according to which *The Castle* is administered touches K. once more in the form of a letter. This time the document is unsigned, as if the sender had wanted to disappear completely. Paradoxically the letter commends K. for labors he has not even begun. It reads in part: "The surveying work that you have carried out thus far has been appreciated by me." But K. has done no surveying yet. Quite the contrary, he has just accepted the job of porter at the village school. To make things worse he has also sullied Klamm's sleigh—another of his "mantles." "The work of the assistants too deserves praise," the official document continues. Yet the assistants have not done anything either; they have engaged in all kinds of mischief; they have followed K. against his strict orders and are molesting him at the very moment when he peruses the letter, so that he has to drive them away with his elbow. "Carry your work to a fortunate conclusion," the letter ends, "I shall keep an eye on you" (154). The last phrase indicates that the author of this missive is identical with the writer of the first letter, K.'s "decree of appointment." There the sender had promised "not to lose sight of you" (*Sie nicht aus den Augen zu verlieren*—30); here he takes the phrase up again to give his promise a still more positive turn. This turn, however, leads K. to the realization that he has neglected his duties, disavowed his own claims to be a Land-Surveyor, and gone astray. The praise is perverted to scorn.

Again, the images of eye and sight are used to function as mirrors with the purpose of confusing K.'s sense of direction. Klamm "keeps an eye" on K. and, by doing so, impresses upon him how far he has strayed from the path of providence. But the phrase has also a less metaphorical meaning, for Klamm appears to have dispatched the two assistants not so much to help the Land-Surveyor as to watch him. "Messengers of Klamm," Frieda describes them. "Their eyes— those ingenuous and yet flashing eyes—remind me somehow of

Klamm's eyes; yes, this is it: it is Klamm's glance that sometimes pierces me from their eyes" (183). At the same time these spies and "eyes" of Klamm mimic K., shadow him, intrude into the privacy of his bed, and covet Frieda; one of them, Jeremias, will actually steal K.'s mistress as K. has stolen Klamm's. They "enact one long parody of K.'s persistence"; [21] on the other hand, they will fade out of sight and vanish as soon as he has dismissed them, thus depriving them of the object of both their vigilance and mimicry. If they are Klamm's eyes, they are also K.'s mirrors. *

Yet Kafka has refined still further the play of mirrors in this labyrinth. As there is on the stage a play within the play, there is an occasional mirror-within-mirror effect in this novel. The most intricate and most confusing among these maneuvers of deception occurs in the thirteenth chapter when Frieda repeats to K. the landlady's utterances about him. At this time a genuine sympathy for Frieda and pity for her lot have begun to get the better of his proprietary instincts. It is in the cadence of a consolation and a compliment that he tells her, "Before I knew you I was going about in a blind circle" (179). Quite some time elapses, and one of the most telling scenes of the book, K.'s meeting with Hans Brunswick, intervenes before Frieda returns to his words:

How startled I was . . . when you said some time today that before you knew me you had gone about in a blind circle. These are perhaps the same words that the landlady used; she too says that it is only since you have known me that you have become aware of your goal. That is because you believe you have secured in me a sweetheart of Klamm's, and so possess a hostage that can only be ransomed at a great price (202–203).

This serves as the introduction to a long tirade in which Frieda enumerates the gloomy views the landlady holds with regard to K. Her recital ends with the following words:

But the landlady said finally, when you see then that you have deceived yourself in everything, in your assumptions and in your hopes, in your ideas of Klamm and in his relations to me, then hell is going to begin for me . . . , since you have no feeling for me but the feeling of ownership (204).

The interplay of various reflections is almost inextricably involved. Who speaks? Frieda or Gardena? Frieda never indicates the occasion at which Gardena said these words, nor does she fully identify with

---

* Eventually, however, it turns out that it was not Klamm at all who had sent the assistants. It was, Jeremiah informs K. (302), Galater, one of Klamm's deputees.

them and take the responsibility for them. She reproduces, however, with utter satisfaction something that originates in a word that K., and not the landlady, has spoken. He said it in good faith and with the best of intentions. And yet his own statement was strangely two-edged. Anyone who is as hostile to him as the landlady can easily turn it against him. He himself had conceded that he needed Frieda very much. Nor can it be denied that he first approached her from utilitarian motives. Gardena certainly displayed considerable ingenuity in reading these motives and spelling them out, but she falls victim to her own animosity when she deduces the course of Frieda's future from K.'s past. His very words which started the conversation prove that K. has developed other sentiments for Frieda than a mere "feeling of ownership."

Frieda then, only seemingly passive, blends K.'s self-reflection and the landlady's reflection of it, twists and turns them, and throws the image back at him. In this process K.'s words have lost all warmth of human kindness and show him to be nothing but a caricature of his former self. Mercilessly exposing the ulterior motives that have inspired K. and just as coldly anticipating the conclusion that his future actions will spring from similar calculations, Frieda exposes K. as a monster. But ulterior motives are at best partial truths, and their discovery usually produces the effect to be expected from splinters, a fragmentation and distortion of reality. In this cruel mirror-within-mirror play Frieda sends K. back to the "blind circles" of the labyrinth along which he had wandered before meeting her. Thereby she demonstrates that their meeting has indeed been in vain. Long before she deserts him in actual fact, she abandons him here. And yet she acts with a certain painful logic: having been taken for a mirror, she shows K. nothing but himself.

Echoes

As can be seen from the few and strangely austere poems he wrote, Franz Kafka was rarely attracted to the sensuous charm of musical language and was not overly gifted as a lyrical poet. Wladimir Weidlé has described Kafka's prose as "almost Mozartian," [22] but the beauty of his style is due to architectural rather than musical qualities. His prose consists primarily of sentences of great latitude, symmetrically structured, phrase following phrase with inexorable necessity, moving along in seemingly unending circles until the whole edifice is broken off suddenly, pointing to further heights which it can no longer reach. The Tower of Babel is one of Kafka's favorite images.

When music is actually heard in Kafka's books, it is almost exclusively meant to signify the invisible and to serve as a symbol of the perennially unattainable, ineffable, and unknowable. From the "unknown nourishment" which the insect craves in "The Metamorphosis" while it listens, fascinated by its sister's violin playing, to the "clear, piercing continuous note which came without variation literally from the remotest distance," to which the "Investigations of a Dog" are devoted (*GW*, 15–16), music holds for Kafka's figures a far from sensual sensation. It is another image of the unimaginable, and more often than not Kafka chooses an animal as the listener in order to stress more strongly the inhuman quality of sound.

Kafka has added a variety of sound effects to the predominantly visual labyrinth of his Castle because of their inhuman quality. To confuse K. as well as the reader, he works with homonyms and identical names: Sortini, the official who persecutes Amalia, is only distinguished by the middle *t* from Sordini, who, K. thinks, has something to do with his affairs (244)—a consonance of names all the more irritating because their bearers never materialize. The little daughter of the Brunswick family is called Frieda (187), like K.'s mistress, and her brother, Hans, like the landlord of the Bridge Inn (105). The proprietress of the Bridge Inn is usually referred to as landlady instead of Gardena, so that she may be more easily mistaken for the Herrenhof landlady, and confusion is almost inevitable when the Bridge Inn landlady emerges in the Herrenhof and behaves as if she were in her own house (140 ff.).

There are still more delicate devices at Kafka's disposal. If mirrors are the instruments of visual deception, then telephones are tools of acoustic seduction. Shortly after K.'s arrival at the Bridge Inn, a young man by the name of Schwarzer ("the black one," "Negro") puts a call through to the Castle. In spite of the late hour the call is answered; the Castle is heard by K. before he has actually seen it. The official on the other end of the wire first denies that a new Land-Surveyor has been appointed; then he calls back to deny the denial. "A mistake," says Schwarzer. The two words do not fail to impress K., who "pricked up his ears. So the Castle had recognized him as the Land-Surveyor" (7). He rejoices too soon; since he never learns the actual content of Schwarzer's conversation, he can only conclude that the Castle has reversed its position in one way or another; the position itself remains hidden from him.

The next day he orders his newly arrived assistants to call again and inquire whether he could appear in their company to requisition a sleigh. This time the information *is* clear: "The 'No' . . . was audible even to K. at his table. . . . But the answer went on . . . : 'Neither tomorrow nor at any other time' " (26). After having acknowledged his Land-Surveyorship by sending the assistants, the Castle once and for all denies him, their master, entrance through its gates. Thereupon K. decides to act and hear for himself. He lifts up the receiver from which presently emanates

a buzz of a kind that K. had never heard before. . . . It was like the hum of countless children's voices—but yet not a hum, the echo rather of voices singing at an infinite distance—blended by sheer impossibility into one high but resonant sound that vibrated on the ear as if it were claiming to penetrate deeper than K.'s miserable hearing would allow.

What penetrates beyond mere hearing is open to any and all interpretations. It may be an inner voice or an outer one. It may be inhuman, or superhuman, or the silence of nothingness that resounds in the ear as the sea is said to resound in an empty shell. Turning inarticulateness into acoustic impression, this sound is the paradox at the core of K.'s parabolical situation. The voices are innumerable; this tallies well with the infinite number X on Klamm's letter, which is delivered onto the scene while K. is engrossed in his telephone conversation with the Castle. Spellbound, he hears the manifold echoes turn "into one high but resonant sound." In the unified variety of this echo turned monotone resound both the merry bell and the depressing tinkling with which the Castle had greeted him before. The whole effect is the acoustic counterpart of the architectural paradox the Castle is soon to offer K. when it actually appears before his eyes: the countless numbers of buildings dominated and thus unified by the tower. The melancholy prevailing on Castle Hill is also heralded by the tone in the receiver "that vibrated on the ears as if it were claiming to penetrate deeper than K.'s miserable hearing would allow" (*so wie wenn sie fordere, tiefer einzudringen als nur in das armselige Gehör*). Here the narrator points to the more than auditive character of the sound; it is meant to speak to K. about the inexpressible which it represents; coming from a sphere beyond words, it aims at a region behind his senses. Obviously K. could learn more about the nature of his antagonist by listening to the Castle than by observing it with his eyes. He is indeed fascinated by this acoustic labyrinth; he forgets himself and his surroundings—"he did not know how long he stood there"—and then enters into a conversation which in its grotesque verbal contradictions sets the pattern of his later actual meanderings through the village.

"Go away!" cries K. to the landlord, who has appeared to announce the arrival of Barnabas with Klamm's "decree of appointment." K.'s "Go away" echoes the "No" the Castle has said to his request for admission to the hill. Promptly it is answered by the Castle; the official on the other side of the wire introduces himself; "Oswald speaking, who is there?" As if to demonstrate that the sound he has heard in the receiver has failed to penetrate his "miserable hearing" and speak to his conscience, K. utters now a half-truth, almost a lie: he does not introduce himself as the Land-Surveyor (which would have been a pretense rather than the complete truth), but as one of his assistants. "What Land-Surveyor? What assistant?" he is asked, whereupon he refers his interrogator rather haughtily to yesterday's conversation. "Ask Fritz," he answers curtly. The answer comes, "Oh, yes, that everlasting Land-Surveyor." On the surface this "everlasting" expresses the Castle's annoyance at being molested once more; at the same time it attributes to K. the epithet "eternal," if only in the sense in which the German language speaks of the Wandering Jew as the Eternal Jew.

The interrogation continues. "What assistant?" the voice asks. "Joseph" (27–28), says K. Here we don't know if he speaks the truth or not. By allowing the hero of *The Castle* to assume the first name of the K. in *The Trial*, Kafka establishes a playful identity between the two figures. And since this is the first and only time in *The Castle* that K.'s Christian name is mentioned, we may even suppose that Joseph is really the name of the Land-Surveyor. Kafka was quite prepared to extend this play with names until it involved himself as well. With an astonished amusement he notes in his diary on January 27, 1922, during a sojourn in the health resort of Spindlermühle: "Despite my having written down my name legibly . . . they have printed Joseph K. down in the guest directory. Shall I enlighten them, or shall I let them enlighten me" (*DII*, 213)? That is, should he let the Information Givers at the Spindlermühle Hotel tell Franz Kafka that he really was Joseph K.? As far as the novel is concerned, Kafka saw to it that such a confusion could not arise. He rewrote the first chapters in which the hero had originally told his story in the first person.* There is, however, some deeper meaning in K.'s adoption of the Christian name of his predecessor in *The Trial*. He does so at the very moment when the Castle comes into personal contact with him, directly accepts his challenge, and seems to begin battle with him. Although Land-Surveyor K. is more active than Bank Clerk Joseph K., they are both at the mercy of the authorities as soon as the officials decide to enter the scene. K. will succumb to them just as hopelessly as does Joseph K., whose mask he borrows here for a brief moment.

The Castle's voice immediately puts K. in his place by giving the names of the assistants. There is no Joseph among them, K. is informed and rebuked; they are called Arthur and Jeremias. This leads to the following exchange: K., "These are the new assistants." Voice, "No, they are the old ones." K., "They are the new ones; I am the old assistant. I followed the Land-Surveyor and came today." Voice (shouting back), "No." K., "Then who am I?" Voice (with a deeper, more authoritative tone), "You are the old assistant" (28). This is the acoustic mirror that the Castle holds before K. It will continue to echo his half-truths and near-lies. Correspondingly Klamm's letters are neither "inconsistent" (31) nor "misunderstandings" (154) as they appear to K., but only give back the sound of the words with which he had presented himself at the Bridge Inn on the first evening: "I am the Land-Surveyor" (5).

It is, to be sure, a response distorted by the unending windings of the labyrinth he has entered. At the end of the telephone conversation the voice asks, "What is it you want?" K. continues to pretend and answers with a counterquestion: "When can my master come to the Castle?" "Never," is the answer. At whom is this "never" directed? At K. or at the fictitious master of an imaginary assistant? He has asked one of the patently false questions that Kafka's heroes are so fond of putting to their fate, and he has been answered accordingly. The spiteful "Very well" with which K. hangs up the receiver indicates that he is willing to measure his strength against an opponent who has already won a victory over him by giving him back his own lie (28).

This echo scene has brought K. into the closest personal contact with the interior of the Castle that he will ever be able to achieve. Acoustically, infinity seems to have reverberated in the telephone

* Brod's Note to the first American edition, now to be found on p. vi of the definitive edition.

in order to expose him to the unending path of self-deception along which he has already begun to wander. Having been allowed to listen to the Castle's paradox in time—infinity vibrating in a simple telephone wire—he is now ready to leave the Bridge Inn and see the Castle as a paradox in space.

Of Time and Space

The Castle covers almost as many pages as *Der Verschollene* and *The Trial* put together. Even though it is fragmentary, it comes near the five hundred pages which Kafka had intended to add to the first chapter of Karl Rossmann's story (*B*, 115). In contrast to *The Trial*, where the narrative covers a whole year, *The Castle* takes place in not more than seven days' time, and even this accounting can be justified only if we consider the evening of K.'s arrival as one day. At the end of the story time does not elapse any more: it fades away. Time indications become rarer and rarer.* When, less than ten pages before the end, the Herrenhof landlady dates a remark K. has dropped about her dress (373) as "made yesterday" (409), we can infer that the novel breaks off on the seventh day. Furthermore, the symptoms of exhaustion which K. displays in his last conversation suggest that he is not going to survive this seventh day.

Kafka seems to parody the seven days of the creation with the week K. spends in the village. In this respect *The Castle* contains a cosmogony in reverse, a "taking back" of the work performed by the hands of the Divine. Instead of a created world which the divine author views on the seventh day with satisfaction, Kafka allows the Castle world to dissolve into nothingness on K.'s seventh day. There is no final chapter extant as there is for *Der Verschollene* or *The Trial;* instead, time and space merge hazily with infinity.

Kafka deals with time in *The Castle* in such a way that half of it has been spent by the end of the third chapter: "When he got up at last on the following morning, he was much refreshed, and it was already the fourth day since his arrival in the village." This happens on page 57; for the remaining half of K.'s week in the village Kafka reserves 365 pages, or about five-sixths of the book.

* For this reason we feel entitled to interpret a remark that Olga makes to K. at the end of the fifth day as an approximation: "You have arrived a week ago." (This remark has been mistranslated in the American edition by "it was a week after your arrival" [294].)

The reason for this distribution may become clearer by a brief comparison of *The Castle* with Thomas Mann's *The Magic Mountain*. Mann's novel also begins with the hero's arrival in a "castle"; the sanatorium Berghof is likewise removed from the common ways of mankind and haunted by a variety of apparitions, including veritable ghosts. K.'s seven days in the neighborhood of the Castle correspond to the seven years which Hans Castorp spends in the Berghof. Yet in the middle of Mann's book, on page 343 of the 716 pages of the American edition, less than one year has passed. The remaining six-sevenths of the time are compressed into the second half of the book. Thomas Mann speeds up the tempo of his tale and reduces the epic material presented as Castorp stays longer on the Magic Mountain, whereas Kafka increases the breadth of narration in direct proportion to the time his hero spends in the vicinity of the Castle. The slow passing of time at Hans Castorp's arrival corresponds to the newness and the wealth of the impressions which he has to gather and digest. The more familiar reality becomes for the hero, the further it recedes into the background and the faster time slips by. Days melt into weeks and these into months and years, boiling down to what Castorp calls, as early as the twenty-first day of his sojourn, "Soup-Everlasting" (*Ewigkeitssuppe*).[23] In other words, Mann treats the time he narrates as empirical time, registered and reflected by the consciousness of the hero according to the laws of psychology. Its speed imitates the tempo in which life itself proceeds and carries the reader along an incline which grows constantly steeper. The more years, the fewer pages to describe them: this is the psychological formula for depicting reality in an epic manner.

Hans Castorp would not be a Thomas Mann hero if he did not oppose this natural flow of time by inner adventures. There is a contrapuntal "inner" time element at work in *The Magic Mountain*—that of Castorp's emotional refinement and intellectual growth—which leads him to see visions, to indulge in dreams, to follow his many mentors on *their* labyrinthine ways, and which contributes eventually, we may suppose, to his death. We can infer how far this subterranean counterflow of "inner" time carries Castorp in the direction of Kafka's Castle from one of the reflections with which Mann accompanies his wanderings:

The contentual time of a story can shrink its actual time out of all measure. We put it in this way on purpose, in order to suggest another element, an illusory, even to speak plainly, a morbid element, which is quite definitely a factor in the situation. I am speaking of cases where the story practises a hermetical magic, a temporal distortion of perspective reminding one of certain abnormal and transcendental experiences in actual life. We have records of opium dreams in which the dreamer, during a brief narcotic sleep, had experiences stretching over a period of ten, thirty, sixty years, or even passing the extreme limit of man's temporal capacity for experience: dreams whose contentual time was enormously greater than their actual . . . time, and in which there obtained an incredible foreshortening of events; the images pressing one upon another with such rapidity that it was as though "something had been taken away, like the spring from a broken watch" from the brain of the sleeper. Such is the description of a hashish eater.[24]

This description brings us to the brink of Kafka's Castle. Yet the abyss which still separates Castorp's Magic Mountain from K.'s Castle Hill can be gauged by the fact that Kafka has actually given artistic shape to an area which Mann has merely reviewed and mapped out in his cerebrations. Moreover, Kafka's Castle did not arise from the dream of a drug addict but from the vision of a mind as painfully alert as that of anyone in his generation.

Mann follows the laws of empirical reality to the very end of his story, using a high degree of irony to mitigate any breach of these laws such as occurs in the "highly questionable"[25] incident of an occultist session. In Kafka, on the other hand, it is reality itself which appears highly questionable. Empirical time is left behind as soon as K. crosses the bridge; it is abandoned once more as he falls asleep after arriving at the inn. When he is awakened, he opens his eyes to the heightened reality of the village. Less than one page is devoted to his arrival at the Bridge Inn, and when he visits the Herrenhof at the end of the second chapter (43), he has acquainted himself with the whole range of the stage on which he is to perform—"the three streets that are in the village" (422). With fearful symmetry K.'s sleep on the first evening is repeated on the sixth day; when he wakes up he is told that "he had slept for well over twelve hours" (375). Sleep is timeless, and this timelessness tears the temporal coherence of the narrated events asunder.

Remembered time as well as sleep serves as an escape from the reality of the present. Whereas Thomas Mann uses the flashback technique in *The Magic Mountain* to enhance the reader's understanding of his hero by setting him off against the background of his youth, Kafka uses K.'s memories in *The Castle* to blur and confuse the contours of the moment he actually narrates. When K. contemplates the Castle for the first time, the recollection of the village at home intrudes upon his mind and proves to be more palpable, more real, than the sight before him. K.'s present goal, the Castle, recedes, and his past, the village which he has left behind, reemerges victoriously. The background of time engulfs the foreground and threatens to devour it.

Kafka uses the memories of the subordinate figures to a similar end in *The Castle*, i.e., to discourage and confuse K. with regard to his future. Flashbacks such as Gardena's story of her affair with Klamm, which happened "considerably over twenty years ago" (103), or Olga's account of Amalia's misfortune, which dates back "more than three years" (244), seem only to lead us back into the past of the persons relating these memories. In actual fact, however, they point to the hopelessness of K.'s future, for they prove to him the absolute intransigence of the authorities, who will reject him just as they withdrew from his informants. These conversations mirror K.'s future in the past of his interlocutors, demonstrating the standstill of time in this Castle: there is no access to it, there was none, and there will be none. To the first message he receives, "Neither tomorrow nor at any other time" (26), they merely add as a new perspective a "nor yesterday."

From the moment of his arrival K. is denied any chance to develop or to acquire the personal growth which would inform his end with the dimension of tragedy. He has no "inner" time to set against the "outer" time he spends circling around an obviously dead center. The nearer he imagines himself to have come to this center, the more time he loses. He does not get wiser; only the days grow longer. The fourth day extends over eight chapters and 109 pages, approximately twice as many pages as the preceding three days had required. When, on the fifth day, he enters the house of Barnabas, he intends to stay "only for a minute or two" (218); yet the minute extends immeasurably. After he has heard Amalia's story, he spends most of the night in Olga's company and finds himself in the end at exactly the same place as before: he has not come any nearer to the secret of the Castle.

Appropriately enough the season is winter. "How much longer is it till spring?" he finally asks Pepi, Frieda's successor in the Herrenhof. "Till spring?" Pepi repeats, as if he were talking about something unknown.

Winter has been with us long, a very long winter, and monotonous. . . . Well, yes, some time spring comes too, and summer, and there is a time for this too, I suppose; but in memory, now, spring and summer seem as short as though they did not last much longer than two days, and even on these days, even during the most beautiful day, even then sometimes snow still falls (407–408).

To be sure, even the village has its spring, but only "some time"— *einmal*—"once upon a time," the words with which fairy tales begin. The spring to come and the summer which is gone are one and the same in Pepi's memory, and even the future past or past future of the "most beautiful day" of the year is astir with flurries of the snow which still envelops and always will envelop the outside of the Castle.

For the barmaid the time of the Castle is filled with the monotony which prevails on glaciers and in arctic nights; for the Land-Surveyor it is filled with the reflections and refractions of mirrors and echoes. Time seems like a labyrinth. In ever more deceiving spirals it spins around a center where either no time at all or eternity prevails.

The Information Givers (Part Three)

There is only one moment in the narrative when K. comes near to penetrating the wall of secrecy that surrounds the Castle. At this moment the fruitless attempts he has made to communicate with the interior of the offices are suddenly met by the Castle's unexpected attention.

Erlanger, one of Klamm's chief secretaries, wishes to see him before five o'clock in the morning of his sixth day in the village. The place of the meeting is to be the Herrenhof. "Tell him that it is very important that I should speak to him," he commissions Barnabas, the messenger (308–309). When Erlanger (whose name means "the one who achieves")[26] finally talks to K., he requests him to send Frieda back to the taproom. This, he makes clear, is not Klamm's wish but a precaution taken by his colleagues to secure the undisturbed progress of their superior's work. However carefully his opponent may hide behind the back of his subordinates, K.'s plan to use Frieda as a kind of hostage seems to have worked at last. The only trouble is that K. is no longer in a position to comply with Erlanger's request: he has found Frieda too indispensable to part from her, he has fallen in love; and more important still, Frieda has left him and returned to the Herrenhof of her own accord, in the dubious company of Jeremias, the assistant. Therefore Erlanger's rather vague offer, "If you show yourself reliable in this trivial affair, it may on some occasion be of use to you in improving your prospects" (354), sounds at best like an ironic echo of

K.'s original intention to secure a hold on Klamm by seducing Frieda. It is no more helpful than were Klamm's previous letters.

K.'s moment of truth does not, however, come in the meeting with Erlanger. Before he passes (and almost misses) Erlanger's door, he has been engaged in a completely unexpected nightlong conversation with another official who introduces himself as Bürgel. This Bürgel is, promisingly enough, a "liaison secretary" (335); yet he is not assigned to Klamm but to a secretary, unknown to K., by the name of Friedrich. Of this Friedrich we learn very little;* we can only note that his name, like Frieda's, alludes to a highly ironical *Frieden* ("peace"). As far as Bürgel's own name is concerned, it is, first and foremost, the diminutive of *Burg*, a synonym of Castle;† this seems to promise that he belongs to the inner circle of the Castle administration and that his liaison with the interior offices is close and effective. At the same time it points to the smallness and unimportance of his person when it is compared with the immensity of the *Burg*, the Castle which he represents. Moreover, his name is also, as Heller has noted, "a diminutive of *Bürge*, guarantor"; [27] and it is this second meaning to which he seems to refer when he talks about the chance which applicants like K. actually have to force their way into the presence of a secretary. Generally speaking, these chances are nil, "but some nights—for who can guarantee (*bürgen*) for everything?—it *does* happen" (347). While he faces Bürgel, the little guarantor who cannot guarantee anything, K. is confronted with this opportunity.

At first K. gives his name, an introduction which, counter to his expectations, seems "to have a good effect" (333). He is even more astonished when the secretary asks him about his surveying although he has not mentioned his profession. All augurs well. When K. complains that he is not employed as a Land-Surveyor, the official jots down a note immediately. "I am prepared," he assures the applicant, "to follow up this matter further. With us here the things are quite certainly not in such a way that an expert employee should be left unused." Yet he is not only willing to further K.'s cause by using his close relations with the Castle—"at every moment I must be prepared to drive up" (336)—he personally offers help to K. by subjecting him immediately to a night interrogation.

* One of the deleted fragments mentions that "Bürgel is not even Friedrich's first secretary" and that "Friedrich's glory has greatly declined in recent years" (422).

† Already the thirteenth-century mystic Meister Eckhart translated the Latin *castellum* (castle) by *bürgelin* (small *Burg*). (*Meister Eckharts Predigten* [ed. Josef Quint] [Stuttgart: Kohlhammer, 1938], 24.)

Such an interrogation is admittedly "a very rare possibility or, rather, one that almost never occurs. It consists in the applicant's coming unannounced in the middle of the night" (343). This condition is fulfilled in the case of K. While looking for Erlanger, he has opened a door in the hope of finding an empty sleeping place. There Bürgel greets him with a faint scream (332). He has indeed appeared uninvited.

The secretaries, Bürgel continues to explain, are, of course, overtired and try to dispose of the applicants one way or the other. Some seem to be so fatigued that they actually fear the interruption of their rest by an untoward applicant. "In any case," Bürgel continues, "it is morbid to be so afraid of him [the applicant] that one hides, say under the quilt" (347). This position, which is, incidentally, also a favorite of the lawyer Huld in *The Trial*, has been relinquished by Bürgel, if only after some hesitation, when K. enters his room: he "pulled the quilt a little off his face, anxiously ready, however, to cover himself up completely if something was not quite all right out there. But then he flung back the quilt without qualms and sat up" (333).

Bürgel goes on enlightening K. The more he describes the resistance offered to the applicants by the other secretaries, the more he seems to emphasize the uniqueness of this one night interrogation which finds him, Bürgel, willing to assist K. To ward off the applicants, Bürgel relates, the officials are accustomed to refer to the system of competences as it is observed by the Castle. (Here Kafka alludes to the efficient defense mechanism Old Austria's bureaucrats devised to protect *their* sleep.) Many an applicant, Bürgel says, "has lost the game because, thinking he was not making enough progress with the competent authority, he tried to slip through by approaching some other, one not competent" (344). Such a train of thought is of course familiar to K.; yet all the circumstances seem to conspire in his favor. He has chanced upon this meeting with Bürgel while he was summoned by a competent authority, Erlanger. However, Bürgel and his chief, Friedrich, may not be so incompetent in the case of the Land-Surveyor as the appearances indicate. For the secret of this Castle administration "lies in the relations regarding competence. The fact is, things are not so constituted . . . that there is only one definite secretary competent to deal with each case." With an expression of deep emotional involvement Bürgel exclaims, "Land-Surveyor, consider the possibility that through some circumstance or other . . . an applicant does, nevertheless, in the middle of the night surprise a secretary who has a certain degree of competence" (346).

At this point Bürgel seems to possess a certain competence.

This coincidence opens completely new vistas before K.; the barriers break down and the tables are turned. Now the official speaks of the distribution of duties in his administration, which is such that suddenly everybody seems to be competent for everybody else. His colleagues, normally so intent on repose, burn with impatience to occupy themselves with any case for which they are in the slightest degree responsible; they are filled with a passionate desire to help. However much they may differ in character and rank, this passion is "always the same, always present in full intensity" (346). Apparently Bürgel himself has been enraptured by this heavenly feeling of ardent charity, and his passion is aimed at none other than K., who, as he sits on the edge of the bed, is "the never beheld, always expected applicant, truly thirstingly expected and always reasonably regarded out of reach."

An official, then, has been waiting for K. just as desperately as K. has been waiting for Klamm. Bürgel's eyes are now resting on him with the same feverish longing with which K. has contemplated the Castle for six long days. A mysterious union between official and applicant is under way, an embrace both actual and metaphysical in nature. Bürgel's pronouncement has acquired a hymnlike quality, which reveals a distinctly erotic coloration. The applicant's presence in his room invites him, as he says, "to penetrate into his poor life. . . . This invitation in the silent night is beguiling." Although Bürgel retains enough official decorum at the climax of this night scene to classify its mystery strictly as "a misuse of official power," he is also carried away by passion to such an extent that he is able to cry: "Nevertheless, we are happy. How suicidal happiness can be" (348–349)! This is the language of love. Possessed by love, the official chooses an imagery consistent with his glowing feelings when he describes the hour of this night interrogation as "the official's hour of labor," which in German is "the difficult hour" (*die schwere Stunde*), the hour when a new being is born. With grandiose labor pains a union between previously fighting forces has been established. The abyss between official and applicant has been bridged, and the gate to the interior of the Castle opens. The impossible has become possible after all. Nobody will be able to deny that this scene possesses a pathos of truly cosmic dimensions.

Nobody except K., that is. For "K. was asleep, impervious to all that was happening" (350). In reply to the salvation Bürgel promises him, K. succumbs to sleep. He exchanges the heightened awareness, the ecstasy which is offered to him, for complete unconsciousness.

While we imagine K. lying there on Bürgel's bed, a motionless heap of extinguished humanity, we encounter some difficulties in following Emrich's evaluation of this scene as "tragic." Emrich's question "whether this tragedy will also lead K. to take a turn to catharsis, to the liberation and purification by a higher consciousness," seems to be irrelevant in view of K.'s complete loss of any consciousness. He is, as the German original says, "locked up against everything" (*abge-schlossen gegen alles*).* This sleeper does not correspond to the description of a "perishing hero" which Emrich gives of him, and the speculation "whether the tragic antinomies in his mind can be over-come" [28] appears strangely farfetched and out of place. These notions apply more readily to one of the heroes of German idealism, Heinrich von Kleist's romantic Prince of Homburg, for example. Kafka's imagi-nation, however, was nourished from different sources.

In Bürgel we can see the last of Kafka's Information Givers. Once more the writer attempted to answer the questions his heroes have been asking throughout his books. In the Fourth Octavo Notebook he spells out the kind of information he and his protagonists were seek-ing. The following imaginary dialogue takes place:

The decisively characteristic thing about this world is its transience. In this sense centuries have no advantage over the present moment. Thus the continuity of transience cannot give any consolation; the fact that new life blossoms among the ruins proves not so much the tenacity of life as that of death. If I wish to fight against this world, I must fight against its de-cisively characteristic element, that is, its transience. Can I do that in this life, and do it really, not only by means of hope and faith?

So you want to fight against the world, fight it with weapons that are more real than hope and faith. There probably are such weapons, but they can be recognized and used only under certain basic assumptions; I want to see first whether these assumptions apply to you.

Look into it. But if I have not got these qualifications, perhaps I can acquire them.

Certainly, but this is a matter in which I could not help you.

So you can only help me if I have already acquired these qualifications.

---

* Emrich supports his thesis with the observation that K. himself is supposed to have given a "painstakingly detailed account" (426) of the night interrogation. Thus, Emrich concludes, K. "does know about the reasons of his failure, about the unique occasion he had missed" (*Franz Kafka* [Bonn: Athenäum, 1958], 389). This piece of indirect evidence is adduced from the fragments, a body of shorter or longer pieces, more or less loosely connected with the main story and, as often as not, contradicting its trend. One may find it attractive to draw on the fragments if one wishes to add color to one's argument; to buttress it with them does not seem altogether advisable.

Yes. To put it more precisely, I cannot help you at all, for if you had these qualifications, you would have everything already.

If this is how things stand, why then did you want to examine me in the first place?

Not in order to show you what you lack, but that you lack something. I might perhaps have been of a certain use to you in this way, for although you know there is something you lack, you do not believe it.

So, in answer to my original question, all you offer me is the proof that I had to ask the question.

I do offer something more, something that you, in accordance with your present state, are now completely incapable of recognizing precisely. I am offering the proof of the fact that you really ought to have asked the original question differently.

So this means: you either will not or cannot answer me.

"Not answer you"—this is it.

And this faith—this is what you can give (*DF*, 95–96).

This minimal insight—the residue of a possible answer—only this kind of information is offered K. And then, it is proffered merely as a chance.

Bürgel, the "little guarantor" is the most sophisticated in the long line of Kafka's doorkeepers. The underporters in the Hotel Occidental, the Information Giver in the Court House, Titorelli, Huld, and even the Prison Chaplain have only been pointing the tortuous way which led to him. Bürgel, too, guards a door, the gate to the interior of the Castle; he, too, deceives K. while informing him; he tempts him with the last, faint opportunity to ask "the original question differently"; he does so by holding a mirror out to K., indeed, by being this mirror himself.

Word by word, image after image, Bürgel shows K. the situation in which he finds himself. Because he mirrors K., he is acquainted with his profession without being told about it. Because he echoes him, he is able to read his innermost thoughts and answer questions which K. never uttered. Thus when K. reminds himself silently not to underestimate the official before him, Bürgel breaks into his reflections with a sudden "no," spoken, as the narrator adds, "as if he were answering a thought of K.'s and were considerately trying to save him the effort of formulating it aloud" (337). The night interrogation and the chance it offers to the applicant appear as K.'s wish dream reflected back to him by the official. This mirage materializes in Bürgel to such an extent that the Information Giver is able to continue his recitation even when K. has withdrawn into sleep. That the dream outlasts the dreamer and the mirrored image is more powerful than the object it mirrors is perhaps the subtlest paradox that the labyrinth of the Castle holds for the reader. Apart from being K.'s mirror, Bürgel is and remains an official; indeed, he is the most hindering helper in the twilight zone of Kafka's intermediaries.

The scene of this night interrogation is set on the threshold of K.'s consciousness. Its time spans the moments between waking and sleep in which unconscious states give way to flashes of insight, reason is submerged and rises to the surface once more, and oblivion alternates with clairvoyance. The six days in the village have readied K. for it: he enters Bürgel's room in a condition of extreme fatigue. In the corridor he had almost sunk down with drowsiness; to make things worse he has emptied to the dregs a little carafe of rum, Frieda's farewell gift (332). In the room he finds, as a mirror of his own tiredness, Bürgel asleep in his bed. Greedily K. surveys this "voluptuous but unfortunately not empty bed" (333), which is mentioned over and over again during the introductory stages of the interrogation: K. longs to lie down on it; Bürgel invites him to sit on its edge; he accepts and cannot prevent his head from leaning against its post. Words like "cover," "tired," and "sleep" occur with increasing frequency. One has only to listen to Bürgel's seemingly innocent comments on his room to see how he manages to trick K. into falling asleep:

Well, I had the choice of getting either a completely furnished room with a narrow hotel bed, or this big bed and nothing else. . . . I chose the big bed; after all, in a bedroom the bed is undoubtedly the main thing! Ah, for anyone who could stretch out and sleep soundly, for a sound sleeper, this bed would surely be truly delicious (334).

This lullaby of lurid suggestiveness is intended to draw the drowsy K. deeper and deeper down the unending coils of half-sleep. Once more K. starts up and in a sudden fit of clearsightedness observes Bürgel smiling "as though he had just succeeded in misleading K. a little" (340).

How far Bürgel succeeds in misleading him we see when K. slips into his own dream vision, a mirage mirrored and duly distorted by the all-encompassing magic of this interrogation. "The tiresome consciousness had gone, he felt free." It is certainly true, his consciousness had receded, but only insofar as it was tiresome; K.'s consciousness of himself, his self-confidence, is rising to unexpected heights. The freedom he feels is but another name for a sudden superiority which he dreams he has gained over his opponent. After all, one of his basic traits is arrogance, the *Anmassung* and *Vermessenheit* of the *Land-vermesser*. Once he had prided himself on having conquered death in the churchyard of his home village; now he braves his dream opponent in a similar way:

And it seemed to him as though . . . he had achieved a great victory . . . and he or someone else raised the champagne glass in honor of this victory. And so that all should know what it was all about, the fight and the victory were repeated once again or perhaps not repeated at all, but only took place now and had already been celebrated earlier and there was no letdown in the celebration, because fortunately the outcome was certain.

K. experiences here the fulfillment of his wishes: his opponent has at long last taken a stand and is prepared to give battle; the mere fact that this battle has come about means victory. Dizzy with dreaming, he does not notice that the time sequences of his vision have been reversed, that the celebration comes before the victory, and the victory precedes the fight. He is beyond space and time, occupied only with the task of asserting himself victoriously. Yet with his time sense his other perspectives have also been reversed: left is right, up is down, truth is lie, and victory, defeat. The phrase "fortunately the outcome was certain" is true if we attribute the conquest to Bürgel, but it is an utter delusion if the victory is claimed by K.

His opponent in the dream is "a secretary, naked, very like the statue of a Greek god." While we can explain the dream image by the sight of "Bürgel's bare chest" in front of K.'s closing eyes (342–343), we are surprised that a Greek god should emerge in the thoroughly un-Hellenic imagination of the Land-Surveyor. We suspect that Kafka is taking over from his dreaming hero and creating this spectre as a sign of the absolute incongruity of the scene. He once wrote about the Prometheus legend that it "tries to explain the inexplicable. As it came out of a substratum of truth it had in turn to end in the inexplicable" (*GW*, 251–252). The substratum of truth in K.'s case, as in that of Prometheus, is the forlornness of man as a result of his presumption.

There is hardly any trace of grandeur in Kafka's treatment of ancient motifs;* instead he stressed the nightmarish quality of a thoroughly modern despair by blending it in a mock-heroic fashion with the inevitability of Greek myth. In a letter written to Brod in April 1921

---

* Cf. also "Poseidon" (*DS*, 195–197) or "The Silence of the Sirens" (*GW*, 248–250).

about certain lives which show a "historical development" and others
which do not, Kafka said:

Sometimes I play with the idea of an anonymous Greek who arrives in
Troy without ever having had the intention of getting there. He has not
yet looked around and is already in the midst of the melee; the gods
themselves do not yet know at all what is at stake, but he has already
been dragged around the city roped to a Trojan chariot; Homer has not
yet started to sing, but he already lies there with his glassy eyes, if not
in the dust of Troy then on the cushions of his deck chair. And why?
Hecuba, of course, is nothing to him; Helena is not decisive either.
Whereas the other Greeks have set out at the bidding of the gods and,
protected by the gods, have fought their battles, he has left because of
a paternal kick in the pants and has fought under a paternal curse. Fortunately there were other Greeks besides him, or world history would
have remained restricted to the two rooms of one's parental apartment
and the threshold between them (*B*, 313–314).

In many respects this ingenious *quid pro quo* of Troy and Prague is
reminiscent of K.'s drowsy vision of himself: here, too, the sense of time
is suspended by a confusion of time sequences; here, too, the result of
the heroic mingling with the trivial is an absurd tragicomedy that
seems to be mocking itself. The "anonymous Greek" is as untragic, as
unheroic, and as locked up in himself as K. Neither figure is allowed
any human development, and the mood of grotesque abandonment
prevailing in both visions is enhanced by the rational and matter-of-fact
tone with which they are reported.

K.'s dream secretary offers him no serious obstacle. "This Greek
god squeaked like a girl being tickled" (343). The statue has come to
life; the half-naked secretary has almost turned into a young female.
K. may remember a saying which is quoted around the Castle and
which Olga had told him the night before: "Official decisions are as
shy as young girls." "This is a good observation," K. had answered;
"the decisions may have other characteristics in common with young
girls" (227). Now as an official decision is near, the official himself
resembles a girl. The girl even opens her mouth, but only to issue a
birdlike and soulless tone. The mechanical sound is the perfect parody
of the mystical humming in the telephone with which the Castle had
once greeted K. His vision remains sharp and pitiless, although his eyes
are closing. Like Joseph K. on the way to his execution, he tries
to keep his "intelligence calm and analytical to the end." He finds this
scene "very funny" (342).

His "fun" consists in projecting all he has learned about the Castle onto this squeaking god, in approaching him with whatever critical acuteness he still possesses, in ridiculing, humiliating, and denigrating him. Bürgel, on his part, keeps talking. There is a distinct counter-movement under way: the more the official is enraptured by his hymnlike peace offer, the more K. opposes it, in the few lucid intervals still permitted to him, with maliciously rational observations. "Clatter, mill, keep clattering," he thinks, "you clatter just for me" (345). Thereby he finally and irrevocably succumbs to the treachery of the labyrinth.

Even in tradition the labyrinth could not be conquered by rational tricks. The more a person tried to find his way through the maze by means of the intellect, the more he was bound to lose himself.[29] The universal nature of the labyrinth reveals itself in the challenge it offers to the *total* existence of man. It is a sign of K.'s arrogance that he mobilizes the forces of his intelligence in the hour of a mystical revelation. Yet so viciously are the circles of this labyrinth constructed that the mystical revelation of its interior is bound to occur in the hour when K. succumbs to his fatigue. Bürgel's droning recitation finally drowns out the last flicker of K.'s reason.

In his dream K. wins out and puts the secretary-turned-god to flight. "And finally he was gone, K. was alone in a large room." Inasmuch as the dream secretary represents Bürgel, the defeat of the former means also the elimination of the chances proferred by the latter. There remain only the splinters of the champagne glass, lying broken on the floor. "K. trampled it to smithereens" (343). The dream is over, the mirror smashed. K. is lost in sleep and Bürgel, his chest still bare, opens his mouth. But instead of a squeak, he utters the promise of K.'s admission into the Castle, a promise which is broken before it is fully made. As K.'s dream contained a declaration of victory before the fight has started, so Bürgel's message of peace is defeated even before it is delivered. The multiple mirrors of the labyrinth have distorted conquest and decline until they form one pernicious glitter, the cutting glitter of the splinters in K.'s dream.

Bürgel talks now about the competence of incompetence, the open gates of the inaccessible, the passion of premeditated deceit. Triumphantly bent over the applicant, the official proves to him that not victory was expected from him but reconciliation. The doors he had tried to force stood open. His inability to be redeemed is confirmed by the announcement that redemption is at hand. There is a shade of poetic justice in the reflection that Bürgel's efforts are also in vain since he preaches to ears deafened by sleep.

Bürgel's "hour of labor" has miscarried. Never will K. be able to "put forward his plea, for which fulfilment is already waiting" (350). He is, in the official's language, an "oddly and quite specially constituted, small, skilful grain" that had almost succeeded in slipping "through the incomparable sieve." More to himself than to the man slumbering before him Bürgel remarks, "You think it cannot happen at all. You are right, it cannot happen at all" (347).

This night interrogation climaxes not only Kafka's *The Castle* but a long series of attempts which European man has undertaken to overcome and exorcize the demonic forces of the universe which throng around him in complete obscurity. The irony of frustration which informs this scene makes it a prime example of grotesque art, its depth and its limitations.[30] As the outcome of Kafka's novel demonstrates, these attempts to penetrate the mystery of the world are bound to end in ultimate failure. Hence Kafka derives the tone of knowing despair which ennobles all truly grotesque representations of human destiny.

Journey's End?

Brod reports that Kafka once told him the end he had had in mind for *The Castle:*

The ostensible Land-Surveyor was to find partial satisfaction at least. He was not to relax in his struggle, but was to die worn out by it. Round his death-bed the villagers were to assemble, and from the Castle itself the word was to come that though K.'s legal claim to live in the village was not valid, yet, taking certain auxiliary circumstances into account, he was to be permitted to live and work there (vi).

Commenting on this plan, Emrich has correctly observed that it offers no more than a repetition of the situation already reached during the night interrogation.[31]

If Kafka had been satisfied with describing K.'s pilgrimage through a modern labyrinth, he could have stopped here, at the end of the eighteenth of twenty chapters. The following scenes do not provide us with any new hints about unexpected turns ahead on K.'s way. The conversation with Erlanger mentioned before, the distribution of the official files in the corridor of the Herrenhof, Pepi's suggestion that K. may follow her to the basement and hibernate in her company, and finally K.'s musings about the landlady's dresses—all this remains, in the end, inconclusive.

To be sure, K. witnesses the destruction of a file which "actually was only . . . a leaf from a note pad," and the suspicion arises in his mind that this file may be his own and that his application may have been dismissed once and for all (362). On the other hand, the landlady restores his courage in an oblique way by claiming that an uproar which suddenly shakes the Inn is coming from some officials who are shouting for help against K., "whom nothing else would cause to waver" (370). The gentlemen from the Castle seem to have started trembling before the Land-Surveyor. But these are only more new doors leading the hero toward new dead ends disguised by new mirrors. Their effectiveness fades before the impact which was already achieved by the night interrogation. Not only K.'s but Kafka's energies seem to be exhausted on these last pages; eventually the labyrinth succeeded in trapping its own creator.

But the Castle is built of more than mirror effects. Its inner chamber not only shelters nothingness but, combined with it in absolute ambiguity, the promise of total existence. Conversely, K. is not only, like the "anonymous Greek," congenitally deprived of any "historical development," he is also exposed to occasions which might have led his story to quite different conclusions. To trace these possibilities hidden in K.'s nature, we have to change our direction and read the book backward. Moving in a circle, we will still follow the basic design of the novel, the periphery of a labyrinth.

The Messengers: Barnabas and Amalia

On the evening of the fourth day K. sends Barnabas to the Castle in order to request a personal interview with Klamm. Whatever he does or says during the next day is colored by his expectation of the messenger's return. High hopes and grave doubts alternate in his mind. Barnabas, by delivering favorable messages, has lived up to his name, which, according to the Acts of the Apostles (4:36), means "son of consolation." [32] On the other hand, these messages, K.'s "decree of appointment," and his laudatory citation as a Land-Surveyor, have also turned out to be malicious specimens of Klamm's peculiar sense of humor in spite of the comfort they offered. There are other reasons for distrusting Barnabas. He had introduced himself with words of

evangelical simplicity: "Barnabas is my name. . . . A messenger am
I," and K. could not help noticing the noble quality of his clothes:
"He was dressed all in white; not in silk, of course, . . . but the
material he was wearing had the softness and dignity of silk" (29).
Yet as soon as he follows Barnabas to his hut, he is disillusioned. He
recognizes that "he had been bewitched by Barnabas's close-fitting,
silken-gleaming jacket, which, now that it was unbuttoned, . . . displayed a coarse, dirty gray shirt patched all over, and beneath it the
huge muscular chest of a farm-laborer" (40). Furthermore, this messenger who looks like a peasant turns out to be a journeyman in the
service of Brunswick, the cobbler, and it seems as if he would let this
menial work interfere with the errands he undertakes at the behest of
K. Barnabas is a cobbler's son and resembles a cobbler much more
than a messenger (in Austrian usage the word *Schuster* ["cobbler"]
has the connotation of "misfit"); nor does the garment which has
drawn K.'s attention by any means represent the livery of an official
Castle servant; it was sewn for him by his sister, Amalia (226). Only
a certain duplicity of behavior identifies him as an envoy of Klamm,
whose ambiguity seems to have influenced the servant: Barnabas
hurries about when carrying out the orders of the Castle but drags
his feet when he is supposed to deliver K.'s answer. The Land-Surveyor
cannot be blamed for bursting out, "It is very bad for me to have only
a messenger like you for important affairs" (157).

It turns out, however, that this ambiguity is inherent only in Barnabas' function as an emissary from the Castle and does not extend to
him as a person. When Olga, his second sister, initiates K. into the
story of her family, the Land-Surveyor discovers that the messenger's
personal intentions toward him are thoroughly honorable. "He did not
sleep all night because you were displeased with him yesterday evening," Olga informs K. (229). It is not his fault when the part he
plays as Klamm's errand boy arouses K.'s suspicions. The Castle bears
the blame, for it makes use of his services without having acknowledged him as its servant. Thus Barnabas finds himself in essentially
the same predicament as K. And yet what seems to be an ordeal to
the Land-Surveyor is at the same time the fulfillment of the most
tender hopes of the messenger and his family. K.'s arrival appears to
them as the turning point after three years of misery. Klamm's letters,
questionable as they are, have meant to them "the first signs of grace"
(296). Barnabas himself is more than willing to serve on sufferance
without any right. He is happy like a little boy, "in spite of all the

doubts that he had about his capability." "He confined these doubts to himself and me," Olga reveals, "but he felt it a point of honor to look like a real messenger." Nor should K. deny him his sympathy, since it is also his point of honor to be a "real" Land-Surveyor.

In spite of his doubtful appearance Barnabas is really a messenger of hope. The hope he offers is a human hope. When K. hears about Barnabas' true feelings, he has an opportunity to realize that his mere presence is able to raise the spirits of others and to comfort them by supporting their expectations. To see this, he has only to desist from mirroring himself in them and to accept them for what they are, just as he demands to be accepted himself. After Barnabas was entrusted with his first letter, Olga informs K. he "laid his head on my shoulder, and cried for several minutes. He was again the little boy he used to be." K.'s response to her tale, though it was fraught with emotion, is cold: "All of you have made pretences" (295). He dismisses as mere fabrication the messenger's outbreak of joy and does not want to have any part of it.

Although K. is groping desperately for help, he refuses to give it to others. When Olga greets him almost jubilantly, "How fortunate that you have come!" he simply turns away, annoyed at such a display of enthusiasm: "He had not come to bring good fortune to anyone. . . . Nobody should greet him as a bearer of good tidings; whoever did this, was liable to confuse his ways, claiming him for causes for which he was at nobody's disposal under such coercion; with the best of intentions he had to refuse." * He is afraid of confusing his ways by being a messenger of good tidings himself. Yet the path before him is already so tortuous that he need not fear to confuse it still further by a simple human response. On the contrary, any kindliness he showed to others might help him along his way. This is one of the passages in *The Castle* where K. actually could have changed his course. But it is no accident that Kafka deleted these sentences in his manuscript; they would have pointed too clearly in a direction neither he nor his hero was prepared to take in their self-inflicted isolation.

Olga is as favorably inclined toward K. as her brother is. It was she who accompanied him on his first walk to the Herrenhof (42 f.). When she exposes the secret of her family to him in a long night's story, she wants to help him as much as to be helped by him. Her very name may be derived from the German equivalent of "holy." [33] There are

---

* From a deleted passage, published by Brod at the end of his postscript to the German edition of *Das Schloss,* p. 497.

striking similarities between their fates. Like him she hopes to establish "a certain connection with the Castle" (286) by making love with its subordinates. Before K. tumbled down to embrace Frieda on the taproom floor, he observed Olga in a mating dance with a number of villagers, and when he emerged, he saw her again, her clothes torn and her hair deranged (50, 55). At that time her debauchery had not particularly surprised him. He took it as a sign of simple sexual jealousy, a revenge for his having preferred Frieda to her. But now he learns that Olga's villagers were in actual fact servants of the Castle: "For more than two years, at least twice a week, I have spent the night with them in the stable" (285). Olga's promiscuity differs from K.'s love-making in one decisive aspect: she does not surrender to the Castle in this indirect and unpromising way to further her own ends. She sacrifices herself to atone for Amalia.

Amalia's story is a novella in its own right, connected to the rest of the narrative by the remarks which K. makes about it. Since he mirrors himself in Amalia, he cannot perceive the true stature of this woman who towers over the village in silent grandeur. One feels that she is present throughout Olga's tale, although she exits from the scene before Olga begins. "She went without taking leave of K., as if she knew he would stay for a long time yet" (223). Unnoticed she slips away and reappears, loses herself again in the darkness of the hut, and yet she seems to dominate it with her personality even when she sleeps. Almost superhuman powers are noticeable in her who dared defy the Castle.

This, then, is Amalia's story: Three years ago, on the third of July, the village celebrated the dedication of an engine which the Castle had presented to the local Fire Brigade. The gift was accompanied by a number of trumpets, "extraordinary instruments on which with the smallest effort . . . one could produce the wildest blasts; to hear them was enough to make one think the Turks had come already" (247). These trumpets produce angelic and satanic sounds, as do the brass instruments used in the Oklahoma theatre in *Der Verschollene;* they indicate that a moment of great importance is at hand and prepare the reader for a meeting between the human and the more-than-human.

At this point, a point remote and vague in Olga's memory, the Castle and the village are united for the first and only time in the novel. Accordingly the season is summer, and on the scene the customary snow and fog are replaced by a green meadow and a murmuring brook. The whole gathering is devoted to a wholesome human purpose, the control of the demonic force of fire. On the other hand, the wild blasts of the trumpets evoke the image of polygamous Turks and these, in turn, the hordes of philandering Castle servants, who, one can surmise, are converging also on this lawn. Nor can one overlook the suggestively ambiguous central image, the fire engine, which is really a big water squirter (*Feuerspritze*).

Even a Castle representative is present, Sortini, who "is supposed to be partly occupied with fire problems." But the joyful occasion has not succeeded in breaking down the barriers traditionally existing between officials and villagers. Keeping close to the Castle's gift, the phallic fire engine, Sortini refuses to mingle with the crowd. Only when Barnabas' father, the third in command of the Fire Brigade, offers apologies to him (for what?), does Sortini react. He lets his eyes rest on Amalia, "to whom he had to look up, for she was much taller than he. At the sight of her he started and leaped over the shaft to get nearer to her; we misunderstood him at first and began to approach him . . . but he held us off with uplifted hand and then waved us away. That was all." It is not all, alas. For the one glance he exchanged with the girl seems to have impressed Amalia unduly. Her stunned silence ever after almost seems to justify a remark made by Brunswick, the cobbler, that "she had fallen head over ears in love" (248). The following morning she receives a letter, couched in most vulgar terms, ordering her to visit Sortini at once at the Herrenhof. The girl tears the letter to pieces and throws the shreds in the face of the messenger who has waited outside the window. This constitutes Amalia's sin (249).

The Castle, in its majestic impassivity, refrains from punishing Amalia in any overt way. But the villagers begin to withdraw from the girl as well as from her relatives. As if the daughter's guilt were by association also the father's, he loses first his honorary post with the Fire Brigade, then his customers. The family becomes anonymous; it is now named after Barnabas, the "least guilty" (273). Amid a community of primitive serfs, the Barnabas family lives in a ghetto assigned to pariahs by the slaves who are their neighbors. The only indication of the Castle's participation in the general ostracism of this family is the fact that it waited for the appearance of so lowly a creature as K. before it allowed Barnabas to go on his semiofficial errands on his behalf. The view of the pariah serving the outcast would indeed be a prime specimen of the double-edged irony indulged in so brilliantly by Klamm and his colleagues.

Now we understand why Barnabas felt called upon to serve the Castle as a messenger; he wanted to atone for the insult inflicted upon Sortini's errand boy. By the same token Olga attempted to expiate Amalia's refusal of Sortini's embrace by becoming the prostitute of the Castle's subordinates. Her sacrifice fails. There is no indication of the official's reconciliation; but then neither he nor the Castle has ever given any indication of having taken offense. Olga comments bitterly, "We had no sign of favor from the Castle in the past, so how could we notice the reverse now" (268)?

A further complication in the story is that it is impossible to establish with certainty the identity of the woman whom Sortini had summoned to the Herrenhof. The letter is addressed to "the girl with the garnet necklace" (249). This disastrous piece of jewelry had passed hands twice before it landed around Amalia's neck. The Bridge Inn landlady, the owner of the Bohemian garnets, had lent them to Olga, and Olga had decorated her sister with them, she did not know why (245). Sortini's summons, then, is directed at each of the three women who had been seen with the jewels at one time or another during this day: at Gardena, who had been Klamm's mistress but being no longer a "girl" was the least probable choice; at Olga, who certainly would have responded to the official's crude beckoning, since she is willing to surrender to the still cruder calls of the servants; and at Amalia, who actually wears the garnets when she is introduced to Sortini. She is the most unlikely to be singled out by Sortini, and this is the very reason why his letter descends upon her as one of those fatal lightning flashes which, bursting forth from indistinct heights, hit the target least expected to be their aim.

Sortini is as elusive as the Castle he represents. His function at the celebration is dubious; "perhaps he was only deputizing for someone else." He is described as "very retiring," and yet he is capable of savage aggression, as his letter shows. He is "small, frail, reflective looking," but backed up by the huge and loudly colored fire engine, he seems to fill the festive scene with his portentous presence. Although he is smaller than Amalia, even his upward look is condescending. Moreover, "one thing about him struck all the people who noticed him at all, his forehead was furrowed; all the furrows . . . were spread fanwise over his forehead, running to the root of his nose" (244).

Imitating the ground plan of a labyrinth, these furrows attract the onlooker and lead him inevitably down to the level of Sortini's eyes, the eyes that have proved so fateful to Amalia.

A rather hectic discussion has developed as to the meaning of this official ever since Brod compared Sortini's letter to Kierkegaard's vision of Mount Moriah, where God asked Abraham to sacrifice his child. For Brod, Sortini's epistle represents "literally a parallel" to Kierkegaard's *Fear and Trembling,* "which starts from the fact that God required of Abraham what was really a crime . . . ; and which uses this paradox to establish triumphantly the conclusion that the categories of morality and religion are by no means identical." [*] Brod's attempt at coordinating God's claim on Isaac and Sortini's design on Amalia has prompted Heller to observe that it means,

> without any polemical exaggeration, to ascribe to the God of Abraham a personal interest in the boy Isaac, worthy rather of a Greek demi-god. Moreover, He, having tested Abraham's absolute obedience, did not accept the sacrifice. Yet Sortini . . . can, to judge by the example of his colleagues, be relied upon not to have summoned Amalia to his bedroom merely to tell her that one does not do such a thing.[34]

Emrich, on the other hand, sees in Sortini an allegory of the spirit per se: "Where spirit is nothing but spirit any more and appears as an isolated and abstract region, it is the very perversion of the human spirit." [35] In the final analysis Emrich is merely translating Brod's theological position into philosophical terms: what is good for the God of Abraham is also good for the spirit of pure abstraction. Heller's rebuttal is strong and sharp enough to puncture Emrich's thesis as well as Brod's. To visualize this Sortini as an absolute of any sort amounts to positing a paradox too paradoxical even for Kafka's wildest imagination. To answer the question raised by Sortini's letter, Kafka would have had to finish the novel and reveal the meaning of the Castle, the secret of which is shared by its officials. Hence we are not surprised to find the image of Sortini veiled by the same insoluble mystery which distinguished the Count Westwest, his master.

There is, however, an element of surprise in the Amalia episode. It offers us at least the hint of a turn to the better, which Kafka may have had in mind for his hero at one point or another. To grasp this hint we have to turn to the heroine rather than to her would-be seducer, Sortini. Amalia astonishes us indeed, and not only because of the space

[*] Postscript to the German edition of *Das Schloss,* 488.

Kafka has devoted to her story. (The scene in her house covers approximately one-sixth of the book.) He granted his heroine what he denied his heroes: the ability to survive, and even transcend, despair.

Amalia is the only female in Kafka's gallery of women who does not conform with the observation he made in a letter to Brod, early in May 1921: "It is strange how little sharp-sightedness women possess; they only notice whether they please, then whether they arouse pity, and finally, whether one is hankering for their compassion; this is all; come to think of it, it may even be enough, generally speaking" (*B*, 323). Amalia is sharp-sighted, although in a very peculiar way. Like Olga she is a "great strapping wench" (41); and yet she is distinguished from her by her "cold, hard eye," which, K. remembers, frightened him when he saw her for the first time (267). To be sure, this does not indicate much more than K.'s inability to view himself in her as he is wont to do in the eyes of Frieda, Gardena, and even Olga. The narrator, more perceptive than his hero, confirms the hardness of Amalia's glance but also mentions its clarity. It was, he adds, "never leveled exactly on the object she was looking at, but in some disturbing way always a little past it, not from weakness, apparently, nor from embarrassment, nor from duplicity, but from a persistent and dominating desire for solitude." Even K. is both startled and spellbound by this look, "which in itself was not ugly but proud and sincere in its taciturnity." Thus he is moved to tell her, "I have never seen a country girl like you" (219). Here the narrator allows K. to articulate an insight more profound than he can consciously grasp. It seems that Kafka himself is subtly playing with his language here, demonstrating once more the inner unity of his imagery. Amalia is no country girl, no feminine version of the man from the country. She is no *Am-ha'aretz* like Joseph K. and K., the Land-Surveyor. She knows, for she has seen.

We shall have to assume that Amalia learned whatever she knows about the Castle from looking at Sortini. We are told precious little about her history before this meeting. She is the youngest member of the family and may have enjoyed the advantages which a family concedes to its youngest child. This is probably the reason why her mother has lent her every bit of her lace for the blouse she is to wear at the celebration, an injustice which induces Olga, the older one, to cry half the night. Both sisters have been looking forward to the occasion, but Amalia seems to be in a state of special expectation. Her father, with the one-track mind of a man, predicts, "Today, mark my words, Amalia will find a husband." Olga, on the other hand, notices her somber glance; "It has kept the same quality since that day, it was high over our heads and involuntarily one had almost literally to bow before her" (245). About the meeting with Sortini we have likewise only negative evidence: although we are told that the official looks up to her, the fact that she returns his glance is not mentioned. (As can be seen from the silence with which Kafka enveloped K.'s transition from the bridge to the village, he refrains from spelling out decisive moments involving the total existence of his figures.) That Amalia's life has been changed here and now we can only guess from her behavior later on in the day: she is even more silent than usual and remains sober among the crowd which has partaken freely of the sweet Castle wine. She preserves this attitude of extreme composure even after she has read Sortini's letter; her gestures reveal no hint of surprise, disgust, or horror; indeed, it is Olga who notices her tiredness— "how I always loved her when she was tired like this"—the deep exhaustion of one who has in a short moment understood and accepted his fate. Tearing the letter to pieces, Amalia appears to perform a ritual. Yet Olga is not quite correct when she concludes the report of this scene by saying: "This was the morning which decided our fate. I say 'decided,' but every minute of the previous afternoon was just as decisive" (249). The decisive moment was the one when Amalia read in Sortini's eyes a secret, the secret of the Castle.

Whatever this secret may be, it forces her to reject Sortini's summons. To defend her on the ground that she is simply trying to maintain her self-respect [36] is to reduce her to the proportions of a sentimental heroine in a tragedy of middle-class manners. After all, there is no greatness in falling in love with a man of higher social rank, and, being disappointed in the most offensive way, she could be expected to react emotionally to the insult. But Amalia's attitude is informed with heroism. "She stood," says Olga, "face to face with the truth and went on living and endured her life then and now." Her experiences afterward only translate the view that opened itself before her into tangible fact: "We saw only the effects, but she looked down into the bottom" ("Sie sah in den Grund"; *Grund* connoting "ground," "reason," and "cause"—272).

Since it is the Castle's secret she saw there at the bottom of Sortini's eyes, it must remain hidden from K. as well as from the reader. When K. tries to obtain information about Barnabas and the Castle from her, Amalia recoils with unusual violence: "I am not initiated, nothing

could induce me to become initiated, nothing at all, not even my consideration for you" (223). This is the voice of a burnt child who has
been asked to discuss the nature of fire, and it sounds so convincing
that K. ceases plying her with questions. Even he understands that
she keeps "her motives locked in her bosom and no one will ever tear
them away from her" (257–258). Yet she is not prevented from talking
by shame or fright—her sharp-sighted eyes have penetrated to regions
deeper than her words could ever reach. Its very ineffability identifies
Amalia's secret with the mystery of Kafka's Castle.

But whatever horror she saw, it did not destroy her; nor did her
defiance of the dreadful prove fatal to her and her house. She goes on
living in the village and enduring her life outside the jurisdiction of
the Castle. She has scorned authority and has paid her price; K.
observes that she has "the ageless look of women who seem not to
grow any older, but seem never to have been young either" (267).
She stands apart, outside any community, even the most intimate com-
munion of sex; exposed to despair, she faces despair upright and cold,
for her eyes have seen beyond it. In the lone figure of this woman
Kafka accepted what became to be known after him and partly through
him as existential solitude. (Had he been able to divulge the content
of Amalia's vision, he could actually be said to have been an existentialist.)

Yet Kafka remained silent. Amalia alone knows what she has seen,
and she is only one episode along the path of the Land-Surveyor. She
is not even a decisive one by his standards, since he can hardly make
use of her. Yet precisely because she refuses to function as his mirror,
she is set opposite him to serve him as an example. She demonstrates
the possibility of living in this village, neither by right nor by sufferance,
but independent of the Castle. Sick and exhausted, she goes on scorning her fate amidst her family, which, while still trying to curry favor
with the authorities, is lost in its own labyrinths. She has dragged them
down along with herself, and they have become strangers to her. Still,
Olga has to admit that "hers is the decisive voice in the family for
better or worse" (225). Each emergency is met by her whose very name
means "labor"; [37] she needs "hardly any sleep, is never alarmed,
never afraid, never impatient, she did everything for the parents;
while we were fluttering around uneasily without being able to help,
she remained cool and quiet whatever happened" (282). Having
resigned from all her claims to humanity, she has become a holy sister
of despair.

In the image of her sister, Olga inadvertently has shown K. a way to survive the Castle, if not to conquer it. This way would also have led him out of the labyrinth. But he remains blind to the door which opens before him. Having been told Amalia's story, he assures Olga that he prefers her and her ways. "If he had to choose between Olga and Amalia it would not cost him much reflection" (300). With these words he takes his leave of Barnabas' hut and gropes his way back into the darkness. It is, presumably, the darkness of his last night.

The Bitter Herb

Amalia's aversion to "Castle gossip" must have aggravated K.'s dislike of her. And yet at one point she interrupts Olga's story to tell him a Castle story of her own: "I heard once of a young man who thought of nothing but the Castle day and night, he neglected everything else, and people feared for his reason, his mind was so wholly absorbed by the Castle." The satirical inference of this remark is unmistakable; Amalia's ridicule is directed against both K. and her own family; in the dark background of the room sleeps her own mother, who has actually lost her mind by thinking beyond endurance about the Castle. "It turned out at length," Amalia continues, "that it was not really the Castle [the young man] was thinking of, but the daughter of a charwoman in the offices up there, so he got the girl and everything was all right again." By reducing the Castle to a sexual wish dream Amalia parodies K.'s relation to Frieda, Olga's escapades in the Herrenhof stable, as well as all those who try to interpret her own defiance as the result of a disappointed love. Moreover, she jeers at the idea of a happy ending in general. He who is desirous of good luck may find it in the end, but he had better not search for it in infinity. She has made her choice against happiness and hides her despair in impenetrable silence. K., however, still hopes for a reconciliation with the irreconcilable. "I think I should like the man," he comments, full of understanding for any carnal approach to the mystery of the Castle. Amalia retorts, maliciously but not unjustifiably, "It is probably his wife you would like."

"Who is the young man she mentioned?" K. asks Olga as soon as the sister has disappeared. "I do not know," Olga replies, "perhaps Brunswick, though it does not fit him exactly. . . . It is not easy to follow her, for often one cannot tell whether she is speaking ironically or in earnest." But K. wants none of Olga's doubts: "Stop interpreting!"

he interrupts her harshly (265–266). He wishes to believe in Bruns-wick's identity with the young man because it fits with one of his plans and points to an auspicious turn his way may still be inclined to take. For once we shall accept the facts presented by Kafka instead of ex-ploring the doubts he casts upon these facts as soon as he has ac-quainted us with them. In other words, we shall adopt K.'s attitude, but for reasons entirely different from his. Kafka has Olga call her explanation into doubt because he seizes upon any detail which would blur still further the labyrinthine contours of his plot. We, on the other hand, are attempting to reconstruct this outline and therefore seem to be entitled to take our cue from Kafka precisely because he obfus-cates it in order to mislead his hero.

If we take up this trace, we arrive at the following result: supposing that Brunswick is indeed identical with the young man in Amalia's story, we find that the charwoman's daughter is no one else but "the girl from the Castle" (18), whom K. meets in tanner Lasemann's house, the first hut he visits in the village. Hers may have been the voice which recognized him as the Land-Surveyor when he entered; in any case, there is an extraordinary quality in the sight she offers:

From a large opening . . . a pale snowy light came in, apparently from the courtyard, and gave a gleam as of silk to the dress of a woman who was almost reclining in a high armchair. She was suckling an infant at her breast. Several children were playing around her, peasant children, as was obvious, but she did not seem to belong among them, though of course illness and weariness give even peasants a look of refinement (16).

Not even a charwoman's daughter can completely strip off the air of gentility once she had been "up there." Her dress resembles Barnabas' livery in that it gives the impression of being silken without having been made of such a noble material. Her kerchief turns out to be silken; its transparency is strangely out of place in a tanner's hut, which, we learn later (188), she is only visiting. On the other hand, the infant asleep on her bosom is a villager's child like the rest of them. An air of sublimity as well as ambiguity emanates from this woman who resembles both the Virgin Mary [38] and a fallen peasant girl. She lies there sick, next to the men stamping around in a steam bath, and does not even look at her child, but sends uncertain glances up, that is, in the direction of the Castle (17). This, then, is the happy ending of Amalia's story about the charwoman's daughter. And Brunswick, the romantic suitor, is described by Olga as "always rather vulgar" (248) and by the Superintendent as "stupid and fanciful" (87). It is as if he had become a spokesman of the village's opposition because he wanted to take his revenge on the power that had turned his wife into a perennial "girl from the Castle."

One offspring of this couple is little Hans, who enters K.'s room with the question, "Can I help you" (185)? The scene is one of the two classrooms in the school. The time is the morning of the fifth day, approximately ten hours before K.'s visit to Barnabas' hut. The boy's unexpected question is superficially concerned with a wound inflicted on K.'s hand by the woman teacher with the help of her cat. At the moment of this incident Hans, a boy of about twelve, had left his desk, touched the bleeding hand of the porter, and uttered a word which K. could not understand because of the noise that had arisen among the children (171–172). After the teacher, the school mistress, and the pupils had left the scene in protest, K. got entangled in the argument with Frieda mentioned above, in which he was incautious enough to admit that he had been lost before meeting her. After a while there is a knock at the door. "Barnabas!" cries K., who upon opening the door is disappointed to be faced by the boy instead of the messenger (185).

K. changes his attitude, however, as soon as Hans gives his name and reminds him of his mother. Gradually he is won over by the boy's appearance and behavior: "There was something imperious in his character, but it was so mingled with childish innocence that one submitted to it gladly, half smilingly, half in earnest." Even Frieda, in spite of her acute distress, surrenders to the charm and authority of the boy, and soon it looks "as if Hans were the teacher, and as if he were examining and passing judgment on the answers, . . . as if he felt quite in general that he alone had the right to ask questions and that by the questions of others some regulation was broken" (186–187). By now K. has been in the village long enough to recognize the child's nobility and to connect it with the Castle. Hans's innocence provokes a barrage of questions from K.; the boy's precocity, on the other hand, shows itself in the way he parries the interrogation with the skill of the initiated. Thus "the question whether he had been in the Castle yet he only answered after it had been repeated several times, and with a 'No.' The same question regarding his mother he did not answer at all" (188). It soon appears that it was his mother who passed on to the youth the superior air of imperviousness shared by all who are related to the region "up there." But Hans's serenity changes to sadness and bitterness when the conversation turns to his

father, the cobbler, and K. gradually gains the impression that Brunswick, on whose support he had counted "even if only on political
grounds," was, though perhaps not his personal enemy, nevertheless "a
bad and dangerous man" (195) and that the boy "was now seeking K.'s
aid against his father" (193).

Obviously Hans has learned to loathe the depressing village and
shares a longing for the heights of Castle Hill with both his mother
and K. A natural alliance is ready to be concluded; a conspiracy and
union for mutual aid presents itself. He would be very happy to help
him, the child assures the grownup, "and if he was not in a position
to help him himself, he would ask his mother to do so, and then it
would be sure to be all right" (189). Hans has an uncanny gift which
enables him to read K.'s mind; he takes the initiative and shoulders
the responsibility for this new move. K. would not be K. if he were to
miss this opportunity. A meeting with Hans's mother could lead to a
new way to the Castle, and he is more than eager to see her and to
talk to her. Hans, however, is a "cautious little man" (208) and must
not be irritated by too candid an approach. Furthermore, he has to be
given assurances as to the part K. intends to play in their alliance.

To accomplish this task, difficult to perform in view of the boy's
extreme acuteness, K. draws once more upon his memories. He had,
he assures Hans, "some medical knowledge and, what was of still
greater value, experience in treating sick people. Many a case that the
doctors had given up he had been able to cure. At home they had called
him 'the bitter herb' on account of his healing powers. In any case he
would be glad to see Hans's mother" (190).

Suspicious Frieda scents the intentions hidden behind K.'s words.
"Your aim was the woman," she reproaches him after the boy's departure. "You were betraying this woman even before you had won her"
(206). But Frieda oversimplifies. Having learned too well the lesson
Gardena taught her, she confuses her own unhappy lot with the future
of Hans's mother. Like all mirrorings, her reflections are both false
and true. K. is quite ready to admit that her words are "not untrue,
they are only hostile" (207). They are hostile in that Frieda fails to see
that K. is taking Hans's lead when the boy indicates that "apparently
it was the climate here that [his mother] could not stand" (191). Enlarging upon this hint, K. cleverly introduces his own objective: "She
need not have to go away for any long time or for any great distance,
even up on Castle Hill the air was quite different" (192). On the surface the therapy he suggests is plain sense, provided only that the

Castle will cooperate. Since the "girl from the Castle" is obviously smarting in exile, a return to the site of her happier past is certainly indicated. Suffering in her marriage, she can but profit by a temporary separation from her inferior husband. No intuition was needed to choose the Castle as a health resort and to recommend a treatment that would never have occurred to the resident doctor because, as an inhabitant of the village, he was too well acquainted with the fact that the Castle was taboo.

On the other hand, Frieda's reproaches are "not untrue" because K. is indeed trying to direct the sick woman back to the Castle in order to gain another foothold there. "What is more natural," he pleads with Frieda, "than to ask [Hans's mother] for advice or even for help? If the landlady only knows the obstacles that keep one from reaching Klamm, then this woman probably knows the way to him, for she has come down here by this way herself" (210). The self-styled doctor has turned into a patient expecting help from the sick whom he had pretended to cure.

Once more we have to think of Amalia, who also "knows healing herbs to soothe . . . pain" (282). But Amalia heals from complete hopelessness. Despairing of the possibility of any cure, she continues to help because the world would be still more hopeless without her efforts. She concentrates on the smallest possible sphere of activity— her family, especially her old parents—and is at least rewarded by seeing that she can delay their ultimate decline. Hers is the minimal gain that can be won in the no man's land between human self-preservation and the absurdity of an inhuman fate.

K., on the other hand, heals from hope—from hope, that is, for himself. To be sure, the promise he holds out to little Hans may, as Frieda implies, be a mere fabrication engendered by the demands of the moment and the opportunities it offers. But we need not accept Frieda's psychology—the malicious surmise of a vengeful woman. When K. remembers the name of "the bitter herb" by which his old patients used to refer to him, he pronounces too profound and multifaceted a truth for us to dismiss lightly his claim that he has "some medical knowledge." Furthermore, the audacity of this Land-Surveyor, who boasts that he has cured "many a case that the doctors have given up," conforms to his earlier dreams: once more he prides himself on being able to conquer death. His healing powers seem to be extraordinary, and we would not be surprised to see him resort to some magic. He has overstepped the customary landmarks of human knowledge just as has Amalia. But his reward consists in the satisfaction of his vanity, in seeing how he outshines the ordinary doctors who remain within the conventional confines of the medical art. Frieda is right when she charges that he uses whatever knowledge he has for his own sake and in his own interest. The bitterness he spreads is the taste he leaves on the lips of his patients.

There is one more difference between Amalia, who "knows healing herbs," and K., who calls himself an herb, albeit a bitter one. The motives behind his words, the intentions of his plans, are hybrid and, as often as not, quite dubious. His very being, like that of a healing herb, seems to make a promise to the suffering. Frieda would not scold him so frantically had she not sensed this promise, believed in it, and found it broken in the end. Olga turns to him intuitively and never stops trusting him and waiting for him. Even Amalia assures him of her willingness to "do many a thing" for him (223) and shows signs of jealousy, the most reliable symptom of female affection, when she finds him with Olga in the dark hut (265). She even enters the abhorred Castle to collect a letter for him (159). In one of the deleted passages an old mother exclaims at the mere sight of him, "This man should not be let go to the dogs" (417). His presence seems to inspire hope in all those who, like these village women, have been sickened by their life in the shadow of the Castle or who, like Hans, are too young to have lost their innocence completely.

When Frieda asks him what he wants to become, Hans replies, "A man like K." It is a quick answer, and yet it is apparent that this wish is not due to any juvenile idealism. Hans is fully aware of K.'s present desperate condition; he even admits candidly that he "would certainly have preferred to shield his mother from K.'s slightest word, even from having to see him." Not only does the astonishingly clear-sighted boy recognize the degradation inflicted upon K.; he even seems to understand that K. himself is at fault when he is humiliated; why else would he want to protect his mother from him? And yet he has come to K. in order to help him and be helped by him whom he thinks able to render assistance in spite of his momentary misery. His own attitude toward K., Hans says, is shared by other people, and "most important of all, it had been his mother herself who had mentioned K.'s name" (196–197).

The name of "the bitter herb" takes on a new meaning through these words of little Hans. Now we see that this bitterness is not only a matter of taste but an integral quality of K. himself. K. not only embitters others by his deeds and words; bitterness is engrained in his life; it is its very substance.

Occasionally K. realizes this himself. The night before this event, the night of his fourth day in the village, he had experienced a moment of extremely severe self-cognition. He had been lying in wait for Klamm and suddenly understood that his waiting was never to succeed. Then it seemed to him as if

all relations with him had been broken off, and as if now in reality he were freer than he had ever been, and at liberty to wait here in this place, usually forbidden to him, as long as he desired, and had won a freedom such as hardly anybody else had ever succeeded in winning, and as if nobody could dare to touch him or drive him away, or even speak to him; but—this conviction was at least equally strong—as if at the same time there was nothing more senseless, nothing more hopeless, than this freedom, this waiting, this inviolability (139).

In one of the most paradoxical passages Kafka has ever written, K. formulates the bitter freedom of the outcast. He is the man without hope to return or ability to arrive, the victor who holds a forbidden ground and the defeated who occupies this ground in vain, the untouchable who boasts of a freedom which severs him from all human contacts and raises him beyond them at the same time. This liberty and invulnerability, however, has lost all meaning because he is deprived of all human standards by which he could measure them. This is the reason why he returns to the human sphere, to argue and attract, to advise and give one rash promise after another. And yet it is not his transparent words but the impenetrable bitterness of his fate behind them that inspires hope in those who turn to him for help. The paradox of his existence appears to the villagers as a guarantee of his healing powers. Even young Hans observes that

these contradictions had engendered in him the belief that though for the moment K. was wretched and giving a horrifying example, yet in an almost unimaginably distant future he would excel everybody. And it was just this absurdly distant future and the magnificent developments that were to lead to it that enticed Hans; that was why he was willing to accept K. even in his present state.

To this the narrator adds:

The peculiar childish-grown-up acuteness of this wish consisted in the fact that Hans looked on K. as on a younger brother whose future would reach further than his own, the future of a little boy (197).

Hans Brunswick's vision opens the horizons of the myth around the figure of this Land-Surveyor. In the boy's eyes he assumes a stature which transcends time and, by the same token, conquers death. He becomes the "everlasting Land-Surveyor," which is a title once used by the Castle for him. But the word which the official had meant merely as an invective has now acquired a more profound meaning. K.'s bitterness will last forever, but so will his capacity to arouse in others expectations that Heller is justified in calling "mysteriously messianic." [39]

K., whose hope has been bolstered by the conversation with Hans —a hope which is "completely groundless, but all the same never more to be put out of his mind" (199)—appears in this scene willing to live up to his paradoxical fate. At the end of his conversation with Hans he seems actually to believe in his ability to heal the boy's mother. As a token he promises that he will carve for the boy a knotted stick even more beautiful than his own, which is lying on the table. Whatever secondary meaning we may feel inclined to attach to this stick —the magician's wand, the physician's Aesculapian serpent stick, the yardstick of the Land-Surveyor—it is, first and foremost, the wanderer's walking stick, K.'s companion when he entered the village. This sign of his identity he intends to duplicate for the boy, thereby adopting him and securing him as his successor. Again Hans seems to comprehend. "It was no longer quite clear whether Hans had not really meant more than the knotted stick, so happy was he made by K.'s promise; and he said good-bye with a radiant face, not without pressing K.'s hand firmly and saying: 'The day after tomorrow, then'" (198). The day after tomorrow, however, is the seventh of K.'s stay in the village, the day on which the novel breaks off. Another name for this day is "never."

Kafka's Land-Surveyor is neither a mythical nor a legendary figure, neither an Eternal Wanderer nor the Wandering Jew. For myth and legend know heaven and hell, a happy or a tragic end. K., however, wanders in circles through the twilight between salvation and damnation, which is the most infernal fate of all. The contradictions of human existence are concentrated in him, but the novel neither affirms this paradox nor solves and conquers it. It simply states it in the form of a parable. If *The Castle* appears as Kafka's masterpiece, it is not because of the insoluble puzzle which K., "the bitter herb," poses to the reader, but because Kafka has found in K.'s antagonist, the Castle, the perfect image to conceal his own uncertainties about man's ulti-

mate destiny and yet to manifest in K.'s meanderings through this
labyrinth his incessant longing for a certainty of one kind or the other.

At no point in the novel has K. come nearer to truth than in the first
paragraph. Leaning on his wanderer's knotted stick, he stands on the
bridge that leads to the village. At this moment the Castle appears
to him as both "great" and "invisible," that is, as palpable yet utterly
immaterial, as holding "an abundance of hope" but not "for us." It is
characteristic of Kafka's labyrinth that one is nearest to truth the
instant before one enters its maze.

CHAPTER VIII

Heightened Redemption

Testaments and Last Stories

Patchwork

ONE of the last pages of Kafka's diary contains the cryptic remark, "Talent for 'patchwork'" (June 5, 1922, *DII*, 230). These three words present only a minor puzzle among the many which Kafka left for posterity to ponder; moreover, they pose a problem which can be easily solved: "patchwork" turns out to be the catchword of a story which occupied Kafka's mind at this time.[1]

Through his Zionist friends Kafka was introduced to the work of Martin Buber, the philosopher and translator of the Hasidic stories. In 1917 Buber published two of Kafka's short stories in his monthly *The Jew* (*DF*, 401). This attention did not prevent Kafka from finding Buber's "last books . . . loathsome and offensive." * Buber had the honor of being rejected alongside Kierkegaard's *Either-Or*. In reality Kafka's attack was directed against himself rather than against the authors he had read. The true meaning of this criticism is revealed when

* Presumably the reference is to *The Mind of Judaism* (*Vom Geist des Judentums*, 1916) and *Events and Meetings* (*Ereignisse und Begegnungen*, 1917). It is, however, hard to understand why the latter book, a collection of quite personal reminiscences and experiences, should have provoked Kafka to such an emotional reaction.

Kafka concludes it with the following observation: "These are books which can only be written and read by someone who retains at least a trace of real superiority. Things being what they are, they grow more and more abominable in my hands" (*B*, 224–225).

In 1922 Buber's *The Great Maggid and His Followers* (*Der Grosse Maggid und seine Nachfolge*) was published. It was an anthology of Hasidic tales centered on Rabbi Dov Baer of Mezrich and his disciples. Kafka's diary mentions the title "Maggid" on May 12 (*DII*, 229). At this time he had probably bought or borrowed the book. Less than a month later he must have noticed one of the stories connected with "The Seer," Rabbi Yaakov Yitzhak of Lublin, one of the Great Maggid's followers. The tale is actually called "Patchwork" and runs as follows:

A hasid of the rabbi of Lublin once fasted from one sabbath to the next. On Friday afternoon he began to suffer such cruel thirst that he thought he would die. He saw a well, went up to it, and prepared to drink. But instantly he realized that because of the one brief hour he had still to endure, he was about to destroy the work of the entire week. He did not drink and went away from the well. Then he was touched by a feeling of pride for having passed this difficult test. When he became aware of it, he said to himself: "Better I go and drink than let my heart fall prey to pride." He went back to the well, but just as he was going to bend down to draw water, he noticed that his thirst had disappeared. When the sabbath had begun, he entered his teacher's house. "Patchwork!" the rabbi called to him, as he crossed the threshold.[2]

It is easy to see why this tale appealed to Kafka. Hasid means "the pious one," and to prove one's piety through asceticism must have seemed to Kafka a most natural way of serving the Divine. That he had ascetic tendencies is demonstrated by his vegetarianism, his abhorrence of uncleanliness, and the ice-cold baths he took even in winter in spite of his frail condition. He could not fail to sympathize both with the hasid, who imposes the cruel task upon himself, and with the teacher, who criticizes his performance harshly but justly.

Applying this same criticism to himself and his literary work, Kafka in this short diary entry meant to say that if he were at all gifted, his talent had exhausted itself in producing patchwork similar to the hasid's. With a shock of recognition he registered this similarity at a time when he had chosen fasting as the theme of his story "A Hunger Artist." The hunger experiments undertaken by the dog in "Investigations of a Dog," a somewhat later tale, read like a conscious parody of the hasid's patchwork (*GW*, 61 ff.).

There is also another side to this diary entry. Patchwork is work
after all, and the pious disciple finally does fulfill his task. He com-
pletes his service and succeeds in doing so under circumstances of
mystical ambiguity. To the hasid, at least, it must have seemed that
the Godhead intervened to dispel his thirst so suddenly. If one believes
in the Divine, then one must conclude that the hasid enjoyed, at the
most critical moment, the help of the Almighty. One might even ask
how any human performance could be more than patchwork without
the participation of the Divine.

The very fact that Kafka measured himself with the standards of
so forgiving and enthusiastic a creed as Hasidism shows that the
tensions straining his mind had lost some of their destructive fury
during the last years of his life. When he says, in a diary entry of the
same time, that his "work draws to an end in the way an unhealed
wound might draw together" (May 8, 1922, *DII*, 228), he not only
laments his suffering but accepts the end with a fair amount of composure. Even here the contradiction remains in full force: the wound
draws together without actually healing. But at least it is allowed to
close, a process that can only take place if it is left undisturbed.

The difference between Kafka's last stories and his earlier works
lies in the greater degree of composure with which they seem to have
been conceived and executed. To be sure, they are still Kafka stories
in that they deliver messages which are essentially incommunicable.
Nor has the threat of a demonically disturbed reality (and the unreality behind it) completely abated. But the threat has somewhat
receded, mostly because Kafka himself has stopped being spellbound
and paralyzed by it. He has gained some distance from himself and
his writings. At times he may even have contemplated his work from
the outside, as the animal views its Burrow in the late story of that title,
and found that it "probably protected me in more ways than I thought
or dared think while I was inside it" (*GW*, 99). His attitude had
changed, not spectacularly perhaps, but nevertheless decidedly. On
January 31, 1922, he entered in his diary:

If I have climbed only the tiniest step, won any security for myself, even
if it be an assurance of the most dubious kind, I then stretch out on my
step and wait for the negative, not to climb after me, indeed, but to drag
me down from it. Hence it is a defensive instinct in me that will not tolerate
my having achieved the slightest degree of lasting ease and smashes the
marriage bed, for example, even before it has been set up.

The tune is familiar, the image of the marital bed broken to pieces repetitive. However, the melody has been transposed into a different key—not major to be sure, but not completely minor either—by the preceding sentence of this entry: "The negative alone, however strong it may be, cannot suffice, as in my unhappiest moments I tend to believe it can" (*DII*, 217).

One extreme difficulty in understanding *The Trial* and *The Castle* stems from the fact that the cases of the two K.'s are argued simultaneously from the points of view of both the heroes and their opponents. In order to interpret these narratives at all, we had to take one side, thereby missing much of what the other side had to say in its favor. In his later stories, however, Kafka's eyes are more determinedly focused on his central figures. He sides with his heroes as much as he is able. At times he even goes so far as to give the impression that he might be identified with them.

Superficially it is as much a personal as a literary phenomenon that during this last period Kafka's style increased in transparency, and his imagery lost some of its most frightening aspects. His body had taken over more and more of the tortures which he used to inflict upon his mind. This change was long in coming; indeed, it reaches as far back as Kafka's fatal sickness itself.

On September 4, 1917, this disease was diagnosed for the first time as a catarrh in the lungs. Brod quotes from his own diary:

There is a danger of T.B. . . . Franz . . . feels himself liberated and defeated at the same time. . . . He considers his illness as a punishment, because he has often wished for a violent solution. But this solution is too drastic for him. He quotes against God, from the *Meistersinger:* "I should have thought him to be more delicate" (*FK*, 162–163).

That Kafka quotes an opera, moreover a Wagnerian one, introduces a touch of irony and stresses the release he felt at hearing the diagnosis rather than the shock he must have suffered. If we put the quotation back into its proper context, we see that these words of reproach are spoken by Eva to Hans Sachs in the second act of the opera. The girl is momentarily upset by the cobbler's refusal to comply with her wishes, but soon she will understand that she has been childish. In spite of her outburst she remains convinced of the master's wisdom; and it is indeed "indelicate" Hans Sachs who steers the action to the end which Eva desires most. Kafka, too, may have been upset by the revelation that his sickness was more than a literary image, namely, a reality which actually endangered his life. But he soon restored its symbolic character and accepted it. If he felt punished by his disease, then he welcomed this punishment.

His condition actually released him from his hated duties at the office. In good conscience he could now allow himself to retire to the country and devote himself completely to writing. Approximately ten days after the diagnosis he writes to Brod from Zürau:

My relation to T.B. is the relation of a child to his mother's apron strings when it clings to them. . . . Constantly I am looking for an explanation for the disease since I am sure that I have not hunted it down all by myself. Sometimes it seems to me as if my brains and my lungs had come to an agreement without informing me. My brains had said: "It cannot go on this way," and after five years my lungs have declared their readiness to help (*B*, 161).

The five years allude to the affair with Felice Bauer as well as to his work, which he considered to have been as inconclusive as his life. But before the year 1917 had drawn to a close, the awareness of his disease helped him break his second engagement to Felice Bauer. (She married another man one and a half years later [*FK*, 167].)

What the diagnosis of tuberculosis meant to Kafka's work we can see from a diary entry, dated September 28, 1917, which was written while he was still under the impact of his doctor's judgment: "I would put myself in death's hands, though. Remnant of faith. Return to a father. Great day of Atonement" (*DII*, 187). This statement is the epitome of Kafka's ambiguity. In German, Day of Atonement (*Versöhnungstag*) indicates more than the breast-beating fervor of penitence that it assumes in Jewish liturgy: as soon as the compound word is split up into its composite parts and these are taken literally, they reveal a universal mildness of reconciliation (*Tag der Versöhnung*). Furthermore, the dative *zum Vater* can be read as referring to both the return to a specific father—the physical one—and to a universal and spiritual Father, for instance, the one in heaven. The entry seems to be a typical Kafka crossroad, where two ways of expression meet for the one moment that is necessary to produce an image. Disease offered him the return to his father's house as a sick child, a dream that actually came true in 1924. It also promised him a homecoming on the level of Novalis' equally ambiguous sentence: "Where do we go? Always home." [3] It is against this ambiguity that the letter to his father must be read.

Dearest Father

Not until two years later, in November 1919, was Kafka ready to compose this epistle of about 15,000 words. On the surface it was an attempt to gain control of a basic conflict that still beset him at the age of thirty-six. The extreme importance he attached to the document can be seen in the fact that he typed it himself (*DF*, 405). Characteristically he did not mail the letter, nor did he deliver it in person. He asked his mother to forward it. But she returned the missive to him "probably with a few comforting words" (*FK*, 16).

At first sight the letter seems intended to reduce Kafka's metaphysical dilemma to the proportions of a family conflict. "You asked me recently," it starts, "why I maintain that I am afraid of you. As usual, I was unable to think of any answer" (138).* The father's question had arisen from the routine of torment that was inherent in a relationship which was disturbed from the very outset. Moreover, it had been, beyond any doubt, rhetorical. But Kafka broke this routine—and his silence—in order to release a flood of material which would have delighted a practicing psychoanalyst.

The bulk of the letter is taken up by a description of his relationship with his father. He was clear-sighted enough to realize that at the roots of the conflict lay the father's abundance of what he himself was most lacking, vitality. He registers the father's

strength, health, appetite, loudness of voice, eloquence, self-satisfaction, superiority in all worldly matters, endurance, presence of mind, knowledge of human nature, a certain largesse, naturally combined with all the weaknesses and failings that go with these merits, weaknesses into which your temperament and sometimes your hot temper drive you (140–141).

This is an adult's appraisal of another adult's character, and it may give us a true likeness of Herrman Kafka. But by a twist closely related to the one that provides the narratives with much of their eerie atmosphere, the letter makes this rather ordinary portrait transparent; it shows the impact of the father on a child who had to bear alone the brunt of so strong a personality.† The letter opens a terrified child's

---

* Numbers without letters in this section refer to the American edition of the letter, *Dearest Father*, 138–196.

† Two older brothers had died as infants; and his oldest sister was six years younger than he.

world to the reader, but it assesses this world with the considerable,
though not always correct, psychological insight of a grownup.

True to the pedagogical indifference of the pre-Freudian era, the
father had developed a system of double standards: at dinnertime the
child had to concentrate on his food while the father, a fast eater,
cleaned and cut his fingernails, sharpened pencils, and poked in his
ears with a toothpick, heaping disgust onto disdain and turning the
family circle into a kind of middle-class inferno. In the sphere of human relations the father was full of vulgar contempt, which was directed particularly against his Czech servants and employees, the
"paid enemies" (161). He distrusted everyone and did his best to
impart his feelings to his son. He undermined the child's confidence
in his environment and, by the same token, raised himself to the stature
of a giant. Franz kept wondering how his father managed to preserve
his own equilibrium in spite of this display of mistrust, but "perhaps
it was only the token of a sovereign" (171). The lonely, high-strung,
and overly critical child probably suffered the most from his father's
irrational self-reliance, which removed him from any ordinary approach by placing him on the arbitrary heights of absolute and infinite power. The letter bristles with epithets like "superior," "sovereign," "despotic," and "tyrannical." Thus he attempted to deify the
father. Reading the letter, one cannot escape the feeling that Kafka,
like his Georg Bendemann, would have thrown himself from a bridge
had his father so ordained.

The letter reports in detail two examples of the pedagogy to which
Kafka had been subjected. The first incident happened when he was a
very young child. He was lying awake in the middle of the night and
kept crying for water. The grown-up letter writer knows, of course,
that the child did not cry because he was thirsty. "I kept on whimper-
ing . . . not, I am certain, because I was thirsty, but partly to annoy
[you], partly to amuse myself" (142–143). Trying to find an excuse, the
grownup does not act as the child's older and mature self; instead he
starts staring at himself with the cold and irate eyes of the father,
whose rest had been disturbed. He ventures into his own unconsciousness, seemingly in search of an explanation, yet what he discovers
there are not the commonly known psychological mechanisms but
an uncommonly large amount of guilt. He always lay in ambush for
his guilt, and when he had trapped it or, rather, had been trapped by
it, he betrayed his original purpose by offering the evidence to his
prosecutor instead of his attorney. This is one of the sources of Kafka's

bitterly masochistic irony. The child kept crying; the father resorted
to threats, and since these threats, according to pattern, only served
to increase the child's forlornness and lament, he took the boy out of
his bed and carried him into the open air. On a balcony he left him
standing in his nightshirt, exposed to complete solitude, surrounded
by darkness.

Even years afterwards I was tormented by the thought that the huge
man, my father, the last resort and supreme judge,* should come, almost
for no reason at all, in the middle of the night, and take me out of my
bed and carry me out onto the balcony, and that therefore I was such
a mere nothing to him (143).

In this "therefore" originate both Kafka's trauma and Kafka's vision:
it turns the clumsy expedient of a pedagogically ignorant father into
a verdict of almost religious depth. (He had, however, prepared this
verdict by indicting himself through a blatant misreading of his own
motives. Therefore he was both right and wrong in a letter to Milena
when he called the epistle to his father an attorney's brief: "And in
reading it try to understand all the lawyer's tricks; it is a lawyer's
letter" [*LM*, 79].)

The second episode occurred during Kafka's adolescence, around
his sixteenth year. He was taking a walk with his parents when he
suddenly started reproaching them that they had left him uninstructed
in "these interesting things." He went on, boasting of great dangers
which he had approached. (He did not say "experienced," for he could
not lie even when he was bragging.) Again the letter writer looks for
a psychological motivation of the boy's aggression: he had broached
the subject because it gave him pleasure,† and also because he wanted
to take revenge on his parents, "somehow for something." The father
parried the provocation by cutting him short. He said something to
the effect that he could counsel him how to carry on "these things"
without incurring any danger. The curt answer is understandable in
view of the father's temperament, his predominantly practical approach, and the general taboo on all things sexual imposed by the
European middle class. And yet it disturbed Kafka to such an extent

---

* The German has simply *"die letzte Instanz."* In *letzter Instanz* means both "in
the last resort" and "without further appeal."

† Kafka says, "Es machte mir Lust (It aroused my desire)." The usual idiom
would have been: "Es machte mir Spass (fun)." By substituting *Lust* ("craving,"
"desire") he opened, so to speak, a linguistic trapdoor into the psychoanalytic
underground.

that he could link this scene with another, when, twenty years later, the father protested against one of his engagements. The actual meaning of that never-forgotten walk with his parents lies in the fact that then, possibly for the first time, the Oedipus situation had become manifest to him. "The thought that you might perhaps have given, before your marriage, similar advice to yourself, was to me utterly inconceivable. So there was almost no smudge of earthly filth on you. And precisely you were pushing me, just as though I was predestined to it, down into this filth, with a few frank words." The letter writer saw this situation also as an archetypal, almost a mythical one. The meaning of what the father had said was, as he very well knew, "unscrupulous in a very modern way." But behind this façade he sensed a "primeval" quality (184–186), namely, the sexual jealousy of a tribal chief claiming for himself the woman whom the son had chosen. Here he was able to express what he had veiled in utter ambiguity in "The Judgment": that the son's basic guilt consisted in his desire to take a wife, to found a family, and to dispossess the father.

We are still deeply involved with autobiographical material here. Indeed, one of the reasons that had touched off the letter was Kafka's latest marriage project. He had proposed to Julie Wohryzek in Želisy, the place where this letter was written. Brod calls the engagement unhappy and short-lived (*FK*, 185 n.). But Kafka had not tarried in informing his father about it. A scene ensued which was stormier than any previous one, at least according to the letter writer. The father, arguing in his crude and businesslike fashion, is reported to have referred to the son's betrothed as "the next best girl. . . . She probably put on some fancy blouse, the thing these Prague Jewesses have a knack of doing, and straightaway, of course, you made up your mind to marry her" (187). As usual, the father hit the son's most vulnerable spot, the self-centered indifference of his life plans. Since he concentrated on his writing, the person of the beloved was, in a deeper sense, really of little relevance to him. He admitted this much when he retorted that both Felice Bauer and J. W. "were chosen by chance" (188). Of course, he was speaking only of the surface reality. The *idea* of marriage had become for him a wish dream and an imperative. As an image matrimony was a touchstone of Kafka's whole existence. In this respect we may see in the engagement controversy with his father an incentive for the composition of this letter.

But there was another reason, and one that leads us away from

Kafka's psychological self-analysis. If one of the focal points in the letter is his sex life, the other is his writing.

In 1919 *A Country Doctor* was published. Kafka himself stressed the importance of this book by dedicating it to his father. To be sure, he had no illusions about the effect that this act of filial devotion would have on the recipient. The letter mentions the father's "proverbial way of hailing the arrival of my books: 'Put it on the bedside table'" (176). There, of course, it would be left unopened. Kafka does not refer to this insult as an individual act of indifference or cruelty, but as an expected reaction, a routine. He does not say that *A Country Doctor* did receive this specific welcome; he had just been expecting a similar rebuff as inevitable. Nevertheless, he embarked once more on an enterprise the outcome of which he clearly could foresee. The dedication is thus blighted by the covert provocation which it contains. And whatever the father's actual reaction to *A Country Doctor* may have been, we can be sure that he stuck stubbornly to the established pattern of their relationship and acted as Franz had expected.

Kafka's relation to his father shows the same ambivalence that the heroes of his books display with regard to the authorities. His scorn and horror were blended with hope and even trust. The letter also contains the following declaration: "I should have been happy to have you as a friend, as a boss, an uncle, a grandfather, even indeed (though this rather more reluctantly) as a father-in-law. Just as father you have been too strong for me" (140). "You are after all basically a kindly and soft-hearted person" (142). "You have, I think, a gift for bringing up children" (147). "Also you have a particularly beautiful, very rare way of quietly, contentedly, approvingly smiling, a way of smiling that can make the person for whom it is meant entirely happy" (155). At the height of his argument he even exclaims:

My writing was all about you; all I did there, after all, was to bemoan what I could not bemoan upon your breast. It was an intentionally long-drawn-out leave-taking from you, only with the exception that although it was brought about by force on your part, it did take its course in the direction I had determined (177).

To be sure, he could determine the direction he gave his writing; he could orient it toward the metaphysical. But he could not reach his goal. The equation father-Father-God is an extremely daring literary venture, and it was as little founded in the reality of Kafka's life as it was upheld in the sphere of religious thinking. Herrman Kafka, the man from the country, resisted being molded into a legendary, let alone a mythical, father figure. Kafka's attempts to carry this image into literature, and beyond it to the realm of belief, come dangerously close to being sacrilege; they prove no other point than that a godhead conceived in the likeness of the older Kafka was no godhead at all. In his darker moments, however, this was the very point Kafka had set out to prove.

The Oedipus situation which the letter described so eloquently had served Kafka as a literary symbol: beyond the father stands a father image which Kafka had created enough like Kafka Senior to prevent it from ever becoming God. Any autobiographical importance or therapeutical intention which this letter might seem to have can be dismissed as a decoy. To be sure, it was written, as its last sentence indicates, "to calm both of us down a little, and make our living and our dying easier" (196). But this intention could only be fulfilled by Kafka the writer. Kafka the son remained true to his quandary. A few sentences earlier he makes his father say:

By means of your dishonesty you have already achieved enough, for you have proved three things: first that you are blameless; secondly, that I am to blame; and thirdly, that out of sheer magnanimity you are pre-pared not only to forgive me but, what is both much more and much less, also to prove and to try to believe it yourself, but I—contrary to the truth, to be sure—am also blameless (194).

Kafka's self-reproaches have become aggressions which he attributes to the father.

On the level of reality Herrman Kafka would surely have dis-missed as extreme nonsense the complexities he was supposed to have uttered. But even on the letter's own level an extreme has been reached: the idea of guilt and forgiveness upon which the letter is founded is being tossed around until it has lost any specific meaning. If it is the privilege—and the basic problem—of modern literature to question by thought and linguistic processes any accepted standards, then a passage like the one above is apt to place the father-son relation-ship under such sharp scrutiny that there is nothing left but two masks grinning at each other in utter despair: a Kafka commentary on the alienation that governed his life.

He had recounted his life as if it had been one of his tales; then he commented upon it as his figures are wont to comment upon their experiences. Although he did not succeed in settling his dispute with the father by writing the letter, at least he raised what he had written to the level of literature. Kafka's "Letter to His Father" is the parable of the Prodigal Son in the twentieth century.

This means that the documentary value of this parable is minimal. It contributes little to our understanding of the "real" Kafka. It neither complements nor explains his literary work. Nor does it offer any information we could not have gathered from the more concentrated, more authentic imagery he created in his tales. It merely adds the mystery of his person to the enigma of his writings, casting, so to speak, new twilight on both. Tongue in cheek, Kafka employed the letter's biographical material for a psychoanalysis of himself by himself. At the same time he sensed all too well that this undertaking constituted a paradox as insoluble as the rest of his work.

On the level of this work, however, he performed one of the strangest and most daring games a writer ever played with the substance of his life. If it was impossible for Kafka the son and Kafka the father to achieve reconciliation, how much more impossible would it be for the heroes in his books to come to a *rapprochement* with the authorities against which they were pitted! There remained nothing but the acceptance of the break which existed in the natural world between the generations and in the supernatural world between the Deity and man. Writing the letter, Kafka seems to have resigned himself to accepting this separation as inevitable and final on both the level of reality and the spiritual level beyond.

The appropriate literary expression of the abyss which yawned between the two worlds is the fragmentariness which distinguishes most of Kafka's major writings. He was incapable of finding an ending which would have both satisfied him and dispelled the doubts that he himself had aroused in the minds of his readers. In some cases he produced variants and settled for one of them as the minor evil. In others he used commentaries to break open a seemingly final form. Others, the best, extend the questions he posed into infinity.

Accepting this break, this fragmentariness, as inescapable, Kafka was ready to compose his two testaments. The letter, too, had been a testament, as can be seen from the "easier death" he expected from having written it. This piece of highly imaginary prose represents indeed one of the purgatories through which he had to pass on his way to the comparative tranquillity of his last days and works.

Franz Kafka's Wills

The change which the disease brought about in Kafka's mind is also revealed by the fact that he paid less and less attention to his diaries after he learned of his illness. There was no entry between November 10, 1917, and June 27, 1919. The diary of 1919 consists of seven notes, only one of which is longer than five lines; the diary of 1920 totals four short entries. On October 15, 1921, he wrote that, a week before, he had entrusted all the earlier notebooks to Milena Jesenská (*DII*, 193). For the next five months he worked hectically on his diaries, waging battles which were the more fierce because he suspected that they represented rearguard actions. During the rest of the year 1922 we find only occasional entries. A few last notes appear on June 12, 1923, somewhat less than a year before Kafka was buried in Prague.

At the same time his literary output increased, due in part to the leisure which his retirement in the country and, later on, his stay at various sanitariums afforded him. As mentioned before, *The Castle* may have been written sometime during this period. Even before he heard the diagnosis of his disease, he had begun work on the eight Octavo Notebooks, filling them with aphorisms, sketches, and fragments which were generally of a less intimate character than the diary entries. His correspondence grew and lasted well into the spring of 1924. Included among his letters of the period between 1920 and 1923 are the documents of his most passionate and most self-destructive love affair, the *Letters to Milena,* which alone constitute a book.

Although at an earlier stage Kafka might have committed his feelings about Milena to paper, he explains in an entry on October 15, 1921, why he had lost interest in his diary:

I could probably write about M., but would not willingly do it, and moreover it would be aimed too directly against myself: I no longer need to make myself so minutely conscious of such things, I am not so forgetful as I used to be in this respect, I am a memory come alive, hence my insomnia (*DII*, 193).

Now he seemed to be capable of concentrating even more on himself and his own fate as a sick man, a lover, and a writer. The opposite side of memory is foreboding; it was precisely the foreboding of an unattainable beyond space and time which had held him spellbound for so long. Now gradually this metaphysical fixation lost its hold on him.

Paradoxically Kafka's increased introversion set some of his energies free and allowed him to turn outward as he had never been able to do before.

His human contacts acquired a certain measure of harmony. As early as 1920 he found in the fellow patient and doctor, Robert Klopstock, a friend who tended him through the last period of his life (*FK*, 186n.). In the summer of 1923 he met Dora Dymant, an eastern European Jewess who came from a Hasidic background. They settled together far from Prague, in Berlin, and although both families opposed their marriage, Dora stayed at his side until his death. It is not difficult to see that Kafka's ironically euphoric happiness was a symptom that he had reached the last stage of his disease. Dora Dymant observed that he "directly welcomed his illness." She touched on a very deep layer of his personality when she remarked that the outbreak of his deadly sickness "came as a liberation for him: now the decision had been taken from his hands." [4]

Yet Kafka was to surrender still another decision to the arbitration of an outside force—the decision about the future of his literary estate. In his postscript to *The Trial* Brod reports that sometime in 1921 Kafka had shown him the outside of a note, saying, "My testament will be quite simple—a request to you to burn everything" (*T*, 330). This note, written in ink, was discovered among Kafka's papers after his death. It is addressed to Brod and in rather general terms asks him to destroy all writings. It directs the executor to the places where he can find the material he is to destroy: his bookcase, the linen cupboard, his desks both at home and in the office "or anywhere else where anything may have got to" (*T*, 328). The letter is undated, yet the reference to the desk in his office indicates that it was written sometime after the fall of 1920, when he had returned once more to work for a short time, and certainly before July 1922, when he retired from the Workers' Accident Insurance Institute for good (*B*, 523–524).

Brod discovered still another testament written in pencil and likewise undated. It reads in part:

Perhaps this time I shall not recover after all. Pneumonia after a whole month's pulmonary fever is all too likely. . . . Of all my writings the only books that can stand are these: "The Judgment," "The Stoker," "The Metamorphosis," "In the Penal Colony," "A Country Doctor" and the short story: "A Hunger Artist." (The few copies of "Meditation" can remain . . . ; but nothing in this volume must be reprinted.) . . . But everything else of mine which is extant . . . , everything without exception in so far as it is discoverable or obtainable from the addresses by request (you know most of them yourself; and whatever happens don't forget the few notebooks in . . . 's possession) . . . all these things without exception are to be burned, and I beg you to do this as soon as possible (*T*, 328–329).

Meno Spann has dated this second document with considerable accuracy.[5] The "few notebooks" are the diaries Kafka gave Milena; therefore the note can only have been written after October 15, 1921. On January 30, 1922, the diary has the entry, "Waiting for pneumonia" (*DII*, 216), and it is more than likely that this fear produced the testament which also refers to pneumonia. He had been acutely ill for a whole month; yet his physical condition was, as the diary shows, both a cause and a reflection of a still more general crisis. His relation with Milena had gone from bad to worse. (The gift of his diaries was a last desperate grasping for her as well as a first farewell.) In January 1922 he was physically and spiritually so close to death that he must have felt compelled to draw up his last will once more.

Contrary to Brod's assumption, it would seem that the penciled note was written later than the one he was shown in 1921. It is by far the more detailed and important testament, and it indicates that their unfinished state was one of the reasons why Kafka wanted his literary remains to be destroyed. He exempted the published books from burning because he had brought them at least formally to a conclusion. "A Hunger Artist," though still unpublished, was probably already accepted for publication. (It appeared in the October 1922 issue of *Die Neue Rundschau*.[6]) Furthermore, this story can boast of a distinct ending.

Kafka clearly distinguishes "Meditation" from the other publications. He decrees that the former *must* not appear again, whereas the latter "*can* stand." Then he elaborates:

When I say that these five books and the story can stand, I do not mean that I wish them to be reprinted and handed down to posterity. On the contrary, should they disappear altogether, this would correspond to my real wishes. Only, since they do exist, I do not wish to hinder anyone who so desires from keeping them (*T*, 329).

The last statement is an extremely hypothetical one; even if Kafka presupposed that Brod would be willing to cooperate fully, he could not expect him to collect each single copy of a Kafka book from owners mostly unknown to him and put them on the pyre. These books had to remain; they were going to stay whether Kafka wished them to stay or not; the mere idea that it could be otherwise was absurd and an exaggeration. Why, then, did he dwell on the superfluous? Was he perhaps not altogether serious? Was he still playing? Was he playing again when he ordained the destruction of his work?

Dora Dymant reports that sometime during the winter of 1923–1924 he forced her to burn a few of his manuscripts before his eyes.[7] He was sick and confined to his bed when he delegated this task to Dora. She was approximately twenty years old, unversed in literary matters, and innocent of the complexities which life with Kafka must have presented; she was devoted to the suffering man and eager to please him. Thus she did what she was instructed to do. Brod, who was entrusted with a similar, though a vastly more comprehensive, task, could be relied upon to resist it. Years later Brod remembered the exact wording of the answer he gave his friend upon the first announcement of what was expected from him: "If you seriously think me capable of such a thing," he said, "let me tell you here and now that I shall not carry out your wishes" (*T*, 330). Why, then, did Kafka insist on retaining Brod as the executor of his will?

The diaries present evidence enough to convince us that Kafka really intended to reject what he had written. He was an inexorable perfectionist and applied the same absolute standards to himself that he did to his contemporaries [*] and, for that matter, to the literature of the past. Yet he must also have felt that his achievements came as close to perfection as was humanly possible—as long as he applied literary criteria to them. This ambivalence resulted in blatant contradictions of conduct. He resisted the printing of almost all of his books, yet finally agreed each time. He also sanctioned the publication of the *A Hunger Artist* volume, in which he added three more stories to the title story, and he did so even after he had forsworn all and sundry publications. Moreover, there was not "much need of long arguments to persuade him to the publication" of his last book (*FK*, 198).

Nor could he have been fully convinced that the unfinished state of

---

[*] See his cruelly incisive comments on Karl Kraus (*J*, 54) and Franz Werfel (*DI*, 182, *DII*, 31, *B*, 424–425 f. *et passim*). Dora Dymant recalls a visit Werfel paid him in Berlin. Werfel read him parts of his latest book. Then Dora saw the visitor leave with tears in his eyes. When she entered the room she found Kafka in a state of profound shock; he had been unable to say a good word about Werfel's work (J. P. Hodin, "Erinnerungen an Franz Kafka," *Der Monat*, I [1949], 93).

his manuscripts sufficed as a reason for their destruction. The fragment had become the very hallmark of his vision and style, distin-
guishing it from the facile conclusiveness of what many among his
contemporaries—the Expressionists—had to say. He was raising questions, not giving answers, since answers could not be given any more
in his day and age. The figure of the Information Giver, which emerges
in varying disguises in the three major novels, testifies to his awareness
that information about authority and order in this world was no longer
obtainable. He may have recognized that this was the message he had
been called upon to deliver and that the imperfection of his delivery
identified him as the legitimate bearer of these painful tidings. He may
have wanted to be forgotten as a teacher of wisdom but to be remembered as a student craving for higher knowledge in spite of his
despair.

On the one hand, Kafka may have wanted his work to perish because in its hopelessness it mirrored the general condition of a world
in shambles. If he were convinced that the decline of this world was
inevitable, then why should he preserve the documents of this decline?
On the other hand, he had been too attentive a reader of Søren
Kierkegaard to overlook his cardinal sentence: "An individual cannot
assist or save a time, he can only express that it is lost." [8] He must have
understood that it was the first and perhaps the only function of literature in a waning age to serve as a witness to its decay and to counter-
balance the horror of decomposition by the fortitude which any genuine testimony requires. The very existence of his writings anticipated
the "hope beyond hopelessness, the transcendence of despair"—which,
more than twenty years after Kafka's death, Thomas Mann discovered
as the ultimate reward held out to the modern artist to compensate
for his torments.[9] Paradoxically the hopelessness of Kafka's writings
contained the only grain of hope that they would be appreciated for
what they were and what they said, and that his name would with-
stand oblivion.

He may even have thought of the destruction of his books as a religious act, a burnt offering. To Dora Dymant he described literature
as "something sacred, absolute, and unimpeachable." What he had
done in the past was worthless; in the future, however, a mystical
"freedom" would inspire him to produce the pure and absolute work
worthy of survival. He considered all previous achievements to be
provisional and intended to divest himself of them in a final effort of
self-purification.[10] But he also knew that the freedom for which he

longed was a freedom beyond all words, a freedom *from* words, if it existed at all for a man like him. Since 1912, when he had Gregor Samsa crave for an "unknown nourishment," his writings had been directed toward this ultimate liberation. Now, ten years later, he realized that this nourishment would not be known to him as long as he lived. Nor would the liberation come to pass during his lifetime. "There is a goal, but no way; what we call a way is hesitation" (*DF*, 36). This "way" had led him in circles around a goal which towered as inaccessibly beyond it as *The Castle* rises beyond the village. His writing testified to this way, this hesitation. On the other hand, this very writing had sustained him during all these years, although it did not guide him toward his aim. Allowing him to express his longing, it had provided him with a foretaste of the freedom to which it was supposed to lead him. The foretaste was all he would ever obtain of the unknown nourishment; the hesitation was all he would ever learn about his aim. He wanted to destroy his writings because they had not reached their aim, and he wanted to save them because in all their imperfection they held out to him a promise that his goal existed.

This was the dilemma he faced when he made out this testament. Since he could not solve the paradox, he delegated it to someone else. By appointing Max Brod to act as executor of his will, he allowed himself to arrive at the decision in principle that his books be burnt, while practically making sure that his decision had a fair chance of being disregarded.

Kafka knew that in all the years of their friendship Brod had identified himself more and more with the work he was now asked to obliterate. Some time before Kafka wrote his will, Brod had published one of the first critical appraisals of Kafka in *Die Neue Rundschau*. There he had exclaimed: "It is perfection, simply perfection, perfection of pure form," which ennobles Kafka's style (*FK*, 131). Brod felt that this perfect style sufficiently justified his decision to disobey the testament of his friend by reediting his published works and granting posterity access to the unpublished ones. "My decision . . ." he says in his postscript to *The Trial*,

rests . . . simply and solely on the fact that Kafka's unpublished work contains the most wonderful treasures, and measured against his own work, the best things he has written. In all honesty I must confess that this one fact of the literary and ethical value of what I am publishing would have been enough to decide me to do so, definitely, finally, and irresistibly (*T*, 332).

Kafka condemned his work because he measured it against a perfection which he knew was beyond his reach. Brod saved it because of its high degree of perfection, which he had been one of the first to see.

Brod has been justified by posterity, if worldly success can ever support a decision which necessitated the solution of an insoluble paradox. In order to perennialize this paradox in the realm of literature, Brod saved Kafka's books. By doing so he acted against Kafka's will and broke asunder the paradox his friend had posed for him and his conscience. Spellbound by the "magic of Kafka's personality," he reacted emotionally when he refused "to perform the holocaust" (*die herostratische Tat*) demanded of him (*T*, 329, 333). His conflict of conscience cannot have been so difficult as he claimed in view of the "fanatical veneration" which he confesses he felt for his friend (*T*, 330). Brod was too sure that Kafka was ultimately a hopeful writer and thinker ever to ask himself in all earnest whether, at least at times when he was overwhelmed by despair, he had not *really* meant that his manuscripts should be destroyed. But it may be demanding too much to expect Brod, who was prejudiced by personal proximity, to have known at such an early date exactly what he was doing and why he was doing it.*

---

* In view of the controversy which has enveloped Max Brod's administration of Kafka's literary estate, a preliminary assessment may be attempted:

1) Max Brod was Kafka's choice and must be accepted as such.

2) He has edited the Kafka papers according to his abilities, which are those of a writer and journalist and not those of a philologist. Recent scholarship has pointed to a number of inaccuracies and discrepancies in the textual material. But none of the inaccuracies have altered the Kafka image decisively.

3) As any other critic, Brod is entitled to his share of misinterpretations. The fact that he was one of the first to analyze Kafka's writings and thereby exerted a great influence on many early Kafka critics must not be held against him. Most of his misconceptions have since been corrected.

4) There are, on the other hand, contradictions in Brod's own interpretation of Kafka. Apropos of Kafka's symbolism he observes: "The happenings he describes . . . are, in the first place, self-explanatory, but they mean also at the same time *not only* themselves. A ray shines out from every detail, pointing to the eternal, the transcendental, the world of ideas. In every great work of art one finds the eternal shining through the mortal forms. In the case of Kafka, however, it has beyond this become a formal principle of his writing; one simply cannot any longer separate content from structure, so intimately have they united" (*FK*, 195; Brod's italics). The last sentence alone should have prevented Brod from changing the structure of *The Castle* arbitrarily by turning it into a theatrical play. (When he met with applause, he attempted a similar change with *Der Verschollene.*) Moreover, he accompanied the performance of his dramatization of *The Castle* in the Berlin Schlosspark-Theater with the following note: "Kafka's genius as a dramatist appears in the tight and sharply drawn structure of each

Brod could not help treating Kafka's testament as a personal document. But it was ultimately a piece of literature, stating once more the problem of Kafka's existence. Was he to destroy himself in his work in spite of the fact that he had sacrificed his life for it? Was he to preserve it in spite of his awareness that it never attained what it had been intended to attain—the unattainable? Just as the "Letter to His Father," Kafka's will deserves to be treated as a work of art, a paradox within a parable demanding interpretation. It also is unable to yield an unambiguous answer.

The Unknown Nourishment

Toward the end of his "Reflections," which date back to the critical years of 1917 and 1918, Kafka noted: " 'But then he returned to his work just as though nothing had happened.' This is a remark with which we are familiar from a vague variety of old stories, although perhaps it does not occur in any of them" (*DF*, 48). After Kafka had

---

scene. Every word in the dialogue 'comes off.' Dramatic above all, is the whole outline of the plot in which the conflict of two worlds unfolds" (*Program Notes, Schlosspark-Theater*, 22 [1953–1954], 13). If content and structure are inseparable in Kafka's novels and if the structure he chose for them is epical, then this structure cannot be dramatic at the same time. If Kafka's epical language is unique in its transparency, then it will not simultaneously "come off" as dialogue on the stage, since the law of genuine dramatic speech requires first and foremost unequivocal precision. That Brod condoned the dramatization of Kafka's works and actively participated in this enterprise cannot be called a misreading. It is a falsification.

5) There is some evidence that Brod monopolized the literary remains of Franz Kafka. His pamphlet *Verzweiflung und Erlösung im Werk Franz Kafkas* ("Despair and Redemption in Franz Kafka's work"), which was published by Fischer in 1959, contains on pp. 29–33 excerpts from letters Kafka wrote about 1914 to a Miss Grete B. These letters are absent from the general collection of Kafka's letters which Brod had edited a year earlier. In his pamphlet Brod also identified Miss Grete B. as the mysterious "Frau M. M.," who, he claimed in his biography, was the mother of Kafka's child. Since "Frau M. M." was deported by the Germans in 1944 without leaving a trace (*FK*, 242), no private considerations can have played a role in the omission of Kafka's letters from the 1958 edition.

Thus it appears that Max Brod was not the fully disinterested editor one would have wished Kafka to choose. Along with the text of his friend's writings he promoted his own interpretations, and he destroyed their form by putting two of Kafka's novels on the stage.

Finally, however, it has to be remembered that Brod could never have violated or misinterpreted Kafka's writings if he had not discovered and preserved them first. We would have preferred to owe Max Brod an unlimited debt of gratitude. But even within the limits he imposed on it, this gratitude is great.

learned about his disease and accepted his approaching death, he took up his old themes, ostensibly at the point where he had left them. But as he passed from crisis to crisis, from the conflict which produced the "Letter to His Father" to the conflict with Milena which precipitated his fear of death to the point where he composed his testament, he succeeded, as we have tried to show, in elevating the raw material of his life to the realm of literature. As life became parable, the parables he actually wrote became more and more personal. He noticed the change himself. "Writing denies itself to me," he remarks in one of the diary fragments.

Hence [my] plan for autobiographical investigations. Not biography but investigation and detection of the smallest possible component parts. Out of these I will then construct myself, as one whose house is unsafe wants to build a safe one next to it, if possible out of the material of the old one (*DF*, 350).

The "Letter" as well as most of the *Hunger Artist* stories * represent investigations of this kind. The term was broad enough to apply easily to a stage in Kafka's development as a writer where the documentary and the imagined merged to form a new unity.

Now art and the artist appear as his preoccupation. The universal anguish which had previously informed his images is being absorbed by his concern for art. To be sure, Kafka's protagonists are still conceived as representatives of humanity, but now they resemble Kafka the writer rather than Kafka the metaphysical outcast. The questions they raise are still far-reaching and profoundly unanswerable, but they are exemplified by figures questioning the possibility of art in a world without law. Repeatedly Kafka seems to return to the scene in *The Trial* where Joseph K., an Everyman of sorts, meets Titorelli, an artist of sorts. But now it is the figure of the artist who commands Kafka's attention; this figure is treated with greater compassion and even a certain amount of sympathy. An air of resignation adds a new shade of irony to these last stories.

Resolutely Kafka put an artist into the center of the title story of the *Hunger Artist* volume, the proofs of which he corrected on his deathbed (*FK*, 211). Aside from this story an artist appears in the charmingly lucid sketch "First Sorrow." A young trapeze artist desires

---

* The collection of four stories under the over-all title of *A Hunger Artist* were published in German as a separate volume in 1924. In English they are included in the volume entitled *The Penal Colony*.

to extend his work from one bar to two bars: "Only the one bar in my hands—how can I go on living!" His manager, a remarkably understanding and benevolent spokesman of reality, promises immediate relief for the artist's sorrow. A second trapeze will be installed right away. And yet, in spite of his matter-of-factness and common sense, the manager loses himself in fearful questions: "Once such ideas began to torment [the artist], would they ever quite leave him alone? Would they not rather increase in urgency? Would they not threaten his very existence" (234)? * The inner movement of this little piece, which is hardly longer than a well-told anecdote, is contrapuntal in a highly ironical fashion. It turns out that the manager—and not the artist—is the real victim of this "first sorrow," and that as far as the artist is concerned, the "first sorrow" may easily prove to be his last. His appetite for more daring and complicated performances once whetted, he may eventually be destroyed by his ever-growing desire for more and more perfection.

To call the next piece, "A Little Woman," a "thoroughly essential small allegory . . . of Kafka's Muse" [11] means to enforce a unity of theme on this volume which Kafka failed to provide. Instead of an allegory it contains the plotless thumbnail sketch of a woman whom Dora Dymant identified as the landlady of one of the apartments which she and Kafka had rented in the Steglitz district of Berlin in the fall of 1923.[12] Taken by itself the brief exercise reaffirms the alienation which existed between the writer and the most accidental among his fellow beings. It is the only one among the four stories contained in *A Hunger Artist* which does not sound the artist theme explicitly, although it is connected to the rest of the volume by the flexibility of its cadences and the ease of its tone.

"A Hunger Artist" itself antedates "A Little Woman" by at least a year and a half; in any case it was written before the January 1922 crisis. Here Kafka returns to the motif of the unknown nourishment which he had introduced in "The Metamorphosis." In the earlier story this image pointed quite generally to the never-to-be disclosed mystery governing man's life. Here it has been integrated in the theme of art, the Hunger Artist's art.

The tale deals with the art of fasting as well as with fasting as an art. The Hunger Artist is willing to dedicate his existence to the perfection of his craft; hence he feels justified in making all-inclusive

---

* Numbers without letters in this and the following section refer to the American edition of *The Penal Colony.*

claims in return. "Just try to explain to anyone the art of fasting!" he exclaims at the height of his career. "Anyone who has no feeling for it cannot be made to understand it" (254). In the original this creed of the Hunger Artist is patterned rhythmically after the words with which Goethe's Faust pronounces the superiority of his all-embracing view of the world over the petty rationalism of his entourage. Even if our artist is not a superman like Goethe's hero, he is certainly a virtuoso, a star of starvation, and his appeal, like the fascination of any romantic hero, is consciously emotional.

His desire for starvation is insatiable. He is convinced that his capacity for fasting has no limits whatever.* He is inspired by the ambition to be "not only the record hunger artist of all time, which presumably he was already," but to surpass himself "by a performance beyond human imagination" (247). This grasp for what can no longer be grasped identifies him as a Kafka hero. So does the paradox that he will have to die from starvation as soon as he succeeds in living up to his noble aim.

His impresario has imposed a forty-day limit on his fasting, a period which is measured, absurdly enough, by a clock instead of a calendar. Yet his reason for limiting the Hunger Artist's enthusiasm for perfection has nothing to do with the performer. He does not act from a realization that the Artist, too, is subject to the necessities of life. Instead, his reason—which Kafka with a touch of malice calls a "good" one—is concerned with the audience. The manager has observed that "for about forty days the interest of the public could be stimulated, . . . but after this the town began to lose interest" (246–247). It is not the Artist, but the public that matters. The performer should be convinced by this argument. But his attitude toward the spectators is as paradoxical as his attitude toward himself and his art.

Not only is this Artist a man driven by the desire to achieve perfection. He is also a showman who needs spectators as he achieves his unheard-of deed. To suffer starvation by himself and for himself would not satisfy him. He depends on the acclaim, the excitement of the crowds, the military bands, the young ladies, and all the other ritual paraphernalia of a popular success. And yet this popular success forces

* According to Meno Spann, the American physician Dr. Henry Tanner actually established a world record by fasting forty days in 1880. This record has long since been broken, thus providing empirical evidence to support our artist's irrational desire to extend his fasting ("Franz Kafka's Leopard," *Germanic Review*, XXXIV [1959], 101).

him to interrupt his achievement long before he has come anywhere
near the stage of accomplishment he feels able to reach. "His public
pretended to admire him so much, why should it have so little patience
with him; if he could endure fasting longer, why should not the public endure it" (247)?

It is the public which answers this question, although in an unexpected way. For reasons unknown to Artist, impresario, and reader alike
the crowds begin to disperse and his fame starts to decline. "Everywhere, as if by secret agreement, a positive revulsion from professional
fasting was in evidence" (250). Thereupon the Artist dismisses the
impresario and hires himself to a circus, a big enterprise which ac-
commodates him somewhere near the animal cages. The former star
has now been moved from the center of attention to the periphery;
the one-man show has degenerated to something less than a side show;
the virtuoso is treated like an animal or even worse; "strictly speaking,
he was only an impediment on the way to the menagerie" (253).

Now he is able to reach perfection by starving himself to death. He
is at liberty to indulge in his life's dream undisturbed. No more limits
are set for him. But the audience he had hoped would watch him
perform his supreme act is gone. He is left to solitude and oblivion.
Time itself is suspended; the little board which used to tell his fasting
days has long been showing the same number, and no more mention
is made of his clock. He is breaking all records, but his achievement
remains unrecorded since the public is absent.

And when once in a time some leisurely passer-by stopped, made merry
over the old figure on the board and spoke of cheating, that was in its
way the stupidest lie ever invented by indifference and inborn malice,
since it was not the Hunger Artist who was cheating, he was working
honestly, but the world was cheating him of his reward (254).

The reward he has in mind is the public acknowledgment that he is
reaching perfection now. Without this acknowledgment perfection will
forever be imperfect.

One of Kafka's "Reflections" reads as follows: "One must not cheat
anyone, not even the world of its victory" (*DF*, 39). But in the case of
the Hunger Artist the world has seen to it that the victory remains in
its possession. Moreover, it forces the dying man to realize the contradictions inherent in his life's occupation. "Forgive me, everybody,"
he whispers with his last strength. If he has really been cheated by

the world, why should he now ask the cheater, the world, to forgive? "I always wanted you to admire my fasting," he continues. The admiration he claimed was based on the assumption that the efforts he devoted to his task were extraordinary. He alone was able to do what he did, and more than common exertions were needed to overcome difficulties that no one but he could master. This is the very nature of records and record breaking. Yet in the same breath he says about his fasting: "But you should not admire it" (255). Kafka has prepared us well to grasp the meaning of this blatant self-contradiction. Early in the story he informs us that this Artist's uniqueness consisted solely in the fact that "he alone knew, what no other initiate knew, how easy it was to fast" (246). The very thought of a meal, we learn, has given him nausea. But only now, with his last words, does he betray his secret: "I have to fast, I cannot help it, . . . because I could not find the food I liked. If I had found it, believe me, I should have made no fuss and stuffed myself like you or anyone else" (255).

The art of this Artist is a negative performance. His fasting represents a passive act, which is a paradox. Running counter to human nature, it may, at least in the minds of a curious crowd, have proved attractive, so long as it was performed as a show of self-denial and a feast of sacrifice. Our Artist, however, was cheating even when he thought that he was working honestly; he could not help starving himself; he was forced into his fanatically pursued profession by the absence of the unknown nourishment appropriate to him and his tastes. His art is produced by a deficiency, and the question whether he is at fault for not finding the right food or whether the world is to be blamed for not providing him with it, this question aims ultimately at the meaning of the role that the artist performs in any kind of human context.

We are not surprised to discover that Kafka refrains from spelling out an answer to this question. He does, however, allow the Artist to die with the conviction that his performance is going to outlast his life. "In his dimming eyes remained the firm though no longer proud conviction that he was still continuing the fast" (255). Disregarding the world and its neglect, humbled by the cognition of the deceit that was his art, he carries the paradox of his existence beyond the threshold of his life. Only there, in the beyond, is the nature of the nourishment that would have satisfied him revealed. Knowing it, he appears to be sated for the first time. He need not strive any longer; he possesses it at last. Therefore his face shows conviction without pride, firmness without the triumph of victory. It is, alas, the face of a dead man.

Previously Kafka had used many images related to food and eating to express the paradox of existence.[13] One of the most persuasive is the following: "He gobbles up the leavings and crumbs that fall from his own table; in this way he is, of course, for a little while more thoroughly sated than all the rest, but he forgets how to eat from the table itself. In this way, however, there cease to be any crumbs and leavings" (*DF*, 42). Unable to lead a fulfilled life, he depleted its very substance by doggishly feeding on its waste. Thus he never came to know the nourishment, the nurturing elements, of his own existence. The Hunger Artist, on the other hand, refuses to accept the waste—and in an act of daring revaluation he declares all ordinary food to be waste. Refusal becomes custom; custom turns into sickness, a sickness unto death. Yet from this sickness he derives fulfillment, the deadly fulfillment of his art. Literally he pays with his life for having partaken of the sublime nourishment, perfection. Kafka seems to revert here to the aesthetic philosophy pronounced in Thomas Mann's "Tonio Kröger." But what was an intellectual disquisition for Tonio Kröger and his author became a fatal reality for this Hunger Artist as well as for his creator.

The story ends with the Hunger Artist's demise and transfiguration. Although the artist's self-fulfillment is alluded to in most discreet tones, Kafka was not satisfied with this comparatively conciliatory ending. He added a more drastic finale. A great cat takes the place of the dead man. The animal, a leopard rather than a panther,[14] is supposed to balance the art of the Artist by the uninhibited vitality of a young animal that has remained completely natural in spite of its imprisonment. "It lacked nothing," while the Artist was consumed by universal want. "The food he liked was brought him without hesitation by the attendants," whereas the impresario had to use dubious tricks to persuade the Artist to accept even a bite. The animal's "noble body, furnished almost to the bursting point with all that it needed, seemed to carry freedom around with it, too" (255). The Artist's freedom, on the other hand, was identical with his deadly idea of perfection. Needless to say, the leopard attracts the crowds that the Artist missed when he tried to find fulfillment.

The image of this leopard is masterfully realized in a few sentences that convey a feeling of the strength which animates the animal. It is nevertheless an oversimplification. If Kafka had wanted to allegorize in his Artist the impotence of the spirit as opposed to the unbroken power of life, the leopard's *joie de vivre* would, by contrast, have revealed the intention of the story. But such a simple antithesis cannot have been Kafka's purpose. His story was meant to show that the Hunger Artist's life problem was a paradox and remained unsolved. Thus the magnificently unequivocal image of the cat was superfluous and, perhaps, even out of place.

On the other hand, Kafka uses the simplicity of the leopard to reveal the complexity with which the figure of the Artist is endowed. He has been interpreted as "a mystic, a holy man, or a priest," as an allegory of "man as a spiritual being" [15] or as a parabolical example of the possibility of achieving a "free spiritual existence" by ascetic practices.[16] In supplying interpretations for this figure, the critics seem to have overlooked the fact that here more than in any previous story the paradox of Kafka's own literary genius has been stated in purely artistic terms. The Hunger Artist shares with his author an insatiable desire for a spiritual security. Yet now his quest is reduced to the sphere of art, and most of the mystery of the story is vested in the artist-hero. There are, in other words, no more intermediaries confusing his dealings with the outside world. Even the impresario is "his partner in an unparalleled career" (251). Nor is there any supreme authority who would summon him or whom he could challenge. The heaven and hell of perfection is bred in his own heart. His conflict, still metaphysical, still insoluble, has been confined to the realm of his art.

This art is fatal since it can only be perfected by the Artist's death. In view of the place it assumes in Kafka's work and the mastery of its execution, this story is a perfection, a fatal fulfillment, or at least comes very close to it. Who, after having read it, would deny the Artist a degree of permanence? One cannot help wondering whether Kafka, by stating in his will that it was to be exempted from unconditional destruction, had not suggested that he himself was willing to perish like his hero and yet harbored the hope that he would, however conditionally, survive in the story itself. The Hunger Artist is dead; may the "Hunger Artist" live!

Something of a Balance

The fourth piece of the *Hunger Artist* collection, the fable "Josephine the Singer, or the Mouse Folk" likewise concentrates on the artist as the central theme. As the title indicates, it adds the countertheme of society to Kafka's exploration of the heroine's character and destiny. "The story," he informed Brod in one of the notes he scribbled when he was no longer able to speak, "is going to have a new title, 'Josephine the Singer, or the Mouse Folk.'" And he continued: "Subtitles like this are not very pretty, it is true, but in this case it has perhaps a special meaning. The title has something of a balance" (*FK*, 205–206). This extension of an artist's portrait to include the group, the folk around him, represented a new venture for Kafka. At the same time it may have been his last word.*

Because of the novelty of this venture Kafka may have wished to remove the tale slightly from the sphere of human experience. He chose an animal mask for his protagonist and made the hero a heroine. Josephine the mouse singer succeeds Joseph K. Thus she is a relative twice removed from her author.

Still, Josephine is much more closely identified with her creator than is Joseph K. Is she really a mouse, and her tale a genuine animal story? It has been observed that the word "mouse" appears only in the title and that with some minor changes the fable could almost as well have been realized on the human level.[17] The addition of the word "mouse" may have yielded the special meaning to which Kafka referred in his deathbed note quoted above. Yet even this change cannot conceal the fact that the story dares to touch once more upon a very personal question. Kafka's attitude toward society was certainly one of his most tormenting problems. Not being able to solve it and ever more hesitant to tackle it explicitly, he had stated it again and again when he allowed the outsider, the bachelor, to appear in his books. Having identified, near his death, the outsider as the artist, he approached the traumatic spot once more and spoke out about it.

The "or" in the title of the story not only sets Josephine apart from the Mouse Folk, it also establishes the coexistence, although precarious, of the heroine and the group around her. The narrator of the fable, who is supposed to represent the Mouse Folk, candidly admits that he is "half in sympathy" with the singer's opponents (259). He stresses the honesty of his report by questioning his own objectivity; at the same time he intimates that the other half of his sympathy belongs to Josephine. If this is not an expression of neutrality, it shows at least that

* "Wagenbach" suggests that the story was written in the spring of 1924, contradicting Brod's surmise that "Investigations of a Dog" was Kafka's last work (Postscript to the German edition of *Beschreibung eines Kampfes*, 350).

he has become conscious of his ambivalence. Consequently, his account is couched in much friendlier terms than, say, the description the landlady gives of K. in *The Castle.*

Furthermore, our narrator may have been induced to greater mildness by the fact that Josephine has vanished, possibly for good. She has thrown tantrums and left the community before, but "this time she has deserted us entirely" (276). Her disappearance is the only element of plot traceable in the story, but it suffices to color the narrator's words with the brighter tones of a near-eulogy. He does not force us to side either with him or with the heroine, or to vacillate between the two sides; the "or" of the title is, so to speak, the beam that holds the two scales of the balance together. The suspense of the story is created by the constant rising and falling of Josephine's scale in the report we are given about her; in the end the narrator even succeeds in achieving an equilibrium of sorts between the Mouse Folk and its singer. To specify the distribution of weight on this balance and to expose the rationale behind this highly precarious equilibrium are the deeper purposes of the tale.

One naturally expects Josephine's existence as an artist to be as contradictory as her art, for mice do not usually sing. The narrator himself keeps wondering whether her song is not just an ordinary piping. "We all pipe, but of course no one dreams of making out that our piping is an art, we pipe without thinking of it, indeed without noticing it, and there are even many among us who are quite unaware that piping is one of our characteristics" (257). Like the Hunger Artist's fasting, Josephine's piping is only the exaggeration of a very common experience. As every man has felt hunger and has conquered his desire to eat, so does every mouse have the ability to pipe. Josephine's piping connects her to her milieu instead of elevating her above the other members of the crowd. In this respect her art is seen as the hypertrophy of the trivial.

Moreover the German word, *pfeifen,* carries distinct overtones of indifference and even scorn. Josephine can be relied upon to bring these overtones to bear on her audience when she is in one of her dark moods. "Ich pfeife auf euren Schutz," she exclaims; a highly idiomatic phrase for which the translation offers only a rather lame equivalent: "Your protection is not worth an old song" (263).

In brighter moments, however, she brings to her performance the magic of her personality. "If you stand before her," the narrator explains, "it is not merely a piping; to comprehend her art it is necessary not only to hear but to see her" (258). Her business is show business, and part of her success is her intimate knowledge of every trick of the trade. But she uses her showmanship primarily to prove a negation: "When you sit before her, you know: this piping of hers is no piping" (259). What her song really is we are never told.

She is the highly professional performer of an art which is at best an illusion, at worst nothing. "A mere nothing in voice, a mere nothing in execution," the narrator describes her in a fit of ungentlemanly frankness (266). The basically negative character of her performance is only one quality that she shares with the Hunger Artist. Like him she is willing to stake her total existence for the execution of her art.

So there she stands, the delicate creature, shaken by vibrations especially below the breast. . . . It is as if she has concentrated all her strength on her song, as if from everything in her that does not directly serve her singing all strength has been withdrawn, almost all power of life, as if she were laid bare and abandoned (260–261).

To be sure, she knows how to dramatize this total commitment and to translate it into an image of tragic infirmity. But behind this apparent weakness she hides the determination to achieve her aim at any price, even at the price of self-sacrifice.

Josephine is driven by an ambition as boundless as the Hunger Artist's; but being a woman and a "frail creature" at that (263), she depends even more than he on the public's recognition. "What she wants," the opposition suspects, "is public, unambiguous, permanent recognition of her art, going far beyond any precedent so far known" (272). She is resolved to conquer time, not by the immortality of her performance, but by the permanence of her reward. This adds realism to her plight and a further human touch to her personality.

For a long time she has been fighting to be relieved of the services which every member of the community has to render. In this desire she displays her shrewdness and her hypochondriac sensitivity. Since the mice spend most of their time thinking about economic affairs, the singer can be assured that the full artistic value of her song has been appreciated only if she is released from the duty of earning her daily bread. (Her problem is like Kafka's own; the fact that it took a fatal sickness to grant him the freedom of creation which society had denied him all his life adds a touch of bitter irony to the singer's demands.) The people reject Josephine's claim; they "listen to her arguments and pay no attention" (271). At least there is no overt hostility in their

refusal; there is even a faint hint of regret. The narrator compares the
Mouse Folk's refusal to comply with the primadonna's wishes to "a
grown-up person deep in thought turning a deaf ear to a child's babble,
fundamentally well disposed but not accessible" (275). Josephine reacts accordingly, that is, she behaves like a child; she feels misunderstood and persecuted. She mopes and pouts. She punishes her public
by cutting her coloraturas—a rare sign of naïveté on her part, for the
Mouse Folk could not care less. After acknowledging her final defeat,
she disappears completely.

Josephine would never admit that such trivialities as economic
reasons prompted her to fight so desperately. Nor, the narrator maintains, has she become so insistent because she realizes that old age is
beginning to show in her appearance and in her art.

For her there is no growing old and no falling off in her voice. If she
makes demands it is not because of outward circumstances but because of
an inner logic. She reaches for the highest garland not because it is momentarily hanging a little lower but because it is the highest; if she had any say
in the matter she would have it still higher (273).

The inner logic the narrator mentions is dictated by the paradox of her
existence: in order to save her self-respect she has to be accepted for
what she obviously is not, a singer. Thus she reaches for the garland of
admiration rather than aspire to reach ultimate perfection in her art.
Her paradox is the dilemma of the performer who wants his personal
appeal to last forever, knowing full well that it is the gift of the moment.
How can Josephine hope for a recognition surviving all times when
she herself is subjected to the passing of time? Yet even if she and her
voice had been blessed with perennial beauty, she would never have
elicited unconditional praise from her nation. For the Mouse Folk is
composed of highly critical individuals engaged in a fierce struggle for
existence. Moreover, they are "completely unmusical" (256).

Her own contradictoriness meets with an equally unresolved contradictoriness on the part of her listeners. The narrator states this in
the third sentence of his account: "There is no one but is carried away
by her singing, a tribute all the greater as we are not a music-loving
race" (256). Traditionally this race is not averse to singing, and it
even treasures songs as part of its national heritage. It is true that
nobody sings these songs any more; nevertheless, Josephine's opponents
use this time-hallowed, though highly derivative, tradition to prove
that her piping does not live up to the accepted standards. In her own

mind she may be what Richard Wagner used to call a *Neutöner,* and her song is likely to appear to her as a kind of "music of the future." But the opposite is true. Even the most stubborn among her critics finds in her song "something of our poor brief childhood, . . . something of lost happiness that can never be found again, but also something of active daily life, of its small gaieties, unaccountable and yet springing up and not to be obliterated" (269). Her audiences wonder why they keep flocking around her, and yet they exert themselves for her as a matter of course; they leave their daily work, they forget the emergencies which seem to be daily occurrences, and they even send out messengers and post sentries in order to assure that the size of the audience will satisfy the artist (261–262).

The mice are a very sober group and the narrator expresses their consensus when he explains that the artist's role consists primarily in representation. This nation has no secular or spiritual leader; it has only the singer. It does not matter that the singer cannot sing as long as her recitals provide the community with the semblance of a center. This train of thought he expresses in a not-so-pious wish: "May Josephine be spared from perceiving that the mere fact of our listening to her is proof that she is no singer" (266). Such an aphorism as this, however cruelly incisive it may be, can never fathom the depth of the relationship that exists between the artist and her public. To be sure, the most malicious among her opponents air their anger by saying, "The sight of Josephine is enough to make us stop laughing." But the narrator takes great pains to elucidate this harsh judgment and even turn it into an indication of hidden affection. The people are not blind to the artist's little mannerisms and considerable eccentricities; they are tempted to ridicule them; "in Josephine there is much to make one laugh." At the same time they have in all sincerity adopted the artist. Although they will never be able to accept Josephine for the singer she pretends to be, they approach her tenderly and seriously. "What is entrusted to one's care one does not laugh at" (262–263). Although her function is to represent, the represented ones refuse to treat her only as a symbol, and Josephine refuses to serve as one.

Brod has identified the Mouse Folk as the Jewish nation (*FK,* 192–193). Following in his footsteps, Carl R. Woodring recently saw Josephine as "a soloist and leading actress, . . . attached to a Jewish theatrical troupe singing plays (operas) in Yiddish, of the kind to which Kafka had become attracted in 1910 and especially in 1911." [18] Something may be said in favor of these interpretations. In a diary note written late in 1911 under the influence of the Yiddish actors, Kafka stresses the importance which literature possesses for the development of small nations. He proceeds in very much the same fashion as that chosen by the Mouse narrator to prove Josephine's importance for her people. A sound literary life, Kafka says in the diary, offers to an endangered and suppressed people

the transitory awakening in the younger generation of higher aspirations, which nevertheless leaves its permanent mark, the acknowledgment of literary events as objects of political solicitude, a dignified antithesis between father and son and the possibility of discussing this, the presentation of national faults in a manner that is very painful, to be sure, but also liberating and deserving forgiveness (*DI*, 192).

Josephine fills a position very much like the one Kafka outlined in his diary, for she, too, addresses herself to the very young, "especially in times of stress" (268). At least on the surface she is the political rather than the artistic rallying point of the nation; her recital is "not so much a performance of song as an assembly of the people" (265). The attitude of the Mouse community toward the artist is a paternal one, and for this reason they take her seriously. This sobriety proves, if nothing else, that the people recognize themselves in her and are ready to forgive her weakness, which only reflects the nation's own plight: her piping, "which rises up where everyone else is pledged to silence, comes almost like a message from the whole people to each individual; Josephine's thin piping amidst grave decisions is almost like our people's precarious existence amidst the tumult of a hostile world" (265–266).

"There are," Kafka continues in his diary note about the small nations,

fewer experts employed in literary history, but literature is less a concern of literary history than of the people, and thus, if not purely, it is at least reliably preserved. For the claim that the national consciousness of a small people makes on the individual is such that everyone must always be prepared to know that part of literature which has come down to him, to support it, to defend it—to defend it even if he does not know it (*DI*, 193).

The ideas young Kafka developed in 1911 stem from Johann Gottfried Herder; [19] they were disseminated throughout the period of Romanticisim and led to the discovery of many folk songs and the emergence of many a folk singer; and when, after 1848, Europe's small nations began to stir and rise, they readily borrowed these ideas and adjusted them to the needs engendered by the awakening of their own national self-awareness. Similar thoughts were still alive among the Czechs when

Kafka wrote this essay in his diary; he cannot have remained blind to their impact on the political aspirations and cultural achievements, especially on the music, of his Slavic neighbors. Kafka applied them, somewhat naïvely it would seem today, to whatever civilization he saw embodied in his Yiddish friends from Warsaw.

The Mouse Folk in his fable, however, do not answer the description of a small nation in the process of national awakening. Josephine will be forgotten, says the narrator in the end, "since we are no historians" (*da wir keine Geschichte treiben*—277). More strongly even than the translation does the original imply that the people who are no historians are also lacking in historical consciousness. Absorbed in their day-to-day struggle for survival they have all but forsworn history. The narrator calls his folk "inured . . . to suffering, not sparing themselves, swift in decision, well acquainted with death, timorous only to the eye in the atmosphere of reckless daring which they constantly breathe, and as prolific as they are bold"—which are all properties necessary to meet the emergencies of the moment and to brave the dangers of the present hour. The people have, he adds, "always somehow managed to save themselves, although at the cost of sacrifices which make historians —generally speaking we ignore historical research entirely—quite horror-struck" (264). This lack of interest by the Mouse Folk in their own history casts considerable doubt on their affinity with the Jews, who are extremely conscious of history, who have produced an important body of historiographical texts, and who were, at the time when "Josephine" was written, engaged in a historical enterprise of some magnitude, Zionism. (Although Brod may attribute too much importance to Kafka's sympathies with this movement, these sympathies existed and prove Kafka's awareness of the historical forces at work in Zionism.)

Even if the Mouse Folk are forgetful of their historical background, they still have preserved a few notions of their prehistoric, mythical past: "In the old days our people did sing; this is mentioned in legends." Whatever memory of antiquity the people still possess is confined to music, and it is here that Josephine comes in as a bearer of nostalgic messages, which remind the individual of his youth and the nation of its past. But these messages are indistinct beyond recognition, and the people are therefore more than doubtful about their roots in tradition: "We have an inkling of what singing is, and Josephine's art does not really correspond to it" (257). Josephine's song cannot play the role Kafka had assigned to literature in a small nation simply because it is not understood to be part of the nation's heritage; still more simply, because it is not understood at all and therefore not appreciated. You do not unite a nation around a symbol which is emptied of its meaning and is therefore both unwilling and unable to serve in such a function.

The Mouse Folk do not look for the messages which Josephine might convey to them if she were a national prophetess. "Is it her singing that enchants us," the narrator asks, "or is it not rather the solemn stillness enclosing her frail little voice" (259)? Is it not, we are tempted to extend this question, the "solemn stillness" behind Josephine's song that holds the ultimate secret of her art and her appeal? For her persecuted and war-stricken people silence has become the sole, though negative, token of the peace which their ancestors may have enjoyed in the past. "Tranquil peace is the music we love best," the narrator admits in the beginning of his report (256). For Kafka himself, on the other hand, this "solemn stillness" is once again a statement of the ineffability of the ineffable. The wordlessness beyond Josephine's song points to a place where words instead of silence promise peace, and it may well be that the Mouse Folk hear this very word, peace, resounding when they flock around the piping singer.

Kafka says in one of his fragments: "Confession and the lie are one and the same. In order to confess, one tells lies. One cannot express what one is; for this *is* precisely what one is; one can communicate only what one is not, that is, the lie. *Only in the chorus there may be a certain truth*" (*DF*, 308; italics mine). Insofar as Josephine is accepted and recognized by her people, she is taken for what she is. The mice do not question whether she is a true artist or not. This does not mean to say that they are convinced of the truth of her artistry. They simply do not ask this question at all. What she says, sings, pretends, and claims is disregarded. Conversely, the report of the narrator, who is, after all, a leader of the Mouse chorus, can be read as an attempt on the part of Kafka to establish the amount of truth which a community can still discover and communicate about itself.

"Our people," the narrator says, "quietly, without visible disappointment, a self-confident mass in perfect equilibrium, . . . our people continue on their way" (277). But whither will their way lead them? A people without history have no aim beyond the sheer continuation of their journey. Their equilibrium is perfect because it is not seriously disturbed either by memories or by expectations. Their self-confidence is gained at the price of their being unconscious of themselves as a nation. Their destination in the future is oblivion. To read into this "truth" a glorification of the people [20] means to disturb the balance of the story and to disregard the wording of the text. The truth about the people lies in its existence and defies an unambiguous statement just as much as does the destiny of the individual or the song of the singer.

Josephine, the narrator sums up, "is a small episode in the eternal history of our people, and the people will get over the loss of her." The people without historians and historic consciousness suddenly appear to possess an eternal history, of which the singer is an example, if only a small one. But a history which is experienced only under the aspect of eternity has lost all human perspective, is not measurable by days, or years, or generations, or epochs. It is, in other words, either a cliché or a paradox to be solved only by him who has seen eternity with his own eyes. This no one has done before the hour of his death.

Josephine is approaching this moment. Whether she deigns to re-appear among her people or not, she is about to depart forever. "Her road . . . must go downhill. The time will soon come when her last notes sound and die into silence." But the narrator has been too rash when he dismisses the loss of Josephine as one simply to be forgotten as soon as possible. Exploring the meaning her death may have to the people, he resorts to questions. "Not that it will be easy for us," he admits, and then begins to ask:

How can our gatherings take place in utter silence? Still, were they not silent even when Josephine was present? Was her actual piping notably louder and more alive than the memory of it will be? Was it even in her lifetime more than a simple memory? Was it not rather because Josephine's singing was past losing in this way that our people in their wisdom esteemed it so highly?

Her singing has been past losing since it is impossible to lose what one does not possess. The "solemn stillness" behind her song will survive her words, will survive her since it is a projection of the people's desire for tranquillity and independent from her and her art. If it is possible to remember silence (which is a negation), then this silence will linger on in the memory of these people who are averse to historical recollections. Thus we see behind the narrator's questions a paradox looming, the paradox which underlies the relationship of Josephine and the Mouse Folk to one another.

Now the narrator is able to predict that "Josephine . . . will happily lose herself in the numberless throng of the heroes of our people, and soon, since we are no historians, will enjoy the heightened redemption of being forgotten like all her brothers" ("[Sie wird] in gesteigerter Erlösung vergessen sein wie alle ihre Brüder"—277). Do these words, "heightened redemption," give us any clue to a positive resolution of Josephine's paradox? Once more we have to stop and ask what they are intended to express.

At first sight they express an absurdity. Redemption is an absolute notion, logically resisting any further degree of comparison. One may believe in redemption or belittle it; one may be granted salvation or be barred from it; in no case, however, will one be able to increase the superlative quality which the word connotes. By heightening Josephine's redemption, Kafka makes relative an absolute and destroys its unconditional character.

In the context of the narrator's last words the phrase assumes a more distinct meaning. Josephine's personal death sets an end to the tribulations and contradictions which had disturbed her life. Thus it can be called a redemption, if only a redemption from her sufferings. Yet she also dies to her nation and is allowed to join "the numberless throngs of heroes" who have died before her. Since the narrator is the spokesman of the collective, he inevitably ranks the group higher than the individual. In this sense her redemption can be heightened. Through it, however, she will enter a mausoleum of oblivion where she will be forgotten with the rest of her brothers, receding like them into the namelessness of an unremembered past. Even this heightened redemption is devoid of any sign pointing to a positive solution. By granting Josephine an oblivion which she will share with the rest of her brothers, Kafka establishes the equilibrium of the balance, the image with which he chose to describe this tale. It is the equilibrium of a perfect paradox.

This paradox sustains the story which Kafka, by implication, had destined to be destroyed and which he was nevertheless busy readying for print on his deathbed. The question of what he understood by oblivion as well as by the redemption to which it leads will remain forever open.

A Castle Within

While the "Hunger Artist" conveys to the reader the unresolved ambiguity of Kafka's attitude toward the relationship between artist and art and "Josephine" is intended to make a similarly noncommittal

statement about the interaction of artist and society, "The Burrow" pronounces with a certain finality on the work of art itself.

It is a very late story. According to Brod, it was written in Kafka's
last year, 1923–1924.[21] "Wagenbach" specifies the fall of 1923 as the
actual time of its composition, whereas Spann calls it the last piece
Kafka ever wrote.[22] Spann is certainly correct in attributing a greater
conclusiveness to "The Burrow" than to the related late fable, "Investigations of a Dog." *

In an almost allegorical way "The Burrow" is identical with Kafka's
own work. Since the story proper is part of his work, it also continually
reflects itself. While the narrator, an anonymous and basically shapeless forest animal, describes the hole it has dug in the soil, Kafka
explains in a multitude of hardly veiled hints that he is about to discuss
the very nature of his own writings. The reader passes through Kafka's
books when he follows the animal through the corridors and fortifications of its cave. The story surrounds the narrator, who remains
somewhat nebulous, with the intricate imagery of his work, which is
described in painstaking detail. Never has Brod chosen a more appropriate title for a Kafka story than when he called this one "The Burrow."

Near the Burrow's entrance (which the animal, characteristically,
refers to as "exit" [91] †), there is a labyrinth, called by the animal
with "a certain sentiment . . . its first achievement" (*dieses Erstlingswerk*—93). Reviewing the Burrow as a totality, the animal is ready
to admit that "it is always a fault to have only one copy" (*ein Exemplar*
—89). The expressions *Erstlingswerk* and *Exemplar* are primarily literary terms; outside of this story it would be absurd to talk of holes in
the ground as "copies." (The German *Exemplar*, semantically much
more closely related to the book trade than the English "copy," carries
also the overtones of *Exempel*, example.) Even at the end of his life

---

* "Investigations" unites the themes of nourishment (material and spiritual),
individual versus community, and art, the latter represented by the mysterious
"soaring dogs" or *Lufthunde* (*GW*, 34). These *Lufthunde* are linguistically patterned after the Yiddish expression *Luftmensch* for swindler, braggart, and finally
anyone who is a bohemian. Moreover, "Investigations" reflects the exploratory nature of Kafka's creativity (Wilhelm Emrich, *Franz Kafka* [Bonn: Athenäum, 1958],
62). Yet these explorations never crystallize into one cogent image and the story
dissolves in imperfection. It may be called an attempt on the part of Kafka at
formulating, ironically, an epistemology; yet this attempt was doomed to failure,
since his thought processes required symbols, not abstractions, in order to become
communicable at all.

† Numbers without letters in this section refer to the American edition of
The Great Wall of China (1948).

Kafka was not willing to observe the natural world except through the looking glass of literature.

From the fact that the Burrow lies hidden deep under the surface of an unknown forest we must not conclude that Kafka is embracing nature and its Creator here. The labyrinthine seclusion of the wood is as much an allegorical image as is the digging of the animal itself. As early as 1904 Kafka wrote to Brod: "We are grubbing through ourselves like the moles and emerge from these sand passages completely blackened, stretching our poor little feet into the air and asking for compassion" (*B*, 29). And on July 12, 1922, he begins another letter to Brod in the same vein: "I am now running around or sitting petrified, just as would a desperate animal in its burrow" (*B*, 390). About the image of the forest, on the other hand, he wrote to Milena:

I, an animal of the forest, was at that time hardly in the forest, lay somewhere in a dirty ditch (dirty only as a result of my being there, of course). . . . Fundamentally I was still only the animal, belonged still only in the forest. . . . You had to recognize oddities which suggested the forest which is my origin and my true homeland. . . . I had to return to the darkness, I could not stand the sun, I was desperate, really, like an animal gone astray. . . . You ask me how I live, this is how I live (*LM*, 199–200).

The cave as origin and true homeland, the forest as a misleading maze, the flight from day into darkness—these are also the primary realities of the animal that hides in the Burrow.

Yet there is another side to the Burrow. To the animal it represents a work of creation, an element of solidity among the nightmarish uncertainties of life. The idea of using the Burrow as the symbol of a writer's work may have occurred to Kafka when he read Thomas Mann's short sketch "The Railway Accident," which was first published by the Vienna *Neue Freie Presse* in 1909. Here the writer-narrator compares his literary output to a "clever foxhole." [23] But the idea of the Burrow was, in its inherent ambiguity, an image that had to impress itself on Kafka regardless of any outside source. The *Bau* * resembles the labyrinth, with which, under Kafka's touch, it acquires an uncanny relationship.

Burrow, maze, and tower, three kinds of construction, predominate in the imagery of Kafka's later writings. Thus the parable "The Great Wall of China" which Brod had originally called *Beim Bau der Chi-*

---

* For the linguistic ambiguity inherent in the German word *Bau* ("burrow," "building"), see p. 136 above.

nesischen Mauer (1917), contains a comparison of the wall with the Tower of Babel (155–157). The Tower of Babel, a labyrinthine edifice, a utopian vision of man's presumption and the inaccessibility of the absolute, in turn casts its shadow over the grand design of *The Castle*. In his third Octavo Notebook Kafka himself seems to establish this connection when he notes: "If it had been possible to build the Tower of Babel without ascending it, it would have been permitted" (*DF*, 36). It seems that he intended to lead the reader back from the lofty heights of the Tower to the tortuous abode of the animal in "The Burrow" (and to the underground corridors of the Herrenhof Inn in *The Castle* as well), for he adds in one of his "Fragments": "What are you building?—I want to dig a subterranean passage. Some progress must be made. My station up there is much too high." Pointedly he concludes: "We are digging the pit of Babel" (*DF*, 349). And the core of all these images may be found in the beginning of an entry in the Fourth Octavo Notebook where he says: "Everything fell in with his intentions and contributed to the building program ("Alles fügte sich ihm zum Bau"—*DF*, 105).

The Tower of Babel resembles *The Castle* in that it represents infinitely more than Kafka's literary output, namely, man's never-to-be fulfilled desire to take part in a dialogue with the "Other," whoever or whatever this "Other" may be. Yet among the many aspects this "Other" exhibited to Kafka was, to be sure, the facet of literary perfection. As early as 1913 he knew that "I am nothing but literature and can and want to be nothing else" (*DI*, 299). His devotion to his work, his *Bau*, was almost religious.

It needed the imminence of his death to let him conceive of the Burrow as the most appropriate cipher for his work. On July 5, 1922, he wrote to Brod in a letter already quoted: *

What I have [only] pretended, is really going to happen. I have not bought myself off by my writing. All my life I have been dying, and now I am going to die in reality. My life was sweeter than the life of others, my death will be all the more frightful. . . . I am enough of a writer to have the desire to enjoy all this with all my senses in complete oblivion of myself—not alertness but self-oblivion is the precondition of writing—or, and this is the same, to tell about it (*B*, 385).

The tale of Kafka's work at the moment of his dying is "The Burrow." The image of the Tower of Babel has turned (one is tempted to say,

* See p. 219 above.

elegantly) into the image of the pit, the grave. Inasmuch as the animal's cave also represents Kafka's tomb, he seems to have intended the story as a way of enjoying his own funeral by participating in it as an eye-witness.

In this story at last Kafka allows himself to enter the Castle, which now turns out to be both his work and his grave. This is a reduction in purpose and a gain in intelligibility. Moreover, the animal is not only granted access to the Castle, a name it gives the "Burrow" with reveal-ing frequency, it has also created it. Literally the creation harbors the creator; moreover, it swallows him up to such an extent that he him-self is denied any identification. Neither an initial like K. nor any physical contour defines the actor-narrator now. All we learn about the animal is that it knows it is growing old (81); that it did not possess strength enough to carry out "the best of the grand plans I thought out in my youth and early manhood" (121); that it has passed its "man-hood's years in childish games" (139), and that, at the time of its telling the story, it is "no longer a young apprentice, but an old architect" (143). The animal's description of itself as an old architect may remind the reader of another example of the late style in European letters. In his drama *The Master Builder* (1892), Henrik Ibsen likewise chose the image of a building, a tower, to describe the ambitions of his own poetic genius as well as the doubts that beset him with regard to the place an artist could still claim for himself within the society of his day.

Needless to say, an element of extreme doubt prevails also in Kafka's animal when it surveys its work. All that can be seen of the Burrow "from outside is a big hole; that, however, really leads nowhere" (79). To the world the fruit of the animal's endeavors is a non-thing, a nothing; and even while it produced this nothingness the animal was, as it gradually realized, to be blamed for its idleness: "I have rested far too often from my labors all my life" (140). Nevertheless, it was per-sonally and physically dedicated to its work: its own forehead served as a stamp hammer. This total devotion even leads the creature to the pious hope that "providence was interested in the preservation of . . . the unique instrument" (90). This hope, in turn, is apt to tinge with slightly more optimistic hues Kafka's dark aphorism from the sequence "He" (1920): "The bones of his own forehead block his way; he batters this forehead bloody by beating it against his own forehead" (264–265). The animal seems to have created the Burrow out of itself, and certainly it has hurt itself in the process: "So I had to run with my forehead thousands and thousands of times, for whole days and nights, against the ground, and I was happy when the blood came, for that was a proof that the walls were beginning to harden; and in this way, as everybody must admit, I richly paid for my Castle Keep" (86). Besides, these labors, these wounds, seem to have been pleasing to providence. Why else would it care to watch over the animal's forehead, its self-destructive weapon and building tool?

Thus it happened that the Burrow could assume in the animal's mind the likeness of an achievement and even play the role of a refuge: "There have been happy times in which I could almost assure myself that the enmity of the world towards me had ceased or been assuaged, or that the strength of the Burrow had raised me above the battle of annihilation" (98–99). Literary work could indeed be an "immense fortress," as Kafka conceded to Brod in a letter dated June 1920; but he himself had not yet entered this castle, "I have suddenly nothing at all, I have only a few beams, and if I were not to support them with my own head, they would collapse" (*B,* 276). But now that the passages and corridors are dug, they seem to last and even to bestow a certain meaning on the animal's struggle for existence: "It is for your sake, passages and rooms, and to answer you, Castle Keep, above all, that I have come, counting my own life as nothing. . . . What do I care for danger now that I am with you? You belong to me, I to you, we are united; what can harm us" (114)? In more than one sense this union of the animal with its cave is unworldly. The dimension of space has ceased to exist in the subterranean corridors. Infinite time prevails there, a timelessness which corresponds with the suspension of chronological sequences in Kafka's own writings. This state is immensely pleasing to the animal: "Within the Burrow I always have endless time,—for whatever I do there is good and important and satisfies me, so to speak." *

Yet the satisfaction that fills the animal within its castle is shortlived, and the importance it attributes to its work still remains open to question. The creature is obsessed with the idea of comparing the secure Burrow with the ordinary life of the forest. That is, it endeavors to remain within the fortifications of its own work and yet to stand outside in order to judge the validity of the security measures it has devised. But as soon as it has left the cave, the animal is gripped by the fear of forfeiting its own work. It is overcome by the equally obsessive urge to return and to descend. Then the freedom of the open

---

* These sentences do not occur in the American edition. In the German edition they precede the sentence quoted above from p. 114.

skies appears as utterly meaningless, "and I tear myself free from all
my doubts and by broad daylight I rush to the door, quite resolved to
raise it now; but I cannot, I rush across it and fling myself into a thorn
bush, deliberately, as a punishment, a punishment for some guilt I do
not know" (102). Here the themes of *The Trial* are sounded too distinctly to be neglected: the image of the door missed by the animal
partly from haste and partly because of its self-torturing reluctance
leads us back to the gate guarded by the doorkeeper in the Prison
Chaplain's parable. The guilt, which is felt by the animal and yet remains unintelligible to it, relates it to the bank clerk Joseph K. Beyond
this, the animal's words gain an almost Biblical depth when it mentions the thorn bush. The image seems to enhance and render still
more mysterious the creature's feeling of guilt without, however, revealing any godhead to it. In this thorn bush the Divine is silent.

Thus, the Burrow not only offers security, it also exerts an irresistible
compulsion. It both attracts the creature and is utterly unable to keep
it within its confines. The animal cannot live within the cave and
likewise is not able to bear the thought of leaving it. This is the self-
critical representation of the spell Kafka's own work cast upon his life.
"My Burrow occupies me too much" (97).

Yet the references to Kafka's writings do not stop with the image of
the door which is being "missed" both in *The Trial* and "The Burrow."
The most complex and enigmatic among these hints is certainly the
animal's allusion to its "first achievement," the labyrinth. Where does
this pointer lead us? "It was there that I began my Burrow," the animal
ruminates,

I began, half in play, at this little corner, and so my first joy in labor exhausted
itself in the construction of a maze which at that time seemed to me the
crown of all Burrows, but which I judge today, perhaps more correctly, to
be too much of an idle *tour de force*, not really worthy of the rest of the
Burrow, though perhaps theoretically brilliant (92).

Did Kafka think here of "The Judgment" which, in his testament, he
mentioned first among the achievements that still could "stand" at that
time? This would justify our assumption that he had preserved "a
certain sentiment" for this early story. Moreover, even the crucial word
"judgment" appears in the reflections of the animal when it contemplates the thin-walled maze of passages which bear testimony to *its*
breakthrough into the work of the Burrow itself: "I am both exasper-
ated and touched when, as sometimes happens, I lose myself for a

moment in my own creation, and my work seems to be still doing its best to prove its *raison d'être* to me, its maker, whose *judgment* has long since been passed on it" (95).*

Or does this labyrinth lead us to *The Castle,* where the maze has become the integral and constituent image? Kafka would have remained thoroughly true to himself and his own doubts if he had considered his most elaborate and mature narrative to bo still a "first achievement" and an "idle *tour de force.*" Measured by the standards of perfection which he expressed in his testament, *The Castle* was as unfinished and questionable, as much of a beginner's timid patchwork, as the stories he had written in 1912. If, however, he really meant the labyrinthine Castle when he described the maze that leads into the Burrow and out of it, then the animal's passageways and corridors indicate those parts of Kafka's work which were still unwritten during the last years of his life and would soon be buried with him, their creator. Then the Burrow would represent a promise Kafka knew he could never keep, a tomb in which he enshrined the hopes he had cherished, knowing very well that they were never to be fulfilled. A mood of bitter-sweet farewell informs the description of the Burrow.

The back and cross references to his own writings which Kafka revealingly hides in "The Burrow" are little more than a literary game, albeit one that is masterfully executed. Furthermore, self-allusions of this kind are not infrequent in the works of writers who feel that they themselves have come late in the development of their craft.† Yet "The Burrow" also contains highly significant statements concerning Kafka's own creative paradox: the conflict which existed in his aims as a writer and a human being.

Not quite in the center of its Burrow the animal has built the main square, or Castle Keep. Here it keeps its stock of supplies.

The place is so spacious that food for half a year hardly fills it. Consequently I can display my stores, walk about among them, play with them, enjoy their plenty and their various smells and have a reliable view of what there actually is. This done, I can always arrange accordingly, and make my calculations and hunting plans for the future (86).

The animal is as little satisfied with its heaped-up supplies as Kafka was with the sum total of his own achievements. Like the animal,

* (Italics mine.) For the biographical relevance of the word "judgment," see pp. 48 ff. above.

† See, e.g., Thomas Mann's characterization of his own writings in *Doctor Faustus,* when Serenus Zeitblom describes Adrian Leverkühn's compositions.

Kafka refused to limit himself, to economize in the use of his intellectual gifts, to "play" with his own figures, to enjoy past performances, or to devise new exploits. The curious beast is haunted by the *idée fixe* that it ought to create a second chamber above the Castle Keep in order to be able to guard the square below without actually having to enter it. Ostensibly it imagines this new room as an ideal playground: "What a joy to lie pressed against the rounded outer wall, pull oneself up, let oneself slide down again, somersault and find oneself on firm ground, and play all these games, so to speak, upon the Castle Keep and yet not within its physical limits." These games may remind the reader of Gregor Samsa's excursions across the walls of his bedroom, but the insect's wanderings were at the same time more sinister as a vision and less weird intellectually than the capers performed by our animal. For the games in the new chamber would enable the creature "to avoid the Castle Keep" and yet not "have to do without it" (121–122). The playground, then, also serves as an observation post; moreover, it offers the animal-on-guard complete control over the supplies in his power without having to touch, protect, and defend them. He could be absent and present at the same time, enjoy his possessions without feeling responsible for them, accumulate goods and yet be unburdened and free. In short, our animal wants to eat its supplies and have them, too.

Again there are darker sides to this happy musing. The animal describes this second chamber as a vacuum (*Hohlraum*). Within the "big hole" of the Burrow our creature visualizes a second emptiness, that is, a negation within a negation. As was the case with the name of Count Westwest,* the reader is at liberty here to interpret this double negation in the affirmative or the negative. This time, too, he will have to remember that the animal never reaches its goal. As little as the Land-Surveyor is admitted into the inner precincts of the Castle district, so little will the animal complete its watch chamber. Moreover, it will not attain what it desires most: it will never find the complete peace for which it is longing, the perfect stillness in which it could hear "the murmur of the silence of the Castle Keep" (122).

This "murmur of silence" is, of course, identical with the sound of the inaudible, the "solemn stillness" behind Josephine's song, and the infinite quiet beyond man's finite word. In this respect "The Burrow" is just a restatement of Kafka's true creative "Self." [24] But the conflict which tore this self asunder and yet forced it to transcend itself in

* See p. 235 above.

unforgettable images is, it seems to me, stated here more clearly than elsewhere in Kafka's work.

It is by the dark clarity of these statements that "The Burrow" acquires its air of finality. A mystical union between the animal and its castle seems to be achieved when it contemplates its work from the outside:

Call it foolish if you like: it gives me infinite pleasure and reassures me. At such times it is as if I were not so much standing before my house as before myself when I was sleeping, experiencing the happiness of being in a profound slumber and simultaneously keeping vigilant guard over myself.

This sentence seems to contain in a nutshell the vision that produced the night interview between K. and Secretary Bürgel in *The Castle*.* Yet Kafka surpasses even further the limits he had imposed on the creature of "The Burrow" when he makes his animal add the following explanation: "I am privileged, as it were, not only to see the spectres of the night in all the helplessness and blind trust of my sleep, but also to confront them in reality at the same time with the calm judgment of one who is fully awake" (97).

Franz Kafka was the ghost seer of our century. As has been seen, "The Burrow" is a vision akin to "The Judgment" which Kafka himself once called "the spectre of one night." In order to conjure up these ghosts he sought a state of trancelike inspiration in which the nightmares would appear. (The many variants in his manuscripts are attempts to reach this state of clairvoyance by writing the same passage all over again.) Yet once he had arrived at the moment of inspiration, his critical mind began to mistrust "all the helplessness and blind trust" of his visionary trance. Then he clamored for the "calm judgment of one who is fully awake." Having put the "Burrow" of his creative unconscious to good use, he asked himself to provide also a sentinel post above the images he had stored in his dream's Castle Keep. In other words, he not only expected his work to show the presence of total inspiration, the mysterious perfection of an entirely successful work of art, but he demanded from himself also a critical alertness that rendered a rational account of the mystical act of creation while this act was still in progress. He was not satisfied with being a visionary; the moment of inspiration had to produce an intellectual distance from his vision as well as an interpretation. Small wonder that the animal never succeeds in constructing its observation post on top of the Castle Keep.

* See pp. 252 ff. above.

"The Burrow" crowns Franz Kafka's late stories by revealing the literary, and personal, roots of his metaphysical conflict. The problem, he seems to be saying at long last, lies in himself and his work rather than in the world outside.

To be sure, his animal feels followed and persecuted; but its enemies, of whom there are many, are still less palpable and definitely less threatening than the antagonists of the earlier novel fragments.

There are, first of all, the field mice and "all sorts of small fry," which the animal decimates by "a certain amount of low hunting" (*Niederjagd*—83). Nevertheless they go on molesting and disquieting the animal which is intent on preserving its peace. There is, next to these negligible opponents,

a huge swarm of little creatures, which as they are audible must certainly be bigger than the small fry but yet cannot be very much bigger, for the sound of their labors is itself very faint. It may be, then, a swarm of unknown creatures on their wanderings, who happen to be passing my way, who disturb me, but will presently cease to do so (124).

Apart from the triviality of this disturbance, it is one which has been imagined by the animal rather than experienced in actuality. Kafka seems to have elaborated on this theme to some extent to indicate the hypothetical character which distinguishes the animal's opponents in general. Are these enemies nothing but sounds of fear, the outward projection of his inner conflict, or does the trouble they are causing really exist?

Even the episode of the animal's "forest brother," some beast of its own kind (103), is no match for the nightmares which used to haunt Kafka before. This animal is, on the one hand, "a lover of peace," but on the other "a dissolute scoundrel who wishes to be housed where he has not built." The evenly sustained tone of our story is badly shattered in a scene where our animal wishes that its "brother's" hindquarters would still show "so that at least . . . I might in my blind rage leap on it, maul it, tear the flesh from its bones, destroy it, drink its blood and fling its corpse among the rest of my spoil" (103). This diatribe sounds more like a personal loss of temper than an integrated part of the story. It certainly does not contribute to our understanding of the animal's plight or the Burrow's structure and meaning.

There is, finally, the great opponent, "some animal unknown to me" (124). This opponent resembles the animal of the Burrow in that it has neither name nor shape nor identity. It produces a "hissing noise" so impersonal that our creature is at first inclined to connect it with the current of air streaming through the passageways. "The noise . . . is a comparatively innocent one; . . . it is not even constant; . . . there are long pauses; . . . it goes on always on the same thin note, with regular pauses, now a hissing, but again like a kind of piping" (115–116). The piping is one more echo of Josephine's song; the hissing, however, leads back to the noises produced by a mole tracked down by Kafka's dog in 1904:

First it amused me and I was especially pleased by the excitement of the mole which was quite desperately looking in vain for a hole in the hard pavement of the street. Suddenly, however, when the dog again struck it with its stretched-out paw, the mole cried out. "Ks, kss," was what it cried. And then it occurred to me—no, nothing occurred to me (to Max Brod, August 28, *B*, 29).

Since Kafka's images are nourished by long-remembered impressions, it is quite possible that the cry of anxiety hissed by a mole in 1904 was turned into the war cry of the animal in "The Burrow." Now, however, the noise no longer expresses fear but provokes it. Still it remains connected with the original feeling of anxiety, and since this enemy resembles our animal, the early reminiscence would lead us to imagine the latter in the shape of a mole rather than a badger, as the critics occasionally presume.[25]

The enemy of the animal in "The Burrow" is as great and as invisible as the Castle appears to K. on the first page of *The Castle*.[*] But the threatening power which the Castle possesses has been transferred to a moving being. The image is reversed. Now the protagonist is trying to be impregnable, and the enemy threatens to storm his bastion. The animal suspects that he "has a plan in view the purpose of which I cannot decipher; I merely assume that the beast . . . is encircling me; it has probably made several circles round my Burrow already since I began to observe it" (136–137). When our animal was young and did not yet possess its Burrow (that is, when it was not yet obsessed by it), it seemed that "the sound of [the enemy's] digging began to weaken, it grew fainter and fainter, as if the digging [antagonist] were gradually diverging from his first route, as if he had decided now to take the diametrically opposite direction and were making straight away from me into the distance" (142). From this we may infer that the enemy's existence is closely related to the importance the Burrow has

[*] See pp. 225 ff. above.

gained in the animal's imagination. If we prefer drastic solutions to delicately woven enigmas, we may even go so far as to say that the enemy represents the spirit of revenge wrought by the Burrow against its inhabitant, the creation against its creator. He almost has become the labyrinth personified, a maze on the move.

Now, however, that the animal is growing old, it will soon have to leave its work, the Burrow, forever. At this late stage of the animal's development it is able to detach itself from its obsession, to overcome its fear, and to do greater justice to its enemy by externalizing him: "The more I reflect upon it, the more improbable it seems to me that the beast has even heard of me; it is possible, though unimaginable, that it can have received news of me through some other channel, but it has probably never heard me." Here, at the very end, it seems that our creature has constructed the Burrow not to secure itself and its provisions, not even to hear the murmurs of silence, which is the source flowing imperceptibly forth from its center. In a contrary-to-fact condition the animal shyly ventures an immensely moving third interpretation: "If [the enemy] had heard me I should have noticed some sign of it, he would at least have stopped his work every now and then to listen" (147). That is, the passageways and corridors of the Burrow had also been a system of communication. The subterranean cave with all its nooks and crannies had been a faint and fearful attempt on the animal's part to give the enemy, the great opponent, the "Other," a sign of its existence. If the Burrow was meant to represent Kafka's work and the hostile beast the spirit of obsession which haunted the writer, then he has, in the penultimate sentence, stated, in veiled and hypothetical form, the dignity of his human expectation to be listened to. This Burrow, like the rest of Kafka's work, was ultimately meant to be the place for an encounter.

The last sentence of the fragment reads: "But all remained unchanged" (147). According to the reminiscences of Dora Dymant, a definite change was to occur on the last pages of the story. There Kafka intended his animal to meet its enemy and be killed in a decisive battle.[26] The validity of these recollections is somewhat impaired by another explanation, ascribed to Kafka by Dora, that she, Dora, "was" the Castle Keep of "The Burrow." [27] This explanation does not rise to a higher level than Brod's own recollection that in everyday conversation Kafka had identified the hostile animal of the story with the tormenting cough that plagued him during the last winter of his life.[28]

At best, these memories prove that Kafka continued to mystify his friends by self-interpretations, which were as playful as they were cunning; comparable, perhaps, to the trap doors with which his animal had secured its refuge. And if, as Brod maintains, Kafka actually finished the manuscript of the story,[29] then we can imagine no other reason for his destroying the last few pages than that he considered the ending, whatever it may have been, inadequate.

On the surface, then, we may assume that "The Burrow" was to end with the animal's defeat, if only in the sense that it had not achieved any change of its fortunes in spite of its lifelong efforts and far-reaching plans. This interpretation has led Wolfgang Kayser to cite this story as a prime example of the nihilistic tendencies inherent in what he terms the grotesque element in art and literature. Calling "The Burrow" "the most typical among Kafka's later stories," Kayser defines the *Bau* as *Abbau,* the construction as destruction. "With a mathematical imagination reminiscent of Edgar Allan Poe's, the animal has secured itself by planning a subterranean structure. Yet while it reports on this structure, all possible ways of finding security are destroyed by its own words." [30]

This *mot* is as ingenious as it is superficial. The forces at work in "The Burrow" are not merely self-defeating. Take the animal itself. Singling it out as a typical Kafka hero, Geoffrey Clive describes its main property as the ability to be "conspicuously persevering":

He never gives up—in spite of the approaching enemy, the neurotic fears, and the multitude of obstacles in his path to perfect security. Like the organization man bent on getting to the top, he stops short of nothing to get to the bottom. With old age already upon him he sets to work again repairing the undermined foundations of his Castle Keep.[31]

This characterization retains its poignancy in spite of the Madison Avenue setting to which Kafka's poor creature has been exposed, and regardless of the observation that the creation, and not the creator, is the central image of this story.

Focusing once more his attention on the Burrow rather than the beast, the reader may feel fortified rather than discouraged by the creature's protestation that all remained unchanged, and that its work, though fragmentary, was allowed to remain intact. Besides, the animal quotes itself in the last sentence of its story. On its return from the forest to the Castle Keep it had heaved this sigh of relief once before, "Everything is unchanged" (113). Far from experiencing this lack of change as a disadvantage, the animal finds support in the preservation of the complex monotony which is its Burrow.

Taken by itself, the animal is as distrustful of reality as any other Kafka hero. "It is comparatively easy," it reflects,

to trust any one if you are supervising him at the same time or at least have the chance of supervising him; perhaps it is possible even to trust some one at a distance; but to trust completely some one outside the Burrow when you are inside (and, so to speak, in a different world), that, it seems to me, is impossible (105).

The reader is given to understand here that no possible means of assurance can ever be devised for a creature like this. And yet this very animal is able to confess in almost the same breath: "But I can only trust myself and the Burrow" ("Vertrauen aber kann ich nur mir und dem Bau"—105–106). The "but," the *aber,* suggests the extreme effort needed to extract a statement like this from a Kafka figure. The unconditional straightforwardness of the statement, however, singles it out as a key sentence.

Of course, the key this sentence offers leads nowhere but back to the Burrow, the work. Now, however, we realize that the story does not treat only the escapades which the animal undertakes to get away from itself and from its abode. It tells also of its returns, its descents into the fragmentary infinity of its own making. To be sure, it finds "great difficulty in summoning the resolution to carry out the actual descent which could be called downright spectacular" (*die an sich geradezu Aufsehen machende Prozedur des Hinabsteigens*—100–101). But return it does; and we are probably not mistaken when we read in this ambiguous phrase * a late reflection of Kafka's own descents into the dark of his creative hours. (See, e.g., the diary entry of September 23, 1912 [*DI*, 275–276].)

We may, with the depth analysts, assume that Kafka was dreaming of his return to the womb when he imagined his Burrow. We may, on the level of plain biography, repeat our point that he allowed himself this return only because the animal's subterranean cave also represented the writer's own tomb. Yet we find a more promising path down the labyrinth of this Burrow when we realize that in this story which is so closely interrelated with the rest of Kafka's life work, the

* *Aufsehen machen* also connotes "drawing attention to oneself," a move which the animal, for obvious reasons, is eager to avoid.

work itself seems to have inspired the writer with a certain amount of trust. The animal's voice is, after all, a voice coming from within a castle. By speaking from inside his work, Kafka has at long last turned this work into a place of some timid inner security, a frail Castle Within.

CHAPTER IX

The True Physician

Franz Kafka and Albert Camus

ON January 21, 1922, two and a half years before his death, Franz Kafka entered in his diary the following remark: "Without forebears, without marriage, without heirs, with a fierce longing for forebears, marriage and heirs. They all stretch their hands to me: forebears, marriage and heirs, but they are too far away for me" (*DII,* 207).

This sentence epitomizes Kafka's personal situation as well as the predicament of his mind. Sharing in the heritage of his race by the vaguest of memories, anticipating its future in the nightmares that haunted him, he cannot be said to have followed willingly any particular literary convention or enjoyed consciously the guidance of anyone among the great masters of the past. He was alone and remained alone.

Nevertheless the Kafka hero has grown into a symbol just as representative of our time as was Goethe's Werther for the late eighteenth century, and Lord Byron's Manfred for the early nineteenth. For Kafka's heroes, like those of Goethe and Byron, reflected a universal discord, a break between man and his world, and they aired the minds of their contemporaries by lifting this conflict above the threshold of their consciousness.

Kafka's ever-increasing fame produced imitators rather than genuine

disciples. The most popular and most misleading corruption of a Kafka hero was achieved by the French actor Jean-Louis Barrault when, aided by André Gide, he dramatized *The Trial* as a melodrama.*
With Barrault the Kafka hero became a withered dancer on the avenues of our sorrow, the charmingly evasive Hamlet of French existentialism after the Second World War.

Franz Kafka could not establish a tradition. He was, as Hermann Broch recognized, a genius "such as is born only once in a century, . . . a primal manifestation of genius (*Ur-Genialität*)." [1] It was only possible to avoid, to imitate, or to reach beyond Kafka. Those who neglected or aped him do not concern us here. In order to go further than he did, it was necessary to comprehend and affirm as the essence of the human in our time that feeling of utter despair which had obsessed Kafka and materialized, as he suspected, in his fatal disease. It also was imperative to remove Kafka's archaic fear from the realm of myth and pursue without fear or frustration the path of self-cognition, in the middle of which Kafka had stopped and died.

Albert Camus set resolutely out to pursue this path. In his *The Myth of Sisyphus* he describes "the wisest and most prudent of mortals," whom the gods condemned "to rolling ceaselessly a rock to the top of a mountain, whence the stone would fall back of its own weight."

---

* This judgment has been rendered obsolete by the film adaptation of *The Trial* by Orson Welles. Welles, whose explosive performance in the title role of *Citizen Kane* once drew crowds to the movie houses, transmogrified Kafka's hero into a petty-bourgeois *Mr. K.* Interpreted by Anthony Perkins as a neurotic playboy, this K. is exposed to a nameless Court which seems to represent all the threats modern society holds in store for a soul without conscience and full of fear. Consequently K. has been transferred from Kafka's Bank to the mammoth office of an anonymous big business concern. There he resides in an elevated glass box surveying "850 office desks, 850 secretaries and 850 clattering typewriters" (*Time,* June 29, 1962, p. 30). Despite the imaginative use of the deserted Paris Gare d'Orsay for settings and despite authentic performances from Romy Schneider as Leni and from Akim Tamiroff as Block the Tradesman, the film presents the audience with a tricked-out and streamlined *Trial,* which is impressive only in its banality. No wonder, then, that K. is tempted to seek information about the proceedings from an electronic brain. He shrinks back from the computer, not as a matter of principle but because he is accused of "a crime so unmentionable that no one can say what it is" (*New York Times,* June 17, 1962, sec. X, p. 9). And since it is a well-known fact that one dies the way one has lived, Orson Welles's K. is not butchered by a knife but blasted to smithereens by an atomic bomb. His demise is no longer a nightmare but a tribute paid to the most common cliché haunting the liberal imagination today. Thus poor K. is doomed to perish in a world which is as little brave as it is new. One reassuring element is that Welles still permits his hero to die "like a dog." This is indeed the appropriate ending for a movie that has turned Kafka's parable into a shaggy underdog story.

This effort is measured by "skyless space" and "a time without depth." It is performed in a world before or beyond all mythological imaginings, a universe of fearless lucidity. Then Sisyphus follows the rock down to the plain.

Camus continues:

It is during that return, that pause, that Sisyphus interests me. A face that toils so close to stones is already stone itself! I see that man going back down with a heavy yet measured step toward the torment of which he will never know the end. That hour like a breathing-space which returns as surely as his suffering, that is the hour of [Sisyphus'] consciousness (*cette heure est celle de la conscience*). At each of those moments . . . he is superior to his fate. He is stronger than his rock.

Camus's *conscience* embraces both the ideas of consciousness and of conscience—a conscience which does not know any guilt. It represents a forceful, and perhaps somewhat forced, conception of tragic awareness, of being alive to universal pain. He has provided his Sisyphus with the unequivocal strength to stand alone, a rock among rocks, yet stronger than his environment and distinguished from it by the clarity of his mind. Neither anguish nor ambiguity are allowed to enter this soul. Camus concludes:

If this myth is tragic, that is because its hero is conscious. . . . Sisyphus, proletarian of the gods, powerless and rebellious, knows the whole extent of his wretched condition: it is what he thinks of during his descent. The lucidity that was to constitute his torture at the same time crowns his victory. There is no fate that cannot be surmounted by scorn.[2]

The image of Sisyphus was too obvious a metaphor of modern man's condition to have escaped Kafka. In 1922, we remember, he bewailed in his diary the solitude of those who have been denied children and likened the king of Greek myth to a contemporary celibate—himself. "Sisyphus was a bachelor."

This image of barren humanity Camus resolutely replaced by what he came to call the "absurd hero." His Sisyphus, who conquers an unintelligible and cruel fate by consciously scorning it, reinstates the dignity of suffering mankind by assuming an attitude which is both absurd and heroic. To be sure, Camus tried to identify his vision of Sisyphus with the tormented shadows of Kafka's principal figures. He did so in a piece of inspired self-defense which he called "Hope and the Absurd in the Work of Franz Kafka," appended to the second edition of *Sisyphus* and all subsequent editions. However, he did not quite succeed in driving this comparison home. For if he says that his Sisyphus "teaches the higher fidelity that negates the gods and raises rocks," and if he ends up in a triumphantly major key by crying: "One must imagine Sisyphus happy," [3] then he fails to describe adequately Kafka's struggle against the authorities, divine, paternal, or otherwise. Kafka negates his gods only conditionally and surreptitiously. If Camus likens Kafka's work to the rock his Sisyphus is perpetually and fruitlessly pushing uphill, then a glance into Kafka's personal documents could have shown him his error. For Kafka's work was a labor enforced not by an outside will but by an inner obsession, and the moments when he interrupted it did not grant him any relaxation, increased consciousness, or victory. Creative relaxation, the *schöpferische Pause,* was an idea congenitally alien to him. He was doubly tormented whenever he had to abstain from the work without which he was totally unable to exist. Yet it is fortunate that Camus misunderstood Kafka; he never could have reached beyond him if he had understood him better.

Camus was born one year after Kafka's breakthrough, in 1913. His hometown was Algiers, and its sunlight fills his first novel, *The Stranger,* just as cruelly as the twilight of Prague submerges most of Kafka's narratives. Camus was by nature and education a "Latin," [4] Kafka at best a Hebrew fallen from the Hebrew tradition and desperately trying to recapture it. Camus fought with the French underground against the tyranny of a totalitarian system which Kafka seems to have anticipated in his nightmares. That is, Camus faced in reality all those persecutions from which Kafka had suffered in his fearful dreams without ever being forced to experience them in their physical brutality. Yet however devastating the German occupation of France may have been, it had its limits and came to an end. Thus the younger writer was spared the limitless horrors the older had imagined in his apocalyptic visions. Finally, Camus had spiritual ancestors: Nietzsche, whose *amor fati* seems to accompany Sisyphus on his descent, Tolstoy and Dostoyevsky, Melville, Gide and Proust, Malraux and Montherlant.[5] And not the last among them was Kafka, the solitary, the man without forebears and heirs.[*]

---

[*] Only the critic who concentrates his attention on Kafka's plots and ignores the cadence of his language, its ironies and ambiguities, is able to doubt his uniqueness. Thus Mark Spilka could say: "Until recently Franz Kafka's reputation for dazzling originality has remained unchallenged. His spectacular opening scenes . . . have seemed unparalleled in serious fiction; and his extension of their

Since in some ways a critical vindication of *The Stranger* is presented in *The Myth of Sisyphus* and its appendix on Kafka, Camus himself has invited a comparison of his first novel and Kafka's work. But while he claimed the older writer as his predecessor and tried to justify his own views by basing them on Kafka's insights, he was already about to abandon them.

Both *The Trial* and *The Stranger* treat of crime and punishment. In Kafka's *The Trial* a drastic punishment is visited upon K. for an undisclosed breach of the Law. Camus's Meursault, on the other hand, commits a definite crime: he shoots an Arab on the shore outside Algiers. Meursault's senses are dimmed by wine and dulled by the inexorable light. Moreover, he acts in a kind of self-defense. The Arab has just wounded one of his friends and brandishes a knife in his hand. Yet Camus manipulates this scene in such a way as to intimate that the crime did not originate in a conscious act of will but was set off by forces beyond the control of the murderer. We have only to follow his description of the act to recognize Meursault's paradoxical innocence:

Then everything began to reel before my eyes, a fiery gust came from the sea, while the sky cracked in two, from end to end, and a great sheet of flame poured through the rift. Every nerve in my body was a steel spring, and my grip closed on the revolver. The trigger gave, and the smooth underbelly of the butt jogged my palm. And so, with that crisp, whipcrack sound, it all began (*S*, 76).[6]

Who commits this crime? Meursault or the murderously blinding light of the day? In Kafka, too, we found such an offense perpetrated on the very threshold of consciousness. Karl Rossmann's crime in *Der Verschollene* is presented in such a roundabout way that the reader is forced to excuse the culprit from all but the guilt of being there on the

---

dreamlike possibilities has reinforced the myth of his uniqueness. There is growing evidence, however, that Kafka was a synthetic writer, . . . and that he was original in the best sense, in his development of the latent tendencies in older forms" (*Comparative Literature*, XI [1959], 289). This statement serves as a blueprint for Spilka's more recent investigation, *Dickens and Kafka* (Bloomington: Indiana University Press, 1963).

Spilka's premises are erroneous, since the earlier interpreters—above all Max Brod—had already pointed to Kafka's indebtedness to all kinds of plots provided by his predecessors. For the student of Kafka who commands a sufficient knowledge of the German language, however, the "dazzling originality" of his work never consisted in his invention of plots and plot motives but in the flux of his sentences and in the texture of his imagery.

scene of his seduction. On the surface of reality, the whole mechanism of revenge released against the young "sinner" seems to be out of proportion.

Camus stresses the incongruity of crime and punishment as well. During Meursault's trial the Public Prosecutor wins the death sentence by proclaiming the murderer guilty of maltreating his mother. "I accuse the prisoner of behaving at his mother's funeral in a way that showed he was already a criminal at heart" (S, 122). Ostensibly the Prosecutor's damaging words have as little relevance as the sweeping gestures satirized by Daumier in his caricatures of French justice. On a deeper level, however, Meursault's lack of affection for his mother is a symptom of his character and a harbinger of his fate. He dies for the sake of his indifference, and because of it. What seems to him— and probably seemed to young Camus—the utmost candor and sincerity is also a deep-seated sluggishness of heart. This, in turn, relates him to Joseph K. in Kafka's *The Trial*, whose guilt remains unexplained and inexplicable.

In one of the unfinished chapters of this novel K. decides to visit his mother once more. Three years have gone by since he saw her last. Before his arrest he was too busy with his own affairs, and afterward he had to concentrate on his trial, that is, on himself again. The only link between mother and son is provided by a cousin who administers the money K. used to send for the old woman.

It is true that his mother's eyesight was failing; but then . . . her general health had improved. . . . His cousin was of the opinion that this was possibly connected with her excessive piety during the last few years. K. had noticed slight signs of this on his last visit with something like repugnance (*T*, 291–292).

The chapter remained a fragment; thus we do not know whether K. did actually visit his mother or what Kafka was driving at; but the place of the fragment would probably have been shortly before K.'s execution,[7] that is, as close to the final catastrophe as the funeral of Meursault's mother in *The Stranger*. Meursault's mother also has been living in a rest home for three years (S, 3); he went to see her too seldom during her last year (S, 4) and tried to make up by meager gifts for the visits which he had failed to make (S, 3). He, too, discovers with considerable annoyance that his mother has turned to religion and expressed a wish for a religious burial (S, 5). Both old women seem to have found secular substitutes for their absent sons: K's mother has the cousin, on whose arm she "stepped out quite vigorously . . . on the way to church" (*T*, 292); Meursault's mother has old Thomas Pérez (*S*, 15), who crumples up like a rag doll at her graveside, while the son yearns to go straight to bed and drown out the tedious incident by a full dose of healthy sleep (*S*, 22).

Considering the symbolic texture of the two novels, a coincidence like this is bound to attract our attention. Neither Kafka nor Camus can be suspected of having based the guilt of the sons on the indifference they displayed toward their mothers. Yet they are related to one another in that they have cut themselves off from their origins and left their past behind. That the maternal image of the Church emerges behind both mothers makes the old women all the more repulsive to their sons.

The coldness between sons and mothers also separates the men from their mistresses. They not only scorn the natural proximity of the generations, they brush aside all deeper affinities between the sexes. Marie asks Meursault whether he wants to marry her. "I said I didn't mind; if she was keen on it, we'd get married. Then she asked me again if I loved her. I replied, much as before, that her question meant nothing or next to nothing—but I supposed I didn't" (*S*, 52). Joseph K. betrays the same lack of interest when he discusses Elsa, whom he used to visit once a week (*T*, 23), with Leni, her successor: " 'Granted that she's your sweetheart,' said Leni, 'you wouldn't miss her very much, all the same, if you were to lose her or exchange her for someone else . . . ?' 'Certainly,' said K., smiling" (*T*, 137).

Despite his indifference K. succumbs to Leni. In this fact we recognize a serious difference between the two heroes: Meursault has reached a level of self-reliance which raises him beyond all emotions, and consequently beyond the fear which drives K. into Leni's caresses. Meursault's relation to Marie is mere play, beginning amidst the waves of the Mediterranean and continuing, almost uninterrupted, in bed. In jail he tries to remember her face—"it was a sun-gold face, lit up with desire" (*S*, 149)—but since he did not share her desire, physical as it was, his imagination fails him, and he gives up his vain effort at recalling her. K., on the other hand, on the way to his execution meets not Leni, who had possessed him, but the shadow of Fräulein Bürstner, who had denied herself to him. He remains totally unaware of the physical presence of a woman's body; he registers only "the warning she had meant for him." K. is attracted by women because they seem to hold a secret key to the mysterious chambers where his trial is being decided. Meursault's case is infinitely simpler: for him women are part of a universe as insignificant in its totality as in its parts.

Paradoxically the murderer Meursault appears to the reader less guilty than K., who superficially has not hurt a hair of anyone's head. This *Stranger*, Maurice Blanchot has said, "relates to himself as if another person would see him and talk about him. . . . He is completely outside. . . . He is all the more himself the less he seems to think, to feel, to be familiar with himself." [8] As it turns out, Meursault's self-alienation is the principal step forward Camus has made beyond Kafka. Because of his continuous and deep concern with himself, K. is unable to discover this self. The resulting uncertainty forces him both to protest his innocence and to display the symptoms of his guilt.

Meursault is persecuted by society; his defiant death sets him free and cleanses him from the prejudices we may have harbored against him. Here is a man, if only a man thoroughly estranged from himself as well as from society. Kafka's K., on the other hand, is persecuted by authorities whose powers extend beyond any social context. Falling prey to their threats, he meets his persecutors halfway and draws the reader along with him into the dizzy torrent of apologies and self-accusations.

The difference between the two men is raised into sharp relief by the conversations they carry on with the priests sent to them by the masters of their trials. Repeatedly Meursault declines the visit of the Prison Chaplain; finally the priest brushes aside all prison etiquette and enters the death cell (S, 145 ff.). K. is less outspoken than Meursault but just as unwilling to partake of the comfort religion may offer him. He merely chances into the Cathedral whither he seems to have been lured by the designs of the Court. The priest appears to him only as the most exalted and therefore the most horrifying among the Information Givers he has met on his way.

Meursault's guilt is proved, but he refuses to see more in it than a criminal offense for which he is ready to pay the penalty (S, 148). Adamantly he resists the clergyman's claim that human justice is only a vague manifestation of divine law, and he has our sympathy since we are aware of the social forces that caused the Prosecutor to clamor for his death in the name of justice. Just as Meursault's guilt is distorted by the court, so, legally speaking, is the way in which K. is prosecuted and executed. Behind the distortion, however, K. suspects not only the corruption of society but the all-pervading chaos of the world. If Kafka had intended to satirize justice, he could easily have confronted K. with his judges and completed *The Trial*. For him, however, the injustice inherent in human justice was but an image, the image of the metaphysical disorder that had befallen mankind. The corrupt warders and lewd magistrates show the mocking grimace on the face of a once-divine countenance. Because of their corruption and lewdness his hero attacks them (and thus allows them to set him one trap after another); because of their hidden authority he can neither escape nor conquer them.

At the time of *The Stranger* Camus was convinced of the godlessness of the world and the dignity of man. Thus he raised Meursault beyond Good and Evil. Yet he was not simply following Nietzsche and the anti-Christian ethics of his Superman. In the stifling cellars of the French underground he acquired a more real, more limpid, more vital sense of man's purpose in a godless universe than self-tormented Nietzsche could ever have hoped to attain in the rarefied air of the Swiss Alps. Whereas Kafka's K. has nothing left but questions and ambiguities, the murderer Meursault insists on his right, even and especially in the face of the clergyman: "I'd been right, I was still right, I was always right" (S, 151). This self-assertion is, of course, the acme of subjectivism, and yet it is the only answer left to a man condemned by the collective subjectivism of a society that sends him to the guillotine for obviously subjective reasons. (Psychologically at least, the unabashed sadism displayed by the officials in K.'s Trial is also an answer to his masochistic nightmares, which are prime specimens of subjectivism.) Only in a system like the one the two clergymen pretend to profess, only in a pre-Nietzschean world where God was not yet dead, could K. and Meursault have accepted their guilt and willingly atoned for it. Only then could a "just" trial have been concluded, that is, a trial the laws of which they (and their readers) could have understood and accepted. As things stand, however, Meursault and K. are victimized by proceedings, the arbitrariness of which mirrors their own rootlessness and homelessness.

Both stories introduce the clergymen at their climax and use them as pivotal figures. Through them a sort of precarious inner balance is reestablished. Confronting men who cannot acknowledge the jurisdiction of the courts prosecuting them, these priests represent, however obscurely and treacherously, an objective, suprapersonal law. With them an order, however shaken and inapplicable, barely touches the chaos which our heroes have grown to take for granted. It is these confrontation scenes which add the meaning of a modern parable to the two novels.

Characteristically both Meursault and K. are eager to prevent the suprapersonal law from entering into their personal spheres of experience. Meursault, aggressive and energetic to the end, takes the priest by the neckband of his cassock and chokes him in a fit "of joy and rage" (S, 151), giving vent to all the thoughts which have been simmering in his brain. Ironically this outburst does not produce one single new idea. On the other hand, Joseph K. is forced to listen to the parable, "Before the Law," without, however, gaining any new insight into his own problem. If the argument with the priest proves anything to him, it is the complete hopelessness of his predicament.

Both Meursault and K. talk in order to drown the words spoken to them. Meursault jolts the Chaplain as if he wanted to shake out of him by physical force an answer to questions he has not even asked. Joseph K. fails to use his small but hectic intelligence to counter the Chaplain's parable with the objection that it does not apply to him. Instead, he loses himself in arguments which bypass or otherwise obscure the basic question of command and obedience. In both scenes a metaphysical truth reverberates in the conscience of men congenitally deaf to such truths. No communication is possible, because the symbols through which the spiritual claims could have expressed themselves have become unintelligible equally to Meursault and K.

Meursault seizes the Chaplain's cassock, thus violating the sanctity of the priest. The pulpit, on which the priest first appears to K., reminds him of a torture instrument (T, 259–260). Cassock and pulpit are treated as material paraphernalia; they are deprived of their symbolic significance. Divorced from the mystery they were once meant to reveal, they have degenerated into meaningless contraptions, bizarre shells of petrified conventions. The disbeliever who repudiates them is entitled to ask what they are doing here at all. Neither Meursault nor K. can see that it is the two clergymen through whom, however distortedly, the "mind projects into the concrete its spiritual tragedy," to use another phrase from Camus's essay on Kafka.[9]

In *The Myth of Sisyphus* Camus distinctly sides with Meursault. "A world," he says,

that can be explained even with bad reasons is a familiar world. But, on the other hand, in a universe suddenly divested of illusions and lights, man feels [himself] an alien, a stranger. His exile is without remedy since he is deprived of the memory of a lost home or the hope of a promised land. This divorce between man and his life, the actor and his setting, is properly the feeling of absurdity.[10]

Thus Meursault is defined and vindicated as an absurd hero. Also Kafka's K. is without memory and hope. He, too, points to the separation between himself and the authorities of his trial when in the end he appears to repudiate, with one last and significant gesture of negation, the here as well as the beyond.

Yet is the scorn shown to the authorities by Kafka's K. strong enough to allow Camus to say that the "flesh wins out" in *The Trial?* [11] K.'s gesture of defiance is steeped in the twilight of ambiguity so that it can also mean acceptance. The questions he raises are not answered. Even if we are prepared to understand them as the expressions of a metaphysical protest, it is hard to see any victory of the flesh in a death as debased as the slaughter which fells K. Camus had to acknowledge the opaqueness which shrouds K.'s death when he noted: "It is the fate and perhaps the greatness of that work that it offers everything and confirms nothing." [12] This sentence divests K. of the title of "absurd hero," which Camus claims to have derived from him.

Even the defiance with which Meursault prepares to die seems to be more radical than it actually is. To be sure, unrelenting to the last, he challenges in his final words the stupidity and corruption of the society which has condemned him to death: "For all to be accomplished, for me to feel less lonely, whatever remained to hope was that on the day of my execution there should be a huge crowd of spectators and that they should greet me with howls of execration" (S, 154). And yet, before he has reached such a high note of contempt, Meursault remembers his mother, for the first time with some degree of sympathy and understanding. He opens his heart to the universe which hitherto had seemed veiled in a mist of indifference, and suddenly a feeling of "tenderness" threatens to well up in his sluggish heart: "Sounds of the countryside came faintly in, and the cool night air, veined with smells of earth and salt, fanned my cheeks. The marvelous peace of the sleepbound summer night flooded through me like a tide" (S, 153).

Is not this feeling, which surges up in him "like the tides of the sea," closely akin to the "oceanic feeling," which Sigmund Freud once diagnosed as an "experience of boundless identification" [13] with a world otherwise thoroughly limited and definable? Does not this night, "spangled with its signs and stars" (S, 154), this "tender" night, give the lie to the indifference Meursault was accustomed to project into it? Does not this union of tenderness and indifference result in the very paradox needed to recapture the puzzle of human existence? The ending of *The Stranger* is a true statement of man's condition in a mysterious universe. As such it is so ambiguous that a critic could ask whether Camus conformed to his own ideas of "absurdity" when he wrote it.[14]

The fascination of both *The Trial* and *The Stranger* for the same European generation—those who were young after the Second World War—arose from the questions posed by these books rather than from any specific answers they were able to give. A multitude of conflicting answers can be found in them, for neither novel is satisfied with copying reality in simple terms. What they contain is the evidence collected by modern man to present at the trial of a world deprived of meaning. It goes without saying that in this trial man cannot hope for any verdict other than the pronouncement of the paradox on which his existence is based.

Parables reach beyond reality. By extending into the metaphysical, they overcome the limits of the physical world. To be sure, Camus presented Meursault's environment with the great skill of an accomplished *littérateur*. We sense the sea, the sand, the houses, and the trees of his Algiers in all their tangible presence. The light, which is the true culprit in *The Stranger*, is vastly more sensible than the symbolic radiance which streams forth from the door of the Law of Kafka's *The Trial*. It is the pure, hot blaze of an everyday sun. Consequently Meursault is vastly more "real" than K. The latter is continuously enveloped by the shadows of the background, whereas Meursault stands in the foreground, *is* foreground. Kafka's trial could not happen to him: on the very first page he would usher out the warders who claimed the right to arrest him. Strong youth that he is, he would get the better of them and their invisible employers.

Since Meursault is near to life, Camus can feel free to tell his story in the first person, whereas Kafka identifies his hero by the first letter of his name. *The Trial* abounds with reminiscences and anticipations, whereas Camus states the paradox of human existence in the immediate present tense. This proximity does not help to solve the paradox though. Meursault in his universal indifference is just as exemplary a modern man as is Joseph K. in his nervous excitement. Again, Kafka is only able to hint at K.'s human dignity, whereas Meursault is allowed to preserve his to the end, an end, to be sure, in which his aloof absurdity is overtaken by the mystery of life. Here even Meursault becomes a "sacrificial victim" [15] of the insolubly paradoxical human condition.

Kafka's heroes are perpetually exposed to an incomprehensible fate, as to a sharp, cold wind. Camus, on the other hand, needs an emergency, an extreme situation, to visualize and make visible the meeting of the natural with the supernatural. In *The Stranger* it was Meursault's death cell; in *The Plague* it is the city of Oran. Suddenly stricken by the plague, this city becomes the hotbed of extraordinary human decisions. A whole community finds itself in a situation which Kafka had anticipated in his "A Country Doctor," written thirty years before *The Plague:* "They have lost their ancient beliefs, . . . but the doctor is supposed to be omnipotent with his tender surgeon's hand." In more ways than one *The Plague* is the story of such a doctor.

Both Kafka and Camus knew that in a godless time the physician assumes the stature of a near-savior. The figure of the medical man has gradually become a leading one in the literature of the post-Freudian era. It dominates the intellectual flights of fancy in Thomas Mann's *The Magic Mountain,* as it holds the center of the more human Odyssey in Boris Pasternak's *Doctor Zhivago.* And it may well be more than an accident that the Nobel Prize Committee has singled out for its award *Doctor Zhivago* as well as Thomas Mann's novel of disease, love, and death, and Camus's parable of Dr. Rieux's struggle against the plague. They may have recognized that the image of the physician holds just as much of man's hope for salvation and redemption as our materialistic age is willing to accept, and that it is this hope which lends the three novels, however different they may otherwise be, their common importance and distinction.

To be sure, Camus exaggerates the contrast between religious redemption and medical cure, so much so that he reduces his parable at times to a mere disputation between an agnostic and a believer. In his novel the parson no longer sits at home "and unravels his vestments, one after another," as he does in Kafka's "A Country Doctor" (*PC*, 141). Camus's priest, Paneloux, fiercely opposes Dr. Rieux. The epidemic drives the Jesuit into the pulpit. Unashamedly he used the plague to reinspire the panicky and stricken ones with a faith they had long since abandoned. He even refuses to accept medical help because it is a human expedient and therefore suspect of counteracting the will of divine Providence.

The dialogue between Meursault and the Prison Chaplain is continued here, with the significant difference that Paneloux is no longer a nameless cog in the machinery of human justice but a determined and sharply profiled crusader, as persuasive by his powerful words as he is by the simple example he sets. Nor is Rieux an indifferent murderer like Meursault but a passionate man revolting against the totality of human suffering. In his essay, *The Rebel,* which serves as the philosophical underpinning of *The Plague,* Camus recalls Dostoyevsky's Ivan Karamazov as saying: "If the suffering of children . . . serves to complete the sum of suffering necessary for the acquisition of truth, I affirm from now onward that truth is not worth such a price." [16] Rieux says the same, but in a simpler and humbler way: "A man can't cure and know at the same time. So let's cure as quickly as we can. That's the more urgent job" (*P,* 189).

In *The Rebel* Camus reminds the reader of the "heartrending cry" of Ivan Karamazov, "If all are not saved, what good is the salvation of one only?" [17] Rieux feels the same way but expresses his feelings without Ivan's nineteenth-century pathos. To Paneloux's admission that he, too, is working for man's salvation, he answers: "Salvation is much too big a word for me. I don't aim so high. I am concerned with man's health; and for me his health comes first" (*P,* 197).

Rieux's experience seems indeed to be limited to awareness of everyday emergencies when we compare it with Kafka's timeless peregrinations through the maze of the mysterious. His Country Doctor is called to visit a boy who appears healthy and yet has "in his right side, near the hip, . . . an open wound as big as the palm" of a hand (*PC,* 141). The boy's sickness is genuine and imagined, visible and yet only a pretense. In other words, it shows the ambiguity characteristic of a neurotic symptom. Kafka was enough of a hypochondriac continuously observing himself, to realize that

all these socalled illnesses, however sad they may look, are facts of belief, the distressed human being's anchorages in some maternal ground or other; thus, it is not surprising that psychoanalysis finds the primal ground of all religions to be precisely the same thing as what causes the individual's "illnesses," true, nowadays there is no sense of religious fellowship (*DF,* 300).

and hence a medical cure is just as impossible as religious redemption. As everywhere, Kafka opened here the vista of the primeval and archaic and lost himself in it. He restated this thought more clearly when he remarked in one of his conversations with Gustav Janouch: "Sin is the root of all illness. This is the reason for mortality" (*J,* 85). If, however, mortality, sickness, and sin are basically one and the same, then they are also universal. Not only is the patient afflicted by them but the physician as well. Since Kafka's Country Doctor finds himself unable to help his young patient, he tries to help himself and, in so doing is defeated in eternity. This is, of course, a cruelly poignant parody of Jesus' saying in the Gospels: "Physician, heal thyself!"

On the other hand, Camus's Dr. Rieux faces a disease, the reality of which is impressed upon him by daily statistics. When the priest suggests to him the identity of disease and sin, he recoils in revolt, the revolt of *The Rebel*. He rejects all that passes human understanding. The priest intimates that we should love what we cannot understand, but Rieux cries out: "No, Father. I've a very different idea of love. And until my dying day I shall refuse to love a scheme of things in which children are put to torture" (*P*, 196–197), like the little Othon who has just writhed to death before them. And while Kafka's Country Doctor complains that he is "misused for sacred ends" (*PC*, 141), confusing his earthly task as a doctor with the holy office of a priest, Rieux limits himself willingly to the human and secular. Since he is aware of his limitations, he remains a rationalist, and since he comes to understand human nature, he becomes a skeptic as well. The fight against the plague means to him a "never-ending defeat," and the ultimate source of his wisdom is "suffering" (*P*, 118). Once he remarks to his friend Tarrou, who has decided to live as a "saint without God": "I feel more fellowship with the defeated than with saints. Heroism and sanctity don't really appeal to me. . . . What interests me is being a man" (*P*, 231). This "being a man" he has long since defined as a "matter of common decency" (*honnêteté*—*P*, 150). To Rieux's understatement of man's purpose Camus adds a more ringing declaration in *The Rebel*: "But he who dedicates himself to the duration of his life, to the house he builds, to the dignity of mankind, dedicates himself to the earth and reaps from it the harvest that sows its seed and sustains the world again and again." [18]

Undoubtedly Camus's vision of man is clearer and simpler than any of Kafka's tormented dreams, but did he not have to pay for his clarity and simplicity by a considerable loss in sophistication? Our contemporary problems are, after all, more complex and subtle than those grasped by the good doctor Rieux; and "in a certain sense the Good is a desolate affair," as Kafka once admitted in the "Reflections" (*DF*, 37). Whereas Kafka seems at times to be obscure because he is unable to control the shadowy throng of his nightmares, Camus's insistence on the merits of humanity occasionally sounds flat and dull to our ears. Whereas

Kafka's images may produce a feeling of soporific abandonment in even the most attentive reader, Camus's images may turn out to be mere allegories, which can easily be deciphered by applying to them the philosophical terms provided in his theoretical writings. Moreover, Kafka's irony permits him to maintain at least a superficial impartiality toward the opponents in his books. Camus, on the other hand, appears to be siding with one of his figures against another: he is partial to Rieux and hostile to Paneloux. On his deathbed the Jesuit is described as a "doubtful case" (*P*, 211), which tends to sound like a moral judgment rather than a medical diagnosis. Besides, on the last page of the book Rieux reveals himself as its chronicler. The author seems to identify himself with his hero and to endorse with his own authority the insights and judgments of his protagonist. The doctor exits by a backdoor, so to speak, and the author takes the stage, occupying the center, the position held thus far by his principal figure.

Yet, paradoxically, this sleight of hand establishes Camus's craftsmanship as a teller of modern parables. For the chronicler of *The Plague* must not be confused with Camus, the journalist, who was as anticlerical as he was anti-Communist. Nor is the author of *The Plague* completely identical with Camus, the philosopher, who held the paradoxical, though highly persuasive, position of a liberal existentialist.[19]

The chronicler of *The Plague* appears as a literary artificer, that is, as a creator of images. At their best these images are symbols like Kafka's symbols, open to more than one interpretation. In this way Camus the novelist, Camus the creator, surpasses the journalist and the philosopher by being able to unite in his imagery the physical and the spiritual planes of our existence.

Lonely Rieux strikes up a friendship with the "godless saint," Tarrou. Almost inadvertently the two men chance upon the idea of sealing their friendship by a night swim in the ocean. On the surface this is a virile gesture meant to express their silent confidence in one another. On a deeper level it touches on associations with submersion in a sort of baptismal bath.[20] Rieux, the chronicler, reports: "The air here reeked of stale wine and fish. . . . Slowly the waters rose and sank, and with their tranquil breathing sudden oily glints formed and flickered over the surface in a haze of broken lights. Before them the darkness stretched out into infinity" (*P*, 232). The word "infinity" is bound to conjure up the same "oceanic feeling" which enveloped Meursault at the climax of his career. Parabolical symbols like "wine," "fish," and "oil" are gathered here so distinctly as to suggest a more than realistic intention on the part of the chronicler. The nocturnal ocean has been turned into a font of rejuvenation, refreshing both body and spirit of the night bathers. But the evidence does not stop here. In the French original the central image of the plague is endowed with ambiguity by Camus's play on the word *fléau,* which, more distinctly than its English equivalent of "scourge," means both a flail and an epidemic. This pun is used as a leitmotiv throughout the novel, just as Kafka plays on the many meanings of the titles and other key words in his works.

In his first sermon Paneloux likens the plague to an immense wooden bar "whirling about the town, striking at random, swinging up again in a shower of drops of blood, and spreading carnage and suffering on earth, 'for the seed-time that shall prepare the harvest of the truth' " (*P,* 89). Rieux himself embarks upon his struggle against disease as one of those "humanists" who "disbelieve in scourges" ("Ils ne croyaient pas aux fléaux"—*P,* 35). In the beginning he is a man from whom any metaphysical meaning of sickness is hidden. This meaning is, however, suggested to him by the plague. Finally he recognizes that he has been wrestling all along with "the angel of plague" thrashing the air above the houses with his flail (*P,* 256–257). The flail image cannot help touching and moving him by its deeper connotations and its more profound meaning.

Of course, this does not amount to saying that Dr. Rieux has been converted, however unconsciously, to the orthodox rigidity of Father Paneloux. But it does indicate that the chronicler has been telling his story of human suffering with such a degree of honesty and completeness that he has reached the limit of his own wisdom. At this outer limit Dr. Rieux is forced to ask questions for which his rational humanism offers no answer. The symbols which he employs are genuine word images which extend into spheres where grammar and logic cannot penetrate. The border line they straddle is also the demarcation line defining the realm of the modern parable.

The plague itself is such a genuine symbol. At no point during his narration does Camus divulge its meaning. We only learn that it was not Rieux who conquered it. The epidemic comes and goes according to its own will and law. It assumes its full value, however, through Rieux's realization that the men he is talking about have now outgrown their physical limitations and are fed and judged by powers outside their ken and beyond their grasp. No longer does the "flesh win out"; the graveyards of Oran bear eloquent witness to man's carnal defeat. Rather does Rieux reiterate his belief in the essential dignity of man on that vantage point of human experience which Rilke must have had in mind when, at the end of his *Requiem* of 1908, he asks: "Who talks of victory?" and answers: "To endure is all" [21]—to endure and survive, that is, in utter isolation and exposure, and on a point of no return. Rieux lives to see the end of the plague, but he is now alone and, as Germaine Brée has put it, "dehumanized." [22]

What, then, is the meaning of the plague? Is it the atonement of sin, as the priest envisages it? Is Tarrou right in explaining it as a symbol of man's inability to manage his own affairs? "They're all mad over murder and they couldn't stop killing men even if they wanted to. . . . We all have plague" (*P*, 228). Is it the inertia of man's heart which renders him deaf and blind to the horrors of history, provided only that they spare him? "I know positively," Tarrou continues, "that each of us has the plague within him; no one, no one on earth is free from it" (*P*, 229). In large sections of *The Rebel* Camus seems to agree with Tarrou's interpretation. Moreover, he has used quite a few of the images developed in *The Plague* to compose an allegory of France's occupation by the Germans in his play, *State of Siege*. Driven by the scourges with which men punish men, all Tarrou can hope for is to be considered "an innocent murderer" (*P*, 230). Or is the truth about the plague recognized by the old, half-crazed drygoodsman who takes to his bed after the outbreak of the epidemic and there counts the time by shifting peas from one saucepan to another (*P*, 107–108)? "What does this mean—'plague'?" he is finally heard asking. And he answers himself: "Just life, no more than that" (*P*, 277). With him, too, Camus seems to sympathize. In his notebooks he comments: "I wish to express, by means of the plague, the feeling of suffocation from which we all suffered and the atmosphere of threat and exile in which we lived. But," he adds immediately, "at the same time I want to extend my interpretation to the notion of existence in general." [23]

The Plague is a parable, and parables are structurally akin to puzzles, the solution of which contains the moral of the parables. But just as adamantly as Kafka does Camus refuse to reveal one unambiguous solution. He only betrays his basic view that everyone is exposed to the plague, rises or falls through it, is given a chance to succumb or conquer—in other words, that everyone is faced with a decision through the plague. The plague means to everyone his own doubt, his own exposure to destiny, and the inevitability of taking a stand. The only general insight Camus's plague conveys to the reader is the realiza-

tion that there are no general insights to be gained. Camus has taken
over from Kafka the very nature of his central parabolical image. And
just as Kafka has placed the parable "Before the Law" in the center of
The Trial, so Camus concentrates the message of his plague chronicle
in one central anecdote. "A hundred years ago," Tarrou tells Rieux,
"plague wiped out the entire population of a town in Persia, with one
exception. And the sole survivor was precisely the man whose job it
was to wash the dead bodies, and who carried on throughout the
epidemic" (*P*, 119). For Camus as for Kafka, the incomprehensible
remains incomprehensible, and a paradox takes the place of any rational maxim conveyed by the narration. It is a kind of meta-didactic
prose: at the core of the secret a new mystery is hidden.

A mystery opens the trial of Kafka's *The Trial,* shrouds the strangeness of Camus's *The Stranger,* and spreads the plague in *The Plague.*
It also causes the fall in Camus's *The Fall.* The hero of this long short
story, the "judge-penitent" Jean-Baptiste Clamence, is neither a peni-
tent nor a judge. His very name holds the paradox of his existence
because he is named after all that which he is not: John, the Baptist,
Clemency. (Translated into the French, Huld, the "inclement" lawyer
in Kafka's *The Trial,* would also be called *Clémence.*) Passively witnessing the plunge of an unknown woman into the Seine, Jean-Baptiste
becomes aware of his fallen state. If he had helped the stranger and
followed her into the river, he might—perhaps—have received the
baptism of divine mercy. His passivity, however, is just as evil as the
misdirected activity of Kafka's Country Doctor, of which it is said: "A
false alarm on the night bell once answered—it cannot be made good,
not ever." As far as Jean-Baptiste is concerned, he profoundly
doubts the salvation he might have found in rescuing this woman. He
knows only one security, the intellectual satisfaction he finds in tormenting himself. A voluntary exile from his home, a fugitive from his
profession, he roams the streets of Amsterdam, scorning, ridiculing,
parodying his self-imposed despair.

For him the world has become a prison without bars. "A hundred
and fifty years ago," he says, "people became sentimental about lakes
and forests. Today we have the lyricism of the prison cell" (*F*, 123–
124). What he means is that he inhabits the same universal and paradoxical dungeon of which Kafka said in his aphorisms, "He," in 1920:

To end as a prisoner—that could be a life's ambition. But it was a barred
cage that he was in. Calmly and insolently, as if at home, the din of the
world streamed out and in through the bars, the prisoner was really free, he

could take part in everything, nothing that went on outside escaped him, he could simply have left the cage, the bars were yards apart, he was not even a prisoner (*GW*, 264).

For Clamence, too, "being sent to a prison" would be "an attractive idea in a way" (*F*, 130). As a matter of fact, he lives in a prison like Kafka's. He, too, is "not even a prisoner," and yet remains a slave whipped through his life by the echo of the mysterious laughter which he has kept hearing ever since the incident on the Pont des Arts.

This laughter turns reality into a veritable inferno. "Have you noticed," Clamence asks, "that Amsterdam's concentric canals resemble the circles of Hell? The middle-class hell, of course, peopled with bad dreams" (*F*, 14). The description fits the shady lanes on which Kafka's Trial is enacted as well as the buildings, petty-bourgeois rather than lordly, of which his Castle is composed.

Not even capable of committing a crime, Clamence has turned into a receiver, more despicable than a thief. Indulging in a whim of sarcastic symbolism, he conceals in his cupboard a panel taken from Van Eyck's famous altarpiece, "The Adoration of the Lamb." The painting itself leaves him cold; what fascinates the "judge-penitent" is the subject of the stolen painting. It represents "The Just Judges," and its unlawful possession gives with glorious irony the lie to the office of a judge, ironically usurped by Clamence. It likewise negates his repentance. Thus he is able to sin without actually committing a crime— he just continues another man's, the chief's, misdeed. The obsessive pleasure he enjoys while doing so is both vicarious and hypothetical. His triumph lies in conquering any feeling of compunction the hidden "Just Judges" may arouse in him. Through this prolonged act of rather complicated symbolism he imagines he has definitely separated justice from innocence, "the latter on the cross and the former in the cupboard" (*F*, 130).

Among Camus's heroes Jean-Baptiste resembles a Kafka figure most in the labyrinthine ways of his thinking and the opaqueness of the images which he chooses to accompany his fall. And yet there remains a difference. Camus keeps as full a distance from his half-deranged hero as Cervantes put between himself and Don Quixote. Kafka, on the other hand, is profoundly serious about the plight of his protagonists. Inasmuch as they resemble their creator, they share with him the inability to laugh. To Milena, Kafka once wrote: "Sometimes I do not understand how human beings have discovered the notion of 'gaiety,' probably it has just been computed as a contrast to sadness" (*LM*,

209). Sadder than this sadness is the idea that gaiety could be achieved by the cerebral process of a calculation.

But all who knew Kafka personally have maintained that he was possessed of the gift of humor to a very high degree. His friend Felix Weltsch has written a book tracing the connection between what he calls Kafka's humor and his religion.[24] Brod has recorded an incident in which the specific coloration of this humor becomes apparent. "We friends of his," Brod recalls, "laughed quite immoderately when he first let us hear the first chapter of *The Trial*. And he himself laughed so much that there were moments when he could not read any further" (*FK*, 178). This laughter is reminiscent of the reaction Heinrich von Kleist experienced when, more than a hundred years earlier, he read his first tragedy to his friends. The arbitrariness of inexorable fate marks Heinrich von Kleist's play, just as it informs Kafka's *Trial*. Kleist was, after all, one of Kafka's favorites. Heinrich Zschokke, one of those present at Kleist's reading, recalls in his autobiography: "One day, when Kleist read to us *The Schroffensteins,* the laughter of his listeners grew so violent and continuous in the end that even the author was forced to join it and thus was prevented from reaching the play's last murder scene." [25] This kind of laughter is a more legitimate, more realistic, and at the same time more ambiguous response to the incomprehensible than the conventional effects of horror tales—the listeners' hair standing proverbially on end, for example. Here, panic terror dissolves into panic laughter, a laughter that eventually envelops even him who has caused the fright. Or, to put it into more general terms, the human condition may be desperate but it is not unequivocally serious. The witnesses of truly absurd horror are still able to react to the frightening and ludicrous scene before them by allowing their tension to be discharged in laughter. To be sure, none of them will be surprised to see tears rolling down their cheeks while they are gripped by this laughter.[26] The nature of horror seems to be as ambivalent as the effect horror has on those stricken by it.

Moreover, Kafka's so-called humor is a direct result of the humorlessness displayed by his characters. His heroes, above all, take themselves so seriously that they are unable to see the seriousness of their condition. Being self-centered, they are blind to the desperate situation to which they are exposed. Seen against this obsessive seriousness of Kafka's heroes, the world cannot but reveal itself as nonsensical. From above and afar one sometimes can hear the echoes of Kafka's laughter at the catastrophic consequences of his heroes' collision with their fate.

By and large Kafka seems to state the case of man against an absurd universe. Camus, on the other hand, sees in his absurd hero the case in point of all things human. Consciously he exposes Clamence's intellectual meanderings before his readers' eyes. *The Fall*, like *The Stranger*, is written in the first person singular, but in the later work Camus uses the form of the monologue, the *récit*, to detach himself even more emphatically from the speaking Ego. He drives his absurd protagonist to the extreme of his absurdity and manages thereby to extricate his own person from the metaphysical exercises of his hero by pitilessly parodying them. The result is a laughter which releases the reader not only from Clamence's obsessions but from the whole complex of crime and punishment which has haunted European letters since that fateful moment when Rodion Raskolnikov entered the old pawnbroker's shop. It is a laughter of sanity restored. More specifically, Jean-Baptiste Clamence's last sigh over his utterly wasted life sounds like an involuntary and highly successful parody of Kafka's tragic frustrations: "It's too late now. It will always be too late. Fortunately" (*F*, 147)!

And yet even Clamence, the contrite charlatan, is representative of a humanity which has lost its place in a God-created universe. Proclaiming the true democracy of all who are guilty (*F*, 136), Clamence is obsessively articulate when he outlines the epidemic he knows he is about to disseminate:

Covered with ashes, tearing my hair, my face scored by clawing, but with piercing eyes, I stand before all humanity recapitulating my shames without losing sight of the effect I am producing, and saying: "I was the lowest of the low." Then imperceptibly I pass from the "I" to the "we." When I get to "This is what we are," the trick has been played and I can tell them off (*F*, 140).

He is genuinely afflicted by the compulsion to unburden himself of his guilt; he cannot choose but talk. His make-up is that of a highly intellectualized clown, but beneath the grease paint, the wit and the sophistry, he is marked like Cain, like Joseph K. Even *The Fall* treats of perdition and salvation.

The reader cannot escape the suspicion that the plague Clamence is intent on spreading originates in his extreme egocentricity. What Clamence suffers from and what he disseminates is the grotesque misery of an Ego hopelessly entangled in its self-reflections. With even greater justification we may apply to *The Fall* what Nathalie

Sarraute said about Kafka's heroes when she tried to set them apart from Camus's Stranger. Jean-Baptiste Clamence too has reached beyond the extreme limits of human existence. "There . . . all feeling has disappeared, even contempt and hatred; there remains nothing but an immense empty stupor, a definite and total inability to understand. One cannot inhabit these parts, nor try to go any further. Those who live on the earth of man can only retrace their steps." [27]

Retracing our steps from *The Fall* to *The Plague*, we can now fully appreciate Dr. Rieux's modesty. His report was a chronicle, not a *récit;* he was able to report his own struggle with the plague in the third, not the first, person. From the very first page of the book he has suppressed the Ego whose struggles and sufferings he has been recounting, replacing the "I" by a "they," the objective and self-denying pronoun. "They" is the city of Oran, and the multitude of its inhabitants, with all their traits and destinies. This, to be sure, is the deeper meaning behind Rieux's remark that he had resolved to write his book "so that he should not be one of those who hold their peace but should bear witness in favor of those plague-stricken people" (*P*, 278). Consequently, he has succeeded in breaking through his isolation and, as a chronicler, in establishing human situations among the individuals populating his report. A man has lost his wife and acquires a friend. Lovers are being separated and reunited. "They knew now that if there is one thing one can always yearn for and sometimes attain, it is human love" (*c'est la tendresse humaine*—*P*, 271). It is more than mere chance that here, as at the end of *The Stranger,* the word "*tendresse*" appears, providing something of a harmonic resolution for the dissonances of man's condition. The image of man is reassembled while the universe around him has kept its inscrutable paradox.

Kafka languished "without forebears, without marriage, without heirs," his vitality constantly drained by the absurdity of a world without grace. Camus faced this absurdity squarely and braved the ambiguities behind which the paradox of existence is hidden. We may miss in his books the tormented nobility of Kafka's high style; instead we find in them human relations reestablished. The hero who holds the center of *The Plague* does not flee backward, like K. in Kafka's *The Trial,* nor forward, like K. in *The Castle.* Instead he is a man standing upright under a low and dark sky, helping, curing, and saving. "There are," Tarrou says,

pestilences and there are victims; no more than that. . . . I grant we should add a third category: that of the true healers. But it's a fact one doesn't come across many of them, and anyhow it must be a hard vocation. That's why I decided to take, in every predicament, the victims' side, so as to reduce the damage done. Among them I can at least try to discover how one attains to the third category; in other words, to peace (*P*, 230).

In this passage the contemporary parable of the tragic and ridiculous isolation of man in an emptied universe can be seen on its way toward a message which it can deliver again from man to man, victoriously crossing all the paradoxes of his existence.

CHAPTER X

Kafka behind the Iron Curtain

ON December 14, 1963, the Prague weekly *Literární noviny* carried the news that Edward Albee's *Who's Afraid of Virginia Woolf?* was to be performed in the Czech capital under the title *Who's Afraid of Kafka?* (*Kdopak by se Kafky bál?*). This news item, which was noted with some glee by the American press, is much less ludicrous than it may appear at first sight: the name Kafka (= kavka) means "jack-daw," and a jackdaw in European folklore is a harbinger of doom.* Thus the Czech translation is a very close approximation of Albee's pun. Indeed, the etymology of Kafka's name served to conceal the impli-cations of the play's title from the Czech state authorities. To be sure, the lilt of the English original is lost, and so is the trenchant irony produced by the linguistic clash between the simplicity of a children's tale and the trite sophistication of the not-so-mature adults in Albee's play. Yet the basic idea is preserved: a literary name of universal renown is used as an image portending disaster.

The real piece of news in this press item, however, was that the Czechs had suddenly started to consider Kafka as a figure of both universal appeal and national importance, and this even though he had been decried by theoreticians everywhere behind the Iron Cur-

* See pp. 90 and 229 above.

tain as a decadent petty bourgeois whose pitiless pessimism made his works an obstacle in the path of proletarian culture. No social realist he.

To be sure, Kafka had not fared too badly in Czech left-wing circles. His friend Jarmila Jesenská, a liberal of pronounced socialist leanings, had translated *The Stoker* as early as 1920. She submitted the translation to Stanislav Kostka Neumann, who filled a whole issue of his literary magazine *Kmen* (*The Stem*) with the story, which he introduced as "belonging to the best narratives in the German language." [1] After Kafka's death in 1924, Neumann published an obituary in the *Communist Review,* in which he called the dead writer "a sensitive mind who glanced deeply into the organism of today's unjust society, who loved the exploited and inexorably punished the rich in an extremely complex and yet moving fashion." [2] The Communist daily *Rudé právo* printed a similar eulogy on August 17, 1924.[3] Moreover, Gustav Janouch remembers that Neumann interpreted *The Stoker,* whose continuation, *Amerika,* was still unknown, as "the first real, altogether unconventional portrait of a modern worker who by his efforts actually sets the ship of our world in motion and keeps it moving." [4] Thus the image of a left-wing Kafka made its appearance in his native city long before West German interpreters like Theodor W. Adorno and, after him, Klaus Wagenbach and Wilhelm Emrich discovered in Kafka the ingenious critic of capitalist society. The Czechs must have preserved traces of this image all through the German occupation and the postwar troubles, so that in 1958, the very year of the Pasternak scandal in Russia, Kafka's *Trial* could be published in Prague, translated by the ever-faithful Paul Eisner.[5] While the public was officially discouraged from reading this most hopeless and reactionary of all bourgeois writers, ten thousand copies of the novel were sold on the first day of its appearance.[6]

But in 1963, eighty years after Kafka's birth, even the official attitude seemed to change. Čedok, the State Travel Agency, began to arrange so-called "Kafka Tours" and invited the international tourist trade to visit the local Kafka shrines.[7] Kafka's tomb in the new Jewish cemetery in Olšany, which the French scholar Marthe Robert had discovered only with difficulty in the fall of 1962,[8] was restored and cleaned. The major development in 1963 was, however, a conference convened in May by the Committee of Czech Germanists. The meeting took place in the castle of Liblice—the property of the Czechoslovak Academy of Sciences—and was attended by seventy local critics and scholars in addition to fourteen guests from East and West Germany, France, Yugoslavia, Austria, Poland, Hungary, and the United States.[9]

Emotions ran high in Liblice. "Kafka also lived for us," the Warsaw literary historian Roman Karst exclaimed. "His work speaks to us, too!" [10] And the Austrian critic Ernst Fischer, a man with a rich Communist past, appealed to the intelligentsia of the Eastern countries: "Let us get Kafka's works back from their involuntary exile! Grant him a permanent visa!" [11]

It is a matter of some doubt whether Kafka's exile would have been altogether involuntary. Overly sensitive to the demands of any authority, this metaphysical anarchist would undoubtedly have taken to his heels before any totalitarian regime. But Fischer's pathos was at least honest: the world of socialism could not offer the exiled writer a homeland but only a residence. He was welcome not by right but on sufferance, a sufferance dictated by political opportunism. As all refugees know, there is nothing more transitory than a permanent visa, which can instantly be abrogated at the slightest whim of authority.

Nevertheless, the conference of Liblice represented a novelty: for the first time an authoritarian state had sanctioned a full-scale discussion of this highly controversial writer. One would suspect that the Czechoslovak Government's wish to promote its tourist trade—and its good relations with the world in general—was an incentive to its participation in the general Kafka boom. Like all the successor states of Old Austria, Czechoslovakia had inherited a healthy interest in *Fremdenverkehr* and potent currency. At the same time the conference bore witness to Czech nationalism, the mystique of a small and repeatedly suppressed nation. Its Czech members catered unabashedly to this nationalism, although, strictly speaking, Kafka was neither a Czech nor a Bohemian but a German-speaking Jew from Prague. Still, the fact remains that the conference seems to have received *carte blanche* from the government to ventilate the problems of Communist literature by grappling with the Kafka problem.

Politically, the conference of Liblice had been prepared by a speech on cultural disarmament that Jean-Paul Sartre had given in Moscow in 1962. To drive home the necessity for intellectual coexistence between East and West, Sartre had stressed Kafka's work, which he described as being universally valid and, at the same time, profoundly unique. The Prague writer was the example and test case of genuine cultural competition. "I asked one of my Soviet friends," Sartre had said, " 'Why don't you translate him?' " The friend answered:

"We shall soon start translating some of his shorter works, but you will understand that Western criticism has distorted him to such an extent that he appears to many among us as our sworn enemy." I replied: "And why did you on your part not publish Marxist reviews and claim him for yourselves? Even in this field you would have been victorious, for your methods surpass those of the Western critics in the interpretation of facts. Or rather, you will surpass them when you have taken over from them the right among so much wrong. In short: genuine cultural competition consists in eliminating all barriers within culture and then challenging the other side peacefully with the question: To whom does Kafka belong, to you or to us—that is, who understands him best? Who profits most from him?" [12]

Considering the fact that Sartre scorns possession and lately even refused to accept the Nobel Prize, he showed a healthy interest in property, if only intellectual property. Perhaps he believed that he had to act as an ambassador: he spoke the language of the party that he felt it was his mission to convince. Stressing the superiority Eastern critics had gained in the explication of fact rather than form, and displaying throughout a utilitarian's approach to literature, he met his hosts more than halfway and undoubtedly opened the road that led from Moscow to Liblice.

Another, albeit less official, turning point in the relations between Czech Communist criticism and Kafka's work dates farther back.[13] A few months before his death in 1957, Louis Fürnberg, coeditor of the East German quarterly *Weimarer Beiträge,* sent a letter to the Prague critic Paul Reimann, in which he said:

It is our task to define our position toward the Kafka problem clearly and unreservedly, concretely and dispassionately, and without failing to appreciate that Kafka was a great writer. This way we shall . . . do more to orient ourselves in the question of Kafka than by continuing in (1) the ignorant flat negation which so far we have allowed to guide us; and (2) the pseudo-objectivity that had as its result our relinquishing Kafka, to the benefit of those circles who face us as mortal enemies.[14]

The author knew Louis Fürnberg well when Fürnberg spent the war years as a refugee in Palestine. He was a mediocre poet, an ardent Communist, and a kindly human being. Hailing from Karlsbad, he had been touched by the civilization of the Habsburg empire and had enjoyed the atmosphere of Masaryk's first republic. He used to perform intellectual egg dances in honor of Rilke and Kafka among his Marxist friends.

Thus he was able to write a poem, "On the Life and Death of F.K.," although he did not dare publish it during his own lifetime:

> How does one get rid of one's ghosts?
> They squat behind the children's bed.
> Is children's fear the poets' fate?
> Are they the father's laughingstock?
>
> And God and father, both in one,
> and endless weakness of the soul,
> and what is mine and what is His,
> and what the sacrament of earth?
>
> And is this all? Nothing but law?
> And this the final consequence:
> A job which one is bound to find,
> As state official, single shift?
>
> And Werfel, Fuchs and Brod and Baum
> and Pollak, Utitz, Weltsch and Kisch?
> And has my dream outgrown its space?
> Are tortures so ingenious?

> Wie wird man die Gespenster los?
> Sie hocken hinterm Kinderbett.
> Ist Kindergrauen Dichterlos?
> Wird man dem Vater zum Gespött?
>
> Und Gott und Vater, beides Eins,
> Und Seelenschwachheit ohne End',
> Und was ist Mein's und was ist Sein's
> Und was der Erde Sakrament?
>
> Und ist dies Alles? Jus und Schluss?
> Und dies die letzte Konsequenz:
> Ein Posten, der sich finden muss,
> Im Staatsdienst, einfacher Frequenz?
>
> Und Werfel, Fuchs und Brod und Baum
> Und Pollak, Utitz, Weltsch und Kisch?

Ist meinem Traum zu eng der Raum?
Sind Qualen so erfinderisch? [15]

These lines are better than they seem. The enumeration of Kafka's Prague friends reproduces the climate, both strenuous and bizarre, that prevailed in German-Jewish Prague. The rhyme of "Kisch" and "erfinderisch" serves to characterize the former, who used to boast that he was a "raving reporter." Above all the stanzas contain a diagnosis: Kafka's vision and work stemmed from infantile neurosis, from his attempt to identify God and father, from the compulsion of his office hours from 8 A.M. to 2 P.M. ("single shift"), from the ludicrous ghetto of the coffeehouses. As long as the West was primarily interested in the circumstances of the writer's life, its critics hardly came forward with a different interpretation. One can safely assume that this poem was written at an early date in Fürnberg's development.

However this may be, the letter Fürnberg wrote Paul Reimann in 1957 so impressed the critic that he reacted immediately and wrote for the fourth issue of *Weimarer Beiträge* (1957) an essay entitled "The Social Problems in Kafka's Novels." This issue had been prepared by Fürnberg just before his death; he must have rejoiced to have found a Communist brother-in-Kafka at long last.

Since, however, the principle of socialist realism was still followed in Russia and her satellites, Reimann remained intent on discovering it in Kafka's writings. He was less concerned with Kafka's stature as a writer than with his acceptability to socialist aesthetics. He continued where Stanislav Kostka Neumann had left off. "*Amerika*," he said, "is a social novel, transparently written, which, apart from some immaterial episodes, contains neither 'puzzles' nor 'secrets.'" [16] But among these "immaterial episodes" belongs the last chapter of the fragment, a vision so mysteriously interwoven of miracle and parody that it could be interpreted both as the hero's confirmation into the Catholic Church and as his journey into the land of death.* Neglecting these passages in a cavalier fashion, Reimann used *Amerika* to exemplify the futility of all attempts "to exploit Kafka for the reactionary purposes of the imperialistic bourgeoisie." [17] For the publication of his essay in book form four years later, he added a significant sentence here: "Kafka was not at all the spokesman of the imperialist bourgeoisie, he was their helpless victim." [18]

* See p. 156 above.

By calling Kafka the victim rather than the mouthpiece of bourgeois society, Reimann eliminated the question of socialist realism, or at least emphatically pushed it to the background. All of a sudden the work of the writer stood out in its uniqueness; nor did it matter much now that its author had been the employee of an insurance company, a sickly littérateur who had intended to seduce coming generations to wallow masochistically in the ruin of their class. Reimann did not overlook the passivity of Kafka's heroes, their lack of resistance, and their lust for losing. But he had begun to distinguish between them and their creator. They were victims, while he pilloried their victimization.

Soon Reimann received assistance from the Viennese critic Ernst Fischer. As early as 1958, Fischer had warned against disposing of Kafka by classifying him as the moribund offspring of a doomed society.[19] In 1962 he demolished the decadence theory in his weighty essay "Alienation, Decadence, and Realism." His approach to Kafka was comparatist. Grouping him with Joyce as a "master of fantastic satire" and adding, for good measure, the names of such decadents as Marcel Proust, William Faulkner, Thomas Mann, and—of all writers —Herman Melville, he denied that decadence in literature was necessarily synonymous with the decline and decomposition of capitalism. "Our time of world-historical transition," he exclaimed, "is characterized by a variety of oscillations, partial decisions and experiments with regard both to the petty-bourgeois producer of art and to the dubiousness of the content and form of his production." And he continued:

In every declining society a new one ripens. There is no lack of antitoxins against decadence, either in the working classes or among the intellectuals. To be sure the writer, the artist, cannot completely escape the influence of his poisoned surroundings; he is not, however, abandoned to it defenselessly either. He may be corrupted; indeed often enough he *is* corrupted. But only rarely does he submit to the ruling classes lastingly and unconditionally. There is the artist's conscience, which cannot easily be paralyzed: his experience of his surroundings is different from the experience of those in power; it is an experience that does not correspond to theirs.[20]

It was not by chance that appearing with Fischer's essay in *Sinn und Form* was a translation of Sartre's "Demilitarization of Culture." The thaw was on. Yet Fischer leaves Sartre far behind when he admits the possibility that despair may take a sudden turn to political action. "Kafka has created total negation," he says; "but in it there is also hidden the negation of negation, the breakthrough from alienation to a decision which bestows upon existence a sudden meaning, and the sense of belonging." [21] By combining the Marxian concept of *Entfremdung* with the idea of *Durchbruch*, which permeates so pessimistic a work as Thomas Mann's *Doctor Faustus*, Ernst Fischer had moved himself close to the border beyond which the left wing of Western Kafka interpreters held sway. He undoubtedly profited from the air of neutrality prevailing in his native Austria, which rendered him less susceptible to the continuous vacillations undergone by the official party line toward literature since Stalin's death and the end of the period of the personality cult. In Fischer's interpretation Kafka was no longer a "slave of circumstance" (as Ludwig Börne had called Goethe) but a figure who, beyond the categories of historical materialism, lingered on in the "no man's land between solitude and community." [22] This, in itself, was heresy. And yet, the time seemed to have come to initiate, perhaps through the criticism of Kafka, a revision of Communist aesthetics in general.

The Liblice conference appears to have been due to the initiative of one man, Eduard Goldstücker. Goldstücker had been jailed during the early fifties, when he was recalled as Minister to Israel and sentenced to life imprisonment, allegedly for having participated in the Slánský conspiracy against the state. After a few years, he was quietly released and appointed Professor of German Language and Literature at the Charles University in Prague. Before Hitler, this chair had been occupied by the venerable Otakar Fischer, the translator and interpreter of Heine, Kleist, and Karl Kraus. At first, the old liberalism of his office seems to have rubbed off on Goldstücker. The paper he read at Liblice included a lengthy comparison of Kafka and Kleist, a sociological complement to Max Brod's early juxtaposition of the two authors in psychological terms. [23] As a precondition of modern Kafka scholarship the Czech professor postulated the abandonment of the sociologizing vulgarisms that had tended to reduce the authorized biography of any writer to a party certificate of good conduct. [24] Yet Goldstücker took back with his left hand what he gave with his right: insisting on the sociological foundation and biographical nature of each work of art, he overstressed the importance of *The Stoker* and, following Wilhelm Emrich, read revolutionary motives even into the land-surveyorship of K. in *The Castle*. (Like his Western predecessor, he neglected the textual evidence which indicates that K. is completely obsessed with his own ordeal and remains profoundly untouched by the sufferings of the proletarians in the village. Having been a victim of political terror, Goldstücker transmogrified Kafka, the visionary of universal pain, into a prophet of atrocities such as Goldstücker himself had endured. For him, Kafka's importance was to be found in his anticipation of Fascist outrages, an interpretation already given by Edwin Muir in 1938, as Peter Demetz has noted.[25] The Prague professor was and remains a stalwart Marxist even though he seems to subscribe to the doctrines of the non-Marxist Sartre concerning nationalism and the "Demilitarization of Culture." Thus he felt compelled to reiterate the words Sartre had spoken in Moscow (thereby connecting the two conferences for all to see): "The profundity of every work springs from the national history, language and traditions, from the special, and in most cases tragic, questions put to the artist by his time and place through the living community of which he is an integral part." [26]

In this attitude he was supported by František Kautman, who addressed the conference on the subject of Franz Kafka and Czech literature. Kautman argued no point other than the intimate relationship of Kafka with the city that had borne and marked him: his presentation was honest and cautious, and he consistently refused to introduce any facile political premises and implications. Like Goldstücker before him, Kautman deflated the myth of Kafka's close personal relations with the Czech anarchists, a commonplace of Kafka interpretation East and West ever since Max Brod had alluded to it in his novel *Stefan Rott*.[27] On the other hand, in establishing a correspondence between the work of Kafka and that of Richard Weiner, Kautman added new traits to the typology of the Jewish writers in Prague—whether their childhood language was German or, as with Weiner, Czech. He quoted two sentences from Weiner's *Lazebník* (*The Barber*, a book written five years after Kafka's death), which in their evocation of human loneliness as well as in their imagery reduplicate the world view of the older writer: "Man never knows what is going to happen when the doorbell rings. Truly, the world is wide, so that he is the wisest who admits that he loses himself in it and, sticking out his head, listens only while shutting his eyes." [28] The emotions conveyed by this aphorism, and especially the cadence, seem to come straight out of Kafka's "Country Doctor" and "Burrow." In Weiner as in Hermann Grab—whose *Stadtpark* of 1935 was not mentioned by Kautman—Kafka appears indeed to have found followers who walked in his footsteps because they, too, had felt the impact of the "clutches of little mother Prague" (*B*, 14).

Nevertheless, Kautman all but failed to acknowledge any direct influence the older authors may have had on contemporary writing. It is true that he cited the claims made by the French surrealists that Kafka was their literary ancestor, claims that would relate their Czech followers, poets like Vítězslav Nezval, even more closely to the nightmares that had haunted Kafka half a century ago. Had not Kafka himself produced a surrealist motto when he remarked to Gustav Janouch: "Actual reality is always unrealistic"? (*J*, 87). Yet Kautman seems to be on the right path again when he points to Dostoyevsky as the ancestor common to Kafka and the surrealists.[29] At best they were relatives twice removed.

Yet during the Second World War the young poet Jiří Orten *was* marked by the sign of Kafka.

> You lie there in your room, it's eleven years ago,
> Sick, having it happen: apple, darkness, bed,
> Exchanging lengthy speeches with your pillows.
>
> . . . . . .
>
> You lie there in your room, you hardly pant, and die
> Without her, me, and any friends and things.
> You go away. Beware that you don't fall.

> "Jsi ve svém pokoji před jedenácti lety.
> Máš příběh. Nemocen . . . Jablko, postel, tma.
> S polštáři dovedeš si dlouze vyprávěti.
>
> . . . . . .
>
> Jsi ve svém pokoji a umíráš a chřadneš,
> beze mne, bez ní, sám, bez věcí, bez přátel.
> A potom odcházíš. Pozor, at' neupadneš!"[30]

This is the stuff that Kafka's bachelors are made of. Yet Orten was exposed not only to Kafka's visions of doom but to the realities of war and persecution. Actually, his experiences proved more tragic as well as more trivial than Kafka's images which had foretold them. They were, however, equally fatal; in 1941, the poet, twenty-two years old, was run over by a *Wehrmacht* truck and refused admittance to the Prague General Hospital because he was a Jew. His relation to Kafka was that of a disciple to a prophet. Both writers belong to the past, but what they saw lingers on today. Inhumanity has survived and the terror may repeat itself. "We cannot complain about a mirror," Kautman exclaimed, "if it reflects the horror in our faces." [31]

Other Czech participants at the conference reacted less emotionally. When the two young philosophers Ivan Sviták and Alexej Kusák addressed the meeting, they left orthodox Marxism resolutely behind. Sviták, who later lost his chair and was expelled from the party, attempted an existentialistic interpretation and quoted Hölderlin. To him creation was "a tragic outcry about man in search of man." [32] Kusák demanded a purely literary explication and denounced the preoccupation of the conference with Kafka's local and class origins. [33] Although the names of Heidegger and of the New Critics were passed over in silence, their ideas and methods must have penetrated some minds in Liblice.

Clearly, there was a revolt in the making. These young men turned to Kafka as a companion in their fight against their elders in much the same way as Kafka himself had once risen against the image of his own father. Their weapons resembled his: they were intellectual integrity and the courage to reject conventions when they had clearly become obsolete.

Paul Reimann retracted. He abandoned the position he had previously taken and deserted his dead friend Fürnberg by inveighing against Kafka. As if he had feared the attack of subversive voices, he opened the discussion by trying, at the same time, to close it. Introducing Kafka, he blamed him for "having hindered us in starting on the way Marx and Lenin had summoned us to go, the way toward a change of the world," and for having "prevented us from solving what has become the life task of our generation: taking the laws of life into our own hands and organizing the world so that people can live and produce." [34] Reimann further compared Kafka with "a mouse which happens to walk into a trap and, looking for an escape, helplessly runs to and fro, and finally, exhausted, collapses." [35] Zoology generally played a prominent role in the conference and its aftermath. When people began to speak of the jackdaw as "a swallow heralding spring," East Germany's *arbiter elegantiarum*, Alfred Kurella, leaped to his feet to announce that he for his part could see no swallows—only bats coming out at nightfall. [36]

Thus it is easy to understand why the East German delegation supported Reimann, adding to his indictment wherever possible. They were led not by the liberal Hans Mayer—at that time still a member of the faculty at Leipzig—but by his faithful student, Helmut Richter —faithful, that is, to the official party line. In Richter's view the German Kafka epigones—Hermann Kasack, Friedrich Dürrenmatt, Martin Walser, and Walter Jens, among others—were all children of the West, a decadent and yet aggressive lot who symbolized the inevitable decline of the civilization they pretended to serve.[37] Eastern Germany, on the other hand, was free of jackdaws, mice, and bats. As a foil to the zealous young men from behind the Berlin wall there appeared the aristocratic profile of Anna Seghers, the veteran novelist. But she refrained from speaking, at least officially, still conscious, perhaps, that *Transit,* her story of 1954, had reminded the critics too strongly of Kafka.[38]

The Hungarian Jenö Krammer spoke only briefly, and said next to nothing. The shadow of a greater man fell over him, and he knew it. But Georg Lukács had not come to Liblice. His spirit, however, loomed large over the convention, especially when Alexej Kusák attacked his pamphlet of 1958, *Against Mistaken Realism.*[39]

Like the rest of the older Communist critics, Lukács had been haunted by the ghost of socialist realism. That this ghost is a subjective specter can be seen from the way Lukács treats Thomas Mann and Franz Kafka. Mann qualifies as a genuine realist "who approaches the milieu of his life in a critical fashion," whereas Kafka is "a classical case of a writer stopped on his way [to realism] by a blind and panic fear of reality." [40] The Hungarian philosopher seems to have forgotten that Mann in his *Reflections of an Unpolitical Man* approached "the milieu of his life" by siding with the cannons of the Prussian Empire, whereas Kafka's diaries reveal the most rebellious sensitivity possible in the circumstances under which he was forced to live. (The anti-Semitic Lord Mayor of Vienna, Dr. Karl Lueger, when asked why he had Jewish friends, replied: "I decide who is a Jew"; in the same way Georg Lukács decides who is a realist—arbitrarily and as a matter of personal preference.) Fundamentally, Lukács could have brought forward the same arguments for Kafka as a realist as he did when discussing Thomas Mann. As a matter of fact, after Russian intervention had ended the uprising of the patriots in the fall of 1956, the Hungarians used to tell a story about "the grand old man from Budapest"; how, when he was arrested, he was taken to Rumania and shut up in some sort of weird castle, where he and his fellow prisoners were treated sometimes like felons and sometimes like guests of honor. After a few days of this, Lukács was supposed to have murmured to himself: "So Kafka was a realist after all!" [41] But Kafka remained for him the mouthpiece of the Western advanced guard to whom the world appeared as an "allegory of transcendental nothingness." [42] He was depicted as staring spellbound at the ghoulishness of the capitalistic everyday; he did not move a finger to exorcise the ghosts. (Didn't he? Was not his writing an act of exorcism?) And since socialist realism does not acknowledge the existence of ghosts, Kafka's books were antisocialist and antirealist, the self-indulgent exercises of a tormented and misguided mind. All this the philosopher had laid down with a maximum of learning and penetration. He did not have to visit Liblice. The man whose judgments determined who were the orthodox and who the revisionists could afford to remain invisible.

At the height of "revisionism," Alexej Kusák had demanded an interpretation of Kafka's works according to their own laws. In a paper, prudently not read at the conference, the Pole Roman Karst met this demand squarely. His essay, "The Immovable Hands of the Clock," is by far the best treatment so far undertaken of the time problem in Kafka. Speaking of the Prague writer as a contemporary and seeing in him a European phenomenon, Karst compares Kafka with Marcel Proust, the hands of whose clock continuously go back, "moved by memory to bring back to us lost experience," and with James Joyce, the hands of whose clock "circle as if crazed, steadily changing their direction, since they are moved by the force of the writer's associations."

The hands on Kafka's clock, however, remain immovable. Proust sets out to regain the past with the help of memory; Kafka wants to efface this past. In the one, the mechanism of recollection is at work; in the other, the mechanism of forgetting. In Kafka memory forms an abyss devouring the past and with it the wealth of what has been experienced. Kafka's figures are men without a personal history, their life consisting only of the moment filled with unrest, because they struggle for a truth unattainable to them. [43]

Karst replaces interpretation through the use of biographical, topological, or sociological facts by exegesis couched in metaphors. He uses Kafka's own key to unlock his secret. A poetic rhapsody rather than a critical analysis, his essay attempts to decipher Kafka's text by approaching it in the language of images, opaque and yet precise. These were new tones, and Karst knew why he kept them to himself in Liblice.

Karst represented a critical approach that had of late been uniquely successful in integrating Kafka. In 1958 the play *The Trial* was performed in the Warsaw Teatr Ateneum, with Jacek Woszczerowicz as Josef K.[44] A year before, the short novels of Bruno Schulz were republished in Cracow.[45] Written in 1934, *The Cinnamon Stores* are, at least thematically, indebted to Kafka, whose *Trial* Schulz had translated in 1936. The world as a labyrinth presided over by a godlike father was the same in Prague and Drohobycz, where Schulz spent most of his life, and where he was shot in 1942 by a Gestapo agent. His style lacks the immediacy as well as the transparence of Kafka's; instead, Schulz displays a predilection for the abrupt and absurd which undoubtedly contributed to the renewed interest in his writings in the wake of Kafka's popularity in Poland.

Recent Polish writers in general seem to have subscribed to Camus's idea of seeing the protagonists of *The Castle* and especially *The Trial* as absurd heroes.[46] Whereas the Czechs had tried to connect Kafka and surrealism, the Poles derived absurd theatre from the situations to which the bank clerk and the land surveyor are exposed in Kafka's novels. Sławomir Mrożek's metaphysical thriller *Striptease*, for example, would be as unthinkable without Kafka's model as it would be without the influence of Sartre's *Huis Clos*. The two nondescript gentlemen who are plunged from a foggy street into a completely empty room play a variation on the theme of Josef K.'s arrest. The mystery of the door is repeated here in the form of theatrical magic: Kafka's mysterious doorkeeper is missing; instead, Mrożek's door shuts without being closed and opens again to let an enormous hand pass through. When one of the gentlemen says: "The most we can do is to preserve our internal dignity and freedom," [47] he is quoting almost word for word Josef K.'s reflections on his way to his execution.[48] As K. lies half naked before his executioners, so the two Everymen in *Striptease* are gradually divested of all that is left of their humanity: their clothes. These men too must perish. Without having discovered the nature of their guilt, they are beckoned to death by a second mammoth hand completely covered by a red glove. Mrożek's theatrical imagination transposes Kafka's epic imagery into scenic pictures that seem both to imitate and to parody their model. He does not dramatize Kafka as Jean-Louis Barrault, André Gide, and Max Brod have done; he rises to meet the challenge of Kafka's world. Black humor takes the place of his predecessor's iridescent irony: the condemned men, who at long last have been handcuffed, stumble and grope around the stage until they have found and picked up their briefcases, each one his own—but these, the last signs of their identity, are exactly the same. Yet tricks and gags notwithstanding, Mrożek's short scene also centers upon the freedom of man when confronted by the inexpressible and when visited by a second reality beyond all human reality. Multifaceted like a Kafka parable, the playlet reduces the older writer's paradox of existence to a metaphor of the absurdity of fate.

The close relationship between Kafka's paradoxicality and the absurdity of the new Polish theatre can be seen even in the Shakespeare interpretations of Jan Kott. Kott had explored the question of ambiguity in an essay, published at the occasion of the performance of *The Trial* in Warsaw, in which he compared the Prague writer with Bruno Schulz and Marc Chagall.[49] From here it was only a short step to his discussion of the elements that contribute to the twilight prevailing in *King Lear:* "In the tragedy," Kott says, "the hero's defeat is tantamount to a confirmation and recognition of the absolute; the defeat of the grotesque hero, on the other hand, means the derision and desecration of the absolute, its change into a blind mechanism, into an automatic tool. Thereby not only the executioner is derided but also the victim, who believed in the justice of the executioner, absolutized the executioner, and invented the executioner because he has acknowledged himself as a victim." [50] As a matter of fact, Kott had thought of Samuel Beckett's absurd *Endgame* when he wrote these lines. Yet they are equally applicable to the endgame in Kafka's *Trial,* where the tragic and the grotesque are united to result in insoluble ambiguity.

The example of the young Czechs as well as the Poles shows that Kafka's spirit seems to emerge wherever a crack opens in the walls of the monolithic system of Communist societies. Kafka, the most self-imprisoned of men, has become a harbinger of freedom: a fact that would have elicited a smile of pained understanding from him before he looked again at the bars of his cage and resumed shaking and fondling them.

After the conference was concluded, Roger Garaudy, a philosopher and a member of the Politbureau of the French Communist Party, gave an interview in which he violently attacked Stalin's *Dialectical and Historical Materialism* as obsolete, as a closed system of the laws of dialectics. Stalin's and Zhdanov's concept of realism, he said, started from a static definition of art, which had been abstracted from the practices of the nineteenth century. Lumping Kafka together with Picasso, of all people, he suggested that the works of neither artist fitted such a definition. "Consequently," he concluded, "either these works must be rejected, which is wrong and ridiculous, or else a new definition of realism must be formed to include [them]." [51]

The logic of this argument is somewhat reminiscent of that of Christian Morgenstern's Palmström, who, after having been run over by a car, concludes that since this sad event would have represented a traffic violation on the part of the driver, it did not happen at all:

> For, he reasons pointedly,
> that which must not, can not be. [52]

> (Weil, so schliesst er messerscharf,
> Nicht sein *kann*, was nicht sein *darf*.)

Yet Roger Garaudy had the courage to apply the Marxian concept of *Entfremdung* not only to the bourgeois class but to socialist society, combining in a bold synthesis the teachings of communism and French existentialism. With the words "Kafka fought against alienation without being able to overcome it," he summed up his interview.

Therefore, Kafka's work is of immediate interest for the capitalist world, in which people live in alienation. It is, however, also of immediate interest for the socialist world, because socialism is the beginning of the fight against alienation, for a total man, but it does not abolish all forms of estrangement. As long as the communist society has not been built, the roots of various forms of alienation continue to exist in socialism. The conference on Kafka presented evidence that literary criticism is ridding itself of dogmatic errors and is aware of the importance of the artistic work in itself. In this sense the conference had a wider and deeper significance and became, because of its clearly antidogmatic and antimechanistic tendency, a stage in the struggle for creative Marxism. [53]

The dream was beautiful, but it would remain only a dream so long as the orthodox members of the conference could count on political support from the state authorities. Still, the results of Liblice were far-reaching, albeit in a less ideological way than Roger Garaudy had outlined. In Prague, a number of official celebrations heralded and followed the conference. Preparations were begun to perform the dramatized versions of *The Trial* and *The Castle*, even though these plays were indeed artistic offenses committed by the West in the wake of the Kafka boom. Popular lectures were given in the Czech capital to acquaint the people with the deliberations of the conference. Radio and television joined in to carry the often esoteric discussions into Czech homes, and on July 3, 1963, the eightieth anniversary of Kafka's birth, state officials spoke at and deposited flowers on Kafka's tomb.[54] A year later Max Brod was to travel from Israel in order to open a Kafka exhibition in the Prague Museum of Czech Literature.[55] A cartoon in the satirical weekly *Dikobraz* (*Porcupine*) showed a little man half hidden behind the giant pages of *Literární časopis*, sighing, "Kafka. Nothing but Kafka." [56] What had once been opium for the people had become their daily bread.

Further east, during an international conference at Leningrad, Ilya Ehrenburg had dwelt on the historical importance of the Prague writer in an address that was as magisterial as it was noncommittal.[57] Thereupon some Kafka stories—"The Metamorphosis" and selected short pieces—were published in the January, 1964, number of *Inostrannaya Literatura* (*Foreign Literature*) in Moscow, accompanied by an essay of S. Knipovitch. To be sure, *Inostrannaya Literatura* took notice of Kafka only "by disqualifying what it had set out to introduce." [58] A month earlier the Ukrainian literary journal *Vsyeswit* (*World*) had printed "The Stoker," "The Metamorphosis," "The Bucket Rider," "Before the Law," and "An Imperial Message." [59] In Rumania, a young writer, S. Damian, praised Kafka, Proust, and Joyce publicly as "explorers who contributed to a better understanding of man." [60] Even Georg Lukács seems to have relented. In his recently published study, *Aesthetics*, he compares Kafka with Charlie Chaplin, whose "world-historical humor," to be sure, is still described as an "objectifying deepening of Kafka's problems." [61] The only two countries behind the Iron Curtain that failed to react favorably to the conference at Liblice were Albania and the German Democratic Republic.

To the eye of the Western observer the Czech convention offered the spectacle of the "Pit of Babel," an image that was coined by Kafka himself (*DF*, 349). Men of diverse opinion talked past each other in many languages; the orthodox and the liberals both dug in where even the unprejudiced could not hope to reach solid rock; the dust of doctrine rose blindingly; and the whole burrow was further undermined by the few young critics who insisted on following Kafka on his own labyrinthine ways, wherever they might lead.

The fear that Kafka inspires is bred by the fear of father, God, or life. It is a terrifying sign of our times that the cry for the freedom to read him as in his lighter moments he meant us to read him, is nothing but the plea for humanity's ultimate liberty: the freedom to be afraid. The uneasiness that led to the conference at Liblice must have been stirred up by the realization that the oldest and most sacred birthright of man was being denied him by the state: his fear and trembling not, to be sure, before the knock on the door at midnight, but before the mystery of creation. The varying shades of approval with which the conference was met behind the Iron Curtain cannot be judged only by the standards of *Kulturpolitik* or politics proper. Humanity, driven to the wall, insisted on its privilege to listen to the almost suffocated voices within itself and to surrender to the awe without which no hope is bred.

To have formulated this paradox is the prime advantage Western criticism has obtained over Kafka's Eastern interpreters. From the paradox, however, it follows also that Kafka the man must be protected from any party, left or right, if Kafka the writer is to be saved.

Ernst Fischer undoubtedly meant well when he sought from Hegel an affidavit to support Kafka's immigration to the East. "Kafka," Fischer said, "tended to give a new meaning to physical actuality by changing it to metaphysics, to petrify the historical moment so that it became [an image of] the permanent condition of man. But his dialectical progress from each answer to a new question, from each thesis to its antithesis, has always worked counter to such a petrification." [62] Yet Kafka was no Hegelian. As early as 1911 he wrote in his diary: "My repugnance for antitheses is certain" (*DI*, 157). This repugnance stems not only from his style of writing and living but from his innermost character. His very being was visionary, a nightmare perhaps, a reflection of the images he had created in his own likeness. His profession as such a creator of images made him insensitive to the clear-cut abstractions of the German philosopher and his left-wing disciples. His life was his complex; his complex was his life. Whenever dialectics seem to emerge from his writings they turn out to be an almost Talmudic shuttling between word and meaning, a profound immersion in the ambiguity of the Scriptures, and a never-fulfilled longing to decipher in a message its unequivocal sense. The social evils of his time were but a sign for him, a fiery writing on the wall, the literal meaning of which remained ultimately hidden. He asked questions in ever new cadences, and what at first seemed an answer turned out to be a fresh question. Thus even the asking of questions became questionable. There is no synthesis in Kafka because his work is not founded on thesis and antithesis. His thesis is the absence of any thesis, his *Grund-Satz* the lack of any *Grundsatz*, and the suspense that his work awakens originates in the total suspension of man beyond place and time, facing a Godhead still invisible to him.

In this last respect, Kafka's questions resemble the questions of Job, from which they are ultimately derived. And there is a certain irony hidden in the realization that in the Castle of Liblice not only the Kafka problem was opened for discussion but the problem of Job as well. Whoever was afraid of Franz Kafka was haunted by the fear of being afraid of a greater and more ancient heritage, a heritage entrusted not only to Kafka but indeed to Everyman.

Notes

Bibliography

and Index

Notes

Chapter I: "Give It Up!"

1. "The Bankruptcy of Faith," *The Kafka Problem*, ed. Angel Flores (New York: New Directions, 1946), 298–318.
2. "Die gesellschaftliche Problematik in Kafkas Romanen," *Weimarer Beiträge,* IV (1957), 598–618.
3. "Schuld und Schuldgefühle," *Merkur,* XI (1957), 722.
4. *Franz Kafka* (Bonn: Athenäum, 1958), 308.
5. "Franz Kafkas Bruch mit der Tradition und sein neues Gesetz," in *Protest und Verheissung* (Bonn: Athenäum, 1960), 243–244.
6. *Tractatus Logico-Philosophicus* (New York: Harcourt, 1933), 6.522.
7. *Mimesis: The Representation of Reality in Western Literature* (Garden City: Doubleday Anchor, 1957), 9.
8. W. K. Wimsatt, *The Verbal Icon* (Lexington: University of Kentucky Press, 1954), especially 3–18.
9. Pp. 9–10.
10. Franz Werfel, *Schlaf und Erwachen* (Berlin: Zsolnay, 1935), 110. For the English version of the poem, I am indebted to Professor Peter Salm, of Wesleyan University, Middletown, Conn.

Chapter II: Juvenilia

1. One of these, "Conversation with the Supplicant," has also been included in *PC,* 9–17. In both cases the title should read "Conversation with the Praying Man" ("Gespräch mit dem Beter").
2. Klaus Wagenbach, *Franz Kafka: Eine Biographie seiner Jugend* (Bern: Francke, 1958), 123.
3. Peter Demetz, *René Rilkes Prager Jahre* (Düsseldorf: Diederichs, 1953), 202–203.
4. Wagenbach, *Kafka,* 84 ff.
5. *Statt einer Literaturgeschichte* (Pfullingen: Neske, 1957), 78.
6. *Tagebücher, Aphorismen, Essays und Reden* (Hamburg: Rowohlt, 1955), 687.

7. Willy Haas, *Die literarische Welt* (Munich: List, 1957), 30.
8. Postscript to the German edition of *Beschreibung eines Kampfes*, 346–347.
9. Wilhelm Emrich, *Franz Kafka* (Bonn: Athenäum, 1958), 99.
10. Wagenbach, *Kafka*, 118–119.
11. Thomas Mann, *Death in Venice and Seven Other Stories*, trans. H. T. Lowe-Porter (New York: Vintage, 1954), 98.
12. *Ibid.*, 102, 99.
13. *Ibid.*, 106.
14. *Ibid.*, 101.

Chapter III: The Breakthrough

1. *Souvenirs sur Gustave Flaubert* (Paris: Ferroud, 1895), 89–90.
2. Claude-Edmonde Magny, "The Objective Depiction of Absurdity," in *The Kafka Problem*, ed. A. Flores (New York: New Directions, 1946), 84–85.
3. Charles Neider, *The Frozen Sea: A Study of Franz Kafka* (New York: Oxford, 1948), 75–76.
4. *Ibid.*
5. H. S. Reiss, *Franz Kafka: Eine Betrachtung seines Werkes* (Heidelberg: Schneider, 1952), 43.
6. Kate Flores, "The Judgment," *Franz Kafka Today*, ed. Angel Flores and Homer Swander (Madison: University of Wisconsin Press, 1958), 13.
7. Wilhelm Emrich, *Franz Kafka* (Bonn: Athenäum, 1958), 125.
8. Clemens Heselhaus, "Franz Kafkas Erzählformen," *Deutsche Vierteljahrsschrift für Literaturwissenschaft und Geistesgeschichte*, XXVI (1952), 356 *et passim.*
9. Walter H. Sokel, "Kafka's 'Metamorphosis': Rebellion and Punishment," *Monatshefte*, XLVIII (1956), 203.

Chapter IV: Parable and Paradox

1. Cf. Heinz Politzer, "The Puzzle of Kafka's Prosecuting Attorney," *PMLA*, LXXV (1960), 438.
2. "Gedanken und Einfälle," in *Heinrich Heines Sämtliche Werke*, ed. O. Walzel, X (Leipzig: Insel, 1915), 261.
3. "Heimkehr 39," in *ibid.*, I (1911), 129.
4. *Ecce Homo*, trans. Anthony M. Ludovici (Edinburgh: Foulis, 1911), 39.
5. *Wissenschaft, Politik und Gnosis* (Munich: Kösel, 1959), 76.
6. Friedrich Nietzsche, *The Joyful Wisdom*, trans. Thomas Common (Edinburgh: Foulis, 1910), 167–169.
7. Luke 15:16, 24.
8. "Der Gottesmord," in *op. cit.*, 63–85.
9. Fyodor Dostoyevsky, *The Brothers Karamazov*, trans. Constance Garnett (New York: Modern Library, 1950), 309–313.
10. *The Variorum Edition of the Poems*, ed. Peter Allt and Russell K. Alspach (New York: Macmillan, 1957), 402.
11. The art historian Heinz Ladendorf has pointed to the relationship between this story and Georges Seurat's painting *"Le Cirque"* of 1890/1891. The painter's equestrienne in front of an amphitheater half filled with puppetlike spectators could impress the viewer as being an illustration for Kafka's "Up in the Gallery," although it antedates the story by roughly a quarter of a century. In both works Ladendorf observes a combination of "lie and pain, beauty and dazzling melo-

drama ('greller Kitsch'), an insoluble and ubiquitously tormenting falseness representing the sadness of existence." The art historian, however, wonders whether Kafka has ever seen Seurat's painting ("Kafka und die Kunstgeschichte," *Wallraf-Richartz-Jahrbuch*, XXIII [1961], 304, 305). To us, the main difference between painting and story lies in the story's pronounced lack of sentimentality as well as in the irony that tempers the melancholy of Kafka's sentences.

12. Johannes Urzidil, "Das Reich des Unerreichbaren: Kafka-Deutungen," *Germanic Review*, XXXVI (1961), 166.

13. Kafka's own interpretation, "The eleven sons are quite simply eleven stories I am working on this very moment" (*FK*, 140), restates the puzzle instead of solving it.

Nevertheless, J. M. S. Pasley believes that he has solved the riddle by equating Kafka's so-called characterizations of the eleven sons with eleven titles preserved in the sixth octavo notebook and designed to serve as a preliminary table of contents for the collection *A Country Doctor*. "And at the foot of this list there appears, for the first time, the title *Elf Söhne*" ("Two Kafka Enigmas: 'Elf Söhne' and 'Die Sorge des Hausvaters,' " *Modern Language Review* [1964], 73). Yet there is another list of the "Eleven Sons" in a letter that Kafka wrote to Kurt Wolff, the publisher of *A Country Doctor*, on Aug. 20, 1917 (*B*, 158–159), anticipating, with one exception, the actual content of the book. Here, however, the sons have multiplied; there are now fifteen titles, in an order radically different from that in the sixth notebook. This can mean only that Kafka neglected his original interpretation when the time came to present the volume to the public. He mystified Max Brod as he would succeed in teasing Pasley almost half a century later. The appearance of the "Eleven Sons" in the published volume indicates that Kafka meant the tale to be more than "quite simply" a characterization of a few of his stories. As critics of Kafka know, he frequently uses the words "quite simply" or their equivalent to hint at a hidden complexity.

In 1964, Pasley undertook to unveil the secret of the engineers as well ("Franz Kafka: 'Ein Besuch im Bergwerk,' " *German Life and Letters*, New Series, XVIII, 40–46). They represented, he said, the contributors to Kurt Wolff's yearbook *Der neue Roman*. Kafka as a narrator of *histoires à clef*? Reducing interpretation to the intellectual level of a *Who's Who in Kafka*? Pasley's "identifications" prove cogently, though not quite intentionally, that Kafka was not concerned with description but with symbolization. And this, as the writer himself once said, "we knew already."

14. *Franz Kafka* (Bonn: Athenäum, 1958), 92–93.

15. An early precursor of Kafka's Odradek can be found in Ferdinand Raimund's magic play, *The Diamond of the Prince of Spirits* (1824). There the ghost of an old magician is conjured up by his son to announce nothing but the message: "I am your father Zephises and have nothing to tell you but this" (*Ich bin dein Vater Zephises und habe dir nichts zu sagen als dieses*). Thereupon he disappears (*Werke*, ed. E. Castle [Leipzig: Hesse & Becker, n.d.], 116).

16. The atavistically festive character of the execution was borrowed, with many another detail, by Shirley Jackson in her short story "The Lottery" (New York: Farrar, Straus, 1949).

17. As was the case with Odradek, the highly technical description of the execution machine owes many a turn of phrase to the professional work Kafka had to perform for the Worker's Accident Insurance Institute. Ironically, one of his special fields of study was the prevention of accidents (Cf. Max Brod, *Franz Kafka* [Frankfort: Fischer, 1954], 83–84, and especially Wagenbach, 314–325).

18. *Franz Kafka als wegweisende Gestalt* (St. Gallen: Tschudy, n.d.).

19. "In the Penal Colony," in *The Kafka Problem*, ed. A. Flores (New York: New Directions, 1946), 140.

Chapter V: Der Verschollene

1. "Aufzeichnungen zu Kafka," in *Prismen* (Berlin and Frankfort: Suhrkamp, 1955), 325.
2. *Franz Kafka* (Bonn: Athenäum, 1958), 227.
3. Klaus Wagenbach, *Franz Kafka* (Bern: Francke, 1958), 62.
4. *Ibid.*, 60.
5. *Ibid.*, 273–274.
6. Adorno, 333.
7. *Ibid.*, 325.
8. Pp. 359, 358.
9. *Kafka*, 233.
10. *Ibid.*, 241; *et alii.*
11. *Ibid.*, 230.
12. Felix Salten, *Josephine Muzenbacher oder die Geschichte einer Wienerischen Dirne von ihr selbst erzählt* (privately printed, 1906).
13. *Wider den missverstandenen Realismus* (Hamburg: Claassen, 1958), 87.
14. *Kafka*, 237–238.
15. Brod assumes the responsibility for this title on p. 359 of the second German edition.
16. Emrich, *Kafka*, 243.
17. *Amerika* (2d German ed.), 354, 353.
18. Norbert Fürst, *Die offenen Geheimtüren Franz Kafkas* (Heidelberg: Rothe, 1956), 54, 55.
19. Alfred Borchardt, *Kafkas zweites Gesicht: Der Unbekannte* (Nuremberg: Glock und Lutz, 1960), 201.
20. Lienhard Bergel, "*Amerika*: Its Meaning," in *Franz Kafka Today*, ed. Angel Flores and Homer Swander (Madison: University of Wisconsin Press, 1958), 122.
21. Emrich, *Kafka*, 257.

Chapter VI: The Trial against the Court

1. *Tagebücher* (2d German ed.), 729.
2. For a more detailed accounting, see Heinz Politzer, "The Puzzle of Kafka's Prosecuting Attorney," *PMLA*, LXXV (1960), 432.
3. Wilhelm Emrich, *Franz Kafka* (Bonn: Athenäum, 1958), 264.
4. Gerhard Kaiser, "Franz Kafkas 'Prozess': Versuch einer Interpretation," *Euphorion*, LII (1958), 40.
5. Hermann Pongs stresses the light imagery in *The Trial* and elsewhere but subjects the text to a moralistic pattern: "Kafka's own tragic ambivalence condemns itself here . . . in the lightlessness of the cathedral scene" (*Franz Kafka: Dichter des Labyrinths* [Heidelberg: Rothe, 1960], 46 *et passim*).
6. Jürgen Born argues similarly ("Max Brod's Kafka," *Books Abroad*, XXXIII [1959], 393–394).
7. Max Brod, *Franz Kafka* (Frankfort: Fischer, 1954), 218–219 n.
8. Emrich, *Kafka*, 260.

9. *Ibid.*, 259.

10. Klaus Wagenbach, *Franz Kafka* (Bern: Francke, 1958), 179 ff.

11. Roy B. Chamberlin and Herman Feldman, *The Dartmouth Bible* (Boston: Houghton Mifflin, 1950), 853 a.

12. *Two Types of Faith* (London: Routledge, 1951), 165–166.

13. New York: Schocken, 1954, 50.

14. *Ibid.*

15. Emrich, *Kafka*, 260.

16. *Sämtliche Werke*, Historisch-Kritische Ausgabe, ed. Richard Werner, I (Berlin: Behr, 1901), 410.

17. *Geschlecht und Charakter* (17th ed.; Vienna: Braumüller, 1917), 288. (Here and in the following quotations from Weininger I am indebted to the American edition of *Sex and Character* [New York: Putnam, n.d.].)

18. Pp. 255–256.

19. P. 254.

20. Pp. 364–365.

21. P. 364.

22. P. 427.

23. "Dostoevsky—in Moderation," in *The Short Novels of Dostoevsky* (New York: Dial, 1945), p. xiv.

24. Emrich, *Kafka*, 280.

25. *Ibid.*, 289.

Chapter VII: The Bitter Herb

1. *Kafka's Castle* (Cambridge: University Press, 1956), 19.

2. Erich Heller, *The Disinherited Mind* (Cambridge: Bowes & Bowes, 1952), 169–170.

3. Wilhelm Emrich, *Franz Kafka* (Bonn: Athenäum, 1958), 300–303.

4. Gustav René Hocke, *Die Welt als Labyrinth* (Hamburg: Rowohlt, 1957), fig. 110.

5. *Franz Kafka, Dichter des Labyrinths* (Heidelberg: Rothe, 1960), 9, 125, 126.

6. "The Labyrinth," in S. H. Hooke, *The Labyrinth* (New York: Macmillan, 1935), 42.

7. P. 101.

8. P. 144.

9. *Manierismus in der Literatur* (Hamburg: Rowohlt, 1959), 272.

10. P. 102.

11. Kurt Seligmann, *The Mirror of Magic* (New York: Pantheon, 1948), 359, 360, (fig. 158).

12. *The Labyrinth of the World and the Paradise of the Heart*, trans. and ed. Count Lutzow (London: Dent, 1905), 17, 81; also Hocke, *Welt*, 102.

13. P. 175.

14. *Wider den missverstandenen Realismus* (Hamburg: Claassen, 1958), 46.

15. *Kafka*, 310.

16. *John Donne*, ed. W. S. Scott (London: Westhouse, 1946), 204.

17. Emrich, *Kafka*, 310.

18. Heller, 170. Karel Kosík suggests the "internal relationship" of the name "Klamm" with the Czech word "klam" = illusion ("Hašek a Kafka," *Plamen*, VI [1963], 99n.).

19. Emrich, *Kafka,* 309.
20. Seligmann, 343.
21. Gray, 54.
22. *Les Abeilles d'Aristée* (Paris: Gallimard, 1954), 310.
23. *The Magic Mountain,* trans. H. T. Lowe-Porter (New York: Knopf, 1951), 183.
24. *Ibid.,* 542.
25. *Ibid.,* 653.
26. Heller, 170.
27. *Ibid.*
28. *Kafka,* 390.
29. Hocke, *Manierismus,* 212.
30. Wolfgang Kayser, *Das Groteske: Seine Gestaltung in Malerei und Dichtung* (Oldenburg: Stalling, 1957), 202 *et passim.*
31. *Kafka,* 410.
32. Herbert Tauber, *Franz Kafka* (New Haven: Yale University Press, 1948), 170 n.
33. Gray, 119.
34. Pp. 176–177.
35. *Kafka,* 363.
36. Gray, 114.
37. Rudolf Kleinpaul, *Die deutschen Personennamen* (Leipzig: Göschen, 1909), 40. (In a later edition [1924] Kleinpaul modified his opinion, claiming that the name Amalia probably was derived from the French name Amélie, which was first cited in German during the sixteenth century.)
38. Gray, 18.
39. P. 181.

Chapter VIII: Heightened Redemption

1. Max Brod, *Franz Kafka als wegweisende Gestalt* (St. Gallen: Tschudy, n.d.), 37–38. My interpretation of Brod's solution of this puzzle differs considerably from his.
2. Martin Buber, *Tales of the Hasidim: The Early Masters,* trans. Olga Marx (New York: Schocken, 1947), 316.
3. "Heinrich von Ofterdingen II," in *Schriften* (Leipzig: Bibliographisches Institut, 1928), 229.
4. J. P. Hodin, "Erinnerungen an Franz Kafka," *Der Monat,* I (1949), 95.
5. "Die beiden Zettel Kafkas," *Monatshefte,* XLVII (1955), 321–328.
6. See Spann's account of the story's publication and its relation to the date of the January 1922 testament (*ibid.,* 324–325).
7. Hodin, 92.
8. *Die Tagebücher,* ed. and trans. Theodor Haecker, 33; quoted from Karl Kraus, *Die Fackel,* XXIX (1928), 773.
9. *Doctor Faustus,* trans. H. T. Lowe-Porter (New York: Knopf, 1948), 491.
10. Hodin, 92.
11. Norbert Fürst, *Die offenen Geheimtüren Franz Kafkas* (Heidelberg: Rothe, 1956), 77.
12. Hodin, 92.
13. For a veritable *catalogue raisonné* of food and starvation imagery in Kafka,

see Meno Spann, "Franz Kafka's Leopard," *Germanic Review*, XXXIV (1959), 85–104, esp. 94–98.

14. *Ibid.*, 91.

15. R. W. Stallman, "A Hunger-Artist," in *Franz Kafka Today*, ed. Angel Flores and Homer Swander (Madison: University of Wisconsin Press, 1958), 64.

16. Benno von Wiese, "Franz Kafka: Ein Hungerkünstler," in *Die deutsche Novelle* (Düsseldorf: Bagel, 1956), 333. Ingeborg Henel ("Ein Hungerkünstler," *Deutsche Vierteljahrsschrift für Literaturwissenschaft und Geistesgeschichte,* XXXVIII [1964], 231 *et passim*) sees the paradox of the story in the Hunger Artist's desire to survive by starvation, a rather simplified interpretation of his multifaceted death wish.

17. Carl R. Woodring, "Josephine the Singer," in *Franz Kafka Today*, 72.

18. *Ibid.*

19. See Robert T. Clark, Jr., *Herder, His Life and Thought* (Berkeley: University of California Press, 1955), 260 *et passim*.

20. Heinz Politzer, *Vor dem Gesetz* (Berlin: Schocken, 1934), 80.

21. *Beschreibung eines Kampfes* (German ed.), 349.

22. "Die beiden Zettel Kafkas," 328.

23. *Gesammelte Werke in zwölf Bänden,* VIII (Frankfort: Fischer, 1960), 423.

24. Wilhelm Emrich, *Franz Kafka* (Bonn: Athenäum, 1958), 172.

25. The image of the mole would then connect our story thematically with the earlier fable fragment "The Village Schoolmaster" (*DS*, 174–201), wrongly titled "The Giant Mole" by Brod. See Fritz Martini, "Ein Manuskript Franz Kafkas: 'Der Dorfschullehrer,'" *Jahrbuch der deutschen Schillergesellschaft*, II (1958), 266–300.

26. *Beschreibung eines Kampfes* (German ed.), 350.

27. Hodin, 92.

28. *Beschreibung eines Kampfes*, 349–350.

29. *Ibid.*, 350.

30. *Das Groteske: Seine Gestaltung in Malerei und Dichtung* (Oldenburg: Stalling, 1957), 161.

31. *The Romantic Enlightenment: Ambiguity and Paradox in the Western Mind (1750–1920)* (New York: Meridian, 1960), 175.

Chapter IX: The True Physician: Franz Kafka and Albert Camus

1. Letter to Waldo Frank, January 12, 1950, in Hermann Broch, *Briefe von 1929 bis 1951*, ed. Robert Pick (Zurich: Rhein-Verlag, 1957), 374.

2. Albert Camus, *The Myth of Sisyphus*, trans. Justin O'Brien (New York: Knopf, 1957), 119–121.

3. *Ibid.*, 123.

4. Maja Goth, *Franz Kafka et les lettres françaises (1928–1955)* (Paris: Corti, 1956), 124.

5. Germaine Brée, *Camus* (New Brunswick: Rutgers University Press, 1959), 241.

6. For the editions of Camus's novels and their abbreviations used in this chapter, see p. xvi.

7. H. Uyttersprot, *Eine neue Ordnung der Werke Kafkas?* (Anvers: De Vries-Brouwers, 1957), 35 *et passim*.

8. "Le roman de l'Étranger," in *Faux pas* (Paris: Gallimard, 1943), 257.

9. *Myth*, 126.

10. P. 6.

11. *Myth*, 129.

12. *Ibid.*, 138 n.

13. Abraham Kaplan, "Freud and Modern Philosophy," in *Freud and the 20th Century*, ed. Benjamin Nelson (New York: Meridian, 1957), 228.

14. Goth, 127–128.

15. Brée, 113.

16. Albert Camus, *The Rebel*, trans. Anthony Bower (New York: Vintage), 56.

17. P. 304.

18. P. 302.

19. *Times Literary Supplement*, Jan. 8, 1960, pp. 13–14.

20. W. M. Frohock, "Camus: Image, Influence and Sensibility," in *Yale French Studies*, II (no. 2, Fourth Study) 91–99.

21. Rainer Maria Rilke, *Requiem*, trans. J. B. Leishman (London: Hogarth, 1957), 141.

22. P. 119.

23. Brée, 125.

24. *Religion und Humor im Leben und Werk Franz Kafkas* (Berlin: Herbig, 1957).

25. Heinrich Zschokke, *Eine Selbstschau* (Aarau, 1842) I, 204 f. Quoted from Helmut Sembdner, ed., *Heinrich von Kleists Lebensspuren: Dokumente und Berichte der Zeitgenossen* (Bremen: Schünemann, 1957), 43–44.

26. See also Walter Höllerer, *Zwischen Klassik und Moderne: Lachen und Weinen in der Dichtung einer Übergangszeit* (Stuttgart: Klett, 1958).

27. "De Dostoevski à Kafka," *L'ère du soupçon, essais sur le roman* (Paris: Gallimard, 1956), 52.

Chapter X: Kafka behind the Iron Curtain

1. "Topič," *Kmen*, IV (1920), 61–72.

2. *Komunistická revue*, III (1924), 479.

3. Paul Reimann, "Kafka a dnešek," in Eduard Goldstücker *et al.* eds., *Franz Kafka. Liblická Konference 1963* (Prague: Nakladetelství Československé akademie věd), 13. (Hereafter quoted as *LK*.)

4. Gustav Janouch, "Die Feuerprobe," *Prager Begegnungen* (Leipzig: List, 1959), 93–120.

5. *Proces* (Prague: Orbis, 1958).

6. "Prager Frühling," *Der Spiegel*, XVII (1963), 66–67.

7. Joe Pelicano, "A Kafka Shrine in Prague," *The Sunday Star* (Washington, D.C.), May 3, 1964.

8. "Prager Tagebuch," *Monat*, XVI (1964), 36–37.

9. Leoš Houška, "Franz Kafka und Prag 1963," *Philologica Pragensia*, VI (1963), 395.

10. "Pokus o záchranu člověka," *LK*, 141.

11. "Kafkovská konference," *LK*, 160.

12. Jean-Paul Sartre, "La démilitarisation de la culture," *France Observateur*, July 17, 1962, 12.

Notes

387

13. Erhard Bahr, "Kafka hinter dem eisernen Vorhang." (Unpublished.)

14. Quoted from Paul Reimann, "Louis Fürnberg—Erinnerungen und Gedanken," *Von Herder bis Kisch* (Berlin: Dietz, 1961), 204–205.

15. "Leben und Sterben F.K.s," *Sinn und Form*, XV (1963), 422.

16. *Weimarer Beiträge*, III (1957), 606.

17. *Ibid.*, 606.

18. "Die gesellschaftliche Problematik in Kafkas Romanen," *Von Herder bis Kisch*, 159.

19. "Das Problem der Wirklichkeit in der modernen Kunst," *Sinn und Form*, X (1958), 473.

20. *Sinn und Form*, XIV (1962), 816–818.

21. "Franz Kafka," *Sinn und Form*, XIV (1962), 553.

22. *Ibid.*

23. "O Franzi Kafkovi z pražské perspektivy 1963," *LK*, 34–35.

24. *Ibid.*, 25.

25. "Ein Band Kafka gegen ein Moped," *Die Zeit*, May 8, 1964.

26. Goldstücker, *LK*, 25. (Omitted from *France Observateur*.)

27. *Stefan Rott oder das Jahr der Entscheidung* (Berlin: Zsolnay, 1931), 351.

28. František Kautman, "Franz Kafka a česká literatura," *LK*, 63. Quote from Richard Weiner, Lazebník (Poetika). (Prague: Aventinum, 1929), 263 (Aventinum, vol. 237).

29. Kautman, *LK*, 73–74.

30. "Devátá elegie," *Deníky Jiřího Ortena* (Prague: Československý spisovatel, 1958), 403.

31. Kautman, *LK*, 74.

32. "Kafka—filosof," *LK*, 96.

33. "Poznámky k marxistické interpretaci Franze Kafky," *LK*, 161–175.

34. "Kafka a dnešek," *LK*, 19.

35. *Ibid.*, 18–19.

36. François Bondy and Hans Mayer, "Literatur und Kommunismus," *Monat*, XVI (1964), 49.

37. Helmut Richter, "O Kafkových epigonech v západoněmecké literatuře," *LK*, 186.

38. Anna Seghers, *Transit* (Berlin: Aufbau, 1954). For reviews see, for example, Paul Rilla, *Essays* (Berlin: Henschel, 1955), 320–324.

39. Kusák, "Poznámky," *LK*, 166–167 *et passim*.

40. *Wider den missverstandenen Realismus* (Hamburg: Claassen, 1953), 86.

41. Bondy and Mayer, "Literatur und Kommunismus," 50.

42. Lukács, "Wider den missverstandenen Realismus," 56.

43. "Unbewegliche Uhrzeiger," *Wort in der Zeit*, IX (1963), 9.

44. Edward Csato, *The Polish Theatre*, trans. Christina Cenkalska (Warsaw: Polonia, 1963), 127.

45. Bruno Schulz, *Sklepy cynamonowe* (Cracow: Wydawnictwo Literackie, 1957).

46. Albert Camus, "L'espoir et l'absurde dans l'œuvre de Franz Kafka," *Le Mythe de Sisyphe* (Paris: Gallimard, 1942), 169 ff.

47. Sławomir Mrożek, *Striptease*, trans. I. A. Langnas and Robert O'Brien, Odyssee, III (1963), 16.

48. "The only thing for me to do is to keep my intelligence calm and analytic to the end" (*P*, 282). See also p. 171 above.

49. "Dziwne myšli o Kafce," *Przegląd Kulturalny*, X (1959), 6.

50. *Szkice o Szekspirze* (Warsaw: Państwowy Instytut Wydawniczy, 1961), 105.

51. "O filosofii, Picassovi a Kafkovi," *Plamen*, V (1963), 1.

52. *Galgenlieder*, trans. Max Knight (Berkeley: University of California Press, 1963), 35.

53. Garaudy, "O filosofii," 3.

54. Houška, "Franz Kafka," 396–397.

55. Harvey Cox, "Kafka East, Kafka West," *Commonweal*, LXXX (1964), 597. Brod's address is reprinted as "Kafka Never Stood Aside" ("Kafka stand niemals beiseite") *Forum*, XI (1964), 495–496.

56. *East Europe*, XII (1963), 25.

57. "Nicht auf Kafka schiessen!" *Der Spiegel*, XVII (1963), 74.

58. Dieter Hasselblatt, *Zauber und Logik. Eine Kafka-Studie* (Cologne: Wissenschaft und Politik, 1964), 15. Hasselblatt adds a thorough analysis of Knipovitch's essay.

59. Hans Mayer and François Bondy, "The Struggle for Kafka and Joyce," *Encounter*, XXII (1964), 83 n.; and Dieter Hasselblatt, "Kafka russisch," *Monat*, XVI (1964), 84.

60. Mihael Vianec, "The Struggle for Kafka and Joyce," *Encounter*, XXIII (1964), 92.

61. *Ästhetik I:2* (*Die Eigenart des Ästhetischen*) (Neuwied: Luchterhand, 1963), 512.

62. "Franz Kafka," *Sinn und Form*, XIV (1962), 523.

Bibliography

Recent Bibliographies of Kafka

Beebe, Maurice, and Naomi Christensen. "Criticism of Franz Kafka: A Selected Checklist." *Modern Fiction Studies*, VIII (1962), 80–100.

Benson, Ann Thornton. "Franz Kafka: An American Bibliography." *Bulletin of Bibliography*, XXII (1958), 112–114.

Flores, Angel. "Bibliographical Index of the Works Available in English" and "Biography and Criticism: A Bibliography," in *Franz Kafka Today*, ed. Angel Flores and Homer Swander. Madison: University of Wisconsin Press, 1958. Pp. 215–285.

Hemmerle, Rudolf. *Franz Kafka: Eine Bibliographie*. Munich: Lerche, 1958.

Järv, Harry. *Die Kafka-Literatur: Eine Bibliographie*. Malmö-Lund: Bo Cavefors, 1961. (Reviewed by Klaus M. Jonas, *Monatshefte*, LV [1963], 39–42.)

Addenda to the Bibliographies Listed Above

Baioni, Giuliano. *Kafka: Romanzo e parabola*. Milano: Feltrinelli, 1963.

Beissner, Friedrich. *Der Schacht von Babel: Zu Kafkas Tagebüchern*. Stuttgart: Kohlhammer, 1963.

Bezzel, Christoph. *Natur bei Kafka: Studien zur Ästhetik des poetischen Zeichens*. Nürnberg: Carl, 1964. (Erlanger Beiträge zur Sprach-und Kunstwissenschaft 15.)

Brod, Max. *Das Schloss: Nach Franz Kafkas gleichnamigen Roman*. Frankfort: Fischer, 1964. (Dramatization of *The Castle*.)

Buber-Neumann, Margarete. *Kafkas Freundin Milena*. Munich: Gotthold Müller, 1963.

Carrouges, Michel. *Kafka contre Kafka*. Paris: Plon, 1962. (In the series "La recherche de l'absolu.")

Dentan, Michel. *Humor et création littéraire dans l'œuvre de Kafka*. Geneva: Droz, 1961.

Flores, Angel, ed. *The Kafka Problem*. New York: Octagon, 1963. (Reprint of the 1946 edition with augmented bibliography.)

Friedman, Maurice. *Problematic Rebel: An Image of Modern Man.* (A Study of Kafka, Melville, Dostoyevsky, and Camus.) New York: Random House, 1963.

Goldstücker, Eduard, *et al.*, eds. *Franz Kafka, Liblická Konference 1963.* (The Conference at Liblice, 1963.) Prague: Nakladetelství Československé akademie věd, 1963.

Gray, Ronald, ed. *Kafka: A Collection of Critical Essays.* Englewood Cliffs: Prentice-Hall, 1962 (*Twentieth Century Views*).

Hasselblatt, Dieter. *Zauber und Logik: Eine Kafka-Studie.* Cologne: Wissenschaft und Politik, 1964.

Hermsdorf, Klaus. *Kafka—Weltbild und Roman.* Berlin: Rütten & Loening, 1961.

Hillmann, Heinz. *Franz Kafka. Dichtungstheorie und Dichtungsgestalt.* Bonn: Bouvier, 1964. (Bonner Arbeiten zur deutschen Literatur, Band 9.)

Järv, Harry. *Introduktion til Kafka.* Vasa: Horisont, 1962 (= Horisont smaskrifter, No. 3).

Jakubec, Joël. *Kafka contre l'absurde.* Lausanne: Cahiers de la Renaissance Vaudoise, 43, 1962 (recte 1963).

Janouch, Gustav. *Franz Kafka und seine Welt: Eine Bildbiographie.* Vienna: Deutsch, 1965.

Mühlberger, Josef. *Die kaiserliche Botschaft.* Graz: Stiasny, 1960.

Politzer, Heinz. *Franz Kafka, der Künstler.* Frankfort: Fischer, 1965.

Rattner, J. *Kafka und das Vaterproblem: Ein Beitrag zum tiefenpsychologischen Problem der Kindererziehung.* Munich: Reinhardt, 1964.

Rhein, Philip H. *The Urge to Live: A Comparative Study of Kafka's* DER PROZESS *and Camus'* L'ETRANGER. Chapel Hill: University of North Carolina Press, 1964.

Richter, Helmut. *Franz Kafka—Werk und Entwurf.* Berlin: Rütten & Loening, 1962 (= Neue Beiträge zur Literaturwissenschaft, XIV).

Sgorlon, Carlo. *Kafka narratore.* Venezia: Neri Pozza, 1961 (= Biblioteca di Cultura, No. 26)

Sokel, Walter H. *Franz Kafka: Tragik und Ironie.* Munich: Langen-Müller, 1964.

Spilka, Mark. *Dickens and Kafka: A Mutual Interpretation.* Bloomington: Indiana University Press, 1963.

Urzidil, Johannes. *Da geht Kafka.* Zurich: Artemis, 1965.

Wagenbach, Klaus. *Franz Kafka in Selbstzeugnissen und Bilddokumenten.* Reinbek bei Hamburg: Rowohlt Taschenbuch, 1964. (Rowohlts Monographien 91.)

Weinberg, Kurt. *Kafkas Dichtungen: Die Travestien des Mythos.* Bern: Francke, 1963.

The Messenger Lectures

THIS book provided the material for six lectures delivered at Cornell University in October 1962, namely, the Messenger Lectures on the Evolution of Civilization. That series was founded and its title prescribed by Hiram J. Messenger, B. Litt., Ph.D., of Hartford, Connecticut, who directed in his will that a portion of his estate be given to Cornell University and used to provide annually a "course or courses of lectures on the evolution of civilization, for the special purpose of raising the moral standard of our political, business, and social life." The lectureship was established in 1923.

Index

NAMES

* An author who is quoted in the text but identified only in the notes is listed
by the page number on which the quotation appears with the note number that
identifies him. Thus the name "Adorno" occurs on page 382 of the Notes.

WORKS OF KAFKA